Using this book

This handbook can answer your questions about writing, grammar, research, and many other subjects. To find answers, you have many routes into the book:

Use a table of contents. The brief contents here shows the book's parts and chapters. The detailed contents inside the back cover shows each chapter's main headings as well.

Use a tabbed divider. On the back of each driver, a detailed outline directs you to the material covered in that part of the book.

Use the glossary. The Glossary of Usage (pp. 427–38) clarifies words that are commonly confused and misused.

Use the index. The index includes every term, concept, and problem word or expression mentioned in the book.

Use the Guide. Just before the detailed contents at the back of the book, this guide indexes all the material for students using standard American English as a second language or second dialect.

Use the elements of the page. Each page of the handbook tells you where you are and what you can find there. See the Preface for Students (p. iii) for sample pages with annotations that highlight the elements.

Why do you need this new edition?

This edition of *The Little, Brown Compact Handbook* differs from the previous edition in countless ways. Here are six that make the book indispensable:

1 More help with college reading and writing ▪ A chapter on **academic writing** explains the key academic skill of synthesizing your own and others' views as you write in response to texts and images. ▪ A chapter on **academic skills** emphasizes the habits you need to succeed in college.

2 More help with research writing ▪ Material on **finding and evaluating sources** covers all kinds of print and electronic resources and shows how to distinguish reliable and unreliable sources. ▪ A **research-paper-in-progress** on the environment follows one student's research and writing process, making it easy to see what's expected of you.

3 Up-to-date, more accessible help with citing sources ▪ Detailed explanations and highlighted examples present the **most recent revisions of MLA,**

APA, and CSE documentation styles and show how to document a wide range of print and electronic sources. A fourth style, **Chicago**, includes models for citing new media. ▪ **Annotated sample sources** show you how to find and format bibliographic information in articles, books, and Web sites.

4 New help with the writing process ▪ A **student work-in-progress** on globalization and jobs illustrates how the writing process can serve you in college work.

5 Current, more accessible help with grammar and usage ▪ Material on **text-message and e-mail shortcuts** gives tips for spotting and editing them in your academic writing. ▪ **Checklist and summary boxes** with **color highlighting** offer quick-reference help with crafting clear and correct sentences.

6 Access to *MyCompLab* ▪ *The Little, Brown Compact Handbook* is even more useful when you combine it with *MyCompLab,* a Web gateway to resources on grammar, writing, and research developed specifically for writers.

PEARSON

PEARSON
mycomplab®

Become a better writer and researcher—and get better grades in all your courses—with *MyCompLab*!

Writing, grammar, and research help are at your fingertips as you draft and revise.

Composing. This dynamic space for composing, revising, and editing is easy to use and built to function like the most popular word-processing programs.

• Use the Writer's Toolkit to search for answers to your writing questions.
• View instructor, peer, and tutor comments on your work in one place.
• Store and manage all your work in one place.
• Access paper review help from experienced tutors through Pearson Tutor Services.

Access instruction, multimedia tutorials, and exercises in the Resources area to help you master skills and get a better grade.

Share e-portfolios of your work with instructors, classmates, and friends.

Portfolio. With this tool, it's easy to create, publish, manage, and share your portfolio. Continue adding material through your college career and beyond!

Manage all your written work and assignments online, in one easy-to-use place.

To Do. This area captures assignments and due dates from your instructor along with the personal writing you've done in *MyCompLab*.

Gradebook. This area shows writing and exercise scores. You can see how you are progressing toward a better grade!

Access an e-book version of your handbook
E-book. Access a searchable electronic version of your handbook anywhere you have an Internet connection.

Register for *MyCompLab* today!

Questions? Go to www.mycomplab.com/help.html and click "Student Support."

If this book did not come packaged with an access code to *MyCompLab*, you can purchase access online at **www.mycomplab.com/buy-access.html** or ask your bookstore to order an access card for you.

Jane E. Aaron

The Little, Brown Compact Handbook

Special Edition for Michigan State University

Taken from:
The Little, Brown Compact Handbook,
Seventh Edition
by Jane E. Aaron

Cover and tab-page designs: Ben Rubinstein.
Ben Rubinstein is a MSU Professional Writing alumnus. Ben is a
graphic designer who can be reached at benrubinstein@gmail.com.

Taken from:

The Little, Brown Compact Handbook, Seventh Edition
by Jane E. Aaron
Copyright © 2010 by Pearson Education, Inc.
Published by Longman
New York, New York 10019

This special edition published in cooperation with Pearson
Learning Solutions.

Pearson Learning Solutions, 501 Boylston Street, Suite 900,
Boston, MA 02116
A Pearson Education Company
www.pearsoned.com

Printed in the United States of America

1 2 3 4 5 6 7 8 9 10 V354 16 15 14 13 12 11

000200010270766671

CT

ISBN 10: 1-256-15400-8
ISBN 13: 978-1-256-15400-6

Preface for Students

This custom edition of *The Little Brown Handbook* is designed to be a useful reference guide throughout your time as an undergraduate student at Michigan State University. We selected this handbook because the basic information and the structure enhance the ways that writing can be understood as opening doors that help you explore your literacy in ways that advance your leadership potential. Your time in the First-Year Writing Program, and in other Programs that support you as you work toward meeting the Tier I Writing Requirement, helps you make effective transitions to writing, reading and researching in higher education in the United States; we accomplish this by focusing on the analytic and generative possibilities of literacy that help you engage in rich inquiry processes and make effective decisions about creating and communicating new knowledge. Inside the pages of this book you will find lots of information that can enrich your writing, reading and researching experiences throughout your time as an undergraduate student at MSU. Customizing this basic text allowed us to address the specific ways in which the missions of the First-Year Writing Program supports the larger mission of the University and the MSU learning outcomes for undergraduate education. The columns below reflect the ways that the mission of the First-Year Writing Program supports the larger mission of the University (http://president.msu.edu/mission).

As a public, research-intensive, land-grant university funded in part by the state of Michigan, our mission is to advance knowledge and transform lives by:

- providing outstanding undergraduate, graduate, and professional education to promising, qualified students in order to prepare them to contribute fully to society as globally engaged citizen leaders
- conducting research of the highest caliber that seeks to answer questions and create solutions in order to expand human understanding and make a positive difference, both locally and globally
- advancing outreach, engagement, and economic development activities that are innovative, research-driven, and lead to a better quality of life for individuals and communities, at home and around the world

As part of the general education requirement, First-Year Writing contributes to this mission by focusing on inquiry-based teaching and learning that encourages students to begin to understand themselves as:

- contributing members of MSU's community of scholars
- committed to asking important questions and to seeking rich responses to those questions
- developing the literacy skills, knowledge and attitudes necessary to improve the quality of life for themselves and others through their scholarly, social, and professional activities

The shared learning outcomes for First-Year Writing focus on supporting the transitions that many students face as they adjust to the expectations for reading, writing, and researching in higher education that are part of moving toward meeting the goals of the University mission. Behind many of these transitions are two more general moves. First, literacy expectations in higher education move readers, writers and researchers away from literacy as an act of consumption and toward literacy as a generative process through which new understanding, ideas, solutions to problems, and motivations inspire participation. Second, literacy activities in higher education ask readers, writers and researchers to move beyond adaptation to what is already known and toward contributions that add to existing knowledge bases and improve on existing practices. The chart below presents the shared learning outcomes for the First-Year Writing Program at Michigan State University.

Writing	Reading	Research
Use writing for purposes of reflection, action, and participation in academic inquiry (Analytical Thinking; Communication)	Engage in reading for the purposes of reflection, critical analysis, decision-making, and inquiry (Analytical Thinking; Integrated Reasoning)	Apply methods of inquiry and conventions to generate new understanding (Analytical Thinking; Integrated Reasoning)
Work within a repertoire of genres and modes to meet appropriate rhetorical purposes (Communication; Analytical Thinking)	Understand that various academic disciplines and fields employ varied genre, voice, syntactical choices, use of evidence, and citation styles (Analytical Thinking; Communication; Integrated Reasoning)	Demonstrate the ability to locate, critically evaluate, and employ a variety of sources for a range of purposes (Analytical Thinking; Integrated Reasoning)
Exercise a flexible repertoire of invention, arrangement, and revision strategies (Communication; Integrated Reasoning)	Read in ways that improve writing, especially by demonstrating an ability to analyze invention, arrangement, and revision strategies at work in a variety of texts (Analytical Thinking; Communication)	Demonstrate the ability to generate and apply research strategies that are purposeful, ethical, and balanced (Integrated Reasoning)
Demonstrate an understanding of writing as an epistemic and recursive process and effectively apply a variety of knowledge-making strategies in writing (Integrated Reasoning)	Demonstrate an understanding of reading as epistemic and recursive meaning making processes (Integrated Reasoning)	Demonstrate an understanding of research as epistemic and recursive processes that arise from and respond back to various communities (Analytical Thinking; Cultural Understanding)
Understand diction, usage, voice, and style, including standard edited English, as conventional and rhetorical features of writing (Analytical Thinking; Communication)	Understand that academic disciplines and fields employ varied genres, styles, syntactical patterns, uses of evidence, and documentation practices that call for a variety of reading strategies (Analytical Thinking; Communication; Integrated Reasoning)	Understand the logics and uses of citation systems and documentation styles and display competence with one citation system/documentation style (Analytical Thinking; Communication)

In addition to supporting the MSU mission, the First-Year Writing program also jump-starts your ability to meet the specific learning goals for undergraduate education at MSU; these are learning goals that you will pursue throughout your undergraduate education. The goals for undergraduate education at MSU appear below. If you look back at the chart that displays the shared learning outcomes for First-Year Writing, you will see that these goals appear in parentheses in the boxes that create connections between these general learning outcomes and the more specific learning outcomes for the First-Year Writing Program.

Undergraduate Learning Goals at MSU: A liberal arts foundation enhances the potential that MSU graduates will be outstanding leaders and life-long learners. These liberal learning goals are intended to provide a framework for students' active engagement in learning both in and out of the classroom. Students who complete an undergraduate degree program at Michigan State University will demonstrate the knowledge, attitudes and skills associated with the following interconnected goals and outcomes:

Analytical Thinking

The MSU graduate uses ways of knowing from mathematics, natural sciences, social sciences, humanities, and arts to access information and critically analyzes complex material in order to evaluate evidence, construct reasoned arguments, and communicate inferences and conclusions.

- Acquires, analyzes, and evaluates information from multiple sources
- Synthesizes and applies the information within and across disciplines
- Identifies and applies, as appropriate, quantitative methods for defining and responding to problems
- Identifies the credibility, use and misuse of scientific, humanistic and artistic methods

Cultural Understanding

The MSU graduate comprehends global and cultural diversity within historical, artistic, and societal contexts.

- Reflects on experiences with diversity to demonstrate knowledge and sensitivity
- Demonstrates awareness of how diversity emerges within and across cultures

Effective Citizenship

The MSU graduate participates as a member of local, national, and global communities and has the capacity to lead in an increasingly interdependent world.

- Understands the structures of local, national, and global governance systems and acts effectively within those structures in both individual and collaborative ways
- Applies knowledge and abilities to solve societal problems in ethical ways

Effective Communication

The MSU graduate uses a variety of media to communicate effectively with diverse audiences.

- Identifies how contexts affect communication strategies and practices
- Engages in effective communication practices in a variety of situations and with a variety of media

Integrated Reasoning

The MSU graduate integrates discipline-based knowledge to make informed decisions that reflect humane social, ethical, and aesthetic values.

- Critically applies liberal arts knowledge in disciplinary contexts and disciplinary knowledge in liberal arts contexts
- Uses a variety of inquiry strategies incorporating multiple views to make value judgments, solve problems, answer questions, and generate new understandings

(http://undergrad.msu.edu/outcomes.html)

Your custom team has worked hard to create a handbook that will enhance your literacy education throughout your time as writers, readers and researchers at MSU and beyond. We hope that helping you see the big picture makes you feel a bit more at ease as you face the challenges and changes that will help you become engaged learners and leaders.

Dr. Nancy C. DeJoy
Dr. Deborah Carmichael
Dr. Christie Daniels
Dr. Joyce Meier
Librarian consultants Sara D. Miller and Ben Oberdick
Editing Assistant Stephanie Amada

Preface for Instructors

The Little, Brown Compact Handbook provides writers with an accessible reference, one that helps them find what they need and then use what they find. Combining the authority of its parent, *The Little, Brown Handbook*, with a briefer and more convenient format, the *Compact Handbook* addresses writers of varying experience, in varying fields, answering common questions about the writing process, grammar and style, research writing, and more.

This new edition improves on the handbook's strengths as a clear, concise, and accessible reference, while keeping pace with rapid changes in writing and its teaching. In the context of the handbook's many reference functions, the following pages highlight as New the most significant additions and changes.

A reference for academic writing

The handbook gives students a solid foundation in the goals and requirements of college writing.

- New A reorganized Part 2 ("Writing in and out of College") proceeds through a chapter each on academic skills in general, critical thinking and reading, academic writing, argument, online writing, oral presentations, and public writing.
- New The revised chapter on academic skills emphasizes taking notes, reading for comprehension, the basics of academic writing, and preparing for exams.
- New The reconceived chapter on academic writing shows students how to write in response to texts.
- New Synthesis receives special emphasis wherever students might need help balancing their own and others' views, such as in responding to texts.
- New Expanded advice on avoiding plagiarism shows students at every turn how to acknowledge borrowed material.
- New A greater stress on opposing views in argument includes discussion of Rogerian approaches.
- Parts 7 and 8 give students a solid foundation in research writing, writing about literature, and writing in other humanities, the social sciences, and the natural and applied sciences. Extensive, specially tabbed sections cover documentation and format in MLA, APA, Chicago, and CSE styles.

A reference for research writing

With detailed advice and a sample MLA paper, the handbook always attends closely to research writing. The discussion stresses using the library as Web gateway, managing information, evaluating and synthesizing sources, integrating source material, and avoiding plagiarism.

- **New** A research-paper-in-progress on green consumerism follows a student through the research process and culminates in an annotated paper documented in MLA style.
- **New** An expanded discussion of evaluating sources illustrates critical criteria with sample articles and Web documents.
- **New** Many kinds of electronic resources—including blogs, wikis, and multimedia as well as Web documents—receive attention as possible sources that require careful evaluation and documentation.
- **New** The advice for generating primary sources now covers conducting observations and surveys.
- **New** Updated source lists in Part 8 provide reliable starting points for research in every discipline.

A reference for documenting sources

The extensive coverage of documentation in three styles—MLA, Chicago, and CSE—reflects each style's latest version and includes many examples of electronic sources.

- **New** MLA style is expanded and completely updated to reflect the 2008 *MLA Handbook for writers of Research Papers*, Seventh Edition.

A reference for the writing process

The handbook takes a practical approach to assessing the writing situation, generating ideas, developing the thesis statement, revising, and other elements of the writing process.

- **New** A student's work-in-progress on globalization and outsourcing illustrates the stages of the writing process.
- **New** Coverage of thesis development now includes discussion and examples of explanatory and argumentative thesis statements.
- An extensive chapter on paragraphs provides twenty-five examples.
- An extensive chapter on document design includes help with using illustrations and a section on designing for readers with vision loss.

A reference on usage, grammar, and punctuation

The handbook's core reference material reliably and concisely explains basic concepts and common errors and provides hundreds of annotated examples from across the curriculum.

■ **New** Five added boxes cover coordination, subordination, helping verbs, sentence patterns, and sentence fragments.

■ **New** Color highlighting in boxes stresses and distinguishes sentence elements for quick reference.

■ **New** Advice on avoiding the informalities common to online communication targets nonstandard grammar, punctuation, abbreviations, and spelling.

A guide for culturally and linguistically diverse writers

At notes and sections labeled ⟨**CULTURE LANGUAGE**⟩, the handbook provides extensive rhetorical and grammatical help for writers whose first language or dialect is not standard American English.

■ Fully integrated coverage, instead of a separate section, means that students can find what they need without having to know which problems they do and don't share with native SAE speakers.

■ The ⟨**CULTURE LANGUAGE**⟩ Guide, just before the back endpapers, orients students with advice on mastering SAE and pulls all the integrated coverage together in one place.

A guide to visual literacy

The handbook helps students process visual information and use it effectively in their writing.

■ **New** The discussion of viewing images critically uses fresh and diverse examples to demonstrate identifying and analyzing visual elements.

■ **New** A student's work illustrates the process of analyzing an advertisement.

■ **New** The discussion of reading and using visual arguments includes a new graph, a new photograph, and new advertisements for analysis.

■ Detailed help with preparing or finding illustrations appears in the discussions of document design, research writing, and Web composition.

■ Illustrations in several of the handbook's student papers show various ways to support written ideas with visual information.

An accessible reference guide

The handbook is an open book for students, with a convenient lay-flat binding, tabbed dividers, and many internal features that help students navigate and use the content.

■ **New** A clean, uncluttered page design uses color and type to distinguish parts of the book and elements of the pages.

■ **New** A brief table of contents inside the front cover provides an at-a-glance overview of the book. As before, a detailed table of contents appears inside the back cover.

■ **New** Color highlighting in boxes and on documentation models distinguishes important elements.

■ A unique approach to terminology facilitates reference and reading. Headings in the text and tables of contents avoid or explain terms. And "Key terms" boxes in the text provide essential definitions, dramatically reducing cross-references and page flipping.

■ An unusually accessible organization groups related problems so that students can easily find what they need.

■ Cross-references give divider numbers in addition to page numbers, sending students directly to the appropriate tabbed section—for instance, "See **3** pp. 130–132."

■ Annotations on both visual and verbal examples connect principles and illustrations.

■ Dictionary-style headers in the index make it easy to find entries.

■ A preface just for students details reference aids and explains the page layout.

Two versions of the handbook

The handbook is available with a full complement of exercises built into the book. Otherwise identical to the book you're holding, *The Little, Brown Compact Handbook with Exercises* includes more than 140 sets of exercises on usage, grammar, punctuation, and mechanics as well as rhetorical concerns such as thesis statements and paraphrasing. The exercises are in connected discourse, and their subjects come from across the academic curriculum.

Supplements

Pearson offers a variety of support materials to make teaching easier and to help students improve as writers. The following are geared specifically to *The Little, Brown Compact Handbook*. Visit *pearsonhighered.com* or contact your local Pearson sales representative for more information on these and scores of additional supplements.

- **New** mycomplab The Web site *MyCompLab* (*mycomplab.com*) integrates instruction, multimedia tutorials, and exercises for writing, grammar, and research with an online composing space and assessment tools. This seamless, flexible environment comes from extensive research in partnership with composition faculty and students across the country. It provides help for writers in the context of their writing, with functions for instructors' and peers' commentary. Special features include an e-portfolio, a bibliography tool, tutoring services, an assignment builder, and a gradebook and course-management organization created specifically for writing classes. In addition, an e-book version of *The Little, Brown Compact Handbook* integrates the many resources of *MyCompLab* into the text.

- **New** Students can subscribe to *The Little, Brown Compact Handbook* as a *CourseSmart* e-textbook. The site includes all of the handbook's content in a format that enables students to search the text, bookmark passages, integrate their notes, and print reading assignments that incorporate lecture notes. For more information, or to subscribe to the *CourseSmart* e-textbook, visit *coursesmart.com*.

- *Exercises to Accompany The Little, Brown Compact Handbook* offers the same activities found in the exercise version of the handbook, all double-spaced so that students can work directly in the book. An answer key is available.

- *Developmental Exercises to Accompany The Little, Brown Compact Handbook* provides activities in workbook format for developmental writers. An answer key is available.

- vango notes *VangoNotes* are study guides in MP3 format that enable students to download handbook information into their own players and then listen to it whenever and wherever they wish. The notes include "need to know" tips for each handbook chapter, practice tests, audio flash cards for learning key concepts and terms, and a rapid review for exams. For more information, visit *VangoNotes.com*.

- *Diagnostic and Editing Tests and Exercises* are cross-referenced to *The Little, Brown Compact Handbook* and are available both in print and online.

Acknowledgments

The Little, Brown Compact Handbook stays fresh and useful because instructors talk with the publisher's sales representatives and editors, answer questionnaires, write detailed reviews, and send me personal notes.

For the seventh edition, the following instructors earn special thanks for detailed reviews in which they drew on their rich experience to offer insights into the handbook and suggestions for its improvement: David L. Anderson, Butler County Community College; Martha Bachman, Camden County College; Mike Barrett, Moberly Area Community College; Debbie Bush, Copiah-Lincoln Community College; Lucia Cherciu, Dutchess Community College; Barbara Goldstein, Hillsborough Community College; Andrew Green, University of Miami; Kathleen Green, Pasadena City College; Harold William Halberg, Montgomery County Community College; Kimberly Harrison, Florida International University; Anne Helms, Alamance Community College; Ann Jagoe, North Central Texas College; Tracy Johnson, Butte College; Michael Lueker, Our Lady of the Lakes University; Angie Macri, Pulaski Technical College; Marilee Motto, Owens Community College; Kathryn Scrivener, Clark College; Nanette Tamer, Villa Julie College; and Lori Truman, Kilgore College.

In responding to the ideas of these thoughtful critics, I had the help of several creative people. Caroline Crouse, George Washington University, guided me through the labyrinth of the contemporary library. Sylvan Barnet, Tufts University, continued to lend his expertise in the chapter "Reading and Writing About Literature," which is adapted from his *Short Guide to Writing About Literature* and *Introduction to Literature* (with William Burto and William E. Cain). Ellen Kuhl provided creative, meticulous, and invaluable help with the material on research writing. And Carol Hollar-Zwick, sine qua non, served brilliantly as originator, sounding board, critic, coordinator, researcher, producer, and friend.

A superb publishing team helped to make this book. At Longman, editors Joe Opiela and Anne Brunell Ehrenworth offered perceptive insights into instructors' and students' needs, while production editor Bob Ginsberg helped resolve sometimes competing production goals in favor of quality and accuracy. At Nesbitt Graphics, Jerilyn Bockorick created the striking new design, and Susan McIntyre performed her usual calm (and calming) miracles of scheduling and management to produce the book. I am grateful to all these collaborators.

PART **1**

The Writing Process

MICHIGAN STATE
UNIVERSITY

1 The Writing Situation

Like most writers (even very experienced ones), you may find writing sometimes easy but more often challenging, sometimes smooth but more often halting. Writing involves creation, and creation requires freedom, experimentation, and even missteps. Instead of proceeding in a straight line on a clear path, you might start writing without knowing what you have to say, circle back to explore a new idea, or keep going even though you're sure you'll have to rewrite later.

As uncertain as the writing process may be, you can bring some control to it by assessing your writing situation, particularly your subject, audience, and purpose.

1a Assessing the writing situation

Any writing you do for others occurs in a context that both limits and clarifies your choices. You are communicating something about a particular subject to a particular audience of readers for a specific reason. You may need to conduct research. You'll probably be up against a length requirement and a deadline. And you may be expected to present your work in a certain format.

These are the elements of the **writing situation,** and analyzing them at the very start of a project can tell you much about how to proceed.

Context

- **What is your writing for?** A course in school? Work? Something else? What do you know of the requirements for writing in this context?
- **Will you present your writing on paper, online, or orally?** What does the presentation method require in preparation time, special skills, and use of technology?
- **How much leeway do you have for this writing?** What does the stated or implied assignment tell you?

Subject (pp. 4–5)

- **What does your writing assignment require you to write about?** If you don't have a specific assignment, what subjects might be appropriate for this situation?

Visit *mycomplab.com* for more resources as well as exercises on the writing situation.

- **What interests you about the subject?** What do you already know about it? What questions do you have about it?
- What does the assignment require you to do with the subject?

Purpose (pp. 5–6)

- **What aim does your assignment specify?** For instance, does it ask you to explain something or argue a point?
- **Why are you writing?**
- **What do you want your work to accomplish?** What effect do you intend it to have on readers?
- **How can you best achieve your purpose?**

Audience (p. 6)

- **Who will read your writing?**
- **What do your readers already know and think about your subject?** Do they have any characteristics—such as educational background, experience in your field, or political views—that could influence their reception of your writing?
- **How should you project yourself in your writing?** What role should you play in relation to readers, and what information should you give? How informal or formal should your writing be?
- **What do you want readers to do or think after they read your writing?**

Research (7 pp. 300–38)

- **What kinds of evidence will best suit your subject, purpose, and audience?** What combination of facts, examples, and expert opinions will support your ideas?
- **Does your assignment require research?** Will you need to consult sources of information or conduct other research, such as interviews, surveys, or experiments?
- **Even if research is not required, what additional information do you need to develop your subject?** How will you obtain it?
- **What style should you use to cite your sources?** (See **7** pp. 336–37 on source documentation in the academic disciplines.)

Deadline and length

- **When is the assignment due?** How will you apportion the work you have to do in the available time?
- **How long should your writing be?** If no length is assigned, what seems appropriate for your subject, purpose, and audience?

Document design

- **What organization and format does the assignment require?** (See p. 44 on format in the academic disciplines and **2** pp. 117–19 on format in public writing.)

- How might you use margins, headings, and other elements to achieve your purpose? (See pp. 45–52.)
- How might you use graphs, photographs, or other illustrations to support ideas and interest readers? (See pp. 52–56 and **2** pp. 96–102 on using illustrations in writing.)

1b Finding your subject

A subject for writing has several basic requirements:

- It should be suitable for the assignment.
- It should be neither too general nor too limited for the assigned deadline and paper length.
- It should be something you are willing to learn more about, even something you care about.

When you receive an assignment, study its wording and its implications about your writing situation to guide your choice of subject:

- **What's wanted from you?** Many writing assignments contain words such as *discuss, describe, analyze, report, interpret, explain, define, argue,* or *evaluate.* These words specify the way you are to approach your subject, what kind of thinking is expected of you, and what your general purpose is. (See pp. 5–6.)
- **For whom are you writing?** Many assignments will specify or imply your readers, but sometimes you will have to figure out for yourself who your audience is and what it expects of you. (For more on analyzing your audience, see p. 6.)
- **What kind of research is required?** An assignment may specify the kinds of sources you are expected to consult, and you can use such information to choose your subject. (If you are unsure whether research is required, check with your instructor.)
- **Does the subject need to be narrowed?** To do the subject justice in the length and time required, you'll often need to limit it. (See below.)

Answering questions about your assignment will help set some boundaries for your choice of subject. Then you can explore your own interests and experiences to narrow the subject so that you can cover it adequately within the space and time assigned. Federal aid to college students could be the subject of a book; the kinds of aid available or why the government should increase aid would be a more appropriate subject for a four-page paper due in a week. Here are some guidelines for narrowing broad subjects:

- **Break your broad subject into as many specific subjects as you can think of.** Make a list.

- **For each specific subject that interests you and fits the assignment, roughly sketch out the main ideas.** Consider how many paragraphs or pages of specific facts, examples, and other details you would need to pin those ideas down. This thinking should give you at least a vague idea of how much work you'd have to do and how long the resulting paper might be.
- **Break a too-broad subject down further,** repeating the previous steps.

The Internet can also help you limit a general subject. On the Web, browse a directory such as *BUBL LINK* (*bubl.ac.uk/link*). As you pursue increasingly narrow categories, you may find a suitably limited topic.

1c Defining your purpose

Your **purpose** in writing is your chief reason for communicating something about your subject to a particular audience of readers. It is your answer to a potential reader's question, "So what?"

Most writing you do will have one of four main purposes:

- **To entertain readers.**
- **To express your feelings or ideas.**
- **To explain something to readers (exposition).**
- **To persuade readers to accept or act on your opinion (argument).**

These purposes often overlap in a single essay, but usually one predominates. And the dominant purpose will influence your slant on your subject, the details you choose, and even the words you use.

Many writing assignments narrow the purpose by using a signal word, such as the following:

- **Report:** Survey, organize, and objectively present the available evidence on the subject.
- **Summarize:** Concisely state the main points in a text, argument, theory, or other work.
- **Discuss:** Examine the main points, competing views, or implications of the subject.
- **Compare and contrast:** Explain the similarities and differences between two subjects. (See also pp. 40–41.)
- **Define:** Specify the meaning of a term or a concept—distinctive characteristics, boundaries, and so on. (See also p. 39.)
- **Analyze:** Identify the elements of the subject, and discuss how they work together. (See also pp. 39–40 and **2** p. 71.)
- **Interpret:** Infer the subject's meaning or implications.

■ **Evaluate:** Judge the quality or significance of the subject, considering pros and cons. (See also **2** pp. 72–73.)

■ **Argue:** Take a position on the subject, and support your position with evidence. (See also **2** pp. 88–96.)

You can conceive of your purpose more specifically, too, in a way that incorporates your particular subject and the outcome you intend:

> To explain how Annie Dillard's "Total Eclipse" builds to its climax so that readers appreciate the author's skill
>
> To explain the methods of an engineering study so that readers understand and accept your conclusions
>
> To explain the steps in a new office procedure so that staffers will be able to follow it without difficulty
>
> To argue against additional regulation of health-maintenance organizations so that readers will perceive the disadvantages for themselves

1d   Considering your audience

The readers likely to see your work—your **audience**—may influence your choice of subject and your definition of purpose. Your audience certainly will influence what you say about your subject and how you say it—for instance, how much background information you give and whether you adopt a serious or a friendly tone.

For much academic and public writing, readers have specific needs and expectations. You still have many choices to make based on audience, but the options are somewhat defined. (See **2** pp. 81–87 and **8** pp. 340–55 on academic writing and **2** pp. 117–28 on public writing.) In other writing situations, the conventions are vaguer and the choices are more open. The following box contains questions that can help you define and make these choices.

Questions about audience

Identity and expectations

■ **Who *are* my readers?**

■ **What are my readers' expectations for the kind of writing I'm doing?** Do they expect features such as a particular organization and format, distinctive kinds of evidence, or a certain style of documenting sources?

■ **What do I want readers to know or do after reading my work?** How should I make that clear to them?

■ **How should I project myself to my readers?** How formal or informal will they expect me to be? What role and tone should I assume?

2 Invention

Writers use a host of techniques to help invent or discover ideas and information about their subjects. **Whichever of the following techniques you use, do your work in writing, not just in your head.** Your ideas will then be retrievable, and the very act of writing will lead you to fresh insights.

CULTURE LANGUAGE The discovery process encouraged here rewards rapid writing without a lot of thinking beforehand about what you will write or how. If your first language is not standard American English, you may find it helpful initially to do this exploratory writing in your native language or dialect and then to translate the worthwhile material for use in your drafts. This process can be productive, but it is extra work. You may want to try it at first and gradually move to composing in standard American English.

2a Keeping a journal

A **journal** is a diary of ideas kept on paper or on a computer. It gives you a place to record your responses, thoughts, and observations about what you read, see, hear, or experience. It can also provide ideas for writing. Because you write for yourself, you can work out your ideas without the pressure of an audience "out there" who will evaluate logic or organization or correctness. If you write every day, even just for a few minutes, the routine will loosen your writing muscles and improve your confidence.

You can use a journal for varied purposes: perhaps to confide your feelings, explore your responses to movies and other media, practice certain kinds of writing (such as poems or news stories), pursue ideas from your course, or think critically about what you read. One student, Katy Moreno, used her journal for the last purpose. Her composition instructor had distributed "It's a Flat World, After All," an essay by Thomas L. Friedman about globalization and the job market. The instructor then gave the following assignment, calling for a response to reading:

In "It's a Flat World, After All," Thomas L. Friedman describes today's global job market, focusing not on manufacturing jobs that have been

mycomplab

Visit *mycomplab.com* for more resources as well as exercises on invention.

7

"outsourced" to overseas workers but on jobs that require a college degree and are no longer immune to outsourcing. Friedman argues that keeping jobs in the United States requires that US students, parents, and educators improve math and science education. As a college student, how do you respond to this analysis of the global market for jobs? Does anything Friedman says cause you to rethink how you will spend your college years or what your major will be?

On first reading the essay, Moreno had found it convincing because Friedman's description of the job market matched her family's experience: her mother had lost her job when it was outsourced to India. After rereading the essay, however, Moreno was not persuaded that more math and science would necessarily improve students' opportunities and preserve their future jobs. She compared Friedman's advice with details she recalled from her mother's experience, and she began to develop a response by writing in her journal:

> Friedman is certainly right that more jobs than we realize are going overseas— that's what happened to Mom's job and we were shocked! But he gives only one way for students like me to compete—take more math and science. At first I thought he's totally right. But then I thought that what he said didn't really explain what happened to Mom—she had lots of math + science + tons of experience, but it was her salary, not better training, that caused her job to be outsourced. An overseas worker would do her job for less money. So she lost her job because of money + because she wasn't a manager. Caught in the middle. I want to major in computer science, but I don't think it's smart to try for the kind of job Mom had—at least not as long as it's so much cheaper for companies to hire workers overseas.

(Further examples of Moreno's writing appear in the next three chapters.)

CULTURE LANGUAGE A journal can be especially helpful if your first language is not standard American English. You can practice writing to improve your fluency, try out sentence patterns, and experiment with vocabulary words. Equally important, you can experiment with applying what you know from experience to what you read and observe.

2b Observing your surroundings

Sometimes you can find a good subject or good ideas by looking around you, not in the half-conscious way most of us move from place to place in our daily lives but deliberately, all senses alert. On a bus, for instance, are there certain types of passengers? What seems to be on the driver's mind? To get the most from observation, you should have a notepad and pen or a handheld computer available for taking notes and making sketches. Back at your desk, study your notes and sketches for oddities or patterns that you'd like to explore further.

2c Freewriting

Writing into a subject

Many writers find subjects or discover ideas by **freewriting:** writing without stopping for a certain amount of time (say, ten minutes) or to a certain length (say, one page). The goal of freewriting is to generate ideas and information from *within* yourself by going around the part of your mind that doesn't want to write or can't think of anything to write. You let words themselves suggest other words. *What* you write is not important; that you *keep* writing is. Don't stop, even if that means repeating the same words until new words come. Don't go back to reread, don't censor ideas that seem dumb or repetitious, and above all don't stop to edit: grammar, punctuation, spelling, and the like are irrelevant at this stage.

If you write on a computer, try this technique for moving forward while freewriting: turn off your computer's monitor, or turn its brightness control all the way down so that the screen is dark. The computer will record what you type but keep it from you and thus prevent you from tinkering with your prose. This **invisible writing** may feel uncomfortable at first, but it can free the mind for very creative results.

CULTURE LANGUAGE Invisible writing can be especially helpful if you are uneasy writing in standard American English and you tend to worry about errors while writing. The blank computer screen leaves you no choice but to explore ideas without regard for their expression. If you choose to write with the monitor on, concentrate on *what* you want to say, not *how* you're saying it.

Focused freewriting

Focused freewriting is more concentrated: you start with your subject and write about it without stopping for, say, fifteen minutes or one full page. As in all freewriting, you push to bypass mental blocks and self-consciousness, not debating what to say or editing what you've written. With focused freewriting, though, you let the physical act of writing take you into and around your subject.

An example of focused freewriting can be found in Katy Moreno's journal response to Thomas L. Friedman's "It's a Flat World, After All" on the previous page. Since she already had an idea about Friedman's essay, Moreno was able to start there and expand on the idea.

2d Brainstorming

A method similar to freewriting is **brainstorming**—focusing intently on a subject for a fixed period (say, fifteen minutes), pushing yourself to list every idea and detail that comes to mind. Like freewriting, brainstorming requires turning off your internal editor so that you keep moving ahead. (The technique of invisible writing on a computer, described above, can help you move forward.)

Here is an example of brainstorming by a student, Johanna Abrams, on what a summer job can teach:

> summer work teaches—
> > how to look busy while doing nothing
> > how to avoid the sun in summer
> > seriously: discipline, budgeting money, value of money
> which job? Burger King cashier? baby sitter? mail-room clerk?
> mail room: how to sort mail into boxes: this is learning??
> how to survive getting fired—humiliation, outrage
> Mrs. King! the mail-room queen as learning experience
> the shock of getting fired: what to tell parents, friends?
> Mrs. K was so rigid—dumb procedures
> initials instead of names on the mail boxes—confusion!
> Mrs. K's anger, resentment: the disadvantages of being smarter than your boss
> The odd thing about working in an office: a world with its own rules for how to act
> what Mr. D said about the pecking order—big chick (Mrs. K) pecks on little
> > chick (me)
> a job can beat you down—make you be mean to other people

2e Clustering

Like freewriting and brainstorming, **clustering** also draws on free association and rapid, unedited work. But it emphasizes the relations between ideas by combining writing and nonlinear drawing. When clustering, you radiate outward from a center point—your subject. When an idea occurs, you pursue related ideas in a branching structure until they seem exhausted. Then you do the same with other ideas, continuously branching out or drawing arrows.

The example below shows how a student used clustering for ten minutes to expand on a subject he arrived at through freewriting: writing as a means of disguise.

2f Asking questions

Asking yourself a set of questions about your subject—and writing out the answers—can help you look at the subject objectively and see fresh possibilities in it.

Clustering

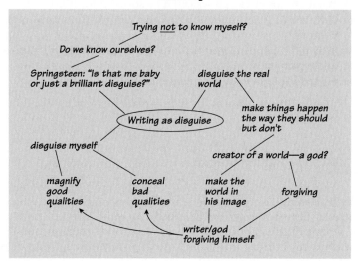

Trying <u>not</u> to know myself?

Do we know ourselves?

Springsteen: "Is that me baby or just a brilliant disguise?"

disguise the real world

Writing as disguise

make things happen the way they should but don't

disguise myself

creator of a world—a god?

magnify good qualities

conceal bad qualities

make the world in his image

forgiving

writer/god forgiving himself

1 Journalist's questions

A journalist with a story to report poses a set of questions:

- Who was involved?
- What happened, and what were the results?
- When did it happen?
- Where did it happen?
- Why did it happen?
- How did it happen?

These questions can also be useful in probing an essay subject, especially when you are telling a story or examining causes and effects.

2 Questions about patterns

We think about and understand a vast range of subjects through patterns such as narration, classification, and comparison and contrast. Asking questions based on the patterns can help you view your subject from many angles. Sometimes you may want to develop an entire essay using just one pattern.

- How did it happen? (Narration)
- How does it look, sound, feel, smell, taste? (Description)
- What are examples of it or reasons for it? (Illustration or support)
- What is it? What does it encompass, and what does it exclude? (Definition)

- **What are its parts or characteristics?** (Division or analysis)
- **What groups or categories can it be sorted into?** (Classification)
- **How is it like, or different from, other things?** (Comparison and contrast)
- **Why did it happen? What results did or could it have?** (Cause-and-effect analysis)
- **How do you do it, or how does it work?** (Process analysis)

For more on these patterns, including paragraph-length examples, see pp. 37–42.

2g The writing process

You have probably used some common pre-writing strategies like brainstorming, freewriting, journaling, mapping, or clustering in the past. These strategies can be effective in some writing situations. In writing situations that ask you to incorporate readings and the insights about writing that come from those readings, however, it is best to have some invention strategies that help you read as a writer. At Michigan State University, we have developed an innovative way to put reading and writing in relationship with one another so that as you read you develop richer, more flexible and more effective approaches to succeeding in a variety of composing situations. Like all inquiry-based approaches to knowledge building, ours begins with a series of questions. You will use these questions both when you read and when you write. The questions ask you to think about five of the major components of literacy: Invention, Arrangement, Revision, Style and Delivery. If you scramble the first letter of each of these elements of literacy you get the word RAIDS, an easy way to remember all five. Here are the questions (the sub-questions that appear in parentheses are examples of things to ask if you are having trouble getting started with the larger questions):

1 Invention

What is invention? (What cognitive, social, and other activities did the writer/writers have to engage in to create the text?)

What's being invented? (What attitudes, beliefs, practices, ideas, etc. emerge from the text? If you get stuck, ask yourself what you know, think, feel, as a result of engaging with the text. What ideas, feelings, beliefs, etc. have changed as a result of your reading?)

2 Arrangement

What's being arranged? (What's being put in relationship with what? What ideas are being put in relationship with one another? What people, cultural practices, etc. are being put in relationship with one another?)

What is arrangement? (How are things being put in relationship with one another? What organizational plans are at work (e.g. inductive, deductive, narrative, categorical)?

3 Revision

What's being revised? (What ideas, attitudes, practices, etc. could change if people adopted the ideas, beliefs, attitudes, practices, etc. suggested by the text?)

What is revision? (What strategies are used specifically to make these changes occur? Note: There are usually some strategies that are used both for invention and for revision.)

4 Style

What style is most prevalent in the text (e.g. high, middle, low, popular, scholarly, etc.)?

How does the style help the writer(s) relate to audience?

How does the style affect the ethos of the writer and the message(s)?

5 Delivery

What mode of delivery is used to present the text? (Remember that more than one mode may have been used. For example, if the text appears in an online course management site you may need to ask questions or do a bit of research to identify the other ways it has been delivered.)

How does the mode of delivery affect writer/reader relationships?

How does the mode of delivery affect the ethos of the writer and the message?

These questions are meant to help you read in ways that enhance understanding and enrich the resources you have to draw from as writers. But, these are more than mere strategies. They set a ground for collaborative literacy work beyond the walls of our individual classrooms and they invoke an inquiry-based critical model appropriate for the mission of our research-intensive institution. At Michigan State University, students are invited to develop literacy skills that position them to be engaged, self-directed, collaborative knowledge builders prepared to take leadership roles in a variety of settings throughout their undergraduate careers and beyond. RAIDS contributes to that process by building strong generative and analytic literacy skills that can be used to create new knowledge and solve problems.

Reading is a common invention strategy in higher education; teachers ask you to read to generate new knowledge, to add to existing knowledge, to get an idea of the general terrain of a field of study, and for a variety of other reasons. Using RAIDS helps you read in ways that facilitate learning about how form and content interact, enhancing your ability to be successful in varied literacy situations.

6 Raids as a generative heuristic across writing situations

RAIDS not only enhances your reading experiences, it also adds depth as you plan and draft your own compositions. In any composing situation, however, there are also at least four factors to consider: Subject; Writer; Audience; Purpose (SWAP). These factors can guide your decisions about Invention, Arrangement, Revision, Style and Delivery to make your creative process more efficient. Here are some examples of how you can use SWAP to make effective decisions about the processes that will inform your composing activities.

Subject: All writers make decisions about which subjects will best help them be successful in any given writing situation. Even when a main subject is assigned, all writers must make decisions about how best to address that subject, and what other topics and sub-subjects will best support their main ideas. Thinking about RAIDS can help.

For example, in the disciplinary literacy assignment in Tier I Writing at MSU, your paper will focus on the major writing, reading, and researching activities connected to the discipline you choose to explore. The purposes for those activities are sure to arise as important related topics, and those purposes are often different from what students expected to discover. That is, writers' ideas about the literacy activities and the purposes for those activities are revised during the inquiry processes connected to the assignment. In addition, the writer must also often deal with the fact that the audience—other undergraduate students interested in the major— will also be surprised by the researcher's findings. In this situation, writers must make decisions about how to create relationships between the readers' assumptions about the subject and the new knowledge being presented.

There are many ways to explore how subjects affect writers' decisions about the elements of RAIDS. At MSU, we assist students in identifying effective and efficient ways to explore these connections. You will be invited to explore Subject/RAIDS connections during each assignment as you prepare to use these strategies outside of the walls of our classrooms. You will gain more from these explorations if you ask questions and engage in the conversations about these issues.

Writer: Making the transition to being a successful writer in higher education in America sometimes challenges assumptions about writing and what it means to be a writer that have informed our educations in the past. In higher education, the expectation that you will be flexible enough as a writer to respond to a variety of composing situations (sometimes simultaneously) in varied ways can sometimes feel overwhelming. Analyzing the SWAP elements of the situation can help us understand the expectations people have for writers and their writing.

For example, in the first paper of the curriculum at MSU, writers are asked to explore some aspect of their own literacy histories. The goal is to say something about the significance of your literacy history as it relates to the themes and ideas presented in the course. Merely telling a story about how you learned to read and/or write isn't enough. You are expected to make connections to the larger literacy issues studied through readings and class discussions. This is your first opportunity to create new knowledge from something known, to go beyond the details and create insights into what your literacy history means in the larger context of literacy studies.

In this situation, the successful writer will be someone who digs deep and asks questions about what things mean outside of the individual contexts in which they occurred, and who communicates that meaning in ways that engage readers. When you think about yourself as a writer who is generating, expressing and communicating meaning, you can be successful in a variety of composing situations. This isn't about faking it. It's about understanding yourself and your literacy as a complex, rich source of your ability to generate creative responses to situations and to communicate those in effective ways.

You already do this. If you think about it, you'll see the ways that you use your literacy differently in different situations all the time. When you talk to parents, for example, you probably approach things differently than when you talk to teachers or to friends at a party. You may write differently in school than on your blog or social networking site. That's because you know that different audiences have different expectations.

As you make the transition to becoming a writer at MSU, you'll find that thinking about the best ways to identify these expectations is to start by asking questions that help you to understand and successfully meet expectations. For example, at some point in the semester you will be asked to write for peers, at another point you will be asked to write for professors, at another point you may be asked to select an audience and justify that choice. Each audience will affect how you think about style and delivery, how you select the appropriate focus for revision and purpose, which invention strategies you'll need to engage to be successful and which arrangement patterns will best help the reader(s) understand your text. You'll talk about this issue in class, but it's also important to think about it in the other writing situations you are presented with outside of any individual course.

7 Audience

Creating effective writer/audience relationships is important in every writing situation. Whether the audience expects you merely to repeat facts accurately or illustrate deeper creative and analytic thinking, knowing the expectations can make your writing process more focused and effective. If your audience is relatively uninformed about all or part of the material you will present, you'll need to explain more and make stronger connections between and among the sections of your paper.

Audience considerations are important to writing processes because different audiences expect you to engage in different invention activities. For example, some audiences expect you to cite only scholarly sources while others see value in citing from a variety of sources. Some audiences expect texts to follow certain arrangement formulas like a lab report for a science professor or a five-paragraph essay for raters of timed essays written for standardized tests. You will spend time in class exploring how each of the elements of **RAIDS** should be considered in relation to audience issues as you compose and revise your texts.

8 Purpose

Purposeful writing often takes the revision of an idea, belief, attitude, or practice into consideration both during the inquiry process and as writers create texts for other audiences. In situations where you are able to pick your own major subject, your purpose often determines what other subjects you will write about, who will be your audience, and how you will present yourself as the writer of the text. In situations where your subject is assigned, the purpose can often be implicit. For example, if you are instructed to write about a certain subject, the purpose is often to learn about that subject and demonstrate your learning in writing. It's a good idea to ask questions about the purpose of a writing assignment before you make too many decisions about which invention activities will be most useful and effective.

In any case, if your purpose for engaging in the inquiry process and your purpose for producing effective products are complementary, your whole experience will be deeper and will lead to stronger connections between and among Subject, Writer, Audience and Purpose, the secret to success in any writing situation!

Thinking about how Subject, Writer, Audience and Purpose affect Invention, Arrangement, Revision, Style and Delivery will take your writing to a new level and help you to identify, understand and respond effectively to the expectations for performance in a variety of literacy situations.[1]

---

[1] Section 2g contributed by the MSU Custom Team.

Shaping your raw material helps you clear away unneeded ideas, spot possible gaps, and energize your subject. The two main operations in shaping material are focusing (below) and organizing ideas (p. 18).

3a | Conceiving a focus

Your readers will expect your essay to be focused on and controlled by a main idea. In your final draft you may express this idea in a **focus statement,** often at the end of your introduction.

CULTURE LANGUAGE — In some cultures it is considered rude or unnecessary for a writer to state his or her main idea outright. When writing in standard American English for school or work, you can assume that readers expect a clear and early idea of your focus.

1 | Development of the focus

A focus will not usually leap fully formed into your head: you will have to develop and shape the idea as you develop and shape your essay. Still, trying to draft a focus early can give you a point of reference when changes inevitably occur.

While you are developing your focus, ask the following questions about each attempt:

Checklist for revising the focus statement

- How well does the **subject** of your statement capture the subject of your paper?
- What **claim** does your statement make about your subject?
- What is the **significance** of the claim? How does it answer "So what?" and convey your purpose?
- How **unified** is the statement? How does each word and phrase contribute to a single idea?

---

mycomplab

Visit *mycomplab.com* for more resources as well as exercises on focus and organization.

3b   Organizing your ideas

Most essays share a basic pattern of introduction (states the subject), body (develops the subject), and conclusion (pulls the essay's ideas together). Introductions and conclusions are discussed on pp. 42–44. Within the body, every paragraph develops some aspect of the essay's main idea, or thesis. For Katy Moreno's essay, with annotations highlighting the body's pattern of support for the thesis statement.

CULTURE LANGUAGE If you are not used to reading and writing American academic prose, its pattern of introduction-body-conclusion and the particular schemes discussed below and on the next page may seem unfamiliar. For instance, instead of introductions that focus quickly on the topic and thesis, you may be used to openings that establish personal connections with readers. And instead of body paragraphs that stress general points and support those points with evidence, you may be used to general statements without support (because writers can assume that readers will supply the evidence themselves) or to evidence without explanation (because writers can assume that readers will infer the general points). When writing American academic prose, you need to take into account readers' expectations for directness and for the statement and support of general points.

1 The general and the specific

To organize material for an essay, you need to distinguish general and specific ideas and see the relations between ideas. General and specific refer to the number of instances or objects included in a group signified by a word. The following "ladder" illustrates a general-to-specific hierarchy:

Most general
↑ life form
│ plant
│ rose
↓ Uncle Dan's prize-winning American Beauty rose
Most specific

As you arrange your material, pick out the general ideas and then the specific points that support them. Set aside points that seem irrelevant to your key ideas. On a computer you can easily experiment with various arrangements of general ideas and supporting information: save your master list of ideas, duplicate it, and then use the Cut and Paste functions to move material around or (a little quicker) drag selected text to where you want it.

2 Schemes for organizing essays

An essay's body paragraphs may be arranged in many ways that are familiar to readers. The choice depends on your subject, purpose, and audience.

- **Spatial:** In describing a person, place, or thing, move through space systematically from a starting point to other features—for instance, top to bottom, near to far, left to right.
- **Chronological:** In recounting a sequence of events, arrange the events as they actually occurred in time, first to last.
- **General to specific:** Begin with an overall discussion of the subject; then fill in details, facts, examples, and other support.
- **Specific to general:** First provide the support; then draw a conclusion from it.
- **Climactic:** Arrange ideas in order of increasing importance to your thesis or increasing interest to the reader.
- **Problem-solution:** First outline a problem that needs solving; then propose a solution.

3 Outlines

It's not essential to craft a detailed outline before you begin drafting an essay; in fact, too detailed a plan could prevent you from discovering ideas while you draft. Still, even a rough scheme can show you patterns of general and specific, suggest proportions, and highlight gaps or overlaps in coverage.

There are several kinds of outlines, some more flexible than others.

Tree diagram

In a tree diagram, ideas and details branch out in increasing specificity. Unlike more linear outlines, this diagram can be supplemented and extended indefinitely, so it is easy to alter. Johanna Abrams developed the following example from her brainstorming about a summer job (p. 10):

A tree diagram or other visual map can be especially useful for planning a project for the Web. The diagram can help you lay out the organization of your project and its links and then later can serve as a site map for your readers. (For more on writing for the Web, see **2** pp. 106–12.)

Subject: Working in a large agency

Tree diagram

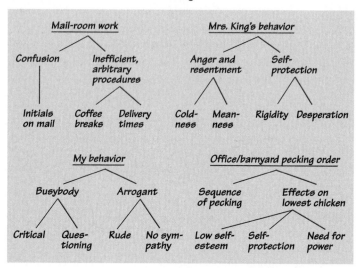

---

4 Unity and coherence

Two qualities of effective writing relate to organization; unity and coherence. When you perceive that someone's writing "flows well," you are probably appreciating these qualities.

To check an outline or draft for **unity**, ask these questions:

- Is each section relevant to the focus of the essay?
- Within main sections, does each example or detail support the principal idea of that section?

To check your outline or draft for **coherence**, ask the following questions:

- Do the ideas follow a clear sequence?
- Are the parts of the essay logically connected?
- Are the connections clear and smooth?

See also pp. 33–37 on unity and coherence in paragraphs.

4 Drafting

Drafting is an occasion for exploration. Don't expect to transcribe solid thoughts into polished prose: solidity and polish will come with revision and editing. Instead, while drafting let the very act of writing help you find and form your meaning.

4a Starting to draft

Beginning a draft sometimes takes courage, even for seasoned professionals. Procrastination may actually help if you let ideas for writing simmer at the same time. At some point, though, you'll have to face the blank paper or computer screen. The following techniques can help you begin:

- **Read over what you've already written**—notes, outlines, and so on—and immediately start your draft with whatever comes to mind.
- **Freewrite** (see p. 9).
- **Skip the opening and start in the middle.** Or write the conclusion.
- **Write a paragraph.** Explain what you think your essay will be about when you finish it.
- **Start writing the part that you understand best.** Using your outline, divide your essay into chunks—say, one for the introduction, another for the first point, and so on. One of these chunks may call out to be written.

4b Maintaining momentum

Drafting requires momentum: the forward movement opens you to fresh ideas and connections. To keep moving while drafting, try one or more of these techniques.

- **Set aside enough time for yourself.** For a brief essay, a first draft is likely to take at least an hour or two.
- **Work in a quiet place.**

mycomplab

Visit *mycomplab.com* for more resources as well as exercises on drafting.

- **If you must stop working, write down what you expect to do next.** Then you can pick up where you stopped with minimal disruption.
- **Be as fluid as possible.** Spontaneity will allow your attitudes toward your subject to surface naturally in your sentences.
- **Keep going.** Skip over sticky spots; leave a blank if you can't find the right word; put alternative ideas or phrasings in brackets so that you can consider them later. If an idea pops out of nowhere but doesn't seem to fit in, quickly jot it down, or write it into the draft and bracket or boldface it for later attention.
- **Resist self-criticism.** Don't worry about your style, grammar, spelling, punctuation, and the like. Don't worry about what your readers will think. These are very important matters, but save them for revision.

If you write on a computer, frequently save the text you're drafting—at least every five or ten minutes and every time you leave the computer.

5   Revising and Editing

During revision—literally "re-seeing"—you shift your focus outward from yourself and your subject toward your readers, concentrating on what will help them respond as you want. It's wise to revise in at least two stages, one devoted to fundamental meaning and structure (here called **revising**) and one devoted to word choice, grammar, punctuation, and other surface features (here called **editing**). Knowing that you will edit later gives you the freedom at first to look beyond the confines of the page or screen to the whole paper.

5a   Revising the whole essay

To revise your writing, you have to read it critically, and that means you have to create some distance between your draft and

mycomplab

Visit *mycomplab.com* for more resources as well as exercises on revising and editing.

yourself. One of the following techniques may help you to see your work objectively.

- **Take a break after finishing the draft.** A few hours may be enough; a whole night or day is preferable.
- **Ask someone to read and react to your draft.** If your instructor encourages collaboration among students, by all means take advantage of the opportunity to hear the responses of others. (See pp. 29–31 for more on collaboration.)
- **Type a handwritten draft.** The act of transcription can reveal gaps in content or problems in structure.
- **Outline your draft.** Highlight the main points supporting the thesis, and convert these sentences to outline form. Then examine the outline you've made for logical order, gaps, and digressions. A formal outline can be especially illuminating because of its careful structure.
- **Listen to your draft.** Read the draft out loud to yourself or a friend or classmate, record and listen to it, or have someone read the draft to you.
- **Ease the pressure.** Don't try to re-see everything in your draft at once. Use the checklist on the next page, making a separate pass through the draft for each item.

1 Revising on a word processor

When you revise on a computer, take a few precautions to avoid losing your work and to keep track of your drafts:

- **Save your work every five to ten minutes.**
- **After doing any major work on a project, create a backup version of the file.**
- **Work on a duplicate of your latest draft.** Then the original will remain intact until you're truly finished with it. On the duplicate you can use your word processor's Track Changes function, which shows changes alongside the original text and allows you to accept or reject alterations later.
- **Save each draft under its own file name.** You may need to consult previous drafts for ideas or phrasings.

2 Titling your essay

The revision stage is a good time to consider a title because attempting to sum up your essay in a phrase can focus your attention sharply on your topic, purpose, and audience. The title should tell

Checklist for revision

Purpose

What is the essay's purpose? Does it conform to the assignment? Is it consistent throughout the paper? (See pp. 5–6.)

Focus

What is the focus of the essay? Where does it become clear? How well do the focus and paper match: Does the paper stray from the focus? (See pp. 17–20.)

Structure

What are the main points of the paper? (List them.) How well does each support the focus? How effective is their arrangement for the paper's purpose? (See pp. 18–20.)

Development

How well do details, examples, and other evidence support each main point? Where, if at all, might readers find support skimpy or have trouble understanding the content? (See pp. 5–6, 37–42.)

Tone

What is the tone of the paper? How do particular words and sentence structures create the tone? How appropriate is it for the purpose, topic, and intended readers? Where is it most and least successful?

Unity

What does each sentence and paragraph contribute to the focus? Where, if at all, do digressions occur? Should these be cut, or can they be rewritten to support the focus? (See p. 20, 33.)

Coherence

How clearly and smoothly does the paper flow? Where does it seem rough or awkward? Can any transitions be improved? (See p. 20, 33–35.)

Title, introduction, conclusion

How accurately and interestingly does the title reflect the essay's content? (See previous page and below.) How well does the introduction engage and focus readers' attention? (See pp. 42–43.) How effective is the conclusion in providing a sense of new understanding? (See pp. 43–44.)

---

the reader what your paper is about, but it should not restate the assignment. Most titles fall into one of these categories:

- A *descriptive title* announces the subject clearly and accurately. Such a title is almost always appropriate and is usually expected for academic writing. Katy Moreno's final title—"Can We Compete? College Education for the Global Economy"—is an example.

■ A *suggestive title* hints at the subject to arouse curiosity. Such a title is common in popular magazines and may be appropriate for writing that is somewhat informal. Moreno might have chosen a suggestive title such as "Training for the New World" or "Education for a Flat World" (echoing Thomas L. Friedman's title).

For more information on essay titles, see **MLA** pp. 402–03 (MLA format), **APA** (APA format), and **6** p. 291 (capitalizing words in a title).

5b Editing the revised draft

After you've revised your essay so that all the content is in place, then turn to the important work of removing any surface problems that could interfere with a reader's understanding or enjoyment of your ideas.

1 Strategies for editing

Try these approaches to discover what needs editing:

■ **Take a break.** Even fifteen minutes can clear your head.
■ **Read the draft slowly, and read what you actually see.** Otherwise, you're likely to read what you intended to write but didn't. (If you have trouble slowing down, try reading your draft from back to front, sentence by sentence.)
■ **Read as if you are encountering the draft for the first time.** Put yourself in the reader's place.
■ **Have a classmate, friend, or relative read your work.** Make sure you understand and consider the reader's suggestions, even if eventually you decide not to take them.
■ **Read the draft aloud or, even better, record it.** Listen for awkward rhythms, repetitive sentence patterns, and missing or clumsy transitions.
■ **Learn from your own experience.** Keep a record of the problems that others have pointed out in your writing. When editing, check your work against this record.

In editing, work first for clear and effective sentences that flow smoothly from one to the next. Then check your sentences for correct-ness. Use the questions in the checklist on the next page to guide your editing, referring to the page numbers in parentheses as needed.

Checklist for editing

Are my sentences clear?

Do my words and sentences mean what I intend them to mean? Is anything confusing? Check especially for these:

Exact language (3 pp. 152–58)
Parallelism (3 pp. 138–40)
Clear modifiers (4 pp. 234–35)
Clear reference of pronouns (4 pp. 219–21)
Complete sentences (4 pp. 236–39)
Sentences separated correctly (4 pp. 239–43)

Are my sentences effective?

How well do words and sentences engage and hold readers' attention? Where does the writing seem wordy, choppy, or dull? Check especially for these:

Emphasis of main ideas (3 pp. 130–38)
Smooth and informative transitions (pp. 36–37)
Variety in sentence length and structure (3 pp. 141–44)
Appropriate language (3 pp. 145–51)
Concise sentences (3 pp. 159–64)

Do my sentences contain errors?

Where do surface errors interfere with the clarity and effectiveness of my sentences? Check especially for these:

- **Spelling errors (6 pp. 282–86)**
- **Sentence fragments (4 pp. 236–39)**
- **Comma splices (4 pp. 239–43)**
- **Verb errors**
  Verb forms, especially -s and -ed endings, correct forms of irregular verbs, and appropriate helping verbs (4 pp. 182–94)
  Verb tenses, especially consistency (4 pp. 194–200)
  Agreement between subjects and verbs, especially when words come between them or the subject is *each, everyone,* or a similar word (4 pp. 204–09)

- **Pronoun errors**
  Pronoun forms, especially subjective (*he, she, they, who*) vs. objective (*him, her, them, whom*) (4 pp. 210–15)
  Agreement between pronouns and antecedents, especially when the antecedent contains *or* or the antecedent is *each, everyone, person,* or a similar word (4 pp. 215–18)

- **Punctuation errors**
  Commas, especially with comma splices (4 pp. 239–43) and with *and* or *but,* with introductory elements, with nonessential elements, and with series (5 pp. 250–61)
  Apostrophes in possessives but not plural nouns (*Dave's/witches*) and in contractions but not possessive personal pronouns (*it's/its*) (5 pp. 267–70)

2 Editing on a computer

When you write on a word processor, consider these additional approaches to editing:

- **Don't rely on a spelling or grammar/style checker to find what needs editing.** See the discussion of these checkers below.
- **If possible, work on a double-spaced paper copy.** Most people find it much harder to spot errors on a computer screen than on paper.
- **Use the Find command to locate and correct your common problems**—certain misspellings, overuse of *there is,* wordy phrases such as *the fact that,* and so on.
- **Resist overediting.** The ease of editing on a computer can lead to rewriting sentences over and over, stealing the life from your prose. If your grammar/style checker contributes to the temptation, consider turning it off.
- **Take special care with additions and omissions.** Make sure you haven't omitted needed words or left in unneeded words.

3 Working with spelling and grammar/style checkers

A spelling checker and grammar/style checker can be helpful *if* you work within their limitations. The programs miss many problems and may even flag items that are actually correct. Further, they know nothing of your purpose and your audience, so they cannot make important decisions about your writing. Always use these tools critically:

- **Read your work yourself to ensure that it's clear and error-free.**
- **Consider a checker's suggestions carefully, weighing each one against your intentions.** If you aren't sure whether to accept a checker's suggestion, consult a dictionary, writing handbook, or other source. Your version may be fine.

Using a spelling checker

Your word processor's spelling checker can be a great ally: it will flag words that are spelled incorrectly and will usually suggest alternative spellings that resemble what you've typed. However, this ally can also undermine you because of its limitations:

- **The checker may flag a word that you've spelled correctly** just because the word does not appear in its dictionary.

- **The checker may suggest incorrect alternatives.** In providing a list of alternative spellings for your word, the checker may highlight the one it considers most likely to be correct. For example, if you misspell *definitely* by typing *definately*, your checker may highlight *defiantly* as the correct option. You need to verify that the alternative suggested by the checker is actually what you intend before selecting it. Consult an online or printed dictionary when you aren't sure about the checker's recommendations.

- **Most important, a spelling checker will not flag words that appear in its dictionary but you have misused.** The jingle in the following screen shot has circulated widely as a warning about spelling checkers.

Spelling checker

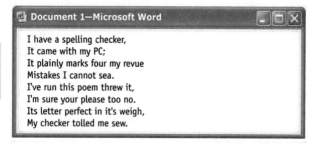

A spelling checker failed to catch any of the thirteen errors in this jingle. Can you spot them?

Document 1—Microsoft Word

I have a spelling checker,
It came with my PC;
It plainly marks four my revue
Mistakes I cannot sea.
I've run this poem threw it,
I'm sure your please too no.
Its letter perfect in it's weigh,
My checker tolled me sew.

Using a grammar/style checker

Grammar/style checkers can flag incorrect grammar or punctuation and wordy or awkward sentences. However, these programs can call your attention only to passages that *may* be faulty. They miss many errors because they are not yet capable of analyzing language in all its complexity. (For instance, they can't accurately distinguish a word's part of speech when there are different possibilities, as *light* can be a noun, a verb, or an adjective.) And they often question passages that don't need editing, such as an appropriate passive verb or a deliberate and emphatic use of repetition.

You can customize a grammar/style checker to suit your needs and habits as a writer. (Select Options under the Tools menu.) Most checkers allow you to specify whether to check grammar only or grammar and style. Some style checkers can be set to the level of writing you intend, such as formal, standard, and informal. (For academic writing choose formal.) You can also instruct the checker to flag specific grammar and style problems that tend to occur in your writing, such as mismatched subjects and verbs, apostrophes in plural nouns, overused passive voice, or a confusion between *its* and *it's*.

5c Formatting and proofreading the final draft

After editing your essay, retype or print it one last time. Follow the wishes of your instructor in formatting your document. Two common formats are discussed and illustrated in this book: MLA (**MLA** pp. 399–401) and APA. In addition, pp. 44–58 treat principles and elements of document design.

Be sure to proofread the final essay several times to spot and correct errors. To increase the accuracy of your proofreading, you may need to experiment with ways to keep yourself from relaxing into the rhythm and the content of your prose. Here are a few tricks, including some used by professional proofreaders:

- **Read printed copy,** even if you will eventually submit the paper electronically. Most people proofread more accurately when reading type on paper than when reading it on a computer screen. (At the same time, don't view the printed copy as error-free just because it's clean. Clean-looking copy may still harbor errors.)
- **Read the paper aloud,** very slowly, and distinctly pronounce exactly what you see.
- **Place a ruler under each line as you read it.**
- **Read "against copy,"** comparing your final draft one sentence at a time against the edited draft.
- **Ignore content.** To keep the content of your writing from distracting you, read the essay backward sentence by sentence. Or print each paragraph on a separate page to isolate it. (Of course, reassemble the paragraphs before submitting the paper.)

5d Revising collaboratively

In many writing courses students work together on writing, most often commenting on each other's work to help with revision. This collaborative writing gives experience in reading written work critically and in reaching others through writing. Collaboration may occur face to face in small groups, via drafts and comments on paper, or on computers.

Whether you collaborate in person, on paper, or on a computer, you will be more comfortable and helpful and will benefit more from others' comments if you follow a few guidelines.

Commenting on others' writing

- **Be sure you know what the writer is saying.** If necessary, summarize the paper to understand its content. (See **2** pp. 63–65.)
- **Address only your most significant concerns with the work.** Use the revision checklist on p. 26 as a guide to what is significant. Unless you have other instructions, ignore mistakes in grammar, punctuation, and the like. (The temptation to focus on such errors may be especially strong if the writer is less experienced than you are with standard American English.) Emphasizing mistakes will contribute little to the writer's revision.
- **Remember that you are the reader, not the writer.** Don't edit sentences, add details, or otherwise assume responsibility for the paper.
- **Phrase your comments carefully.** Avoid misunderstandings by making sure comments are both clear and respectful. If you are responding on paper or online, not face to face with the writer, remember that the writer has nothing but your written words to go on. He or she can't ask you for immediate clarification and can't infer your attitudes from gestures, facial expressions, and tone of voice.
- **Be specific.** If something confuses you, say *why*. If you disagree with a conclusion, say *why*.
- **Be supportive as well as honest.** Tell the writer what you like about the paper. Word comments positively: instead of *This paragraph doesn't interest me,* say *You have an interesting detail here that I almost missed.* Question the writer in a way that emphasizes the effect of the work on you, the reader: *This paragraph confuses me because. . . .* And avoid measuring the work against a set of external standards: *This essay is poorly organized. Your thesis statement is inadequate.*
- **While reading, make your comments in writing.** Even if you will be delivering your comments in person later on, the written record will help you recall what you thought.
- **Link comments to specific parts of a paper.** Especially if you are reading the paper on a computer, be clear about what in the paper each comment relates to. You can embed your comments directly into the paper, distinguishing them with highlighting or color, or you can use a word processor's Comment function.

Benefiting from comments on your writing

- **Think of your readers as counselors or coaches.** They can help you see the virtues and flaws in your work and sharpen your awareness of readers' needs.
- **Read or listen to comments closely.**
- **Know what the critic is saying.** If you need more information, ask for it, or consult the appropriate section of this handbook.
- **Don't become defensive.** Letting comments offend you will only erect a barrier to improvement in your writing. As one writing teacher advises, "Leave your ego at the door."
- **Revise your work in response to appropriate comments,** even if you are not required to do so. You will learn more from actually revising than from just thinking about it.
- **Remember that you are the final authority on your work.** You should be open to suggestions, but you are free to decline advice when you think it is inappropriate.
- **Keep track of both the strengths and weaknesses others identify.** Then in later assignments you can build on your successes and give special attention to problem areas.

CULTURE LANGUAGE In some cultures writers do not expect criticism from readers, or readers do not expect to think and speak critically about what they read. If critical responses are uncommon in your native culture, collaboration may at first be uncomfortable for you. As a writer, think of a draft or even a final paper as more an exploration of ideas than the last word on your subject; then you may be more receptive to readers' suggestions. As a reader, allow yourself to approach a text skeptically, and know that your tactful questions and suggestions will usually be considered appropriate.

5e | Preparing a writing portfolio

Your writing instructor may ask you to assemble samples of your writing into a portfolio, or folder, once or more during the course. Such a portfolio gives you a chance to consider all your writing over a period and to showcase your best work.

Although the requirements for portfolios vary, most instructors are looking for a range of writing that demonstrates your progress and strengths as a writer. You, in turn, see how you have advanced from one assignment to the next, as you've had time for new knowledge to sink in and time for practice. Instructors often allow students to revise papers before placing them in the portfolio, even if the papers were submitted earlier. In that case, every paper in the portfolio can benefit from all your learning.

An assignment to assemble a writing portfolio will probably also provide guidelines for what to include, how the portfolio will be evaluated, and how (or whether) it will be weighted for a grade. Be sure you understand the purpose of the portfolio and who will read it. For instance, if your composition instructor will be the only reader and his or her guidelines encourage you to show evidence of progress, you might include a paper that took big risks but never entirely succeeded. In contrast, if a committee of instructors will read your work and the guidelines urge you to demonstrate your competence as a writer, you might include only papers that did succeed.

Unless the guidelines specify otherwise, provide error-free copies of your final drafts, label all your samples with your name, and assemble them all in a folder. Add a cover letter or memo that lists the samples, explains why you've included each one, and evaluates your progress as a writer. The self-evaluation involved should be a learning experience for you and will help your readers assess your development as a writer.

6 Paragraphs

A **paragraph** is a group of related sentences set off by a beginning indention or, sometimes, by extra space. Paragraphs give you and your readers a breather from long stretches of text, and they indicate key steps in the development of your thesis.

This chapter discusses the three qualities of an effective body paragraph: unity (below), coherence (next page), and development (p. 37). In addition, the chapter discusses two special kinds of paragraphs: introductions and conclusions (pp. 42 and 43).

CULTURE / LANGUAGE Not all cultures share the paragraphing conventions of American academic writing. In some other languages, writing moves differently from English—not from left to right, but from right to left or down rows from top to bottom. Even in languages that move as English does, writers may not use paragraphs at all. Or they may use paragraphs but not state the central ideas or provide transitional expressions to show readers how sentences relate. If your native language is not English and you have difficulty with paragraphs, don't worry about paragraphing during drafting. Instead, during a separate step of revision, divide your text into parts that develop your main points. Mark those parts with indentions.

mycomplab

Visit *mycomplab.com* for more resources as well as exercises on paragraphs.

6a   Maintaining paragraph unity

Checklist for revising paragraphs

- **Is the paragraph unified?** Does it adhere to one general idea that is either stated in a topic sentence or otherwise apparent? (See previous page and below.)
- **Is the paragraph coherent?** Do the sentences follow a clear sequence? Are the sentences linked as needed by parallelism, repetition or restatement, pronouns, consistency, and transitional expressions? (See below.)
- **Is the paragraph developed?** Is the general idea of the paragraph well supported with specific evidence such as details, facts, examples, and reasons? (See p. 37.)

6b   Achieving paragraph coherence

When a paragraph is **coherent,** readers can see how it holds together: the sentences seem to flow logically and smoothly into one another. Exactly the opposite happens with this paragraph:

1 Paragraph organization

A coherent paragraph organizes information so that readers can easily follow along. These are common paragraph schemes:

- **General to specific:** Sentences downshift from more general statements to more specific ones. (See the paragraph by Rosenbaum on the previous page.)
- **Climactic:** Sentences increase in drama or interest, ending in a climax. (See the paragraph below about sleep.)
- **Spatial:** Sentences scan a person, place, or object from top to bottom, from side to side, or in some other way that approximates the way people actually look at things. (See the paragraph by Woolf on p. 38.)
- **Chronological:** Sentences present events as they occurred in time, earlier to later. (See the paragraph by LaFrank on p. 36.)

2 Parallelism

Parallelism helps tie sentences together. In the following paragraph the underlined parallel structures of *She* and a verb link all sentences to the first one. Parallelism also appears *within* many of the sentences. Aphra Behn (1640–89) was the first Englishwoman to write professionally.

In addition to her busy career as a writer, Aphra Behn also found time to briefly marry and spend a little while in debtor's prison. She found time to take up a career as a spy for the English in their war against the Dutch. She made the long and difficult voyage to Suriname [in South America] and became involved in a slave rebellion there. She plunged into political debate at Will's Coffee House and defended her position from the stage of the Drury Lane Theater. She actively argued for women's rights to be educated and to marry whom they pleased, or not at all. She defied the seventeenth-century dictum that ladies must be "modest" and wrote freely about sex.

—Angeline Goreau, "Aphra Behn"

3 Repetition and restatement

Repeating or restating key words helps make a paragraph coherent and also reminds readers what the topic is. In the following paragraph note the underlined repetition of *sleep* and the restatement of *adults*.

Perhaps the simplest fact about sleep is that individual needs for it vary widely. Most adults sleep between seven and nine hours, but occasionally people turn up who need twelve hours or so, while some rare types can get by on three or four. Rarest of all are those legendary types who require almost no sleep at all; respected researchers have recently studied three such people. One of them—a healthy, happy woman in her seventies—sleeps about an hour every two or three days. The other two are men in early middle age, who get by on a few minutes a night. One of them complains about the daily fifteen minutes or so he's forced to "waste" in sleeping.

—Lawrence A. Mayer, "The Confounding Enemy of Sleep"

4 Pronouns

Because pronouns refer to nouns, they can help relate sentences to each other. In the paragraph on the previous page by Angeline Goreau, *she* works just this way by substituting for *Aphra Behn* in every sentence after the first.

5 Consistency

Consistency (or the lack of it) occurs primarily in the person and number of nouns and pronouns and in the tense of verbs. Any

---

Key term

parallelism The use of similar grammatical structures for similar elements of meaning within or among sentences: *The book caused a stir in the media and aroused debate in Congress*. (See also **3** pp. 138–40.)

inconsistencies not required by meaning will interfere with a reader's ability to follow the development of ideas.

Note the underlined inconsistencies in the next paragraphs:

Shifts in tense

In the Hopi religion, water is the driving force. Since the Hopi lived in the Arizona desert, they needed water urgently for drinking, cooking, and irrigating crops. Their complex beliefs are focused in part on gaining the assistance of supernatural forces in obtaining water. Many of the Hopi kachinas, or spirit essences, were directly concerned with clouds, rain, and snow.

Shifts in number

Kachinas represent the things and events of the real world, such as clouds, mischief, cornmeal, and even death. A kachina is not worshiped as a god but regarded as an interested friend. They visit the Hopi from December through July in the form of men who dress in kachina costumes and perform dances and other rituals.

Shifts in person

Unlike the man, the Hopi woman does not keep contact with ka-chinas through costumes and dancing. Instead, one receives a small likeness of a kachina, called a *tihu*, from the man impersonating the kachina. You are more likely to receive a tihu as a girl approaching marriage, though a child or older woman may receive one, too.

Grammar checkers A grammar checker cannot help you locate shifts in tense, number, or person among sentences. Shifts are sometimes necessary (as when tenses change to reflect actual differences in time). Furthermore, a passage with needless shifts may still consist of sentences that are grammatically correct, as all the sentences are in the preceding examples.

Key terms

pronoun A word that refers to and functions as a noun, such as *I, you, he, she, it, we, they: The bush had a beehive in it.* (See **4** p. 167.)

tense The form of a verb that indicates the time of its action, such as present (*I run*), past (*I ran*), or future (*I will run*). (See **4** p. 194.)

number The form of a noun, pronoun, or verb that indicates whether it is singular (one) or plural (more than one): *boy is, boys are.*

person The form of a pronoun that indicates whether the subject is speaking (first person: *I, we*), spoken to (second person: *you*), or spoken about (third person: *he, she, it, they*). All nouns are in the third person.

6 Transitional expressions

Transitional expressions such as *therefore, in contrast,* or *meanwhile* can forge specific connections between sentences, as do the underlined expressions in this paragraph:

> Medical science has thus succeeded in identifying the hundreds of viruses that can cause the common cold. It has also discovered the most effective means of prevention. One person transmits the cold viruses to another most often by hand. For instance, an infected person covers his mouth to cough. He then picks up the telephone. Half an hour later, his daughter picks up the same telephone. Immediately afterward, she rubs her eyes. Within a few days, she, too, has a cold. And thus it spreads. To avoid colds, therefore, people should wash their hands often and keep their hands away from their faces.
>
> —Kathleen LaFrank (student), "Colds: Myth and Science"

Note that you can use transitional expressions to link paragraphs as well as sentences. In the first sentence of LaFrank's paragraph, the word *thus* signals that the sentence refers to an effect discussed in the preceding paragraph.

The following box lists many transitional expressions by the functions they perform.

Transitional expressions

To add or show sequence
again, also, and, and then, besides, equally important, finally, first, further, furthermore, in addition, in the first place, last, moreover, next, second, still, too

To compare
also, in the same way, likewise, similarly

To contrast
although, and yet, but, but at the same time, despite, even so, even though, for all that, however, in contrast, in spite of, nevertheless, notwithstanding, on the contrary, on the other hand, regardless, still, though, yet

To give examples or intensify
after all, an illustration of, even, for example, for instance, indeed, in fact, it is true, of course, specifically, that is, to illustrate, truly

To indicate place
above, adjacent to, below, elsewhere, farther on, here, near, nearby, on the other side, opposite to, there, to the east, to the left

To indicate time

after a while, afterward, as long as, as soon as, at last, at length, at that time, before, earlier, eventually, formerly, immediately, in the meantime, in the past, lately, later, meanwhile, now, presently, shortly, simultaneously, since, so far, soon, subsequently, suddenly, then, thereafter, until, until now, when

To repeat, summarize, or conclude

all in all, altogether, as has been said, in brief, in conclusion, in other words, in particular, in short, in simpler terms, in summary, on the whole, that is, therefore, to put it differently, to summarize

To show cause or effect

accordingly, as a result, because, consequently, for this purpose, hence, otherwise, since, then, therefore, thereupon, thus, to this end, with this object

Note Draw carefully on this list of transitional expressions because the ones in each group are not interchangeable. For instance, *besides, finally,* and *second* may all be used to add information, but each has its own distinct meaning.

CULTURE LANGUAGE   If transitional expressions are not common in your native language, you may be tempted to compensate when writing in English by adding them to the beginnings of most sentences. But such explicit transitions aren't needed everywhere, and in fact too many can be intrusive and awkward. When inserting transitional expressions, consider the reader's need for a signal: often the connection from sentence to sentence is already clear from the context or can be made clear by relating the content of sentences more closely (see **3** pp. 132–34). When you do need transitional expressions, try varying their positions in your sentences, as illustrated in the sample paragraph on the previous page.

6c Developing paragraphs

An effective, well-developed paragraph always provides the specific information that readers need and expect in order to understand you and to stay interested in what you say. Paragraph length can be a rough gauge of development: anything much shorter than 100 to 150 words may leave readers with a sense of incompleteness.

To develop or shape an idea in a paragraph, one or more of the following patterns may help. (These patterns may also be used to develop entire essays. See pp. 10–11.)

1 Narration

Narration retells a significant sequence of events, usually in the order of their occurrence (that is, chronologically). A narrator is concerned not just with the sequence of events but also with their consequence, their importance to the whole.

> Jill's story is typical for "recruits" to religious cults. She was very lonely in college and appreciated the attention of the nice young men and women who lived in a house near campus. They persuaded her to share their meals and then to move in with them. Between intense bombardments of "love," they deprived her of sleep and sometimes threatened to throw her out. Jill became increasingly confused and dependent, losing touch with any reality besides the one in the group. She dropped out of school and refused to see or communicate with her family. Before long she, too, was preying on lonely college students.
> —Hillary Begas (student), "The Love Bombers"

2 Description

Description details the sensory qualities of a person, scene, thing, or feeling, using concrete and specific words to convey a dominant mood, illustrate an idea, or achieve some other purpose.

> The sun struck straight upon the house, making the white walls glare between the dark windows. Their panes, woven thickly with green branches, held circles of impenetrable darkness. Sharp-edged wedges of light lay upon the window-sill and showed inside the room plates with blue rings, cups with curved handles, the bulge of a great bowl, the crisscross pattern in the rug, and the formidable corners and lines of cabinets and bookcases. Behind their conglomeration hung a zone of shadow in which might be a further shape to be disencumbered of shadow or still denser depths of darkness.   —Virginia Woolf, *The Waves*

3 Illustration or support

An idea may be developed with several specific examples, or with a single extended example, as in the next paragraph:

> The language problem that I was attacking loomed larger and larger as I began to learn more. When I would describe in English certain concepts and objects enmeshed in Korean emotion and imagination, I became slowly aware of nuances, of differences between two languages even in simple expression. The remark "Kim entered the house" seems to be simple enough, yet, unless a reader has a clear visual image of a Korean house, his understanding of the sentence is not complete. When a Korean says he is "in the house," he may be in his courtyard, or on his porch, or in his small room! If I wanted to give a specific picture of entering the house in the Western sense, I had to say

"room" instead of house—sometimes. I say "sometimes" because many Koreans entertain their guests on their porches and still are considered to be hospitable, and in the Korean sense, going into the "room" may be a more intimate act than it would be in the English sense. Such problems!

—Kim Yong Ik, "A Book-Writing Venture"

Sometimes you can develop a paragraph by providing your reasons for stating a general idea. For instance:

There are three reasons, quite apart from scientific considerations, that mankind needs to travel in space. The first reason is the need for garbage disposal: we need to transfer industrial processes into space, so that the earth may remain a green and pleasant place for our grandchildren to live in. The second reason is the need to escape material impoverishment: the resources of this planet are finite, and we shall not forgo forever the abundant solar energy and minerals and living space that are spread out all around us. The third reason is our spiritual need for an open frontier: the ultimate purpose of space travel is to bring to humanity not only scientific discoveries and an occasional spectacular show on television but a real expansion of our spirit.

—Freeman Dyson, "Disturbing the Universe"

4 Definition

Defining a complicated, abstract, or controversial term often requires extended explanation. The following definition comes from an essay asserting that "quality in product and effort has become a vanishing element of current civilization." Notice how the writer pins down meaning with examples and contrasts.

In the hope of possibly reducing the hail of censure which is certain to greet this essay (I am thinking of going to Alaska or possibly Patagonia in the week it is published), let me say that quality, as I understand it, means investment of the best skill and effort possible to produce the finest and most admirable result possible. Its presence or absence in some degree characterizes every manmade object, service, skilled or unskilled labor—laying bricks, painting a picture, ironing shirts, practicing medicine, shoemaking, scholarship, writing a book. You do it well or you do it half-well. Materials are sound and durable or they are sleazy; method is painstaking or whatever is easiest. Quality is achieving or reaching for the highest standard as against being satisfied with the sloppy or fraudulent. It is honesty of purpose as against catering to cheap or sensational sentiment. It does not allow compromise with the second-rate.   —Barbara Tuchman, "The Decline of Quality"

5 Division or analysis

With division or analysis, you separate something into its elements—for instance, you might divide a newspaper into its sections. You may also approach the elements critically, interpreting their meaning and significance (see also **2** pp. 70–73):

> The surface realism of the soap opera conjures up an illusion of "liveness." The domestic settings and easygoing rhythms encourage the viewer to believe that the drama, however ridiculous, is simply an extension of daily life. The conversation is so slow that some have called it "radio with pictures." (Advertisers have always assumed that busy housewives would listen, rather than watch.) Conversation is casual and colloquial, as though one were eavesdropping on neighbors. There is plenty of time to "read" the character's face; close-ups establish intimacy. The sets are comfortably familiar: well-lit interiors of living rooms, restaurants, offices, and hospitals. Daytime soaps have little of the glamour of their prime-time relations. The viewer easily imagines that the conversation is taking place in real time.
>
> —Ruth Rosen, "Search for Yesterday"

6 Classification

When you classify items, you sort them into groups. The classification allows you to see and explain the relations among the items. The following paragraph identifies three groups, or classes, of parents:

> In my experience, the parents who hire daytime sitters for their school-age children tend to fall into one of three groups. The first group includes parents who work and want someone to be at home when the children return from school. These parents are looking for an extension of themselves, someone who will give the care they would give if they were at home. The second group includes parents who may be home all day themselves but are too disorganized or too frazzled by their children's demands to handle child care alone. They are looking for an organizer and helpmate. The third and final group includes parents who do not want to be bothered by their children, whether they are home all day or not. Unlike the parents in the first two groups, who care for their children however they can, these parents seek a permanent substitute for themselves.   —Nancy Whittle (student), "Modern Parenting"

7 Comparison and contrast

Comparison and contrast may be used separately or together to develop an idea. The following paragraph illustrates one of two common ways of organizing a comparison and contrast: **subject by subject**, first one subject and then the other.

> Consider the differences also in the behavior of rock and classical music audiences. At a rock concert, the audience members yell, whistle, sing along, and stamp their feet. They may even stand during the entire performance. The better the music, the more active they'll be. At a classical concert, in contrast, the better the performance, the more *still* the audience is. Members of the classical audience are so highly disciplined that they refrain from even clearing their throats or coughing.

No matter what effect the powerful music has on their intellects and feelings, they sit on their hands.
—Tony Nahm (student), "Rock and Roll Is Here to Stay"

The next paragraph illustrates the other common organization: **point by point,** with the two subjects discussed side by side and matched feature for feature:

> Arguing is often equated with fighting, but there are key differences between the two. Participants in an argument approach the subject to find common ground, or points on which both sides agree, while people engaged in a fight usually approach the subject with an "us-versus-them" attitude. Participants in an argument are careful to use respectful, polite language, in contrast to the insults and worse that people in a fight use to get the better of their opponents. Finally, participants in an argument commonly have the goal of reaching a new understanding or larger truth about the subject they're debating, while those in a fight have winning as their only goal.
> —Erica Ito (student), "Is an Argument Always a Fight?"

8 Cause-and-effect analysis

When you use analysis to explain why something happened or what did or may happen, then you are determining causes or effects. In the following paragraph the author looks at the cause of an effect—Japanese collectivism:

> The *shinkansen* or "bullet train" speeds across the rural areas of Japan giving a quick view of cluster after cluster of farmhouses surrounded by rice paddies. This particular pattern did not develop purely by chance, but as a consequence of the technology peculiar to the growing of rice, the staple of the Japanese diet. The growing of rice requires the construction and maintenance of an irrigation system, something that takes many hands to build. More importantly, the planting and the harvesting of rice can only be done efficiently with the cooperation of twenty or more people. The "bottom line" is that a single family working alone cannot produce enough rice to survive, but a dozen families working together can produce a surplus. Thus the Japanese have had to develop the capacity to work together in harmony, no matter what the forces of disagreement or social disintegration, in order to survive.   —William Ouchi, *Theory Z*

9 Process analysis

When you analyze how to do something or how something works, you explain a process. The following example identifies a process, describes the equipment needed, and details the steps in the process:

> As a car owner, you waste money when you pay a mechanic to change the engine oil. The job is not difficult, even if you know little

about cars. All you need is a wrench to remove the drain plug, a large, flat pan to collect the draining oil, plastic bottles to dispose of the used oil, and fresh oil. First, warm up the car's engine so that the oil will flow more easily. When the engine is warm, shut it off and remove its oil-filler cap (the owner's manual shows where this cap is). Then locate the drain plug under the engine (again consulting the owner's manual for its location) and place the flat pan under the plug. Remove the plug with the wrench, letting the oil flow into the pan. When the oil stops flowing, replace the plug and, at the engine's filler hole, add the amount and kind of fresh oil specified by the owner's manual. Pour the used oil into the plastic bottles and take it to a waste-oil collector, which any garage mechanic can recommend.

—Anthony Andreas (student), "Do-It-Yourself Car Care"

6d Writing introductory and concluding paragraphs

1 Introductions

An introduction draws readers from their world into yours.

- It focuses readers' attention on the topic and arouses their curiosity about what you have to say.
- It specifies your subject and implies your attitude.
- Often it includes your thesis statement.
- It is concise and sincere.

The box below gives options for focusing readers' attention.

Some strategies for introductions

- Ask a question.
- Relate an incident.
- Use a vivid quotation.
- Create a visual image that represents your subject.
- Offer a surprising statistic or other fact.
- Provide background.
- State an opinion related to your thesis.

- Outline the argument your thesis refutes.
- Make a historical comparison or contrast.
- Outline a problem or dilemma.
- Define a word central to your subject.
- In some business or technical writing, simply state your main idea.

CULTURE LANGUAGE These options for an introduction may not be what you are used to if your native language is not English. In other cultures readers may seek familiarity or reassurance from an author's introduction, or they may prefer an indirect approach to the subject. In academic and business English, however, writers and readers prefer concise, direct expression.

Openings to avoid

When writing and revising your introduction, avoid approaches that are likely to bore or confuse readers:

- **A vague generality or truth.** Don't extend your reach too wide with a line such as *Throughout human history . . .* or *In today's world. . . .* You may have needed a warm-up paragraph to start drafting, but your readers can do without it.
- **A flat announcement.** Don't start with *The purpose of this essay is . . .* , *In this essay I will . . .* , or any similar presentation of your intention or topic.
- **A reference to the essay's title.** Don't refer to the title of the essay in the first sentence—for example, *This is a big problem* or *This book is about the history of the guitar.*
- **According to Webster. . . .** Don't start by citing a dictionary definition. A definition can be an effective springboard to an essay, but this kind of lead-in has become dull with overuse.
- **An apology.** Don't fault your opinion or your knowledge with *I'm not sure if I'm right, but I think . . .* , *I don't know much about this, but . . .* , or a similar line.

2 | Conclusions

Your conclusion finishes off your essay and tells readers where you think you have brought them. It answers the question "So what?"

Effective conclusions

Usually set off in its own paragraph, the conclusion may consist of a single sentence or a group of sentences. It may take one or more of the approaches listed in the box below.

Some strategies for conclusions

- Recommend a course of action.
- Summarize the paper.
- Echo the approach of the introduction.
- Restate your thesis and reflect on its implications.
- Strike a note of hope or despair.
- Give a symbolic or powerful fact or other detail.
- Give an especially compelling example.
- Create an image that represents your subject.
- Use a quotation.

Conclusions to avoid

Several kinds of conclusions rarely work well:

- **A repeat of the introduction.** Don't simply replay your introduction. The conclusion should capture what the paragraphs of the body have added to the introduction.
- **A new direction.** Don't introduce a subject different from the one your essay has been about.
- **A sweeping generalization.** Don't conclude more than you reasonably can from the evidence you have presented. If your essay is about your frustrating experience trying to clear a parking ticket, you cannot reasonably conclude that *all* local police forces are too tied up in red tape to be of service to the people.
- **An apology.** Don't cast doubt on your essay. Don't say, *Even though I'm no expert* or *This may not be convincing, but I believe it's true* or anything similar. Rather, to win your readers' confidence, display confidence.

7 Document Design

Imaginehowharditwouldbetoreadandwriteiftextlookedlikethis. To make reading and writing easier, we place spaces between words. This convention and many others—such as page margins, paragraph breaks, and headings—have evolved over time to help writers communicate clearly with readers.

7a Designing academic papers and other documents

The design guidelines offered in this chapter apply to all types of documents, including academic papers, Web sites, business reports, flyers, and newsletters. Each type has specific requirements as well, covered elsewhere in this book.

1 Designing academic papers

Many academic disciplines prefer specific formats for students' papers. This book details two such formats:

- **Modern Language Association,** used in English, foreign languages, and other humanities (**MLA** pp. 399–401).

my**comp**lab

Visit *mycomplab.com* for more resources as well as exercises on document design.

- **American Psychological Association,** used in the social sciences and some natural and applied sciences.

Other academic formats can be found in the discipline style guides listed in **8** pp. 349, 352, and 355.

The design guidelines in this chapter extend the range of elements and options covered by most academic styles. Your instructors may want you to adhere strictly to a particular style or may allow some latitude in design. Ask them for their preferences.

2 Writing online

In and out of school, you are likely to do a lot of online writing—certainly e-mail and possibly blogs and other Web sites. The purposes and audiences for online writing vary widely, and so do readers' expectations for its design. See **2** pp. 102–12 for the approaches you can take in different online writing situations.

3 Designing business documents and other public writing

When you write outside your college courses, your audience will have certain expectations for how your documents should look and read. Guidelines for such writing appear later in this book:

- **Public writing,** including letters, job applications, reports, proposals, flyers, newsletters, and brochures (**2** pp. 117–28).
- **Oral presentations,** including *PowerPoint* slides and other visual aids (**2** pp. 112–17).

7b Considering principles of design

Most of the principles of design respond to the ways we read. White space, for instance, relieves our eyes and helps to lead us through a document. Groupings or lists help to show relationships. Type sizes, images, and color add variety and help to emphasize important elements.

The sample documents on these two pages illustrate quite different ways of presenting a report for a marketing course. Even at a glance, the second document is easier to scan and read. It makes better use of white space, groups similar elements, uses bullets and fonts for emphasis, and more successfully integrates the visual data of the chart.

As you design your own documents, think about your purpose, the expectations of your readers, and how readers will move through your document. Also consider the following general principles, noting that they overlap and support one another:

- **Conduct readers through the document.** Establish flow, a pattern for the eye to follow, with headings, lists, and other elements.

Original design

Runs title and subtitle together. Does not distinguish title from text.	
Crowds the page with minimal margins.	
Downplays paragraph breaks with small indentions.	
Buries statistics in a paragraph. Obscures relationships with non-parallel wording.	

Generation Online: College Students and the Internet

College life once meant classrooms of students listening to teachers or groups of students talking over lunch in the union. But the reality today is more complex: students interact with their peers and professors by computer as much as face to face. As these students graduate and enter the workforce, all of society will be affected by their experience.

According to the Pew Internet Research Center (2008), today's college students are practiced computer and Internet users. The Pew Center reports that 24 percent of students in college today started using computers between ages five and eight. By age eighteen all students were using computers. Almost all college students, 92 percent, rely on the Internet, with 66 percent of students using more than one e-mail address. Computer ownership among this group is also very high: 85 percent have purchased or have been given at least one computer.

Students are eager to tap into the Internet's benefits and convenience.

Does not introduce the figure, leaving readers to infer its meaning and purpose.

Overemphasizes the figure with large size and excessive white space.

Presents the figure undynamically, flat on.

Don't know 2%
Use library more 9%
Use Internet and library about the same 13%
Use Internet more 76%

Figure 1

Does not caption the figure to explain what it shows, offering only a figure number and a partial text explanation.

The Internet has eclipsed the library as the site of college students' research, as shown in Figure 1 from the Pew Report. In fact, a mere 9 percent of students

- **Use white space to ease crowding and focus readers' attention.** Provide ample margins, and give breathing room to headings, lists, and other elements. Even the space indicating new paragraphs (indentions or blank lines) gives readers a break and reassures them that ideas are divided into manageable chunks.
- **Group information to show relationships.** Use headings (like those in this chapter) and lists (like the one you're reading) to convey the similarities and differences among parts of a document.
- **Emphasize important elements.** Establish hierarchies of information with type fonts and sizes, headings, indentions, color, boxes, and white space. In this book, for example, the importance of headings is clear from their size and color and from the presence of decorative elements, such as the box around 7c in the heading on the next page.

Revised design

Generation Online:
College Students and the Internet

College life once meant classrooms of students listening to teachers or groups of students talking over lunch in the union. But the reality today is more complex: students interact with their peers and professors by computer as much as face to face. As these students graduate and enter the workforce, all of society will be affected by their experience.

According to the Pew Internet Research Center (2008), today's college students are practiced computer users and Internet users.

- They started young: 24 percent were using computers between ages five and eight, and all were using them by age eighteen.
- They rely on the Internet: 92 percent have used the network, and 66 percent use more than one e-mail address.
- They own computers: 85 percent have purchased or have been given at least one computer.

Students are eager to tap into the Internet's benefits and convenience. Figure 1, from the Pew Report, shows that the Internet has eclipsed the library as the site of college students' research. In fact, a mere 9 percent of students reported using the library more than the Internet as a starting point for research.

☐13% ☐9% ☐2% ■76%   ■ Use Internet more
                        ■ Use Internet and library
                          about the same
                        ■ Use library more
                        ☐ Don't know

Figure 1. College students' use of the Internet and the library for research

Distinguishes title from subtitle and both from text.

Provides adequate margins.

Emphasizes paragraph breaks with white space.

Groups statistics in a bulleted list set off with white space. Uses parallel wording for parallel information.

Introduces the figure to indicate its meaning and purpose.

Reduces white space around the figure.

Presents the figure to emphasize the most significant segment.

Captions the figure so that it can be read independently from the text.

■ **Standardize to create and fulfill expectations.** Help direct readers through a document by, for instance, using the same size and color for all headings at the same level of importance. Standardizing also reduces clutter, making it easier for readers to determine the significance of the parts.

7c Using the elements of design

Applying the preceding principles involves margins, text, lists, headings, color, and illustrations. You won't use all these elements for every project, and in many writing situations you will be required to follow a prescribed format (see p. 44 on formats in academic writing). If you are addressing readers who have vision loss, consider the additional guidelines discussed on p. 56.

Note Your word processor may provide wizards or templates for many kinds of documents, such as letters, memos, reports, agendas, résumés, and brochures. **Wizards** guide you through setting up and writing complicated documents. **Templates** are preset forms to which you add your own text, headings, and other elements. Wizards and templates can be helpful, but not if they lead you to create cookie-cutter documents no matter what the writing situation. Always keep in mind that a document should be appropriate for your subject, audience, and purpose.

1 Setting margins

Margins at the top, bottom, and sides of a page help to prevent the page from overwhelming readers with unpleasant crowding. Most academic and business documents use a minimum one-inch margin on all sides. Publicity documents, such as flyers and brochures, often use narrower margins, compensating with white space between elements. (See **2** pp. 125–28.)

2 Creating readable text

A document must be readable. You can make text readable by attending to line spacing, type fonts and sizes, highlighting, word spacing, and line breaks.

Line spacing

Most academic documents are double-spaced, with an initial indention for paragraphs, while most business documents are single-spaced, with an extra line of space between paragraphs. Double or triple spacing sets off headings in both types. Web sites and publicity documents, such as flyers and brochures, tend to use more line spacing to separate and group distinct parts of the content.

Type fonts and sizes

The readability of text also derives from the type fonts (or faces) and their sizes. For academic and business documents, generally choose a type size of 10 or 12 points, as in these samples:

```
10-point Courier        10-point Times New Roman
12-point Courier        12-point Times New Roman
```

These fonts and the one you're reading have **serifs**—the small lines that finish the letters. Serif fonts are suitable for formal writing and are often easier to read on paper. **Sans serif** fonts (*sans* means "without" in French) include this one found on many word processors:

10-point Arial   12-point Arial

Sans serif fonts can be easier to read on a computer screen and are clearer on paper for readers with some vision loss (see p. 58).

Your word processor probably offers many decorative fonts:

10-point Bodega Sans   **10-POINT COMIC**
10-POINT STENCIL   *10-point Park Avenue*

Decorative fonts are generally inappropriate for academic and business writing, where letter forms should be conventional and regular. But on some Web sites and in publicity documents, decorative fonts can attract attention, create motion, and reinforce a theme.

Note The point size of a type font is often an unreliable guide to its actual size, as the decorative fonts above illustrate. Before you use a font, print out a sample to be sure it is the size you want.

Highlighting

Within a document's text, underlined, *italic*, **boldface,** or even color type can emphasize key words or sentences. Underlining is rarest these days, having been replaced by italics. Both academic and business writing sometimes use boldface for strong emphasis—as with a term being defined—and publicity documents often rely extensively on boldface to draw the reader's eye. Neither academic nor business writing generally uses color within passages of text. In Web and publicity documents, however, color may be effective if it is dark enough to be readable. (See p. 51 for more on color.)

No matter what your writing situation, use highlighting selectively to complement your meaning, not merely for decoration.

Word spacing

In most writing situations, follow these guidelines for spacing within and between words:

- **Leave one space between words.**
- **Leave one space after all punctuation, with these exceptions:**

Dash (two hyphens or the so-called em dash on a computer)	book--its	book—its
Hyphen	one-half	
Apostrophe within a word	book's	
Two or more adjacent marks	book.")	
Opening quotation mark, parenthesis, or bracket	("book	[book

- **Leave one space before and after an ellipsis mark.** In the examples below, ellipsis marks indicate omissions within a sentence and at the end of a sentence. See **5** pp. 277–79 for additional examples.

  book . . . in   book. . . . The

Line breaks

Your word processor will generally insert appropriate breaks between lines of continuous text: it will not, for instance, automatically begin a line with a comma or period, and it will not end a line with an opening parenthesis or bracket. However, you will have to prevent it from breaking a two-hyphen dash or a three-dot ellipsis mark by spacing to push the beginning of each mark to the next line.

When you instruct it to do so (usually under the Tools menu), your word processor will also automatically hyphenate words to prevent very short lines. If you must decide yourself where to break words, see **6** pp. 286–87.

3 Using lists

Lists give visual reinforcement to the relations between like items—for example, the steps in a process or the elements of a proposal. A list is easier to read than a paragraph and adds white space to the page.

When wording a list, work for parallelism among items—for instance, all complete sentences or all phrases (see also **3** p. 140). Set the list with space above and below and with numbering or bullets (centered dots or other devices, such as the blue squares used in this book). On most word processors you can format a numbered or bulleted list automatically using the Format menu.

4 Using headings

Headings are signposts: they direct the reader's attention by focusing the eye on a document's most significant content. Most Web and publicity documents use headings both decoratively and functionally, to capture and then direct readers' attention. In contrast, most academic and business documents use headings only functionally, to divide text, orient readers, and create emphasis.

When you use headings in academic and business documents, follow these guidelines:

- **Use one, two, or three levels of headings** depending on the needs of your material and the length of your document. Some level of heading every two or so pages will help keep readers on track.

- **Create an outline of your document** to plan where headings should go. Use the first level of heading for the main points (and sections) of your document. Use a second and perhaps a third level of heading to mark subsections of supporting information.

- **Keep headings as short as possible** while making them specific about the material that follows.
- **Word headings consistently**—for instance, all questions (*What Is the Scientific Method?*), all phrases with *-ing* words (*Understanding the Scientific Method*), or all phrases with nouns (*The Scientific Method*).
- **Indicate the relative importance of headings** with type size, positioning, and highlighting, such as capital letters, underlining, or boldface.

First-Level Heading

Second-Level Heading

Third-Level Heading

Generally, you can use the same type font and size for headings as for the text.

- **Don't break a page immediately after a heading.** Push the heading to the next page.

Note Document format in psychology and some other social sciences requires a particular treatment of headings.

5 | Using color

With a computer and a color printer, most writers can produce documents that use color for bullets, headings, borders, boxes, illustrations, and other elements. Web and publicity documents almost always use color, whereas academic and business documents consisting only of headings and text may not need color at all. (Ask your instructor or supervisor for his or her preferences.) If you do use color in an academic document, follow these guidelines:

- **Print text in black,** not red, blue, or another color.
- **Make sure that color headings are dark enough to be readable.**
- **Stick to the same color for all headings at the same level**— for instance, red for main headings, black for secondary headings.
- **Use color for bullets, lines, and other nontext elements.** But use no more than a few colors to keep pages clean.
- **Use color to distinguish the parts of illustrations**—the segments of charts, the lines of graphs, and the parts of diagrams. Use only as many colors as you need to make your illustration clear.

See also p. 56 on the use of color for readers who have vision loss.

7d Using illustrations

An illustration can often make a point for you more efficiently than words can. Tables present data. Figures (such as graphs and charts) usually recast data in visual form. Diagrams, drawings, and photographs can explain processes, represent what something looks like, or add emphasis.

1 Using illustrations appropriately for the writing situation

Academic and many business documents tend to use illustrations differently from publicity documents. In the latter, illustrations generally attract attention, enliven the piece, or emphasize a point, and they may not be linked directly to the document's text. In academic and business writing, however, illustrations directly reinforce and amplify the text. Follow these guidelines for academic and most business writing:

- **Focus on a purpose for each illustration**—a reason for including it and a point you want it to make. Otherwise, readers may find it irrelevant or confusing.
- **Provide a source note for someone else's independent material**—whether data or an entire illustration (see **7** p. 313). Each discipline has a slightly different style for such source notes: those in the illustrations on the next several pages reflect MLA style for English and some other humanities.
- **Number figures, photographs, and other images together:** Figure 1, Figure 2, and so on.
- **Number and label tables separately:** Table 1, Table 2, and so on.
- **Refer to each illustration in your text**—for instance, "See fig. 2." Place the reference at the point(s) in the text where readers will benefit by consulting the illustration.
- **Determine the placement of illustrations.** The social sciences and some other disciplines require each illustration to fall on a page by itself immediately after the text reference to it. You may want to follow this rule in other situations as well if you have a large number of illustrations. Otherwise, you can embed them in your text pages just after you refer to them. When embedding illustrations, consider where they will help but not distract readers.

2 Using tables

Tables usually present raw data, making complex information accessible to readers. The data may show how variables relate to one another, how variables change over time, or how two or more groups contrast. The following table emphasizes the last function.

Table

A self-explanatory title falls above the table. Self-explanatory headings label horizontal rows and vertical columns.	The layout of rows and columns is clear: headings align with their data, and numbers align vertically down columns.

Table 1

Public- and private-school enrollment of US students age five and older, 2006

	Number of students	Percentage in public school	Percentage in private school
All students	74,220,937	83.2	16.8
Kindergarten	4,012,680	86.0	14.0
Grades 1-4	15,758,734	88.8	11.2
Grades 5-8	16,498,217	89.4	10.6
Grades 9-12	17,500,473	90.5	9.5
College (undergraduate)	17,063,732	77.0	23.0
Graduate and professional school	3,387,101	59.8	40.2

Source: Data from *2006 American Community Survey*; US Census Bureau, n.d.; Web; 10 Oct. 2008; table S1404.

3 Using figures

Figures represent data or show concepts visually. They include charts, graphs, diagrams, and photographs.

Pie charts

Pie charts show the relations among the parts of a whole. The whole totals 100 percent, and each pie slice is proportional in size to its share of the whole. Use a pie chart when shares, not the underlying data, are your focus.

Pie chart

Fig. 1. Marital status in 2006 of adults age eighteen and over. Data from *Statistical Abstract of the United States: 2008*; US Census Bureau, 27 Mar. 2007; Web; 10 Oct. 2008.

Color distinguishes segments of the chart. Use distinct shades of gray, black, and white if your paper will not be read in color.
Segment percentages total 100.
Every segment is clearly labeled. You can also use a key, as in the chart on p. 57.
Self-explanatory caption falls below the chart.

Bar charts

Bar charts compare groups or time periods on a measure such as quantity or frequency. Use a bar chart when relative size is your focus. Be sure to start with a zero point in the lower left corner so that the values on the vertical axis are clear.

Bar chart

Vertical scale shows and clearly labels the values being measured. Zero point clarifies values.

Horizontal scale shows and clearly labels the groups being compared.

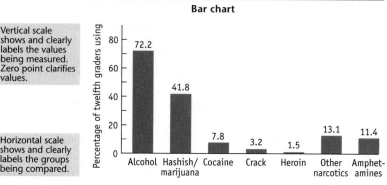

Self-explanatory caption falls below the chart.

Fig. 2. Lifetime prevalence of use of alcohol and other drugs among twelfth graders in 2007. Data from *Monitoring the Future: A Continuing Study of American Youth*; U of Michigan, 11 Dec. 2007; Web; 10 Aug. 2008.

Line graphs

Line graphs show change over time in one or more subjects. They are an economical and highly visual way to compare many points of data. Be sure to start with a zero point in the lower left corner so that the values on the vertical axis are clear.

Line graph

Vertical scale shows and clearly labels the values being measured. Zero point clarifies values.

Color and labels distinguish the subjects being compared. Use dotted and dashed black lines if your paper will not be read in color.

Horizontal scale shows and clearly labels the range of dates.

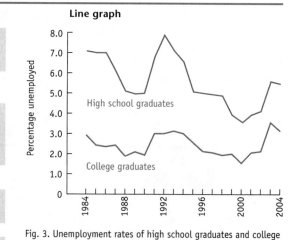

Self-explanatory caption falls below the graph.

Fig. 3. Unemployment rates of high school graduates and college graduates, 1984-2004. Data from Antony Davies; *The Economics of College Tuition*; Mercatus Center, George Mason U, 3 Mar. 2005; Web; 26 June 2008.

Diagrams

Diagrams show concepts visually, such as the structure of an organization, the way something works or looks, or the relations among subjects. Often, diagrams show what can't be described economically in words.

Diagram

Diagram makes concept comprehensible.

Fig. 4. RGB color theory, applied to televisions and computer monitors, in which all possible colors and white are created from red, green, and blue. From "Color Theory"; *Wikipedia*; Wikimedia, 15 Mar. 2005; Web; 13 May 2008.

Self-explanatory caption falls below the diagram.

Photographs and other images

Sometimes you may focus an entire paper on analyzing an image such as a photograph, painting, or advertisement. But most commonly you'll use images to add substance to ideas or to enliven them. You might clarify a psychology paper with a photograph from a key experiment, add information to an analysis of a novel with a drawing of the author, or capture the theme of a brochure with a cartoon. Images grab readers' attention, so use them carefully to explain, reinforce, or enhance your writing.

Note When using an image prepared by someone else—for instance, a photograph downloaded from the Web—you must verify that the source permits reproduction of the image before you use it. In most documents, but especially in academic papers, you must also fully cite the source of any borrowed image. See **7** pp. 335–36 on copyright issues with Internet sources.

Photograph

Photograph shows subject more economically and dramatically than words could.

Self-explanatory caption falls below the image.

Fig. 5. View of Saturn from the *Cassini* spacecraft, showing the planet and its rings. From United States, Natl. Atmospheric and Space Administration, Jet Propulsion Laboratory; *Cassini-Huygens: Mission to Saturn and Titan*; NASA, 24 Feb. 2005; Web; 26 Apr. 2008.

7e   Considering readers with vision loss

Your audience may include readers who have low vision, problems with color perception, or difficulties processing visual information. If so, consider adapting your design to meet these readers' needs. Here are a few pointers:

- **Use large type fonts.** Most guidelines call for 14 points or larger.
- **Use standard type fonts.** Many people with low vision find it easier to read sans serif fonts such as Arial than serif fonts (see pp. 48–49). Avoid decorative fonts with unusual flourishes, even in headings.
- **Avoid words in all-capital letters.**
- **Avoid relying on color alone to distinguish elements.** Label elements, and distinguish them by position or size.
- **Use red and green selectively.** To readers who are red-green colorblind, these colors will appear in shades of gray, yellow, or blue.
- **Use contrasting colors.** To make colors distinct, choose them from opposite sides of the color spectrum—violet and yellow, for instance, or orange and blue.
- **Use only light colors for tints behind type.** Make the type itself black or a very dark color.

7f   Designing documents at MSU

The documents produced in the First-Year Writing program at Michigan State University can and do take a variety of forms. The guidelines in this section are good general advice for the most typical assignments. However, since the First-Year Writing courses at MSU use an inquiry-based approach, composing assignments requires students to consider the rhetorical situation of each assignment and make rhetorical decisions about what fulfills the needs of each individual situation. You can employ the RAIDS (revision, arrangement, invention, delivery, and style) heuristic to help you fully consider the needs of any rhetorical situation. This consideration extends beyond merely what you write to how you present your work. Thinking about the RAIDS heuristic in this expanded way helps you plan and compose all of the assignments in the course, both written and otherwise.

Design is often thought to be something a writer is concerned with at the end of a project. However, this is not always true. Design impacts the effectiveness of a piece of discourse and it is, therefore, an important consideration during the entire process of composing. What you are designing (e.g. a brochure) and how you design (e.g. as a trifold document) has dramatic implications for the content itself as well as its presentation. So, when designing your work use the following questions to guide you:

- What is invention? (What activities should you engage in to create the text?)
- What is being invented? (What ideas, practices, arguments, etc. are you trying to present in the text?)
- What is being arranged? (What concepts, ideas, and/or objects are you putting in relation to what?)
- What is arrangement? (How should things be put in relation to one another? How can you use the design of your document to create effective arrangement patterns?)
- What is being revised? (What are you trying to change (e.g. what ideas, practices, etc.? and how will you use the design to help you accomplish this?))
- What is revision? (What design elements are most likely to support your revisionary purpose?)
- What style will you use and how will that help you relate to your audience? (How formal or informal should your document be? What font faces and sizes will you use for different

kinds of text such as headings and body text? Why have you made these choices?)

- What mode of delivery will you use to present your ideas and what is the effect of using that mode upon the audience? (Will you solely be using text? Do you have information that you can and/or should deliver visually?)

The importance of considering the rhetorical impact of every design choice that you make is crucial to creating an effective document. Depending on the assignment and your instructor, you may be given great latitude to make these decisions on your own. Well-considered design choices enhance a document's effectiveness and readability. Conversely, not considering these issues as you put together a document can adversely affect your audience's ability to understand your ideas and/or provoke an undesirable response from your audience.[1]

---

[1] Section 7f contributed by the MSU Custom Team.

PART 2

Writing in and out of College

MICHIGAN STATE
UNIVERSITY

8 Academic Skills

When you take college courses, you enter an academic discipline—a community of instructors and students whose basic goal is to build knowledge about a subject, whether it is English, history, engineering, or something else. You participate in a discipline community first by studying a subject, acquiring its vocabulary, and learning to express yourself in its ways. As you gain experience and knowledge, you contribute to the community by asking questions and communicating your answers in writing. This active, involved learning is the core of academic work. It may seem beyond you at first, as you try to grasp the content of readings and identify important ideas. But the transition will be easier if you follow this chapter's advice for getting the most from your classes, understanding assigned reading, becoming an academic writer, and preparing for exams.

8a Listening and taking notes in class

When you begin each class meeting, push aside other concerns so that you can focus and listen. Either on paper or on a computer, record what you hear as completely as possible while sorting out the main ideas from the secondary and supporting ones. (See the following box.) Such active note taking will help you understand the instructor's approach to the course and provide you with complete material for later study.

Tips for taking class notes

- **Use your own words.** You will understand and retain the material better if you rephrase it. But use the speaker's words if necessary to catch everything.
- **Leave space in your notes if you miss something.** Ask someone for the missing information as soon as possible after class.
- **Include any reading content mentioned by your instructor.** Use your notes to integrate all the components of the course—your instructor's views, your own thoughts, and the assigned reading.

(continued)

Visit *mycomplab.com* for more resources on academic skills.

Tips for taking class notes
(continued)

- **Review your notes shortly after class.** Reinforce your new knowledge when it is fresh by underlining key words and ideas, adding headings and comments in the margins, converting your notes to questions, or outlining the lecture based on your notes.

8b | Reading for comprehension

The assigned reading you do for college courses—such as textbooks, journal articles, essays, and works of literature—requires a greater focus on understanding and retention than does the reading you do for entertainment or for practical information. The process outlined below may seem time consuming, but with practice you'll become efficient at it.

Note The following process stresses ways of understanding what you read. In critical reading, covered in the next chapter, you extend this process to analyze and evaluate what you read and see.

1 Writing while reading

Reading for comprehension is an *active* process. Students often believe they are reading actively when they roll a highlighter over the important ideas in a text, but truly engaged reading requires more than that. If you take notes while reading, you "translate" the work into your own words and reconstruct it for yourself.

The substance of your reading notes will change as you preview, read, and summarize. At first, you may jot quick, short notes in the margins, on separate pages, or on a computer. (Use the last two for material you don't own or are reading online.) As you delve into the work, the notes should become more detailed, restating important points, asking questions, connecting ideas. (See p. 69 for an example of a text annotated in this way by a student.) For some reading, you may want to keep a reading journal that records both what the work says and what you think about it.

2 Previewing

For most course reading, you should skim before reading word for word. Skimming gives you an overview of the material: its length and difficulty, organization, and principal ideas.

- **Gauge length and level.** Is the material brief and straightforward enough to read in one sitting, or do you need more time?
- **Examine the title and introduction.** The title and first couple of paragraphs will give you a sense of the topic, the author's approach, and the main ideas. As you read them, ask yourself what you already know about the subject so that you can integrate new information with old.
- **Move from heading to heading or paragraph to paragraph.** Viewing the headings as headlines or as the levels of an outline will give you a feeling for which ideas the author sees as primary and which subordinate. In a text without headings, reading the first sentence of each paragraph will give you a sense of the author's important ideas.
- **Note highlighted words.** You will likely need to learn the meanings of terms in **bold**, *italic,* or color.
- **Slow down for pictures, diagrams, tables, graphs, and other illustrations.** They often contain concentrated information.
- **Read the summary or conclusion.** These paragraphs often recap the main ideas.
- **Think over what you've skimmed.** Try to recall the central idea, or thesis, and the sequence of ideas.

3 Reading

After previewing a text, you can settle into it to learn what it has to say.

First reading

The first time through new material, read as steadily and smoothly as possible, trying to get the gist of what the author is saying.

- **Read in a place where you can concentrate.** Choose a quiet environment away from distractions such as music or talking.
- **Give yourself time.** Rushing yourself or worrying about something else you have to do will prevent you from grasping what you read.
- **Try to enjoy the work.** Seek connections between it and what you already know. Appreciate new information, interesting relationships, forceful writing, humor, good examples.
- **Make notes sparingly during this first reading.** Mark major stumbling blocks—such as a paragraph you don't understand—so that you can try to resolve them before rereading.

CULTURE • LANGUAGE   If English is not your first language and you come across unfamiliar words don't stop and look up every one. You will lose more in concentration than you will gain in understanding. Instead, try to guess the meanings of unfamiliar words from their contexts, circle them, and look them up later.

Rereading

After the first reading, plan on at least one other. This time read *slowly*. Your main concern should be to grasp the content and how it is constructed. That means rereading a paragraph if you didn't get the point or using a dictionary to look up words you don't know.

Use your pen, pencil, or keyboard freely to highlight and distill the text:

- **Distinguish main ideas from supporting ideas.** Look for the central idea, or thesis, for the main idea of each paragraph or section, and for the evidence supporting ideas.
- **Learn key terms.** Understand both their meanings and their applications.
- **Discern the connections among ideas.** Be sure you see why the author moves from point A to point B to point C and how those points work together to support the central idea. It often helps to outline the text or summarize it (see below).
- **Add your own comments.** In the margins or separately, note links to other readings or to class discussions, questions to explore further, possible topics for your writing, points you find especially strong or weak. (This last category will occupy much of your time when you are expected to read critically. See pp. 70–73.)

4 Summarizing

A good way to master the content of a text is to summarize it: reduce it to its main points, in your own words.

Writing a summary

- **Understand the meaning.** Look up words or concepts you don't know so that you understand the author's sentences and how they relate to one another.
- **Understand the organization.** Work through the text to identify its sections—single paragraphs or groups of paragraphs focused on a single topic. To understand how parts of a work relate to one another, try drawing a tree diagram or creating an outline (1 pp. 19–20).
- **Distill each section.** Write a one- or two-sentence summary of each section you identify. Focus on the main point of the section, omitting examples, facts, and other supporting evidence.

> ■ **State the main idea.** Write a sentence or two capturing the author's central idea.
> ■ **Support the main idea.** Write a full paragraph (or more, if needed) that begins with the central idea and supports it with the sentences that summarize sections of the work. The paragraph should concisely and accurately state the thrust of the entire work.
> ■ *Use your own words.* By writing, you re-create the meaning of the work in a way that makes sense for you.

Summarizing even a passage of text can be tricky. Below is one attempt to summarize the following material from an introductory biology textbook.

Original text

As astronomers study newly discovered planets orbiting distant stars, they hope to find evidence of water on these far-off celestial bodies, for water is the substance that makes possible life as we know it here on Earth. All organisms familiar to us are made mostly of water and live in an environment dominated by water. They require water more than any other substance. Human beings, for example, can survive for quite a few weeks without food, but only a week or so without water. Molecules of water participate in many chemical reactions necessary to sustain life. Most cells are surrounded by water, and cells themselves are about 70–95% water. Three-quarters of Earth's surface is submerged in water. Although most of this water is in liquid form, water is also present on Earth as ice and vapor. Water is the only common substance to exist in the natural environment in all three physical states of matter: solid, liquid, and gas.

—Neil A. Campbell and Jane B. Reece, *Biology*

Draft summary

Astronomers look for water in outer space because life depends on it. It is the most common substance on Earth and in living cells, and it can be a liquid, a solid (ice), or a gas (vapor).

This summary accurately restates ideas in the original, but it does not pare the passage to its essence. The work of astronomers and the three physical states of water add color and texture to the original, but they are asides to the key concept that water sustains life because of its role in life. The following revision narrows the summary to this concept:

Revised summary

Water is the most essential support for life—the dominant substance on Earth and in living cells and a component of life-sustaining chemical processes.

Note Do not count on the AutoSummarize function on your word processor for summarizing texts that you may have copied onto your computer. The summaries are rarely accurate, and you will not gain the experience of interacting with the texts on your own.

8c Becoming an academic writer

As a member of an academic community, you will communicate with other members mainly through writing. Chapter 10 provides a detailed introduction to academic writing, and **8** (Chapters 55–56) treats writing in specific disciplines. The disciplines do differ in their conventions for writing, but in all of them you will be expected to do the following:

- **Know the writing situation posed in each assignment.** Most assignments will at least suggest possible subjects and imply a purpose and an audience. In that context, you refine your subject, your purpose, and your sense of audience as you proceed through the writing process. For a review of assessing the writing situation, see **1** pp. 2–5.
- **Develop and organize your writing.** Most academic papers center on a main point, or thesis, and support the thesis with evidence. For more on developing a thesis and organizing a paper, see **1** pp. 17–20.
- **Synthesize your own and others' ideas.** Academic writing often involves interacting with the works of other writers—responding to them, comparing them, and using them to answer questions. Such interaction requires you to read critically (the subject of the next chapter) and to **synthesize**, or integrate, others' ideas into your own. For more on synthesis, see p. 83.
- **Revise and edit your writing.** Academic writing is careful writing. Allow yourself enough time to revise and edit so that readers can see your main ideas, follow your train of thought, and make sense of your sentences. Consult this book's revision and editing checklists in **1** pp. 24 and 26.
- **Acknowledge your sources.** Academic writers build on the work of others by fully crediting borrowed ideas and information. Always record the publication information of any source you consult so that you can cite it if you decide to use it later in your writing. See **7** pp. 330–37 for a discussion of avoiding plagiarism. For guides to specific documentation styles, see **MLA** pp. 358–401 (English and some other humanities).

8d Preparing for exams

Studying for an exam involves three main steps, each requiring about a third of the preparation time: reviewing the material, organizing summaries of the material, and testing yourself. Your main goals are to strengthen your understanding of the subject, making both its ideas and its details more memorable, and to increase the flexibility of your new knowledge so that you can apply it in new contexts.

Note Cramming for an exam is about the least effective way of preparing for one. It takes longer to learn under stress, and the learning is shallower, more difficult to apply, and more quickly forgotten. Information learned under stress is even harder to apply in stressful situations such as taking an exam. And the lack of sleep that usually accompanies cramming makes a good performance even more unlikely. If you must cram for a test, face the fact that you can't learn everything. Spend your time reviewing main concepts and facts.

1 Reviewing and memorizing the material

Divide your class notes and reading assignments into manageable units. Reread the material, recite or write out the main ideas and selected supporting ideas and examples, and then skim for an overview. Proceed in this way through all the units of the course, returning to earlier ones as needed to refresh your memory or to relate ideas.

During this stage you should be memorizing what you don't already know by heart. Try these strategies for strengthening your memory:

- **Link new and known information.** For instance, to remember a sequence of four dates in twentieth-century African history, link the dates to simultaneous and more familiar events in the United States.
- **Create groups of ideas or facts that make sense to you.** For instance, memorize French vocabulary words in related groups, such as words for parts of the body or parts of a house. Keep the groups small: research has shown that we can easily memorize about seven items at a time but have trouble with more.
- **Create narratives and visual images.** You may recall a story or a picture more easily than words. For instance, to remember how the economic laws of supply and demand affect the market for rental housing, you could tie the principles to a narrative about the aftermath of the 1906 San Francisco earthquake, when half the population was suddenly homeless. Or you could visualize a person who has dollar signs for eyes and is converting a spare

room into a high-priced rental unit, as many did after the earth-quake to meet the new demand for housing.

- Use *mnemonic devices,* **or tricks for remembering.** Say the history dates you want to remember are separated by five years, then four, then nine. By memorizing the first date and recalling 5 + 4 = 9, you'll have command of all four dates.

2 Organizing summaries of the material

Allow time to reorganize the material in your own way, creating categories that will help you apply the information in various contexts. For instance, in studying for a biology exam, work to understand a process, such as how a plant develops or how photosynthesis occurs. Or in studying for an American government test, explain the structures of the local, state, and federal levels of government. Other useful categories include advantages/disadvantages and causes/effects. Such analytical thinking will improve your mastery of the course material and may even prepare you directly for specific essay questions.

3 Testing yourself

Convert each heading in your lecture notes and course reading into a question. Answer in writing, going back to the course material to fill in what you don't yet know. Be sure you can define and explain all key terms. For subjects that require solving problems (such as mathematics, statistics, or physics), work out a difficult problem for every type on which you will be tested. For all subjects, focus on the main themes and questions of the course. In a psychology course, for example, be certain you understand principal theories and their implications. In a literature course, test your knowledge of literary movements and genres or the relations among specific works.

When you are satisfied with your preparation, stop studying. If your exam is the next day, get as much sleep as your schedule allows. You will be able to think more clearly on exam day if you are rested.

9 Critical Thinking and Reading

Throughout college and beyond, you will be expected to think, read, and write critically. **Critical** here does not mean "negative" but "skeptical," "exacting," "creative." You already operate critically every day as you figure out why things happen to you or what your experiences mean. This chapter introduces more formal methods for reading texts critically (below), developing a critical response (p. 70), and viewing images critically (p. 73).

Note Critical thinking plays a large role in research writing. See **7** pp. 316–23 on evaluating print and online sources and **7** pp. 303–04 on synthesizing sources.

9a Using techniques of critical reading

In college and work, much of your critical thinking will focus on written texts (a short story, a journal article, a blog) or on visual objects (a photograph, a chart, a film). Like all subjects worthy of critical consideration, such works operate on at least three levels: (1) what the creator actually says or shows, (2) what the creator does not say or show explicitly but builds into the work (intentionally or not), and (3) what you think. Discovering the first of these levels—reading for comprehension—is discussed in the preceding chapter as part of academic skills (see pp. 61–63). This chapter builds on the earlier material to help you discover the other two levels.

CULTURE LANGUAGE The idea of reading critically may require you to make some adjustments if readers in your native culture tend to seek understanding or agreement more than engagement from what they read. Readers of English use texts for all kinds of reasons, including pleasure, reinforcement, and information. But they also read skeptically, critically, to see the author's motives, test their own ideas, and arrive at new knowledge.

1 Previewing the material

When you're reading a work of literature, such as a short story or a poem, it's often best just to plunge right in. But for critical reading of other works, it's worthwhile to skim before reading word for word, forming expectations and even some preliminary questions. The preview will make your reading more informed and fruitful.

mycomplab

Visit *mycomplab.com* for more resources on critical thinking and reading.

- **What is the work's subject and structure?** Following the steps outlined on p. 62, gauge the length and level, read the title and introduction for clues to the topic and main ideas, read the headings, note highlighted words (defined terms), examine illustrations, and read the summary or conclusion.
- **What are the facts of publication?** Does the date of publication suggest currency or datedness? Does the publisher or publication specialize in a particular kind of material—for instance, scholarly articles or popular books? For a Web document, who or what sponsors the site: an individual? a nonprofit organization? an academic institution? a corporation? a government body?
- **What do you know about the author?** Does a biography tell you about the author's publications, interests, biases, and reputation in the field? For an online source, which may be posted by an unfamiliar or anonymous author, what can you gather about the author from his or her words? If possible, trace unfamiliar authors to learn more about them.
- **What is your preliminary response?** What do you already know about the author's subject? What questions do you have about either the subject or the author's approach to it? What biases of your own might influence your reception of the work—for instance, curiosity, boredom, or an outlook similar or opposed to the author's?

2 Reading

Reading is itself more than a one-step process. You want to understand the first level on which the text operates—what the author actually says—and begin to form your impressions.

A procedure for this stage appears in the preceding chapter (pp. 62–63). To recap: Read once through fairly smoothly, trying to appreciate the work and keeping your notes to a minimum. Then read again more carefully, this time making detailed notes, to grasp the ideas and their connections and to pose questions. In the following example, a student, Charlene Robinson, annotates the first four paragraphs of "Student Loans":

> The first lesson of economics is scarcity: There is never enough of anything to fully satisfy all those who want it.
>
> The first lesson of politics is to disregard the first lesson of economics. When politicians discover some group that is being vocal about not having as much as they want, the "solution" is to give them more. Where do politicians get this "more"? They rob Peter to pay Paul.

Basic contradiction between economics and politics

← *biblical reference?*

After a while, of course, they discover that Peter doesn't have enough. Bursting with compassion, politicians rush to the rescue. Needless to say, they do not admit that robbing Peter to pay Paul was a dumb idea in the first place. On the contrary, they now rob Tom, Dick, and Harry to help Peter.

ironic and dismissive language

The latest chapter in this long-running saga is that politicians have now suddenly discovered that many college students graduate heavily in debt. To politicians it follows, as the night follows the day, that the government should come to their rescue with the taxpayers' money.

politicians = fools? or irresponsible

3 Summarizing

Summarizing a text—distilling it to its essential ideas, in your own words—is an important step for comprehending it and is discussed in detail in the previous chapter (pp. 63–65). Here, we'll look at how Charlene Robinson summarized paragraphs 1–4 of Thomas Sowell's "Student Loans." She first drafted this sentence:

Draft summary

As much as politicians would like to satisfy voters by giving them everything they ask for, the government cannot afford a student loan program.

Reading the sentence and Sowell's paragraphs, Robinson saw that this draft misread the text by asserting that the government cannot afford student loans. She realized that Sowell's point is more complicated than that and rewrote her summary:

Revised summary

As their support of the government's student loan program illustrates, politicians ignore the economic reality that using resources to benefit one group (students in debt) involves taking the resources from another group (taxpayers).

Note Using your own words when writing a summary not only helps you understand the meaning but also constitutes the first step in avoiding plagiarism. The second step is to cite the source when you use it in something written for others. See **7** pp. 330–37.

9b Developing a critical response

Once you've grasped the content of what you're reading—what the author says—then you can turn to understanding what the author does not say outright but suggests or implies or even lets slip. At this stage you are concerned with the purpose or intention of the author and with how he or she carries it out.

Critical thinking and reading consist of four overlapping operations: analyzing, interpreting, synthesizing, and (often) evaluating.

1 Analyzing

Analysis is the separation of something into its parts or elements, the better to understand it. To see these elements in what you are reading, begin with a question that reflects your purpose in analyzing the text: why you're curious about it or what you're trying to make out of it. This question will serve as a kind of lens that highlights some features and not others.

Analyzing Thomas Sowell's "Student Loans", you might ask one of these questions:

Questions for analysis	Elements
What is Sowell's attitude toward politicians?	References to politicians: content, words, tone
How does Sowell support his assertions about the loan program's costs?	Support: evidence, such as statistics and examples

2 Interpreting

Identifying the elements of something is only a start: you also need to interpret the meaning or significance of the elements and of the whole. Interpretation usually requires you to infer the author's **assumptions**—opinions or beliefs about what is or what could or should be. (*Infer* means to draw a conclusion based on evidence.)

Assumptions are pervasive: we all adhere to certain values, beliefs, and opinions. But assumptions are not always stated outright. Speakers and writers may judge that their audience already understands and accepts their assumptions; they may not even be aware of their assumptions; or they may deliberately refrain from stating their assumptions for fear that the audience will disagree. That is why your job as a critical thinker is to interpret what the assumptions are.

Thomas Sowell's "Student Loans" is based on certain assumptions, some obvious, some not. Analyzing Sowell's attitude toward politicians requires focusing on the statements about them. They "disregard the first lesson of economics" (paragraph 2), which implies that they ignore important principles (knowing that Sowell is an economist himself makes this a reasonable assumption). Politicians also "rob Peter to pay Paul," are "[b]ursting with compassion," "do not admit . . . a dumb idea," are characters in a "long-running saga," and arrive at the solution of spending taxes "as the night follows the day"—that is, inevitably (paragraphs 2–4). From these statements and others, we can infer the following:

> Sowell assumes that politicians become compassionate when a cause is loud and popular, not necessarily just, and they act irresponsibly by trying to solve the problem with other people's (taxpayers') money.

3 Synthesizing

If you stopped at analysis and interpretation, critical thinking and reading might leave you with a pile of elements and possible meanings but no vision of the whole. With **synthesis** you make connections among parts *or* among wholes. You use your perspective—your knowledge and beliefs—to create a new whole by drawing conclusions about relationships and implications.

A key component of academic reading and writing, synthesis receives attention in the next chapter (p. 83) and then in the context of research writing (see **7** pp. 303–04). Sometimes you'll respond directly to a text, as in the following statement about Thomas Sowell's essay "Student Loans," which connects Sowell's assumptions about politicians to a larger idea also implied by the essay:

> Sowell's view that politicians are irresponsible with taxpayers' money reflects his overall opinion that the laws of economics, not politics, should drive government.

Often synthesis will take you outside the text to its surroundings. The following questions can help you investigate the context of a work:

- **How does the work compare with works by others?** For instance, how have other writers responded to Sowell's views on student loans?
- **How does the work fit into the context of other works by the same author or group?** How do Sowell's views on student loans typify, or not, the author's other writing on political and economic issues?
- **What cultural, economic, or political forces influence the work?** What other examples might Sowell have given to illustrate his view that economics, not politics, should determine government spending?
- **What historical forces influence the work?** How has the indebtedness of college students changed over the past four decades?

4 Evaluating

Critical reading and writing often end at synthesis: you form and explain your understanding of what the work says and doesn't say. If you are also expected to **evaluate** the work, however, you will go further to judge its quality and significance. You may be evaluating a source you've discovered in research (see **7** pp. 316–23), or you may be completing an assignment to state and defend a judgment, such as *Thomas Sowell does not summon the evidence to support his case.* You can read Charlene Robinson's critical response to Thomas

Sowell's "Student Loans" by following the links in the e-book version of this handbook at *mycomplab.com.*

Evaluation takes a certain amount of confidence. You may think that you lack the expertise to cast judgment on another's work, especially if the work is difficult or the author well known. True, the more informed you are, the better a critical reader you are. But conscientious reading and analysis will give you the internal authority to judge a work *as it stands* and *as it seems to you,* against your own unique bundle of experiences, observations, and attitudes.

5 Using RAIDS for analysis

The First-Year Writing Program has developed RAIDS as a heuristic that you can use for both the generation of ideas as well as analyzing the ideas of others. As you consider the ideas you encounter, you will want to consider the following questions. You can see a full explanation of the RAIDS concepts in section 2g.

- What is invention?
- What is being invented?
- What is being arranged?
- What is arrangement?
- What is revision?
- What is being revised?
- What style is being used and how did that help the writer relate to his/her audience?
- What mode of delivery is being used and what is the effect of using that mode upon the audience?

Considering these questions will provide you with great insight into not only what is being said but also what motivates that discourse as well. Additionally, by using RAIDS consistently and frequently, you will also learn how authors construct texts, which will give you rhetorical tools that you can use in your own writing.

9c Viewing images critically

Every day we are bombarded with images—pictures on billboards, commercials on television, graphs and charts in newspapers and textbooks, to name just a few examples. Most images slide by without our noticing them, or so we think. But images, sometimes even more than text, can influence us covertly. Their creators have purposes, some worthy, some not, and understanding those purposes requires critical reading. The method parallels that in the previous section for reading text critically: preview, read for comprehension, analyze, interpret, synthesize, and (often) evaluate.

1 Previewing an image

Your first step in exploring an image is to form initial impressions of the work's origin and purpose and to note distinctive features. This previewing process is like the one for previewing a text (pp. 68–69):

- **What do you see?** What is most striking about the image? What is its subject? What is the gist of any text or symbols? What is the overall effect of the image?
- **What are the facts of publication?** Where did you first see the image? Do you think the image was created especially for that location or for others as well? What can you tell about when the image was created?
- **What do you know about the person or group that created the image?** For instance, was the creator an artist, scholar, news organization, or corporation? What seems to have been the creator's purpose?
- **What is your preliminary response?** What about the image interests, confuses, or disturbs you? Are the form, style, and subject familiar or unfamiliar? How might your knowledge, experiences, and values influence your reception of the image?

If possible, print a copy of the image or scan it into your reading journal, and write comments in the image margins or separately.

2 Reading an image

Reading an image requires the same level of concentration as reading a text. Try to answer the following questions about the image. If some answers aren't clear at this point, skip the question until later.

- **What is the purpose of the image?** Is it mainly explanatory, conveying information, or is it argumentative, trying to convince readers of something or to persuade them to act? What information or point of view does it seem intended to get across?
- **Who is the intended audience for the image?** What does the source of the image, including its publication facts, tell about the image creator's expectations for readers' knowledge, interests, and attitudes? What do the features of the image itself add to your impression?
- **What do any words or symbols add to the image?** Whether located on the image or outside it (such as in a caption), do words

or symbols add information, focus your attention, or alter your impression of the image?

- **What people, places, things, or action does the image show?** Does the image tell a story? Do its characters or other features tap into your knowledge, or are they unfamiliar?
- **What is the form of the image?** Is it a photograph, advertisement, painting, graph, diagram, cartoon, or something else? How do its content and apparent purpose and audience relate to its form?

The illustration below shows the notes that a student, Matthew Greene, made on an advertisement for *BoostUp.org*.

Annotation of an image

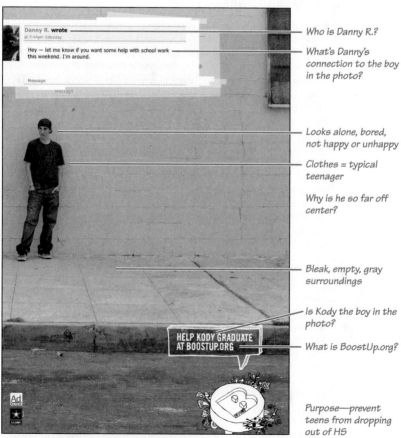

Advertisement for *BoostUp.org*, 2007

3 Analyzing an image

Elements for analysis

As when analyzing a written work, you analyze an image by identifying its elements. The image elements you might consider appear in the box below. Keep in mind that an image is a visual *composition* whose every element likely reflects a deliberate effort to communicate. Still, few images include all the elements, and you can narrow the list further by posing a question about the image you are reading, as illustrated opposite.

Elements of images

- **Emphasis:** Most images pull your eyes to certain features: a graph line moving sharply upward, a provocative figure, bright color, thick lines, and so on. The cropping of a photograph or the date range in a chart will also reflect what the image creator considers important.

- **Narration:** Most images tell stories, whether in a sequence (a TV commercial or a graph showing changes over time) or at a single moment (a photograph, a painting, or a pie chart). Sometimes dialog or a title or caption contributes to the story.

- **Point of view:** The image creator influences responses by taking account of both the viewer's physical relation to the image subject—for instance, whether it is seen head-on or from above—and the viewer's assumed attitude toward the subject.

- **Arrangement:** Patterns among colors or forms, figures in the foreground and background, and elements that are juxtaposed or set apart contribute to the image's meaning and effect.

- **Color:** An image's colors can direct the viewer's attention and convey the creator's attitude toward the subject. Color may also suggest a mood, an era, a cultural connection, or another frame in which to view the image.

- **Characterization:** The figures and objects in an image have certain qualities—sympathetic or not, desirable or not, and so on. Their characteristics reflect the roles they play in the image's story.

- **Context:** The source of an image or the background in an image affects its meaning, whether it is a graph from a scholarly journal or a photo of a car on a sunny beach.

- **Tension:** Images often communicate a problem or seize attention with features that seem wrong, such as misspelled or misaligned words, distorted figures, or controversial relations between characters.

- **Allusions:** An **allusion** is a reference to something the audience is likely to recognize and respond to. Examples include a cultural symbol such as a dollar sign, a mythological figure such as a unicorn, or a familiar movie character such as Darth Vader from *Star Wars*.

Question for analysis

You can focus your analysis of elements by framing your main interest in the image as a question. Matthew Greene posed this question about the *BoostUp.org* ad: *Does the ad move readers to learn more about* BoostUp.org *and how they can help teens to graduate?* The question led Greene to focus on certain elements of the ad:

Image elements	Responses
Emphasis	The ad's grayness and placement of Kody at the far left puts primary emphasis on the boy's isolation. Danny R.'s message, breaking up the gray, receives secondary emphasis.
Narration	The taped-on message suggests a story and connection between Kody and Danny R. Danny R. might be a friend, relative, or mentor. Based on the direct appeal in the word bubble, it appears that Danny R. is trying to help Kody graduate by offering to help him with schoolwork.
Arrangement	The ad places Danny R. and Kody together on the left side of the page, with Danny's message a bright spot on the dull landscape. The appeal to help Kody graduate is subtle and set on its own—the last thing readers look at. It also pulls the elements together so that the ad makes sense.
Color	The lack of color in most of the photo emphasizes Kody's isolation. The whiteness of Danny R.'s message relieves the grayness, like a ray of hope.

Sample Web pages for analysis

The screen shots on the next page are from *AIDS Clock*, an interactive Web site sponsored by the United Nations Population Fund (*www.unfpa.org/aids_clock*). The top image is the home page, displaying a traditional world map. The bottom image appears when viewers click on "Resize the map": now each country's size reflects the number of its people who live with HIV, the virus that causes AIDS. (For example, South Africa grows while the United States shrinks.) The large red number in the upper right changes every fifteen seconds. The "Wake up video" to its left scrolls through photos of people along with text urging viewers to join the World AIDS Campaign. Try to answer the questions in the annotations above the screen shots.

4 Interpreting an image

The strategies for interpreting an image parallel those for interpreting a written text (p. 71). In this process you look more deeply at the elements, considering them in relation to the image creator's

Elements of Web pages

Emphasis and color: What elements on these pages draw your attention? How does color distinguish and emphasize elements?

Narration: What story do the two Web pages tell? What does each map contribute to the story? What does the red number contribute? (Notice that the number changes from the first screen to the second.)

Arrangement: What does the arrangement of elements on the pages contribute to the story being told?

Tension: How do you respond to the distorted map in the second image? What does the distortion contribute to your view of the Web site's effectiveness?

Context: How does knowing the Web site's sponsoring organization, the United Nations Population Fund, affect your response to these images?

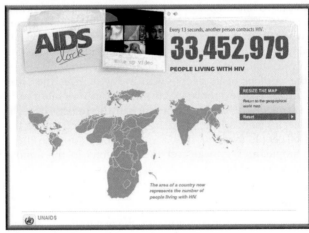

AIDS Clock Web pages, 2008

likely assumptions and intentions. You aim to draw reasonable inferences about *why* the image looks as it does, such as this inference about the *BoostUp.org* advertisement on p. 75:

> The creators of the *BoostUp.org* ad assume that readers want students to graduate from high school.

This statement is supported by the ad's text: the word bubble connecting to the *BoostUp.org* logo specifically says, "Help Kody graduate at BoostUp.org."

5 Synthesizing ideas about an image

As discussed on p. 72, with synthesis you take analysis and interpretation a step further to consider how a work's elements and underlying assumptions relate and what the overall message is. You may also expand your synthesis to view the whole image in a larger context: How does the work fit into the context of other works? What cultural, economic, political, or historical forces influence the work?

Placing an image in its context often requires research. For instance, to learn more about the assumptions underlying the *BoostUp.org* advertisement and the goals of the larger ad campaign, Matthew Greene visited the Web sites of *BoostUp.org* and the Ad Council, one of the ad's sponsors. The following entry from his reading journal synthesizes this research and his own ideas about the ad:

> The *BoostUp.org* magazine ad that features Kody is part of a larger campaign designed to raise public awareness about high school dropouts and encourage pubic support to help teens stay in school. Sponsored by the US Army and the nonprofit Ad Council, *BoostUp.org* profiles high school seniors who are at risk of dropping out and asks individuals to write the students personal messages of support. Ads like "Kody" are the first point of contact between the public and the teens, but they don't by themselves actually help the teens. For that, readers need to visit *BoostUp.org*. Thus the ad's elements work together like pieces of a puzzle, with the solution to be found only on the Web site.

6 Evaluating an image

If your critical reading moves on to evaluation, you'll form judgments about the quality and significance of the image: Is the message of the image accurate and fair, or is it distorted and biased? Can you support, refute, or extend the message? Does the image achieve its apparent purpose, and is the purpose worthwhile? How does the image affect you?

You can read Matthew Greene's response to the *BoostUp.org* advertisement by following the links in the e-book version of this handbook at *mycomplab.com*.

7 Analyzing multimedia with RAIDS

You can also use RAIDS to analyze literacy artifacts that are not traditional academic texts. For instance, in order to analyze visual images and/or multimedia objects like video, you can use the questions below:

- What is invention? (What activities did the composer(s) have to engage in to create the text?)
- What is being invented? (What ideas, practices, arguments, etc. are created through the text?)
- What is being arranged? (What is being put in relation to what?)
- What is arrangement? (How are things being put in relation to one another? How is the image composed? What are the parts of a video (text, visual, audio, ambient sound, motion, color, camera angle, etc.) that contribute to the overall message and how are they used)?
- What is being revised? (What is the composer(s) trying to change (e.g. what ideas, practices, etc.?))
- What is revision? (What is being or has been done to accomplish those revisions?)
- What style is being used and how did that help the composer relate to his/her audience?
- What mode of delivery is being used and what is the effect of using that mode upon the audience?

In using the above questions to analyze a multimedia object, you will acquire a greater awareness of how images and multimedia content are created. This is important for coming to a greater understanding about the media that you encounter on a daily basis. Also, knowing how images and multimedia are put together will be invaluable throughout the Remix assignment.[1]

---

[1]Sections 9b.5 and 9c.7 contributed by the MSU Custom Team.

10 Academic Writing

The academic disciplines differ widely in their subjects and approaches, but they all share the common goal of building knowledge through questioning, research, and communication. The differences among disciplines lie mainly in the kinds of questions asked, the kinds of research done to find the answers, and the **genres,** or types of writing, used to communicate the answers, such as case studies, research reports, literary analyses, and reviews of others' writings.

Both a discipline's concerns and the kind of writing create an academic writing situation, which in turn shapes a writer's choice of subject, conception of audience, definition of purpose, choice of structure and content, and even choice of language. This chapter introduces academic writing situations in general. See **8** (Chapters 55–56) for the particular goals and expectations of writing about literature and in other humanities, the social sciences, and the natural and applied sciences.

10a Writing in response to texts

Academic knowledge building depends on reading, analyzing, and expanding on the work of others. Thus many academic writing assignments require you to respond to one or more texts—not only to written products such as short stories and journal articles but also to visual communications such as images, charts, films, and advertisements. As you form a response to a text, you will synthesize, or integrate, its ideas and information with yours to come to your own conclusions.

Note A common academic assignment, the research paper, expects you to consult and respond to multiple texts in order to support and extend your ideas. See **7** (Chapters 50–54). This section focuses on responding directly to a single text, but the skills involved apply to research writing as well.

1 Deciding how to respond

When an assignment asks you to respond directly to a text, you might take one of the following approaches. (Note that the word

Visit *mycomplab.com* for more resources on academic writing.

author refers to a photographer, painter, or other creator as well as to a writer.)

- ■ **Agree with and extend the author's ideas,** exploring related ideas and providing additional examples.
- ■ **Agree with the author on some points but disagree on others.**
- ■ **Disagree with the author on one or more main points.**
- ■ **Explain how the author achieves a particular effect,** such as evoking a historical period or balancing opposing views.
- ■ **Analyze the overall effectiveness of a text**—for example, how well a writer supports a thesis with convincing evidence or whether an advertisement succeeds in its unstated purpose.

2 Forming a response

You will likely have an immediate response to at least some of the texts you analyze: you may agree or disagree strongly with what the author is saying. But for some other responses, you may need time and thought to determine what the author is saying and what you think about it.

Whatever your assignment, your first task is to examine the text thoroughly so that you're sure you understand what the author says outright and also assumes or implies. You can use the process of critical reading described in the previous chapter to take notes on the text, summarize it, and develop a critical response. Then, as you write, you can use the tips in the following box to convey your response to readers.

Responding to a text

- ■ **Make sure your writing has a point**—a central idea, or thesis, that focuses your response. (For more on developing a thesis, see 1 p. 17.)
- ■ **Include a very brief summary if readers may be unfamiliar with your subject.** But remember that your job is not just to report what the text says or what an image shows; it is to *respond* to the work from your own critical perspective. (For more on summary, see pp. 63–65.)
- ■ **Center each paragraph on an idea of your own that supports your thesis.** Generally, state the idea outright, in your own voice.
- ■ **Support the paragraph idea with evidence from the text**—quotations, paraphrases, details, and examples.
- ■ **Conclude each paragraph with your interpretation of the evidence.** As a general rule, avoid ending paragraphs with source evidence; instead, end with at least a sentence that explains what the evidence shows.

3 Emphasizing synthesis in your response

Following the suggestions in the preceding box will lead you to show readers the synthesis you achieved by thinking critically about the text. That is, you integrate your perspective with that of the author in order to support a conclusion of your own about the work.

A key to synthesis is deciding how to present evidence from your reading and observation in your writing. Especially when you are writing about a relatively unfamiliar subject, you may be tempted to let a text or other source do the talking for you through extensive summary or quotations. However, readers of your academic writing will expect to see you managing ideas and information to make your points. Thus a typical paragraph of text-based writing should open with your own idea, give evidence from the text, and conclude with your interpretation of the evidence. You can see examples of this paragraph pattern in the research paper in **MLA** pp. 403–11.

Note Effective synthesis requires careful handling of evidence from the text (quotations and paraphrases) so that it meshes smoothly into your sentences yet is clearly distinct from your own ideas. See **7** pp. 326–30 on integrating borrowed material.

10b Determining purpose

For most academic writing, your general purpose will be mainly explanatory or mainly argumentative. That is, you will aim to clarify your subject so that readers understand it as you do, or you will aim to gain readers' agreement with a debatable idea about the subject. (See **1** pp. 5–6 for more on general purposes and pp. 88–102 for more on argument.)

Your specific purpose—including your subject and how you hope readers will respond—depends on the kind of writing you're doing. For instance, in a literature review for a biology class, you want readers to understand the research area you're covering, the recent contributions made by researchers, the issues needing further research, and the sources you consulted. Not coincidentally, these topics correspond to the major sections of a literature review. In following the standard format, you both help to define your purpose and begin to meet the discipline's (and thus your instructor's) expectations.

Your specific purpose will be more complex as well. You take a course to learn about a subject and the ways experts think about it. Your writing, in return, contributes to the discipline through the knowledge you uncover and the lens of your perspective. At the same time, as a student you want to demonstrate your competence with research, evidence, format, and other requirements of the discipline.

10c Analyzing audience

Many academic writing assignments will specify or assume an educated audience or an academic audience. Such readers look for writing that is clear, balanced, well organized, and well reasoned, among other qualities discussed in the next section. Other assignments will specify or assume an audience of experts on your subject, readers who look in addition for writing that meets the subject's requirements for claims and evidence, organization, language, format, and other qualities.

Of course, much of your academic writing will have only one reader besides you: the instructor of the course for which you are writing. Instructors fill two main roles as readers:

- **They represent the audience you are addressing.** They may actually be members of the audience, as when you address academic readers or subject experts. Or they may imagine themselves as members of your audience—reading, for instance, as if they sat on the city council. In either case, they're interested in how effectively you write for the audience.
- **They serve as coaches,** guiding you toward achieving the goals of the course and, more broadly, toward the academic aims of building and communicating knowledge.

Like everyone else, instructors have preferences and peeves, but you'll waste time and energy trying to anticipate them. Do attend to written and spoken directions for assignments, of course. But otherwise view your instructors as representatives of the community you are writing for. Their responses will be guided by the community's aims and expectations and by a desire to teach you about them.

10d Choosing structure and content

Many academic writing assignments will at least imply how you should organize your paper and even how you should develop your ideas. Like the literature review mentioned opposite, the type of paper required will break into discrete parts, each with its own requirements for content.

No matter what type of paper an assignment specifies, the broad academic aims of building and exchanging knowledge determine features that are common across disciplines. Follow these general guidelines for your academic writing, supplementing them as indicated with others elsewhere in this book:

- **Develop a thesis**—a central idea or claim to which everything in the paper clearly relates. Usually, state your thesis near the beginning of the paper. For more on theses, see **1** p. 17.

- **Support the thesis with evidence,** drawn usually from research and sometimes from your own experience. The kinds of evidence will depend on the discipline you're writing in and the type of paper you're doing. For more on evidence in the disciplines, see **8** p. 347 (other humanities), 349–51 (social sciences), and 352 (natural and applied sciences).

- **Synthesize.** Put your sources to work for you by thinking critically about them. Integrate them into your own perspective using your own voice. For more on synthesis, see p. 83 and **7** pp. 303–04 in the discussion of research writing.

- **Acknowledge sources fully, including online sources.** *Not* acknowledging sources undermines the knowledge-sharing foundation of academic writing and opens you to charges of plagiarism, which can be punishable (see **7** pp. 330–36). For lists of disciplines' documentation guides, see **8** pp. 349, 352, and 355. For documentation guidelines and samples, see **MLA** pp. 358–67 (English and some other humanities).

- **Organize clearly within the framework of the type of writing you're doing.** Develop your ideas as simply and directly as your purpose and content allow. Clearly relate sentences, paragraphs, and sections so that readers always know where they are in the paper's development.

(CULTURE LANGUAGE) These features are far from universal. In other cultures, for instance, academic writers may be indirect or may not have to acknowledge well-known sources. Recognizing such differences between practices in your native culture and in the United States can help you adapt to US academic writing.

10e Using academic language

American academic writing relies on a dialect called standard American English. The dialect is also used in business, the professions, government, the media, and other sites of social and economic power where people of diverse backgrounds must communicate with one another. It is "standard" not because it is better than other forms of English, but because it is accepted as the common language, much as the dollar bill is accepted as the common currency.

Standard American English varies a great deal, from the formal English of a President's State of the Union address through the middle formality of this handbook to the informal chitchat between anchors on morning TV. Even in academic writing, standard American English allows much room for the writer's own tone and voice, as these passages on the same topic show:

More formal

Two complicated sentences, one explaining the technique and one giving the example	Using the technique of "color engineering," manufacturers and advertisers can heighten the interest of consumers in a product by adding color that does not contribute to the utility of the product but appeals more to emotions. In one example from the 1920s, manufacturers of fountain pens, which had previously been made of hard black rubber, dramatically increased sales simply by producing the pens in bright colors.
Drawn-out phrasing, such as *interest of consumers* instead of *consumers' interest*	
Formal vocabulary, such as *heighten, contribute,* and *utility*	

Less formal

Four sentences, two each for explaining the technique and giving the example	A touch of "color engineering" can sharpen the emotional appeal of a product or its ad. New color can boost sales even when the color serves no use. In the 1920s, for example, fountain-pen makers introduced brightly colored pens along with the familiar ones of hard black rubber. Sales shot up.
More informal phrasing, such as *Sales shot up*	
More informal vocabulary, such as *touch, boost,* and *ad*	

As different as they are, both examples illustrate several common features of academic language:

- **It follows the conventions of standard American English for grammar and usage.** These conventions are described in guides to the dialect, such as this handbook. Note that standard American English excludes many forms that are encouraged by rapid communication in e-mail and in text or instant messaging, such as incomplete sentences, no capital letters, and shortened spellings (*u* for *you, b4* for *before, thru* for *through,* and so on). (See **3** p. 146 for more on these forms.)
- **It uses a standard vocabulary,** not one that only some groups understand, such as slang, an ethnic or regional dialect, or another language. (See **3** pp. 145–46 and 147–48 for more on specialized vocabularies.)
- **It creates some distance between writer and reader with the third person** (*he, she, it, they*). The first person (*I, we*) is sometimes appropriate to express personal opinions or invite readers to think along, but not with a strongly explanatory purpose (*I discovered that "color engineering" can heighten . . .*). The second person (*you*) is appropriate only in addressing readers directly

(as in this handbook), and even then it may seem condescending or too chummy (*You should know that "color engineering" can heighten . . .*).

■ **It is authoritative and neutral.** In the preceding examples, the writers express themselves confidently, not timidly (as in *One possible example of color engineering that might be considered in this case is . . .*). They also refrain from hostility (*Advertisers will stop at nothing to achieve their goals*) and enthusiasm (*Color engineering is genius at work*).

At first, the diverse demands of academic writing may leave you groping for an appropriate voice. In an effort to sound fresh and confident, you may write too casually:

Too casual

"Color engineering" is a great way to get at consumers' feelings. . . . When the guys jazzed up the color, sales shot through the roof.

In an effort to sound "academic," you may produce wordy and awkward sentences:

Wordy and awkward

The emotions of consumers can be made more engaged by the technique known as "color engineering." . . . A very large increase in the sales of fountain pens was achieved by the manufacturers of the pens as a result of this color enhancement technique. [The passive voice in this example, such as *increase . . . was achieved* instead of *the manufacturers achieved,* adds to its wordiness and indirection. See **4** pp. 204–05 for more on verb voice.]

A cure for writing too informally or too stiffly is to read academic writing so that the language and style become familiar and to edit your writing (see **1** pp. 25–26).

CULTURE LANGUAGE   If your first language is not English or is an English dialect besides standard American, you know well the power of communicating with others who share your language. Learning to write standard American English in no way requires you to abandon your first language. Like most multilingual people, you are probably already adept at switching between languages as the situation demands—speaking one way with your relatives, say, and another way with an employer. As you practice aca-demic writing, you'll develop the same flexibility with it.

11 Argument

Argument is writing that attempts to solve a problem, open readers' minds to an opinion, change readers' own opinions, or move readers to action. Using a variety of techniques, you engage readers to find common ground and narrow the distance between your views and theirs.

(CULTURE · LANGUAGE) The ways of conceiving and writing arguments described here may be initially uncomfortable to you if your native culture approaches such writing differently. In some cultures, for example, a writer is expected to begin indirectly, to avoid asserting his or her opinion outright, to rely for evidence on appeals to tradition, or to establish a compromise rather than argue a position. In American academic and business settings, writers aim for a well-articulated opinion, evidence gathered from many sources, and a direct and concise argument for the opinion.

11a Understanding and using the elements of argument

An argument has four main elements: subject, claims, evidence, and assumptions. (The last three are adapted from the work of the British philosopher Stephen Toulmin.)

1 The subject

An argument starts with a subject and often with a view of the subject as well—that is, an idea that makes you want to write about the subject. (If you don't have a subject or you aren't sure what you think, see **1** pp. 7–16 for some invention techniques.) Your subject should meet several requirements:

- **It can be disputed:** reasonable people can disagree over it.
- **It *will* be disputed:** it is controversial.
- **It is narrow enough to research and argue in the space and time available.**

On the flip side of these requirements are several kinds of subjects that will not work as the starting place of argument: indisputable facts, such as the functions of the human liver; personal preferences or beliefs, such as a moral commitment to vegetarianism; and ideas that few would disagree with, such as the virtues of a secure home.

2 Claims

Claims are statements that require support. In an argument you develop your subject into a central claim or **thesis,** asserted outright in a **thesis statement** (see **1** p. 17). This central claim is what the argument is about.

A thesis statement is always an **opinion**—that is, a judgment based on facts and arguable on the basis of facts. It may be one of the following:

- **A claim about past or present reality:**

    In both its space and its equipment, the college's chemistry laboratory is outdated.

    Academic cheating increases with students' economic insecurity.

- **A claim of value:**

    The new room fees are unjustified given the condition of the dormitories.

    Computer music pirates undermine the system that encourages the very creation of music.

- **A recommendation for a course of action,** often a solution to a perceived problem:

    The college's outdated chemistry laboratory should be replaced incrementally over the next five years.

    Schools and businesses can help to resolve the region's traffic congestion by implementing car pools and rewarding participants.

The backbone of an argument consists of specific claims that support the thesis statement. These may also be statements of opinion, or they may fall into one of two other categories:

- **Statements of** *fact,* including facts that are generally known or are verifiable (such as the cost of tuition at your school) and those that can be inferred from verifiable facts (such as the monetary value of a college education).
- **Statements of** *belief,* or convictions based on personal faith or values, such as *The primary goal of government should be to provide equality of opportunity for all.* Although seemingly arguable, a statement of belief is not based on facts and so cannot be contested on the basis of facts.

3 Evidence

Evidence demonstrates the validity of your claims. The evidence to support the claim that the school needs a new chemistry lab might include the present lab's age, an inventory of facilities and equipment, and the testimony of chemistry professors.

There are several kinds of evidence:

- **Facts,** statements whose truth can be verified or inferred: *Poland is slightly smaller than New Mexico.*
- **Statistics,** facts expressed as numbers: *Of those polled, 22 percent prefer a flat tax.*
- **Examples,** specific instances of the point being made: *Many groups, such as the elderly and people with disabilities, would benefit from this policy.*
- **Expert opinions,** the judgments formed by authorities on the basis of their own examination of the facts: *Affirmative action is necessary to right past injustices, a point argued by Howard Glickstein, a past director of the US Commission on Civil Rights.*
- **Appeals to readers' beliefs or needs,** statements that ask readers to accept a claim in part because it states something they already accept as true without evidence: *The shabby, antiquated chemistry lab shames the school, making it seem a second-rate institution.*

Evidence must be reliable to be convincing. Ask these questions about your evidence:

- **Is it accurate**—trustworthy, exact, and undistorted?
- **Is it relevant**—authoritative, pertinent, and current?
- **Is it representative**—true to its context, neither under- nor overrepresenting any element of the sample it's drawn from?
- **Is it adequate**—plentiful and specific?

4 Assumptions

An **assumption** is an opinion, a principle, or a belief that ties evidence to claims: the assumption explains why a particular piece of evidence is relevant to a particular claim. For instance:

Claim: The college needs a new chemistry laboratory.
Evidence (in part): The testimony of chemistry professors.
Assumption: Chemistry professors are the most capable of evaluating the present lab's quality.

Assumptions are not flaws in arguments but necessities: we all acquire beliefs and opinions that shape our views of the world. Interpreting a work's assumptions is a significant part of critical reading and viewing (see p. 71 and 77–78), and discovering your own assumptions is a significant part of argument. If your readers do not share your assumptions or if they perceive that you are not forthright about your biases, they will be less receptive to your argument.

11b Writing reasonably

Reasonableness is essential if an argument is to establish common ground between you and your readers. Readers expect logical thinking, appropriate appeals, fairness toward the opposition, and, combining all of these, writing that is free of fallacies.

1 Logical thinking

The thesis of your argument is a conclusion you reach by reasoning about evidence. Two processes of reasoning, induction and deduction, are familiar to you even if you aren't familiar with their names.

Induction

When you're about to buy a used car, you consult friends, relatives, and consumer guides before deciding what kind of car to buy. Using **induction**, or **inductive reasoning**, you make specific observations about cars (your evidence) and you induce, or infer, a **generalization** that Car X is most reliable. The generalization is a claim supported by your observations.

You might also use inductive reasoning in a term paper on print advertising:

> **Evidence:** Advertisements in newspapers and magazines.
> **Evidence:** Comments by advertisers and publishers.
> **Evidence:** Data on the effectiveness of advertising.
> **Generalization or claim:** Print is the most cost-effective medium for advertising.

Reasoning inductively, you connect your evidence to your generalization by assuming that what is true in one set of circumstances (the evidence you examine) is also true in a similar set of circumstances (evidence you do not examine). With induction you create new knowledge out of old.

The more evidence you accumulate, the more probable it is that your generalization is true. Note, however, that absolute certainty is not possible. At some point you must *assume* that your evidence justifies your generalization, for yourself and your readers. Most errors in inductive reasoning involve oversimplifying either the evidence or the generalization. See pp. 93–95 on fallacies.

Deduction

You use **deduction**, or **deductive reasoning**, when you proceed from your generalization that Car X is the most reliable used car to your own specific circumstances (you want to buy a used car) to the conclusion that you should buy Car X. In deduction your assumption is a generalization, principle, or belief that you think is true. It links the evidence (new information) to the claim (the conclusion you draw). With deduction you apply old information to new.

Say that you want the school administration to postpone new room fees for one dormitory. You can base your argument on a deductive **syllogism**:

> **Premise:** The administration should not raise fees on dorm rooms in poor condition. [A generalization or belief that you assume to be true.]
>
> **Premise:** The rooms in Polk Hall are in poor condition. [New information: a specific case of the first premise.]
>
> **Conclusion:** The administration should not raise fees on the rooms in Polk Hall. [Your claim.]

As long as the premises of a syllogism are true, the conclusion derives logically and certainly from them. Errors in constructing syllogisms lie behind many of the fallacies discussed on pp. 93–95.

2 Rational, emotional, and ethical appeals

In most arguments you will combine **rational appeals** to readers' capacities for logical reasoning with **emotional appeals** to readers' beliefs and feelings. The following example illustrates both: the second sentence makes a rational appeal (to the logic of financial gain), and the third sentence makes an emotional appeal (to the sense of fairness and open-mindedness).

> Advertising should show more physically challenged people. The millions of Americans with disabilities have considerable buying power, yet so far advertisers have made no attempt to tap that power. Further, by keeping people with disabilities out of the mainstream depicted in ads, advertisers encourage widespread prejudice against disability, prejudice that frightens and demeans those who hold it.

For an emotional appeal to be successful, it must be appropriate for the audience and the argument:

- **It must not misjudge readers' actual feelings.**
- **It must not raise emotional issues that are irrelevant to the claims and the evidence.** See p. 94 on specific inappropriate appeals, such as bandwagon and ad hominem.

A third kind of approach to readers, the **ethical appeal,** is the sense you give of being a competent, fair person who is worth heeding. A rational appeal and an appropriate emotional appeal contribute to your ethical appeal, and so does your acknowledging opposing views (see the next page). An argument that is concisely written and correct in grammar, spelling, and other matters will underscore your competence. In addition, a sincere and even tone will assure readers that you are a balanced person who wants to reason with them.

A sincere and even tone need not exclude language with emotional appeal—words such as *frightens* and *demeans* at the end of the example about advertising. But avoid certain forms of expression that will mark you as unfair:

- **Insulting words,** such as *idiotic* or *fascist.*
- **Biased language,** such as *fags* or *broads* (see **3** pp. 148–51).
- **Sarcasm,** such as the phrase *What a brilliant idea* to indicate contempt for the idea and its originator.
- **Exclamation points!** They'll make you sound shrill!

3 Acknowledgment of opposing views

A good test of your fairness in argument is how you handle possible objections. Assuming your thesis is indeed arguable, then others can marshal their own evidence to support a different view or views. By dealing squarely with these opposing views, you show yourself to be honest and fair. You strengthen your ethical appeal and thus your entire argument.

Before or while you draft your essay, list for yourself all the opposing views you can think of. You'll find them in your research, by talking to friends and classmates, and by critically thinking about your own ideas. You can also look for a range of views in an online discussion that deals with your subject. Two places to start are the *Yahoo!* archive of discussion groups at *groups.yahoo.com* and the *Google* blog directory at *blogsearch.google.com.*

A common way to handle opposing views is to state them, refute those you can, grant the validity of others, and demonstrate why, despite their validity, the opposing views are less compelling than your own. A somewhat different approach, developed by the psychologist Carl Rogers, emphasizes the search for common ground. In a **Rogerian argument** you start by showing that you understand readers' views and by establishing points on which you and readers agree and disagree. Creating a connection in this way can be especially helpful when you expect readers to resist your argument, as it encourages them to hear you out as you develop your claims.

4 Fallacies

Fallacies—errors in argument—either evade the issue of the argument or treat the argument as if it were much simpler than it is.

Evasions

An effective argument squarely faces the central issue or question it addresses. An ineffective argument may dodge the issue in one of the following ways:

■ **Begging the question:** treating an opinion that is open to question as if it were already proved or disproved.

> The college library's expenses should be reduced by cutting subscriptions to useless periodicals. [Begged questions: Are some of the library's periodicals useless? Useless to whom?]

■ **Non sequitur** (Latin: "It does not follow"): linking two or more ideas that in fact have no logical connection.

> She uses a wheelchair, so she must be unhappy. [The second clause does not follow from the first.]

■ **Red herring:** introducing an irrelevant issue intended to distract readers from the relevant issues.

> A campus speech code is essential to protect students, who already have enough problems coping with rising tuition. [Tuition costs and speech codes are different subjects. What protections do students need that a speech code will provide?]

■ **Appeal to readers' fear or pity:** substituting emotions for reasoning.

> She should not have to pay taxes because she is an aged widow with no friends or relatives. [Appeals to people's pity. Should age and loneliness, rather than income, determine a person's tax obligation?]

■ **Bandwagon:** inviting readers to accept a claim because everyone else does.

> As everyone knows, marijuana use leads to heroin addiction. [What is the evidence?]

■ **Ad hominem** (Latin: "to the man"): attacking the qualities of the people holding an opposing view rather than the substance of the view itself.

> One of the scientists has been treated for emotional problems, so his pessimism about nuclear waste merits no attention. [Do the scientist's previous emotional problems invalidate his current views?]

Oversimplifications

In a vain attempt to create something neatly convincing, an ineffective argument may conceal or ignore complexities in one of the following ways:

■ **Hasty generalization:** making a claim on the basis of inadequate evidence.

> It is disturbing that several of the youths who shot up schools were users of violent video games. Obviously, these games can breed violence, and they should be banned. [A few cases do not establish the relation between the games and violent behavior. Most youths who play violent video games do not behave violently.]

■ **Sweeping generalization:** making an insupportable statement. Many sweeping generalizations are **absolute statements** involving words such as *all, always, never,* and *no one* that allow no exceptions. Others are **stereotypes,** conventional and oversimplified characterizations of a group of people:

People who live in cities are unfriendly.
Californians are fad-crazy.
Women are emotional.
Men can't express their feelings.

(See also **3** pp. 148–51 on sexist and other biased language.)

■ **Reductive fallacy:** oversimplifying (reducing) the relation between causes and effects.

Poverty causes crime. [If so, then why do people who are not poor commit crimes? And why aren't all poor people criminals?]

■ **Post hoc fallacy** (from Latin, *post hoc, ergo propter hoc:* "after this, therefore because of this"): assuming that because *A* preceded *B,* then *A* must have caused *B.*

The town council erred in permitting the adult bookstore to open, for shortly afterward two women were assaulted. [It cannot be assumed without evidence that the women's assailants visited or were influenced by the bookstore.]

■ **Either/or fallacy:** assuming that a complicated question has only two answers, one good and one bad, both good, or both bad.

Either we permit mandatory drug testing in the workplace or productivity will continue to decline. [Productivity is not necessarily dependent on drug testing.]

11c Organizing an argument

All arguments include the same parts:

■ **The** *introduction* **establishes the significance of the subject and provides background.** The introduction may run a paragraph or two, and it generally includes the thesis statement. However, the thesis statement may come later in the paper if you think readers may have difficulty accepting it before they see at least some support for it. (See **1** pp. 42–43 for more on introductions.)

■ **The** *body* **states and develops the claims supporting the thesis.** In one or more paragraphs, the body develops each claim with relevant evidence. See the next page on organizing the body.

■ **The** *response to opposing views* details and addresses those views, either conceding them or demonstrating your argument's greater strengths. See the next page on organizing this response.

■ The *conclusion* **completes the argument,** restating the thesis, summarizing the supporting claims, and making a final appeal to readers. (See **1** pp. 43–44 for more on conclusions.)

The structure of the body and the response to opposing views depends on your subject, purpose, audience, and form of reasoning. Here are several possible arrangements:

A common scheme	A variation
Claim 1 and evidence	Claim 1 and evidence
Claim 2 and evidence	Response to opposing views
Claim X and evidence	Claim 2 and evidence
Response to opposing views	Response to opposing views
	Claim X and evidence
	Response to opposing views

The Rogerian scheme	The problem-solution scheme
Common ground and concession to opposing views	The problem: claims and evidence
Claim 1 and evidence	The solution: claims and evidence
Claim 2 and evidence	Response to opposing views
Claim X and evidence	

11d Using visual arguments

In a **visual argument** you use one or more images to engage and convince readers. Advertisements often provide the most vivid and memorable examples of visual arguments, but writers in almost every academic discipline support their claims with images. The main elements of written arguments discussed on pp. 89–90—claims, evidence, and assumptions—appear also in visual arguments.

1 Claims

The claims in an image may be made by composition as well as by content, with or without accompanying words. For instance:

Image A photograph framing hundreds of chickens crammed into small cages, resembling familiar images of World War II concentration camps.

Claim Commercial poultry-raising practices are cruel and unethical.

Image A chart with dramatically contrasting bars that represent the optimism, stress, and heart disease reported by people before and after they participated in a program of daily walking.

Claim Daily exercise leads to a healthier and happier life.

The following advertisement is one of a series featuring unnamed but well-known people as milk drinkers. The celebrity here is Serena Williams, a tennis champion. The ad makes several claims both in the photograph and in the text.

Claims in an image

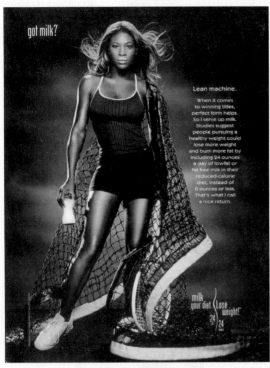

Image claim: Strong, shapely women drink milk.

Image claim: Attractive people drink milk.

Image claim: Athletes drink milk.

Text claim: Milk can help dieters reduce to a healthy weight.

got milk?

Lean machine.

When it comes to winning titles, perfect form helps. So I serve up milk. Studies suggest people pursuing a healthy weight could lose more weight and burn more fat by including 24 ounces a day of lowfat or fat free milk in their reduced-calorie diet, instead of 8 ounces or less. That's what I call a nice return.

milk your diet. Lose weight!

Advertisement by the Milk Processor
Education Program

2 Evidence

The kinds of evidence offered by images parallel those found in written arguments:

- **Facts:** You might provide facts in the form of data, as in a graph showing a five-year rise in oil prices. Or you might draw an inference from data, as the ad above does by stating that milk can help dieters "lose weight and burn more fat."
- **Examples:** Most often, you'll use examples to focus on an instance of your argument's claims, as Serena Williams represents milk drinkers in the ad above.

- **Expert opinions:** You might present a chart from an expert showing a trend in unemployment among high school graduates.
- **Appeals to beliefs or needs:** You might depict how things clearly ought to be (an anti-drug brochure featuring a teenager who is confidently refusing peer pressure) or, in contrast, show how things clearly should not be (a Web site for an anti-hunger campaign featuring images of emaciated children).

To make an image work hard as evidence, be sure it relates directly to a point in your argument, adds to that point, and gives readers something to think about. Always include a caption that provides source information and that explicitly ties the image to your text, so that readers don't have to puzzle out your intentions. Number images in sequence (Fig. 1, Fig. 2, and so on), and refer to them by number at the appropriate points in your text. (See **1** pp. 52–56 for more on captioning and numbering illustrations.)

The images below and on the next page supported an argument with this thesis: *Despite proof that the depiction of smoking in movies encourages children and teens to smoke, studios continue to release youth-oriented movies that show stars smoking.*

Image as evidence

Photograph of an actress smoking in a PG-13 movie —a visual example of the claim that youth-oriented movies depict smoking

Caption explaining the image, tying it to the text of the paper and providing source information

Fig. 1. The actress Kate Hudson in *Raising Helen,* one of many PG-13 movies released each year in which characters smoke. Photograph by Peggy Storm; *gettyimages.com*; Getty Images, 2003; Web; 21 Apr. 2008.

Image as evidence

[One in a Series]

Eighty percent of this year's nominated movies feature smoking. And the winner is

the global tobacco industry. It gains at least $4 billion in lifetime sales revenue, in the U.S. alone, from the new teen smokers recruited to smoke by films each year. In 2007, two-thirds of new U.S. releases featured smoking: 39% of G/PG movies, 66% of PG-13 films, 84% of R-rated films. Together, these movies delivered **6.6 billion tobacco impressions** to North American theater audiences. R-rating smoking is reasonable, responsible—and inevitable. You'll still be able to include smoking in any film, just like this year's R-rated nominees for Best Picture. Yet by keeping smoking out of the G/PG/PG-13 films that kids see most, you'll save 60,000 lives a year. So who's trying to stop the "R"? Must be somebody with a lot to lose.

SMOKE FREE MOVIES

SmokeFreeMovies.ucsf.edu

Smoke Free Movies policies—the R-rating, certification of no payoffs, anti-tobacco spots, and an end to brand display—are endorsed by the World Health Organization, American Medical Association, AMA Alliance, American Academy of Pediatrics, American Heart Association, American Legacy Foundation, American Lung Association, Campaign for Tobacco-Free Kids, Society for Adolescent Medicine, Los Angeles County Department of Health Services, New York State PTA, and others. To explore this critical health issue, visit our web site or write Smoke Free Movies, UCSF School of Medicine, San Francisco, CA 94143-1390.

Advertisement by a reputable research and advocacy group, reinforcing the thesis and providing data about depictions of smoking in movies

Fig. 2. Advertisement by the research and advocacy group Smoke Free Movies, providing data on the depiction of smoking in movies and linking the tobacco industry to the practice. From "Our Ads"; *Smoke Free Movies*; U of California, San Francisco, Cardiovascular Research Inst., 2008; Web; 23 Apr. 2008.

Caption interpreting the ad and providing source information

3 Assumptions

Like a written argument, a visual argument is based on assumptions—your ideas about the relation between evidence and claims (p. 89). Look again at the milk ad featuring Serena Williams (p. 97). The advertiser seems to have assumed that a celebrity endorsement would strengthen the claims and evidence about the benefits of drinking milk. In addition, the photograph of Williams emphasizes qualities that the advertiser presumably thought would appeal to readers: strength, shapeliness, beauty, even glamour.

As in written arguments, the assumptions in visual arguments must be appropriate for your readers if the argument is to succeed with them. The milk ad originally appeared in sports magazines, so the advertiser could assume that readers knew of and admired Williams. But to readers uninterested in sports or tennis, the photograph might actually undermine the ad's effectiveness.

4 Appeals

Images can help to strengthen the rational, emotional, and ethical appeals of your written argument (pp. 92–93):

- **Images can contribute evidence,** as long as they come from reliable sources, present information accurately and fairly, and relate clearly to the argument's claims.
- **Images can appeal to a host of ideas and emotions,** including patriotism, curiosity, moral values, sympathy, and anger. Any such appeal should correctly gauge readers' beliefs and feelings, and it should be clearly relevant to the argument.
- **Images can show that you are a competent, fair, and trustworthy source of information,** largely through their relevance, reliability, and sensitivity to readers' needs and feelings.

This image illustrates the writer's claim that television can ease loneliness.

Appeals in an image

Rational appeal: Backs up the writer's claim that TV can ease loneliness: the man appears to live alone (only one chair is visible) and is interacting enthusiastically with the TV

Emotional appeal: Reinforces the benefits of TV watching: the man's isolation may be disturbing, but his excitement is pleasing

Ethical appeal: Conveys the writer's competence through the appropriateness of the image for the point being made

Fig. 1. Television can be a source of companionship for people whose living situations and limited mobility leave them lonely. Photograph by Jean Michel Foujols; *Corbis*; Corbis, 2005; Web; 13 Oct. 2008.

5 Recognizing fallacies

When making a visual argument, you'll need to guard against all the fallacies discussed on pp. 93–95. Here we'll focus on specific visual examples. The first, the milk ad on p. 97, uses Serena Williams for snob appeal, inviting readers to be like someone they admire. If you drink milk, the ad says subtly, you too may become strong, beautiful, and fearless (notice that Williams looks unguardedly into the camera). The ad does have some substance in its specific and verifiable claim that drinking "24 ounces a day of lowfat or fat free milk" could help people reduce to a healthy weight, but Williams herself, with her milk mustache, makes a stronger claim.

Another example of a visual fallacy is the hasty generalization, a claim that is based on too little evidence or that misrepresents the facts. This fallacy appears in the following graph, which is intended to support this claim: *After a steep decline over the preceding five years, the teen birthrate shot up in 2006.* At first glance, the graph seems to demonstrate the claim, but a close look reveals that it badly misrepresents the data. If the graph were not distorted, the line would be nearly flat.

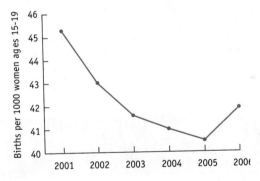

Fallacy in an image

The vertical axis lacks a zero point and covers a small span, thus misrepresenting and exaggerating both the decline and the increase in the birthrate.

Fig. 2. Steep decline and sharp increase in the birthrate among women ages 15 to 19 in the United States, 2001-06. Data from Brady E. Hamilton et al.; *National Vital Statistics Reports*; US Dept. of Health and Human Services, Centers for Disease Control and Prevention, 1 May 2008; Web; 10 July 2008.

6 Choice of images

You can wait until you've drafted an argument before concentrating on what images to include. This approach keeps your focus on the research and writing needed to craft the best argument from sources. But you can also begin thinking visually at the beginning of a project, as you might if your initial interest in the subject was sparked by a compelling image. Either way, ask yourself some basic questions as you consider visual options:

- **Which parts of your argument require visual evidence or can use visual reinforcement?** Do readers need a visual to understand your argument? Can a claim be explained better visually than verbally? Can a graph or chart present data compactly and interestingly? Can a photograph appeal effectively to readers' beliefs and values?
- **What are the limitations or requirements of your writing situation?** What do the type of writing you're doing and its format allow? Look through examples of similar writing to gauge the kinds of illustrations readers will expect.
- **What kinds of visuals are readily available on your subject?** As you researched your subject, what images seemed especially effective? What sources have you not yet explored? (See **7** pp. 313–14 for tips on locating images.)
- **Should you create original images tailored to your argument?** Instead of searching for existing images, would your time be better spent taking your own photographs or using computer software to compose visual explanations, such as charts and graphs?

Note Any image you include in a paper requires the same detailed citation as a written source. If you plan to publish your argument online, you will also need to seek permission from the author. See **7** pp. 330–37 on citing sources and obtaining permissions.

12 Online Writing

In and out of college, you will write extensively online. Many forms of online writing expand your options as a writer, but they also present distinctive challenges. This chapter discusses some of the options and challenges of e-mail (next page), online collaboration (p. 105), and Web composition (p. 106).

Visit *mycomplab.com* for more resources as well as exercises on online writing.

12a Using e-mail

To use e-mail productively for college work, pause to weigh each element of the message. Consider especially your audience and purpose and how your tone will come across to readers. In the message shown below, the writer knows the recipients well and yet has serious information to convey to them, so he writes informally but states his points and concerns carefully. Writing to the corporation mentioned in the message, the writer would be more formal in both tone and approach. Although e-mail is typically more casual than printed correspondence, in academic settings a crafted message is more likely to achieve the intended purpose. Proofread all but the most informal messages for errors in grammar, punctuation, and spelling.

For more on using e-mail to interact with other students in a course, see p. 105. For more on using e-mail as a research tool, see **7** p. 311.

1 Addressing messages

Send a message only to the people who need to read it. As a general rule, avoid sending messages to many recipients at once— all the students in a course, say, or all the participants in a discussion group—unless what you have to say applies to all of them. Occasionally, you may indeed have a worthwhile idea or important

E-mail message

Consider who needs to read your message as you address it.

Use the *Subject* line to describe accurately the content of the message.

To: Sara Ling; Bob Riggins
From: Franklin Potter
Subject: Student Loan Project: My Sections
Attached: Potter.P1.doc

Attach files of shared work.

Hi. I've attached the draft of my sections of our paper to this message. One thing I'm a bit unsure about in my sections is how evenhanded I am when I talk about the private loan consolidation companies. I want to make sure that I point out problems while still recognizing that they are businesses and have a right to operate for a profit. Anyway, keep that in mind as you read the sections.

Adjust the content and tone to the intended audience.

Use short paragraphs with space between them.

I also e-mailed the people at Federated Loan Consolidation Corporation and asked them whether they were affiliated with a federal agency and about the kinds of guarantees they provide for fixed interest rates. I guess one issue I really want to get at is how these private corporations represent themselves. I'll pass on any information they send me. See you in class. Frank information that everyone on the list will want to know. But spamming—flooding entire lists with irrelevant messages—is rude and irritating.

Similarly, avoid sending frivolous messages to all the members of a group. Instead of dashing off "I agree" and distributing the two-word message widely, put some time into composing a thoughtful response and send it only to those who will be interested.

2 Composing messages

The messages you send are going to people, not just inboxes, so craft your messages with the recipients in mind.

- **Don't say or do anything you wouldn't say or do face to face.**
- **Use names.** In the body of your message, address your reader(s) by name if possible and sign off with your own name and information on how to contact you. Your own name is especially important if your e-mail address does not spell it out.
- **Pay careful attention to tone.** Refrain from flaming, or attacking, correspondents. Don't use all capital letters, which SHOUT. And use irony or sarcasm only cautiously: in the absence of facial expressions, either one can lead to misunderstanding. To indicate irony and emotions, you can use an emoticon such as the smiley :-). These sideways faces can easily be overused, though, and should not substitute for thoughtfully worded opinions.
- **Avoid saying anything in e-mail that you would not say in a printed document such as a letter or memo.** E-mail can usually be retrieved from the server, and in business and academic settings it may well be retrieved in disputes over contracts, grades, and other matters.

3 Reading and responding to messages

When you read and respond to messages, again consider the people behind them.

- **Be a forgiving reader.** Avoid nitpicking over spelling or other surface errors. And because attitudes are sometimes difficult to convey, give authors an initial benefit of the doubt: a writer who at first seems hostile may simply have tried too hard to be concise; a writer who at first seems unserious may simply have failed at injecting humor into a worthwhile message.
- **Consider who will read your response.** The Reply function will automatically address the person who wrote you, whereas the

Reply All function will address others who may have been sent copies of the original message. Before you send the message, choose the readers who need to see it.

- **Respect others' privacy.** Forward messages only with permission or only if you know that the author of the message won't mind. If you add more recipients to your response, make sure not to pass on previous private messages by mistake.
- **Avoid participating in flame "wars,"** overheated dialogs that contribute little or no information or understanding. If a war breaks out in a discussion, ignore it: don't rush to defend someone who is being attacked, and don't respond even if you are under attack yourself.

12b Collaborating online

Many instructors integrate online collaboration into their courses, encouraging students to work in groups for discussing ideas and exchanging and commenting on drafts of projects.

1 Participating in discussions

Online conversations in your courses will occur either in real-time chat, which occurs immediately, like a telephone conversation, or in a delayed medium such as e-mail, a blog, or a wiki. Chat discussions can be fast-paced and often work better for brain-storming topics and exchanging impressions than for careful articulation of ideas. Delayed conversations allow detailed, thoughtful messages and responses, so they are good places to develop ideas, explore assignments, and respond to others' work. For either type of conversation, observe the guidelines for composing and responding to messages in the preceding section.

2 Working on drafts

In writing and other courses, you and your fellow students may be invited to exchange and respond to one another's projects by e-mail or over the Web. To guide your reading of others' work, use the revision checklist in **1** p. 24 and the collaboration tips in **1** pp. 29–31. Focus on the deep issues in others' drafts, especially early drafts: thesis, purpose, audience, organization, and support for the thesis. Hold comments on style, grammar, punctuation, and other surface matters until you're reviewing later drafts, if indeed you are expected to comment on them at all.

12c | Creating Web compositions

Creating a Web page or site is sometimes as simple as saving a document in a different format, but more often it means thinking in a new way.

The diagrams on the next page show a key difference between traditional printed documents and Web sites. Most traditional documents are meant to be read in sequence from start to finish. In contrast, most Web sites are intended to be examined in whatever order readers choose as they follow links to pages within the site and to other sites. A Web site thus requires careful planning of the links between pages and thoughtful cues to orient readers.

When you create a composition for the Web, it will likely fall into one of two categories: pages such as class papers that resemble printed documents in being linear and text-heavy and that call for familiar ways of writing and reading; or "native" hypertext documents that you build from scratch, which call for screen-oriented writing and reading. These two categories are discussed on pp. 108–12.

Note If you anticipate that some of your readers may have visual, hearing, or reading disabilities, you'll need to consider their needs while designing Web sites. Some of these considerations are covered under document design in **1** p. 56, and others are fundamental to any effective Web design, as discussed in this section. In addition, avoid any content that relies exclusively on images or sound, instead supplementing such elements with text descriptions, and try to provide key concepts both as text and as images and sound. For more on Web design for readers with disabilities, visit the World Wide Web Consortium at *www.w3.org/WAI* or the American Council for the Blind at *acb.org/accessible-formats.html*.

1 | Using HTML

Most Web pages are created using hypertext markup language, or HTML, and an HTML editor. The HTML editing program inserts command codes into your document that achieve the effects you want when the material appears on the Web.

From the user's point of view, most HTML editors work much as word processors do, with similar options for sizing, formatting, and highlighting copy and with a display that shows what you will see in the final version. You can compose a Web page without bothering at all about the behind-the-scenes HTML coding. As you gain experience with Web building, however, you may want to create more sophisticated pages by editing the codes themselves.

Traditional print document

Web site

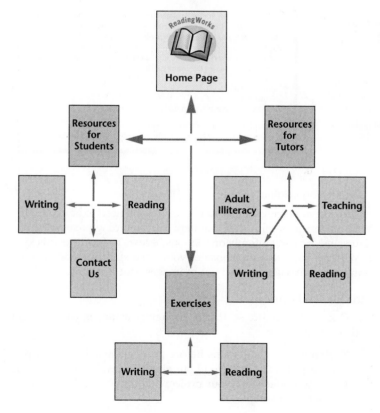

2 Creating online papers

If an instructor asks you to post a paper to a Web site or blog, you can compose it on your word processor and then use the Save As HTML function available on most word processors to translate it into a Web page. After translating the paper, your word processor should allow you to modify some of the elements on the page, or you can open the translated document in an HTML editor. The illustration below shows the opening screen of a student's project for a composition course.

Paper submitted on the Web

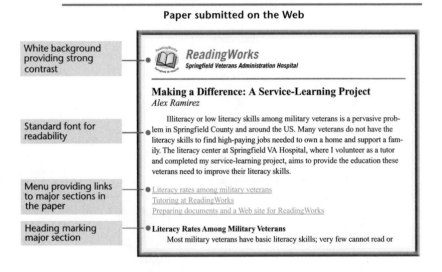

White background providing strong contrast

Standard font for readability

Menu providing links to major sections in the paper

Heading marking major section

ReadingWorks
Springfield Veterans Administration Hospital

Making a Difference: A Service-Learning Project
Alex Ramirez

Illiteracy or low literacy skills among military veterans is a pervasive problem in Springfield County and around the US. Many veterans do not have the literacy skills to find high-paying jobs needed to own a home and support a family. The literacy center at Springfield VA Hospital, where I volunteer as a tutor and completed my service-learning project, aims to provide the education these veterans need to improve their literacy skills.

Literacy rates among military veterans
Tutoring at ReadingWorks
Preparing documents and a Web site for ReadingWorks

Literacy Rates Among Military Veterans
Most military veterans have basic literacy skills; very few cannot read or

3 Creating original sites

When you create an original Web site, you need to be aware that Web readers generally alternate between skimming pages for highlights and focusing intently on sections of text. To facilitate this kind of reading, you'll want to consider your site's structure and content, flow, ease of navigation, and use of images, video, and sound.

Structure and content

Organize your site so that it efficiently arranges your content and orients readers:

■ **Sketch possible site plans before getting started.** (See the previous page for an example.) Your aim is to develop a sense of the major components of your project and to create a logical space for each component.

- Consider how menus on the site's pages can provide overviews of the organization as well as direct access to the pages. The Web page below includes a menu on the left.

- Treat the first few sentences of any page as a get-acquainted space for you and your readers. On the page below, the text hooks readers with questions and then orients them with general information.

- Distill your text so that it includes only essential information. Concise prose is essential in any writing situation, of course. But Web readers expect to scan text quickly and, in any event, have difficulty following long text passages on a computer screen.

Original Web site

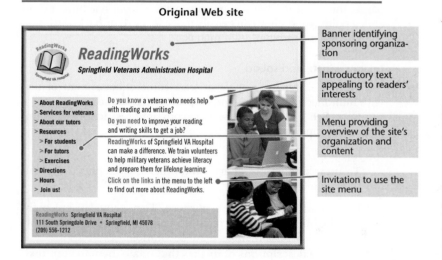

Flow

Beginning Web authors sometimes start at the top of the page and then add element upon element until information proceeds down the screen much as it would in a printed document. However, by thinking about how information will flow on a page, you can take better advantage of the Web's visual nature. Follow these guidelines:

- Standardize elements of your design to create expectations in readers and to fulfill those expectations. For instance, develop a uniform style for the main headings of pages, for headings within pages, and for menus.

- Make scanning easy for readers. Focus readers on crucial text by adding space around it or enlarging it. Add headings to break up text and to highlight content. Use lists to reinforce the parallel importance of items. (See **1** pp. 50–51 for more on headings and lists.)

Easy navigation

A Web site of more than a few pages requires a menu on every page that lists the features of the site, giving its plan at a glance. By clicking on any item in the menu, readers can go directly to a page that interests them.

You can embed a menu at the top, side, or bottom of a page. Menus at the top or side are best on short pages because they will not scroll off the screen as readers move down the page. On longer pages, menus at the bottom prevent readers from reaching a dead end, a point where they can't easily move forward or backward. You can also use a combination of menus.

Images, video, and sound

Most Web readers expect at least some enhancement of text with multimedia elements—images, video, and sound.

Note See **7** p. 336 on observing copyright restrictions with images, video, and sound.

Images

To use photographs, charts, and other images effectively, follow these guidelines:

- **Use visual elements for a purpose.** They should supplement text, highlight important features, and direct the flow of information. Don't use them as mere decoration.
- **Compose descriptions of images that relate them to your text.** Don't ask the elements to convey your meaning by themselves.
- **Provide alternative descriptions of images** for readers with vision loss or readers whose Web browsers can't display the images.

Video and sound

Video and sound files can provide information that is simply unavailable in printed documents. For instance, as part of a film review you might show and analyze a short clip from the film. Or as part of a project on a controversial issue you might provide links to sound files containing political speeches.

Video and sound files can be difficult to work with and can be slow to download at the reader's end. Make sure they're worth the time: they should provide essential information and should be well integrated with the rest of your composition.

Sources of multimedia elements

You can use your own multimedia elements or obtain them from other sources:

- **Create your own graphs, diagrams, and other illustrations using a graphics program.** Any graphics program requires learning and practice to be used efficiently but can produce professional-looking illustrations.
- **Incorporate your own artwork, photographs, video clips, and sound recordings.** You may be able to find the needed equipment and software at your campus computer lab.
- **Obtain icons, video, and other multimedia elements from other electronic sources.** Be sure to acknowledge your sources and to obtain reprint permission if needed (see **7** pp. 335–36).

4 Multimedia composing using RAIDS

The First-Year Writing program recognizes that writing and composing are activities that occur in a variety of settings and media. To this end, one assignment in the course, the Remix assignment, asks you to transmediate a given piece of your own writing to a new form/media. Once you know what type of media you will be using, you will need to think about how to plan and compose your Remix project. The following questions will help you consider important issues.

- What is invention? (What activities will you engage in to create the project? Do you need to do research? Do you need to take video? Do you need to conduct interviews or surveys?)
- What is being invented? (What ideas, practices, arguments, etc. will you create through the project?)
- What is being arranged? (What concepts, ideas, and/or objects are you putting in relation to what?)
- What is arrangement? (How will you put things in relation to one another? If writing for the web, how will you structure the website and distribute its content? For video, what is the arc of the narrative? What information will you present? Where will it be presented? What modalities (audio, text, visual etc.) will you use to communicate information?)
- What is being revised? (What are you trying to change (e.g. what ideas, practices, etc.?) What is your purpose? What are you trying to accomplish?)
- What is revision? (What is/has to be done to accomplish those changes?)

It is important to think about these issues before and during the creation of your project so that its effectiveness is maximized. Every part of your project, no matter its form, should help you achieve your purpose. If you create a video, including background music should be done deliberately with a consideration and understanding of how that music serves the overall purpose of your project. Even the seemingly smallest choices such as what font face to use (which is actually a very important decision) should be made only after the careful consideration of the rhetorical impact and/or consequences of that choice upon your project as a whole.[1]

13 Oral Presentations

Effective speakers use organization, voice, and other techniques to help their audiences follow and appreciate their presentations.

13a Composing presentations with RAIDS

You may be called on to present either formally or informally as part of the requirements for your First-Year Writing course. While the above recommendations are helpful suggestions for most presentations, remember that you may be asked to present in a way that is unique to your individual course and/or instructor. So, as with the other tasks you will complete, you will want to approach your presentation as a unique situation and use the RAIDS heuristic to think about the content, arrangement, and delivery of your presentation. You can use the following questions as you plan and compose your presentation:

- What is invention? (What activities will you engage in to generate the content of your presentation?)
- What is being invented? (What ideas, practices, arguments, etc. are created through the presentation? What do you need to say?)
- What is being arranged? (What is being put in relation to what?)
- What is arrangement? (How are things being put in relation to one another? What is the best way to organize and present information?)

---

[1]Section 12c.4 contributed by the MSU Custom Team.

Visit *mycomplab.com* for more resources as well as exercises on oral presentations.

- What is being revised? (What are you trying to change (e.g. what ideas, practices, etc.?) What are you trying to accomplish? What is your purpose?)
- What is revision? (What will you have to do to accomplish those changes?)
- What style is being used and how will that help you relate to your audience? (Is your presentation formal or informal? What style is appropriate to your purpose? Which fonts and color selections serve the purpose of your individual presentation?)
- What mode of delivery is being used and what is the effect of using that mode upon the audience? (Will you use PowerPoint and if so, how? What information will you deliver through PowerPoint? How will your slide design assist you in achieving your purpose?)

It is also important to think about the use of tools for your presentation. Some presentations are better suited to using technological tools such as PowerPoint while others are not. Additionally, while PowerPoint is one of the most widespread pieces of presentation software, programs such as Keynote and Prezi may support your presentation in different ways and should be considered if they help your presentation's effectiveness.[1]

13b Organizing the presentation

Give your oral presentation a recognizable shape so that listeners can see how ideas and details relate to each other.

The introduction

The beginning of an oral presentation should try to accomplish three goals:

- **Gain the audience's attention and interest.** Begin with a question, an unusual example or statistic, or a short, relevant story.
- **Put yourself in the speech.** Demonstrate your expertise, experience, or concern to gain the interest and trust of your audience.
- **Introduce and preview your topic and purpose.** By the time your introduction is over, listeners should know what your subject is and the direction you'll take to develop your ideas.

---

[1]Section 13a contributed by the MSU Custom Team.

Your introduction should prepare your audience for your main points but not give them away. Think of it as a sneak preview of your speech, not the place for an apology such as *I wish I'd had more time to prepare* . . . or a dull statement such as *My speech is about*. . . .

Supporting material

Just as you do when writing, you should use facts, statistics, examples, and expert opinions to support the main points of your oral presentation. In addition, you can make your points more memorable with vivid description, well-chosen quotations, true or fictional stories, and analogies.

The conclusion

You want your conclusion to be clear, of course, but you also want it to be memorable. Remind listeners of how your topic and main idea connect to their needs and interests. If your speech was motivational, tap an emotion that matches your message. If your speech was informational, give some tips on how to remember important details.

13c Delivering the presentation

Methods of delivery

You can deliver an oral presentation in several ways:

- **Impromptu, without preparation:** Make a presentation without planning what you will say. Impromptu speaking requires confidence and excellent general preparation.
- **Extemporaneously:** Prepare notes to glance at but not read from. This method allows you to look and sound natural while ensuring that you don't forget anything.
- **Speaking from a text:** Read aloud from a written presentation. You won't lose your way, but you may lose your audience. Avoid reading for an entire presentation.
- **Speaking from memory:** Deliver a prepared presentation without notes. You can look at your audience every minute, but the stress of retrieving the next words may make you seem tense and unresponsive.

Vocal delivery

The sound of your voice will influence how listeners receive you. Rehearse your presentation several times until you are confident that you are speaking loudly, slowly, and clearly enough for your audience to understand you.

Physical delivery

You are more than your spoken words when you make an oral presentation. If you are able, stand up to deliver your presentation, turning your body toward one side of the room and then the other, stepping out from behind any lectern or desk, and gesturing as appropriate. Above all, make eye contact with your audience as you speak. Looking directly in your listeners' eyes conveys your honesty, your confidence, and your control of the material.

Visual aids

You can supplement an oral presentation with visual aids such as posters, models, slides, or videos.

- **Use visual aids to underscore your points.** Short lists of key ideas, illustrations such as graphs or photographs, or objects such as models can make your presentation more interesting and memorable. But use visual aids judiciously: a battery of illustrations or objects will bury your message rather than amplify it.
- **Coordinate visual aids with your message.** Time each visual to reinforce a point you're making. Tell listeners what they're looking at. Give them enough viewing time so they don't mind turning their attention back to you.
- **Show visual aids only while they're needed.** To regain your audience's attention, remove or turn off any aid as soon as you have finished with it.

Many speakers use *PowerPoint* or other software to present visual aids. Screens of brief points supported by data, images, or video can help listeners follow your main points. (See the next page for examples.) To use *PowerPoint* or other software effectively, follow the guidelines above and also the following:

- **Don't put your whole presentation on screen.** Select your key points, and distill them to as few words as possible. Think of the slides as quick, easy-to-remember summaries.
- **Use a simple design.** Avoid turning your presentation into a show about the software's many capabilities.
- **Use a consistent design.** For optimal flow through the presentation, each slide should be formatted similarly.
- **Add only relevant illustrations.** Avoid loading the presentation with mere decoration.

Practice

Take time to rehearse your presentation out loud, with the notes you will be using. Gauge your performance by making an audio- or videotape of yourself or by practicing in front of a mirror.

PowerPoint **slides**

First slide, introducing the project and presentation

Simple, consistent slide design focusing viewers' attention on information, not *PowerPoint* features

> ## *Making a Difference?*
>
> ### *A Service-Learning Project at ReadingWorks*
>
> Springfield Veterans
> Administration Hospital
>
> Jessica Cho
> Nathan Hall
> Alex Ramirez
>
> **FALL 2008**
>
> ReadingWorks
> Springfield VA Hospital

Later slide, using brief, bulleted points to be explained by the speaker

Photographs reinforcing the project's activities

> ## *Semester goals*
>
> * Tutor military veterans
> * Research adult literacy
> * Keep a journal
> * Collaborate on documents for ReadingWorks
> * Report experiences and findings

Practicing out loud will also tell you if your presentation is running too long or too short.

If you plan to use visual aids, you'll need to practice with them, too. Your goal is to eliminate hitches (upside-down slides, missing charts) and to weave the visuals seamlessly into your presentation.

Stage fright

Many people report that speaking in front of an audience is their number-one fear. Even many experienced and polished speakers have some anxiety about delivering an oral presentation, but they use this nervous energy to their advantage, letting it propel them into working hard on each presentation. Several techniques can help you reduce anxiety:

- **Use simple relaxation exercises.** Deep breathing or tensing and relaxing your stomach muscles can ease some of the physical symptoms of speech anxiety—stomachache, rapid heartbeat, and shaky hands, legs, and voice.
- **Think positively.** Instead of worrying about the mistakes you might make, concentrate on how well you've prepared and practiced your presentation and how significant your ideas are.
- **Don't avoid opportunities to speak in public.** Practice and experience build speaking skills and offer the best insurance for success.

14 Public Writing

Writing outside of school, such as for business or for community work, resembles academic writing in many ways. It usually involves the same basic writing process, discussed in **1** pp. 2–28: assessing the writing situation, developing what you want to say, freely working out your meaning in a draft, and revising and editing so that your writing will achieve your purpose with readers. It often involves research, as discussed in **7** pp. 300–37. And it involves the standards of conciseness, appropriate and exact language, and correct grammar and usage discussed in **3** through **6**.

But public writing has its own conventions, too. They vary widely, depending on what you're writing and why, whether it's a proposal for your job or a flyer for a community group. This chapter covers several types of public writing: business letters and résumés (next page); memos, reports, and proposals (p. 123); and flyers, newsletters, and brochures for community work (p. 125).

CULTURE LANGUAGE Public writing in the United States, especially business writing, favors efficiency and may seem abrupt or impolite compared with such writing in your native culture. For instance, a business letter elsewhere may be expected to begin with polite questions about the addressee or with compliments for the addressee's company, whereas US business letters are expected to get right to the point.

mycomplab

Visit *mycomplab.com* for more resources as well as exercises on public writing.

14a Writing business letters and résumés

When you write for business, you are addressing busy people who want to see quickly why you are writing and how they should respond to you. Follow these general guidelines:

- **State your purpose right at the start.**
- **Be straightforward, clear, concise, objective, and courteous.**
- **Observe conventions of grammar and usage,** which make your writing clear and impress your reader with your care.

1 Business letter format

For any business letter, use either unlined white paper measuring 8½" × 11" or what is called letterhead stationery with your address printed at the top of the sheet. Type the letter single-spaced (with double spacing between elements) on only one side of a sheet. A common business-letter form is illustrated on the next page:

- The *return-address heading* gives your address and the date. Do not include your name. If you are using stationery with a printed heading, you need only give the date.
- The *inside address* shows the name, title, and complete address of the person you are writing to.
- The *salutation* greets the addressee. Whenever possible, address your letter to a specific person. (Call the company or department to ask whom to address.) If you can't find a person's name, then use a job title (*Dear Human Resources Manager, Dear Customer Service Manager*) or use a general salutation (*Dear Smythe Shoes*). Use *Ms.* as the title for a woman when she has no other title, when you don't know how she prefers to be addressed, or when you know that she prefers *Ms.*
- The *body* contains the substance. Instead of indenting the first line of each paragraph, double-space between paragraphs.
- The *close* should reflect the level of formality in the salutation: *Respectfully, Cordially, Yours truly,* and *Sincerely* are more formal closes; *Regards* and *Best wishes* are less formal.
- The *signature* has two parts: your name typed four lines below the close, and your handwritten signature in the space between. Give your name as you sign checks and other documents.
- **Include any additional information below the signature,** such as *Enc.* (indicating an enclosure with the letter) or *cc: Margaret Zusky* (indicating that a copy is being sent to the person named).

Use an envelope that will accommodate the letter once it is folded horizontally in thirds. The envelope should show your name and address in the upper left corner and the addressee's name, title,

Business letter (job application)

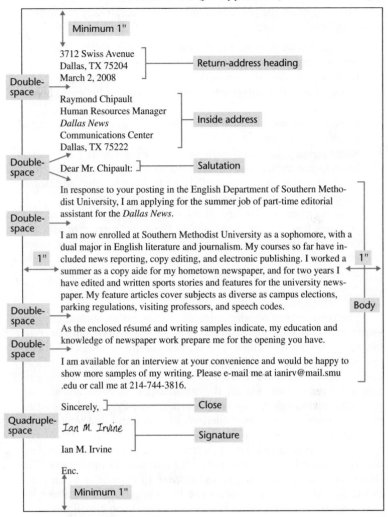

and address in the center. For easy machine reading, the United States Postal Service recommends all capital letters and no punctuation (spaces separate the elements on a line), as in this address:

RAYMOND CHIPAULT
HUMAN RESOURCES MANAGER
DALLAS NEWS
COMMUNICATIONS CENTER
DALLAS TX 75222-0188

2 Job-application letter

The sample on the preceding page illustrates the key features of a job-application letter:

- **Interpret your résumé for the particular job.** Don't detail your entire résumé, reciting your job history. Instead, highlight and reshape only the relevant parts.
- **Announce at the outset what job you seek and how you heard about it.**
- **Include any special reason you have for applying,** such as a specific career goal.
- **Summarize your qualifications for this particular job,** including relevant facts about education and employment history and emphasizing notable accomplishments. Mention that additional information appears in an accompanying résumé.
- **Describe your availability.** At the end of the letter, mention that you are free for an interview at the convenience of the addressee, or specify when you will be available (for instance, when your current job or classes leave you free, or when you could travel to the employer's city).

3 Résumé

The résumé that accompanies a job application should provide information in table format that allows a potential employer to evaluate your qualifications. The résumé should include your name and address, a career objective, your education and employment history, special skills or awards, and information about how to obtain your references. Fit all the information on one uncrowded page unless your education and experience are extensive. The sample on the next page gives guidelines for a résumé that you submit in print.

Employers may ask for an electronic version of your résumé so that they can add it to a computerized database of applicants. The employers may scan your printed résumé to convert it to an electronic file, which they can then store in an appropriate database, or they may request that you embed your résumé in an e-mail message. To produce a scannable or electronic résumé, follow the guidelines below and consult the sample on p. 122.

- **Keep the design simple for accurate scanning or electronic transmittal.** Avoid images, unusual type, more than one column, vertical or horizontal lines, italics, and underlining.
- **Use concise, specific words to describe your skills and experience.** The employer's computer may use keywords (often nouns) to identify the résumés of suitable job candidates, and you want to ensure that your résumé includes the appropriate

Résumé (print)

Ian M. Irvine	3712 Swiss Avenue Dallas, TX 75204 214-744-3816 ianirv@mail.smu.edu	Name and contact information
Position desired	Part-time editorial assistant.	Career objective stated simply and clearly
Education	*Southern Methodist University*, 2006 to present. Current standing: sophomore. Major: English literature and journalism. Journalism courses: news reporting, copy editing, electronic publishing, communication arts, broadcast journalism. *Abilene (Texas) Senior High School*, 2002-06. Graduated with academic, college-preparatory degree.	Education before work experience for most college students
Employment history	2006 to present. Reporter, *Daily Campus*, student newspaper of Southern Methodist University. Write regular coverage of baseball, track, and soccer teams. Write feature stories on campus policies and events. Edit sports news, campus listings, features. Summer 2007. Copy aide, *Abilene Reporter-News*. Assisted reporters with copy routing and research. Summer 2006. Painter, Longhorn Painters, Abilene. Prepared and painted exteriors and interiors of houses.	Headings marking sections, set off with space and highlighting Conventional use of capital letters: yes for proper nouns and after periods; no for job titles, course names, department names, and so on
Special skills	Fluent in Spanish. Proficient in Internet research and word processing.	
References	Available on request: Placement Office Southern Methodist University Dallas, TX 75275	Standard, consistent type font

keywords. Name your specific skills—for example, the computer programs you can operate—and write concretely with words like *manager* (not *person with responsibility for*) and *reporter* (not *staff member who reports*). Look for likely keywords in the employer's description of the job you seek.

4 Electronic communication

Electronic communication—mainly e-mail and faxes—adds a few twists to business writing. E-mail now plays such a prominent

Résumé (scannable or electronic)

Ian M. Irvine
3712 Swiss Avenue
Dallas, TX 75204
214-744-3816
ianirv@mail.smu.edu

> Accurate key-words, allowing the employer to place the résumé into an appropriate database

KEYWORDS: Editor, editorial assistant, publishing, electronic publishing.

OBJECTIVE
Part-time editorial assistant.

> Simple design, avoiding un-usual type, italics, multiple columns, deco-rative lines, and images

EDUCATION
Southern Methodist University, 2006 to present.
Major: English literature and journalism.
Journalism courses: news reporting, copy editing, electronic publishing, communication arts, broadcast journalism.

Abilene (Texas) Senior High School, 2002-06.
Academic, college preparatory degree.

> Standard font easily read by scanners

EMPLOYMENT HISTORY
Reporter, Daily Campus, Southern Methodist University, 2006 to present.
Writer of articles for student newspaper on sports teams, campus policies, and local events. Editor of sports news, campus listings, and features.

> Every line align-ing at left margin

Copy aide, Abilene Reporter-News, Abilene, summer 2007.
Assistant to reporters, routing copy and doing research.

Painter, Longhorn Painters, Abilene, summer 2006.
Preparation and painting of exteriors and interiors of houses.

SPECIAL SKILLS
Fluent in Spanish.
Proficient in Internet research and word processing.

REFERENCES
Available on request:
Placement Office
Southern Methodist University
Dallas, TX 75275

role in communication of all sorts that it is discussed extensively as part of writing online (see pp. 103–05). Generally, the standards for business e-mail are the same as for other business correspondence.

Faxes follow closely the formats of print documents, but there are unique concerns:

- **Consider legibility.** Small type, photographs, horizontal lines, and other elements that look fine on your copy may not be legible to the addressee.

- **Include a cover sheet.** Most faxes require a cover sheet with the addressee's name, company, and fax number; the date, time, and subject; your own name and fax and telephone numbers; and the total number of pages (including the cover sheet) in the fax.
- **Advise your addressee to expect a fax.** Fax transmissions can go astray. The advice is essential if the fax is confidential, because the machine is often shared.
- **Consider urgency.** Transmission by fax can imply that the correspondence is urgent. If yours isn't, you may want to use the mail instead.

14b Writing memos, reports, and proposals

1 Memos

Business memorandums (memos, for short) address people within the same organization. Most memos deal briefly with a specific topic, such as an answer to a question or an evaluation.

Both the form and the structure of a memo are designed to get to the point and dispose of it quickly (see the sample on the next page). State your reason for writing in the first sentence. Devote the first paragraph to a concise presentation of your answer, conclusion, or evaluation. In the rest of the memo explain your reasoning or evidence. Use headings or lists as appropriate to highlight key information.

2 Reports and proposals

Reports and proposals are text-heavy documents, sometimes lengthy, that convey information such as the results of research, a plan for action, or a recommendation for change. As with other business correspondence, you will prepare a report or proposal for a specific purpose, and you will be addressing interested but busy readers.

Reports and proposals usually divide into sections. The sections vary depending on the purpose of the document, but usually they include an overview or summary, which tells the reader what the document is about; a statement of the problem or need, which justifies the report or proposal; a statement of the plan or solution, which responds to the need or problem; and a recommendation or evaluation. Consider the following guidelines as you prepare a report or proposal:

- **Do your research.** The standard formats of reports and proposals require you to be well informed, so be alert to where you have enough information or where you don't.
- **Focus on the purpose of each section.** Stick to the point of each section, saying only what you need to say, even if you have

Business memo

Bigelow Wax Company

Heading: company's name, addressee's name, writer's name and initials, date, and subject description

TO: Aileen Rosen, Director of Sales
FROM: Patricia Phillips, Territory 12   *PP*
DATE: March 17, 2008
SUBJECT: 2007 sales of Quick Wax in Territory 12

Body: single-spaced with double spacing between paragraphs; paragraphs not indented

Since it was introduced in January 2007, Quick Wax has been unsuccessful in Territory 12 and has not affected the sales of our Easy Shine. Discussions with customers and my own analysis of Quick Wax suggest three reasons for its failure to compete with our product.

1. Quick Wax has not received the promotion necessary for a new product. Advertising—primarily on radio—has been sporadic and has not developed a clear, consistent image for the product. In addition, the Quick Wax sales representative in Territory 12 is new and inexperienced; he is not known to customers, and his sales pitch (which I once overheard) is weak. As far as I can tell, his efforts are not supported by phone calls or mailings from his home office.

2. When Quick Wax does make it to the store shelves, buyers do not choose it over our product. Though priced competitively with our product, Quick Wax is poorly packaged. The container seems smaller than ours, though in fact it holds the same eight ounces. The lettering on the Quick Wax package (red on blue) is difficult to read, in contrast to the white-on-green lettering on the Easy Shine package.

3. Our special purchase offers and my increased efforts to serve existing customers have had the intended effect of keeping customers satisfied with our product and reducing their inclination to stock something new.

People receiving copies

Copies: L. Mendes, Director of Marketing
       J. MacGregor, Customer Service Manager

additional information. Each section should accomplish its purpose and contribute to the whole.

- **Follow an appropriate format.** In many businesses, reports and proposals have specific formatting requirements. If you are unsure about the requirements, ask your supervisor.

A sample report appears on the next page. For a sample proposal, follow the links in the e-book version of this handbook at *mycomplab.com*.

Report

Canada Geese at ABC Institute: **An Environmental Problem**	Descriptive title conveying report's contents
Summary The flock of Canada geese on and around ABC Institute's grounds has grown dramatically in recent years to become a nuisance and an environmental problem. This report reviews the problem, considers possible solutions, and proposes that ABC Institute and the US Fish and Wildlife Service cooperate to reduce the flock by humane means.	Standard format: summary, statement of the problem, solutions, and (not shown) recommendations
The Problem Canada geese began living at Taylor Lake next to ABC Institute when they were relocated there in 1985 by the state game department. As a nonmigratory flock, the geese are present year-round, with the highest population each year occurring in early spring. In recent years the flock has grown dramatically. The Audubon Society's annual Christmas bird census shows a thirty-fold increase from the 37 geese counted in 1986 to the 1125 counted in 2008.	Major sections delineated by headings
The principal environmental problem caused by the geese is pollution of grass and water by defecation. Geese droppings cover the ABC Institute's grounds as well as the park's picnicking areas. The runoff from these droppings into Taylor Lake has substantially affected the quality of the lake's water, so that local authorities have twice (2007 and 2008) issued warnings against swimming.	Formal tone, appropriate to a business-writing situation
Possible Solutions The goose overpopulation and resulting environmental problems have several possible solutions:	Single spacing with double spacing between paragraphs and around the list
• Harass the geese with dogs and audiovisual effects (light and noise) so that the geese choose to leave. This solution is inhumane to the geese and unpleasant for human neighbors. • Feed the geese a chemical that will weaken the shells of their eggs and thus reduce growth of the flock. This solution is inhumane to the geese and also impractical, because geese are long-lived. • Kill adult geese. This solution is, obviously, inhumane to the geese. • Thin the goose population by trapping and removing many geese (perhaps 600) to areas less populated by humans, such as wildlife preserves.	Bulleted list emphasizing alternative solutions
Though costly (see figures below), the last solution is the most humane. It would be harmless to the geese, provided that sizable netted enclosures are used for traps. [Discussion of solution and "Recommendations" section follow.]	

14c Writing for community work

At some point in your life, you're likely to volunteer for a community organization such as a soup kitchen, a daycare center, or a literacy program. Many college courses involve service learning, in which you do such volunteer work, write about the experience for your course, and write *for* the organization you're helping.

The writing you do for a community group may range from flyers to grant proposals. Two guidelines will help you prepare effective projects like the ones here, for a literacy program.

- ■ **Craft each document for its purpose and audience.** You are trying to achieve a specific aim with your readers, and the approach and tone you use will influence their responses. If, for example, you are writing letters to local businesses to raise funds for a homeless shelter, bring to mind the people who will

---

Flyer

FIRST ANNUAL AWARDS DINNER

ReadingWorks

Springfield VA Hospital

Large type and color focusing a distant reader's attention on important information: what's happening, when, where, and who is invited

White space drawing viewers' eyes to main message and creating flow among elements

WHEN
Friday night
May 23
7:30 to 10:30

For information
contact ReadingWorks
209-556-1212

Color highlighting only key information

WHERE
Suite 42
Springfield VA Hospital

WHO
Students, tutors, and their families are invited to join us for an evening of food and music as we celebrate their efforts and accomplishments.

Less important information set in smaller type

ReadingWorks of Springfield Veterans Administration Hospital
111 South Springdale Drive
Springfield, MI 45078

read your letter. How can you best persuade those readers to donate money?

- **Expect to work with others.** Much public writing is the work of more than one person. Even if you draft the document on your own, others will review the content, tone, and design. Such collaboration is rewarding, but it sometimes requires patience and goodwill. See **1** pp. 29–31 for advice on collaborating.

Newsletter

ReadingWorks

Springfield Veterans Administration Hospital   **SUMMER 2008**

From the director

Can you help? With more and more learners in the ReadingWorks program, we need more and more tutors. You may know people who would be interested in participating in the program, if only they knew about it.

Those of you who have been tutoring VA patients in reading and writing know both the great need you fulfill and the great benefits you bring to the students. New tutors need no special skills—we'll provide the training—only patience and an interest in helping others.

We've scheduled an orientation meeting for Friday, September 12, at 6:30 PM. Please come and bring a friend who is willing to contribute a couple of hours a week to our work.

Thanks,
Kate Goodman

FIRST ANNUAL AWARDS DINNER

A festive night for students and tutors

The first annual Reading-Works Awards Dinner on May 23rd was a great success. Springfield's own Golden Fork provided tasty food and Amber Allen supplied lively music. The students decorated Suite 42 on the theme of books and reading. In all, 127 people attended.

The highlight of the night was the awards ceremony. Nine students, recommended by their tutors, received certificates recognizing their efforts and special accomplishments in learning to read and write:

Ramon Berva
Edward Byar
David Dunbar
Tony Garnier
Chris Guigni
Akili Haynes
Josh Livingston
Alex Obeld
B. J. Resnansky

In addition, nine tutors received certificates commemorating five years of service to ReadingWorks:

Anita Crumpton
Felix Cruz-Rivera
Bette Elgen
Kayleah Bortoluzzi
Harriotte Henderson
Ben Obiso
Meggie Puente
Max Smith
Sara Villante

Congratulations to all!

PTSD: New Guidelines

Most of us are working with veterans who have been diagnosed with post-traumatic stress disorder. Because this disorder is often complicated by alcoholism, depression, anxiety, and other problems, the National Center for PTSD has issued some guidelines for helping PTSD patients in ways that reduce their stress.

- The hospital must know your tutoring schedule, and you need to sign in and out before and after each tutoring session.

- To protect patients' privacy, meet them only in designated visiting and tutoring areas, never in their rooms.

- Treat patients with dignity and respect, even when (as sometimes happens) they grow frustrated and angry. Seek help from a nurse or orderly if you need it.

Multicolumn format allowing room for headings, articles, and other elements on a single page

Two-column heading emphasizing the main article

Elements helping readers skim for highlights: spacing, varied font sizes, lines, and a bulleted list

Color focusing readers' attention on banner, headlines, and table of contents

Lively but uncluttered overall appearance

Box in the first column highlighting table of contents

Brochure

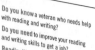

Do you know a veteran who needs help with reading and writing?

Do you need to improve your reading and writing skills to get a job?

ReadingWorks can make a difference. We organize volunteers to help military veterans achieve literacy and to prepare them for life-long learning.

For more information about our services, call Kate Goodman at 209-556-1212 or visit www.readingworks.org.

ReadingWorks
Springfield VA Hospital
111 South Springdale Drive
Springfield, MI 45078

 ReadingWorks
Springfield VA Hospital

Helping
military
veterans
achieve
literacy

Panel 2: The right page when the cover is opened, the first one readers see, containing key information

Panel 6: The back, usually including the return address and space for a mailing label and postage

Panel 1: The cover, drawing readers' attention to the group's name, purpose, and affiliation

---

 ReadingWorks
Springfield VA Hospital

OUR MISSION
- We provide workshops and formal lessons for veterans wishing to develop their reading and writing skills
- We train volunteers to tutor veterans one on one.
- We maintain outreach programs to provide access to literacy training for all veterans.
- We create literacy resources and share them with others who promote literacy for veterans.

OUR SERVICES

One-on-one tutoring
One to three hours a week with a trained volunteer tutor.

Workshops and classes
Small-group meetings centered on reading and writing, computer skills, and English as a second language.

Library
Books and other resources for students at various literacy levels.

Computer lab
Five computers with high-speed Internet access and a full range of software.

OUR TUTORS
The goodwill and generosity of our volunteer tutors allows us to reach out to those who have served our country.

If you or someone you know can join our team, contact Kate Goodman at 209-556-1212.

Hours
12:00 to 8:00, Mon., Wed.
9:00 to 5:00, Tues., Thurs., Fri.

Eligibility
Any veteran of the US military is eligible for our services.

How to reach us
Springfield VA Hospital
Room 172, first floor
111 South Springdale Drive
Springfield, MI 45078

209-556-1212
www.readingworks.org

Panel 3: The left page when the cover is opened, reinforcing the message of panel 2

Varied type, color, and photographs, adding visual interest and focusing readers' attention

Panels 4 and 5: The inside panels, containing contact information and other details

Clarity and Style

MICHIGAN STATE
UNIVERSITY

15 Emphasis

Emphatic writing leads readers to see your main ideas both within and among sentences. You can achieve emphasis by attending to your subjects and verbs (below), using sentence beginnings and endings (p. 132), coordinating equally important ideas (p. 134), and subordinating less important ideas (p. 136). In addition, emphatic writing is concise writing, the subject of Chapter 20.

Grammar checkers A grammar checker may spot some problems with emphasis, such as nouns made from verbs, passive voice, wordy phrases, and long sentences that may also be flabby and unemphatic. However, no checker can help you identify the important ideas in your sentences or determine whether those ideas receive appropriate emphasis.

15a Using subjects and verbs effectively

The heart of every sentence is its subject, which usually names the actor, and its predicate verb, which usually specifies the subject's action: *Children* [subject] *grow* [verb]. When these elements do not identify the key actor and action in the sentence, readers must find that information elsewhere and the sentence may be wordy and unemphatic.

In the following sentences, the subjects and verbs are underlined.

> Unemphatic   The intention of the company was to expand its workforce. A proposal was also made to diversify the backgrounds and abilities of employees.

These sentences are unemphatic because their key ideas do not appear in their subjects and verbs. In the revision on the next page the sentences are not only clearer but more concise.

Key terms

subject Who or what a sentence is about: *Biologists often study animals.* (See **4** pp. 172–73.)

predicate The part of a sentence containing a verb that asserts something about the subject: *Biologists often study animals.* (See **4** pp. 172–73.)

---

mycomplab

Visit *mycomplab.com* for more resources as well as exercises on emphasis.

Revised	The <u>company</u> <u>intended</u> to expand its workforce. It also <u>proposed</u> to diversify the backgrounds and abilities of employees.

The constructions discussed below and opposite usually drain meaning from a sentence's subject and verb.

Nouns made from verbs

Nouns made from verbs can obscure the key actions of sentences and add words. These nouns include *intention* (from *intend*), *proposal* (from *propose*), *decision* (from *decide*), *expectation* (from *expect*), and *inclusion* (from *include*).

Unemphatic	After the company made a <u>decision</u> to hire more workers with disabilities, its next <u>step</u> was the <u>construction</u> of wheelchair ramps and other facilities.
Revised	After the company <u>decided</u> to hire more workers with disabilities, it next <u>constructed</u> wheelchair ramps and other facilities.

Weak verbs

Weak verbs, such as *made* and *was* in the unemphatic sentence above, tend to stall sentences just where they should be moving and often bury key actions:

Unemphatic	The company <u>is</u> now the leader among businesses in complying with the 1990 disabilities act. Its officers <u>make</u> frequent speeches on the act to business groups.
Revised	The company now <u>leads</u> other businesses in complying with the 1990 disabilities act. Its officers frequently <u>speak</u> on the act to business groups.

Forms of *be, have,* and *make* are often weak, but don't try to eliminate every use of them: *be* and *have* are essential as helping verbs (*is going*, <u>has</u> *written*); *be* links subjects and words describing them (*Planes* <u>are</u> *noisy*); and *have* and *make* have independent meanings (among them "possess" and "force," respectively). But do consider replacing forms of *be, have,* and *make* when one of the words following the verb could be made into a strong verb itself, as in the following examples.

Key terms

noun A word that names a person, thing, quality, place, or idea: *student, desk, happiness, city, democracy.* (See **4** pp. 166–67.)

helping verb A verb used with another verb to convey time, obligation, and other meanings: <u>was</u> *drilling,* <u>would have been</u> *drilling.* (See **4** p. 169.)

Unemphatic	Emphatic
was influential	influenced
is a glorification	glorifies
have a preference	prefer
had the appearance	appeared, seemed
made a claim	claimed

Passive voice

Verbs in the passive voice state actions received by, not performed by, their subjects. Thus the passive de-emphasizes the true actor of the sentence, sometimes omitting it entirely. Generally, prefer the active voice, in which the subject performs the action. (See also **4** pp. 202–03 for help with editing the passive voice.)

Unemphatic	The 1990 law is seen by most businesses as fair, but the costs of complying have sometimes been objected to.
Revised	Most businesses see the 1990 law as fair, but some have objected to the costs of complying.

15b Using sentence beginnings and endings

Readers automatically seek a writer's principal meaning in the main clause of a sentence—essentially, in the subject that names the actor and in the verb that usually specifies the action (see p. 130). Thus you can help readers understand the meaning you intend by controlling the information in your subjects and the relation of the main clause to any modifiers attached to it.

Old and new information

Generally, readers expect the beginning of a sentence to contain information that they already know or that you have already introduced. They then look to the ending for new information. In the

---

Key terms

passive voice The verb form when the subject names the *receiver* of the verb's action: *The house was destroyed by the tornado.*

active voice The verb form when the subject names the *performer* of the verb's action: *The tornado destroyed the house.*

main clause A word group that can stand alone as a sentence, containing a subject and a predicate and not beginning with a subordinating word: *The books were expensive.* (See **4** p. 179.)

modifier A word or word group that describes another word or word group: *sweet candy, running in the park.* (See **4** pp. 169–70 and 177–79.)

unemphatic passage below, the second and third sentences both begin with new topics, while the old topics appear at the ends of the sentences. The pattern of the passage is A→B. C→B. D→A.

Unemphatic   Education often means controversy these days, with rising costs and constant complaints about its inadequacies. But the value of schooling should not be obscured by the controversy. The single best means of economic advancement, despite its shortcomings, remains education.

In the more emphatic revision, the old information begins each sentence and new information ends the sentence. The passage follows the pattern A→B. B→C. A→D.

Revised   Education often means controversy these days, with rising costs and constant complaints about its inadequacies. But the controversy should not obscure the value of schooling. Education remains, despite its shortcomings, the single best means of economic advancement.

Cumulative and periodic sentences

You can call attention to information by placing it first or last in a sentence, reserving the middle for incidentals:

Unemphatic   Education remains the single best means of economic advancement, despite its shortcomings. [Emphasizes shortcomings.]

Revised   Despite its shortcomings, education remains the single best means of economic advancement. [Emphasizes advancement more than shortcomings.]

Revised   Education remains, despite its shortcomings, the single best means of economic advancement. [De-emphasizes shortcomings.]

A sentence that adds modifiers to the main clause is called **cumulative** because it accumulates information as it proceeds:

Cumulative   Education has no equal in opening minds, instilling values, and creating opportunities.

Cumulative   Most of the Great American Desert is made up of bare rock, rugged cliffs, mesas, canyons, mountains, separated from one another by broad flat basins covered with sunbaked mud and alkali, supporting a sparse and measured growth

of sagebrush or creosote or saltbush, depending on location and elevation.   —Edward Abbey

The opposite kind of sentence, called **periodic**, saves the main
clause until just before the end (the period) of the sentence. Everything before the main clause points toward it:

Periodic	In opening minds, instilling values, and creating opportu-
nities, education has no equal.
Periodic	With people from all over the world—Korean doctors, Ja-
maican cricket players, Vietnamese engineers, Haitian cab-
drivers, Chinese grocers, Indian restaurant owners—the
American mosaic is continually changing.

The periodic sentence creates suspense by reserving important
information for the end. But readers should already have an idea of
the sentence's subject—because it was mentioned in the preceding
sentence—so that they know what the opening modifiers describe.

15c Using coordination

Use **coordination** to show that two or more elements in a sentence are equally important in meaning and thus to clarify the relationship between them:

Ways to coordinate information in sentences

- **Link main clauses with a comma and a coordinating conjunction:**
  and, but, or, nor, for, so, yet.

  Independence Hall in Philadelphia is faithfully restored **,** but many
  years ago it was in bad shape.

- **Relate main clauses with a semicolon alone or a semicolon and a
  conjunctive adverb:** *however, indeed, thus,* etc.

  The building was standing **;** however, it suffered from neglect.

- **Within clauses, link words and phrases with a coordinating conjunction:** *and, but, or, nor.*

  The people and officials of the nation were indifferent to independence Hall or took it for granted.

- **Link main clauses, words, or phrases with a correlative conjunction:** *both . . . and, not only . . . but also,* etc.

  People not only took the building for granted but also neglected it.

Grammar checkers A grammar checker may spot some errors in punctuating coordinated elements, and it can usually flag long sentences that may contain excessive coordination. But otherwise a checker can provide little help with coordination because it cannot recognize the relations among ideas in sentences.

1 Coordinating to relate equal ideas

Coordination shows the equality between elements, as illustrated by the examples in the preceding box. At the same time that it clarifies meaning, it can also help smooth choppy sentences:

| Choppy sentences | We should not rely so heavily on oil. Coal and uranium are also overused. We have a substantial energy resource in the moving waters of our rivers. Smaller streams add to the total volume of water. The resource renews itself. Oil and coal are irreplaceable. Uranium is also irreplaceable. The cost of water does not increase much over time. The costs of coal, oil, and uranium rise dramatically. |

The revision groups coal, oil, and uranium and clearly opposes them to water (the connecting words are underlined):

| Ideas coordinated | We should not rely so heavily on oil, coal, and uranium, for we have a substantial energy resource in the moving waters of our rivers and streams. Oil, coal, and uranium are irreplaceable and thus subject to dramatic cost increases; water, however, is self-renewing and more stable in cost. |

2 Coordinating effectively

Use coordination only to express the *equality* of ideas or details. A string of coordinated elements—especially main clauses—implies that all points are equally important:

| Excessive coordination | The weeks leading up to the resignation of President Nixon were eventful, and the Supreme Court and the Congress closed in on him, and the Senate Judiciary Committee voted to begin impeachment proceedings, and finally the President resigned on August 9, 1974. |

Key terms

coordinating conjunctions *And, but, or, nor,* and sometimes *for, so, yet.* (See **4** p. 171.)

conjunctive adverbs Modifiers that describe the relation of the ideas in two clauses, such as *hence, however, indeed,* and *thus.* (See **4** p. 243.)

correlative conjunctions Pairs of connecting words, such as *both . . . and, either . . . or, not only . . . but also.* (See **4** p. 172.)

Such a passage needs editing to stress the important points (under-lined below) and to de-emphasize the less important information:

> **Revised** The weeks leading up to the resignation of President Nixon were eventful, as the Supreme Court and the Congress closed in on him and the Senate Judiciary Committee voted to begin impeachment proceedings. Finally, the President resigned on August 9, 1974.

Even within a single sentence, coordination should express a logical equality between ideas:

> **Faulty** John Stuart Mill was a nineteenth-century utilitarian, and he believed that actions should be judged by their usefulness or by the happiness they cause. [The two clauses are not sepa-rate and equal: the second expands on the first by explaining what a utilitarian such as Mill believed.]
>
> **Revised** John Stuart Mill, a nineteenth-century utilitarian, believed that actions should be judged by their usefulness or by the happi-ness they cause.

15d Using subordination

Use **subordination** to indicate that some elements in a sentence are less important than others for your meaning. Usually, the main idea appears in the main clause, and supporting details appear in subordinate structures:

Ways to subordinate information in sentences

- **Use a subordinate clause beginning with a subordinating word:** *who (whom), that, which, although, because, if,* etc.

  Although some citizens had tried to rescue Independence Hall, they had not gained substantial public support.

  The first strong step was taken by the federal government, which made the building a national monument.

- **Use a phrase.**

  Like most national monuments, Independence Hall is protected by the National Park Service.

  Protecting many popular tourist sites, the service is a highly visible gov-ernment agency.

- **Use a short modifier.**

  At the red brick Independence Hall, park rangers give guided tours and protect the irreplaceable building from vandalism.

Grammar checkers A grammar checker may spot some errors in punctuating subordinated elements, and it can usually flag long sentences that may contain excessive subordination. But otherwise a checker can provide little help with subordination because it cannot recognize the relations among ideas in sentences.

1 Subordinating to emphasize main ideas

A string of main clauses can make everything in a passage seem equally important:

String of main clauses	Computer prices have dropped, and production costs have dropped more slowly, and computer manufacturers have had to struggle, for their profits have been shrinking.

Emphasis comes from keeping the truly important information in the main clause (underlined) and subordinating the less important details:

Revised	Because production costs have dropped more slowly than prices, <u>computer manufacturers have had to struggle with shrinking profits</u>.

2 Subordinating effectively

Use subordination only for the less important information in a sentence.

Faulty	Ms. Angelo was in her first year of teaching, although she was a better instructor than others with many years of experience.

The preceding sentence suggests that Angelo's inexperience is the main idea, whereas the writer intended to stress her skill *despite* her inexperience. Reducing the inexperience to a subordinate clause and elevating the skill to the main clause (underlined) gives appropriate emphasis:

Revised	Although Ms. Angelo was in her first year of teaching, <u>she was a better instructor than others with many years of experience</u>.

Key terms

subordinate clause A word group that contains a subject and verb, begins with a subordinating word such as *because* or *who,* and is not a question: *Words can do damage <u>when they hurt feelings</u>.* (See **4** p. 179.)

phrase A word group that lacks a subject or predicate or both: *Words can do damage <u>by hurting feelings</u>.* (See **4** pp. 175–76.)

Subordination loses its power to organize and emphasize when too much loosely related detail crowds into one long, meandering sentence:

Overloaded The boats that were moored at the dock when the hurricane, which was one of the worst in three decades, struck were ripped from their moorings, because the owners had not been adequately prepared, since the weather service had predicted that the storm would blow out to sea, which they do at this time of year.

The revision stresses important information in the main clauses (underlined):

Revised Struck by one of the worst hurricanes in three decades, <u>the boats at the dock were ripped from their moorings.</u> <u>The owners were unprepared</u> because the weather service had said that hurricanes at this time of year blow out to sea.

16 Parallelism

Parallelism gives similar grammatical form to sentence elements that have similar function and importance.

The air is dirtied by <u>factories belching smoke</u>
and
<u>cars spewing exhaust.</u>

In this example the two underlined phrases have the same function and importance (both specify sources of air pollution), so they also have the same grammatical construction. Parallelism makes form follow meaning.

Grammar checkers A grammar checker cannot recognize faulty parallelism because it cannot recognize the relations among ideas.

16a Using parallelism with *and, but, or, nor, yet*

The coordinating conjunctions *and, or, nor,* and *yet* always signal a need for parallelism.

mycomplab

Visit *mycomplab.com* for more resources as well as exercises on parallelism.

The industrial base was <u>shifting</u> and <u>shrinking</u>. [Parallel words.]

Politicians rarely <u>acknowledged the problem</u> or <u>proposed alternatives</u>. [Parallel phrases.]

Industrial workers were understandably disturbed <u>that they were losing their jobs</u> and <u>that no one seemed to care</u>. [Parallel clauses.]

When sentence elements linked by coordinating conjunctions are not parallel in structure, the sentence is awkward and distracting:

Nonparallel	The reasons steel companies kept losing money were <u>that their plants were inefficient</u>, <u>high labor costs</u>, and <u>foreign competition was increasing</u>.
Revised	The reasons steel companies kept losing money were <u>inefficient plants</u>, <u>high labor costs</u>, and <u>increasing foreign competition</u>.
Nonparallel	Success was difficult even for efficient companies because of <u>the shift away from all manufacturing in the United States</u> and <u>the fact that steel production was shifting toward emerging nations</u>.
Revised	Success was difficult even for efficient companies because of <u>the shift away from all manufacturing in the United States</u> and <u>toward steel production in emerging nations</u>.

All the words required by idiom or grammar must be stated in compound constructions (see also p. 158):

Faulty	Given training, workers can acquire the <u>skills</u> and <u>interest</u> in other jobs. [Idiom dictates different prepositions with *skills* and *interest*.]
Revised	Given training, workers can acquire the skills <u>for</u> and interest in other jobs.

16b Using parallelism with *both . . . and, not . . . but,* or another correlative conjunction

Correlative conjunctions stress equality and balance between elements. Parallelism confirms the equality.

Key terms

coordinating conjunctions Words that connect elements of the same kind and importance: *and, but, or, nor,* and sometimes *for, so, yet.* (See **4** p. 171.)

correlative conjunctions Pairs of words that connect elements of the same kind and importance, such as *but . . . and, either . . . or, neither . . . nor, not . . . but, not only . . . but also.* (See **4** p. 172.)

It is not a tax bill but a tax relief bill, providing relief not for the needy but for the greedy.

—Franklin Delano Roosevelt

With correlative conjunctions, the element after the second connector must match the element after the first connector:

| Nonparallel | Huck Finn learns not only that human beings have an enormous capacity for folly but also enormous dignity. [The first element includes *that human beings have;* the second element does not.] |
| Revised | Huck Finn learns that human beings have not only an enormous capacity for folly but also enormous dignity. [Repositioning *that human beings have* makes the two elements parallel.] |

16c Using parallelism in comparisons

Parallelism confirms the likeness or difference between two elements being compared using *than* or *as:*

| Nonparallel | Huck Finn proves less a bad boy than to be an independent spirit. In the end he is every bit as determined in rejecting help as he is to leave for "the territory." |
| Revised | Huck Finn proves less a bad boy than an independent spirit. In the end he is every bit as determined to reject help as he is to leave for "the territory." |

(See also **4** pp. 224–25 on making comparisons logical.)

16d Using parallelism with lists, headings, and outlines

The items in a list or outline are coordinate and should be parallel. Parallelism is essential in a formal topic outline and in the headings that divide a paper into sections. (See **1** pp. 19–20 and 50–51 for more on outlines and headings.)

Nonparallel	Revised
Changes in Renaissance England	Changes in Renaissance England
1. Extension of trade routes	1. Extension of trade routes
2. Merchant class became more powerful	2. Increased power of the merchant class
3. The death of feudalism	3. Death of feudalism
4. Upsurging of the arts	4. Upsurge of the arts
5. Religious quarrels began	5. Rise of religious quarrels

17 Variety and Details

Writing that's interesting as well as clear has at least two features: the sentences vary in length and structure, and they are well textured with details.

Grammar checkers Some grammar checkers will flag long sentences, and you can check for appropriate variety in a series of such sentences. But generally these programs cannot help you see where variety may be needed because they cannot recognize the relative importance and complexity of your ideas.

17a Varying sentence length

In most contemporary writing, sentences tend to vary from about ten to about forty words. When sentences are all at one extreme or the other, readers may have difficulty focusing on main ideas and seeing the relations among them.

- **Long sentences.** If most of your sentences contain thirty-five words or more, your main ideas may not stand out from the details that support them. Break some of the long sentences into shorter, simpler ones.
- **Short sentences.** If most of your sentences contain fewer than ten or fifteen words, all your ideas may seem equally important and the links between them may not be clear. Try combining sentences with coordination (p. 134) and subordination (p. 136) to show relationships and stress main ideas over supporting information.

17b Varying sentence structure

A passage will be monotonous if all its sentences follow the same pattern, like soldiers marching in a parade. Try the following techniques for varying structure.

1 Subordination

A string of main clauses in simple or compound sentences can be especially plodding.

Visit *mycomplab.com* for more resources on variety and details.

Monotonous   The moon is now drifting away from the earth. It moves away at the rate of about one inch a year. This movement is lengthening our days. They increase a thousandth of a second every century. Forty-seven of our present days will someday make up a month. We might eventually lose the moon altogether. Such great planetary movement rightly concerns astronomers, but it need not worry us. It will take 50 million years.

Enliven such writing—and make the main ideas stand out—by expressing the less important information in subordinate clauses and phrases. In the revision below, underlining indicates subordinate structures that used to be main clauses:

Revised   The moon is now drifting away from the earth <u>about one inch a year</u>. <u>At a thousandth of a second every century</u>, this movement is lengthening our days. Forty-seven of our present days will someday make up a month, <u>if we don't eventually lose the moon altogether</u>. Such great planetary movement rightly concerns astronomers, but it need not worry us. It will take 50 million years.

2   Sentence combining

As the preceding example shows, subordinating to achieve variety often involves combining short, choppy sentences into longer units that link related information and stress main ideas. Here is another unvaried passage:

Monotonous   Astronomy may seem a remote science. It may seem to have little to do with people's daily lives. Many astronomers find otherwise. They see their science as soothing. It gives perspective to everyday routines and problems.

Key terms

main clause A word group that can stand alone as a sentence because it contains a subject and a predicate and does not begin with a subordinating word: *Tourism is an industry. It brings in over $2 billion a year.* (See **4** p. 179.)

subordinate clause A word group that contains a subject and predicate, begins with a subordinating word such as *because* or *who,* and is not a question: *Tourism is an industry <u>that brings in over $2 billion a year</u>.* (See **4** p. 179.)

phrase A word group that lacks a subject or predicate or both: *Tourism is an industry <u>valued at over $2 billion a year</u>.* (See **4** p. 177.)

Combining five sentences into one, the following revision is both clearer and easier to read. Underlining highlights the changes.

> **Revised**   Astronomy may seem a remote science <u>having</u> little to do with people's daily lives, <u>but</u> many astronomers <u>find their science soothing</u> because it gives perspective to everyday routines and problems.

3 | Varied sentence beginnings

An English sentence often begins with its subject, which generally captures old information from a preceding sentence (see p. 132):

> The defendant's <u>lawyer</u> was determined to break the prosecution's witness. <u>He</u> relentlessly cross-examined the stubborn witness for a week.

However, an unbroken sequence of sentences beginning with the subject quickly becomes monotonous:

> **Monotonous**   The defendant's lawyer was determined to break the prosecution's witness. He relentlessly cross-examined the witness for a week. The witness had expected to be dismissed within an hour and was visibly irritated. She did not cooperate. She was reprimanded by the judge.

Beginning some of these sentences with other expressions improves readability and clarity:

> **Revised**   The defendant's lawyer was determined to break the prosecution's witness. <u>For a week</u> he relentlessly cross-examined the witness. <u>Expecting to be dismissed within an hour,</u> the witness was visibly irritated. She did not cooperate. <u>Indeed,</u> she was reprimanded by the judge.

The underlined expressions represent the most common choices for varying sentence beginnings:

- **Adverb modifiers,** such as *For a week* (modifies the verb *cross-examined*).
- **Adjective modifiers,** such as *Expecting to be dismissed within an hour* (modifies *witness*).
- **Transitional expressions,** such as *Indeed.* (See **1** pp. 36–37 for a list.)

Key terms

adverb A word or word group that describes a verb, an adjective, another adverb, or a whole sentence: *dressed <u>sharply</u>, <u>clearly</u> unhappy, soaring <u>from the mountain</u>.* (See **4** pp. 169–70.)

adjective A word or word group that describes a noun or pronoun: *<u>sweet</u> smile, <u>certain</u> someone.* (See **4** p. 169.)

CULTURE LANGUAGE · In standard American English, placing certain adverb modifiers at the beginning of a sentence requires you to alter the normal subject-verb order as well. The most common of these modifiers are negatives, including *seldom, rarely, in no case, not since,* and *not until.*

	adverb subject verb phrase
Faulty	Seldom a witness has held the stand so long.

	adverb helping verb subject main verb
Revised	Seldom has a witness held the stand so long.

4 Varied word order

Occasionally you can vary a sentence and emphasize it at the same time by inverting the usual order of parts:

A dozen witnesses testified for the prosecution, and the defense attorney barely questioned eleven of them. The twelfth, however, he grilled. [Normal word order: *He grilled the twelfth, however.*]

Inverted sentences used without need are artificial. Use them only when emphasis demands.

17c Adding details

Relevant details such as facts and examples create the texture and life that keep readers awake and help them grasp your meaning. For instance:

Flat	Constructed after World War II, Levittown, New York, consisted of thousands of houses in two basic styles. Over the decades, residents have altered the houses so dramatically that the original styles are often unrecognizable.
Detailed	Constructed on potato fields after World War II, Levittown, New York, consisted of more than seventeen thousand houses in Cape Cod and ranch styles. Over the decades, residents have added expansive front porches, punched dormer windows through roofs, converted garages to sun porches, and otherwise altered the houses so dramatically that the original styles are often unrecognizable.

18 Appropriate and Exact Language

The clarity and effectiveness of your writing will depend greatly on the use of language that is appropriate for your writing situation (below) and that expresses your meaning exactly (p. 152).

18a Choosing appropriate language

Appropriate language suits your writing situation—your subject, purpose, and audience. In most college and career writing you should rely on what's called **standard American English,** the dialect of English normally expected and used in school, business, the professions, government, and the communications media. (For more on its role in academic writing, see **2** pp. 85–87.)

The vocabulary of standard American English is huge, allowing expression of an infinite range of ideas and feelings; but it does exclude words that only some groups of people use, understand, or find inoffensive. Some of these more limited vocabularies should be avoided altogether; others should be used cautiously and in relevant situations, as when aiming for a special effect with an audience you know will appreciate it. Whenever you doubt a word's status, consult a dictionary (see p. 152).

Grammar checkers A grammar checker can often be set to flag potentially inappropriate words, such as nonstandard dialect, slang, colloquialisms, and gender-specific terms (*manmade, mailman*). However, the checker can flag only words listed in its dictionary of questionable words. For example, a checker flagged *businessman* as potentially sexist in *A successful businessman puts clients first,* but the checker did not flag *his* in *A successful businessperson listens to his clients.* If you use a checker to review your language, you'll need to determine whether a flagged word is or is not appropriate for your writing situation.

1 Nonstandard dialect CULTURE LANGUAGE

Like many countries, the United States includes scores of regional, social, and ethnic groups with their own distinct **dialects,** or versions of English. Standard American English is one of those dialects, and so are Black English, Appalachian English, Creole, and

mycomplab

Visit *mycomplab.com* for more resources as well as exercises on appropriate and exact language.

145

the English of coastal Maine. All the dialects of English share many features, but each also has its own vocabulary, pronunciation, and grammar.

If you speak a dialect of English besides standard American English, be careful about using your dialect in situations where standard English is the norm, such as in academic or business writing. Dialects are not wrong in themselves, but forms imported from one dialect into another may still be perceived as unclear or incorrect. When you know standard English is expected in your writing, edit to eliminate expressions in your dialect that you know (or have been told) differ from standard English. These expressions may include *theirselves, his, them books,* and others labeled "nonstandard" by a dictionary. They may also include certain verb forms, as discussed in **4** pp. 182–94. For help identifying and editing nonstandard language, see the ⟨CULTURE LANGUAGE⟩ Guide just before the back endpapers of this book.

Your participation in the community of standard English does not require you to abandon your own dialect. You may want to use it in writing you do for yourself, such as journals, notes, and drafts, which should be composed as freely as possible. You may want to quote it in an academic paper, as when analyzing or reporting conversation in dialect. And, of course, you will want to use it with others who speak it.

2 | **Shortcuts of online communication**

Rapid communication by e-mail and text or instant messaging encourages some informalities that are inappropriate for academic writing. If you use these media frequently, you may need to proofread your academic papers especially to identify and revise errors such as the following:

- **Sentence fragments.** Make sure every sentence has a subject and a predicate. Avoid fragments such as *Observing the results* or *After the meeting.* For more on fragments, see **4** pp. 236–39.
- **Missing punctuation.** Between and within sentences, use standard punctuation marks. Check especially for missing commas within sentences and missing apostrophes in possessives and contractions. See **5** pp. 250–61 and 267–70.
- **Missing capital letters.** Use capital letters at the beginnings of sentences, for proper nouns and adjectives, and in titles. See **6** pp. 288–91.
- **Nonstandard abbreviations and spellings.** Avoid forms such as *2* for *to* or *too, b4* for *before, bc* for *because, ur* for *you are* or *you're,* and + or & for *and.* See **6** pp. 282–86 and 294–96.

3 | Slang

Slang is the language used by a group, such as musicians or computer programmers, to reflect common experiences and to make technical references efficient. The following example is from an essay on the slang of "skaters" (skateboarders):

> Curtis slashed ultra-punk crunchers on his longboard, while the Rube-man flailed his usual Gumbyness on tweaked frontsides and lofty fakie ollies.
> —Miles Orkin, "Mucho Slingage by the Pool"

Among those who understand it, slang may be vivid and forceful. It often occurs in dialog, and an occasional slang expression can enliven an informal essay. But most slang is too flippant and imprecise for effective communication, and it is generally inappropriate for college or business writing. Notice the gain in seriousness and precision achieved in the following revision:

Slang	Many students start out pretty together but then get weird.
Revised	Many students start out with clear goals but then lose their direction.

4 | Colloquial language

Colloquial language is the everyday spoken language, including expressions such as *get together, go crazy, do the dirty work,* and *get along.*

When you write informally, colloquial language may be appropriate to achieve the casual, relaxed effect of conversation. An occasional colloquial word dropped into otherwise more formal writing can also help you achieve a desired emphasis. But most colloquial language is not precise enough for college or career writing. In such writing you should generally avoid any words and expressions labeled "informal" or "colloquial" in your dictionary.

Colloquial	According to a Native American myth, the Great Creator had a dog hanging around with him when he created the earth.
Revised	According to a Native American myth, the Great Creator was accompanied by a dog when he created the earth.

5 | Technical words

All disciplines and professions rely on specialized language that allows the members to communicate precisely and efficiently with each other. Chemists, for instance, have their *phosphatides,* and literary critics have their *motifs* and *subtexts*. Without explanation, technical words are meaningless to nonspecialists. When you are writing for nonspecialists, avoid unnecessary technical terms and carefully define terms you must use.

6 Indirect and pretentious writing

Small, plain, and direct words are almost always preferable to big, showy, or evasive words. Take special care to avoid euphemisms, double talk, and pretentious writing.

A **euphemism** is a presumably inoffensive word that a writer or speaker substitutes for a word deemed potentially offensive or too blunt, such as *passed away* for *died* or *misspeak* for *lie*. Use euphemisms only when you know that blunt, truthful words would needlessly hurt or offend members of your audience.

A kind of euphemism that deliberately evades the truth is **double talk** (also called **doublespeak** or **weasel words**): language intended to confuse or to be misunderstood. Today double talk is unfortunately common in politics and advertising—the *revenue enhancement* that is really a tax, the *peace-keeping function* that is really war making, the *biodegradable* bags that last decades. Double talk has no place in honest writing.

Euphemism and sometimes double talk seem to keep company with **pretentious writing**, fancy language that is more elaborate than its subject requires. Choose your words for their exactness and economy. The big, ornate word may be tempting, but pass it up. Your readers will be grateful.

Pretentious	To perpetuate our endeavor of providing funds for our elderly citizens as we do at the present moment, we will face the exigency of enhanced contributions from all our citizens.
Revised	We cannot continue to fund Social Security and Medicare for the elderly unless we raise taxes.

7 Sexist and other biased language

Even when we do not mean it to, our language can reflect and perpetuate hurtful prejudices toward groups of people. Such biased language can be obvious—words such as *nigger, honky, mick, kike, fag, dyke,* and *broad.* But it can also be subtle, generalizing about groups in ways that may be familiar but that are also inaccurate or unfair.

Biased language reflects poorly on the user, not on the person or persons whom it mischaracterizes or insults. Unbiased language does not submit to false generalizations. It treats people respectfully as individuals and labels groups as they wish to be labeled.

Stereotypes of race, ethnicity, religion, age, and other characteristics

A **stereotype** is a generalization based on poor evidence, a kind of formula for understanding and judging people simply because of their membership in a group:

Men are uncommunicative.
Women are emotional.
Liberals want to raise taxes.
Conservatives are affluent.

At best, stereotypes betray a noncritical writer, one who is not thinking beyond notions received from others. In your writing, be alert for statements that characterize whole groups of people:

Stereotype	Elderly drivers should have their licenses limited to daytime driving only. [Asserts that all elderly people are poor night drivers.]
Revised	Drivers with impaired night vision should have their licenses limited to daytime driving only.

Some stereotypes have become part of the language, but they are still potentially offensive:

Stereotype	The administrators are too blind to see the need for a new gymnasium. [Equates vision loss and lack of understanding.]
Revised	The administrators do not understand the need for a new gymnasium.

Sexist language

Among the most subtle and persistent biased language is that expressing narrow ideas about men's and women's roles, position, and value in society. Like other stereotypes, this **sexist language** can wound or irritate readers, and it indicates the writer's thoughtlessness or unfairness. The box on the next two pages suggests some ways of eliminating sexist language.

CULTURE LANGUAGE Forms of address vary widely from culture to culture. In some cultures, for instance, one shows respect by referring to all older women as if they were married, using the equivalent of *Mrs.* Usage in the United States is changing toward making no assumptions about marital status, rank, or other characteristics—for instance, addressing a woman as *Ms.* unless she is known to prefer *Mrs.* or *Miss.*

Eliminating sexist language

■ **Avoid demeaning and patronizing language:**

Sexist   <u>Dr. Keith Kim</u> and <u>Lydia Hawkins</u> coauthored the article.

Revised   Dr. Keith Kim and Dr. Lydia Hawkins coauthored the article.

Revised   Keith Kim and Lydia Hawkins coauthored the article.

Sexist   <u>Ladies</u> are entering almost every occupation formerly filled by men.

Revised   Women are entering almost every occupation formerly filled by men.

■ **Avoid occupational or social stereotypes:**

Sexist   The considerate doctor commends a nurse when <u>she</u> provides <u>his</u> patients with good care.

Revised   The considerate doctor commends a nurse who provides good care for patients.

Sexist   The grocery shopper should save <u>her</u> coupons.

Revised   Grocery shoppers should save their coupons.

■ **Avoid referring needlessly to gender:**

Sexist   Marie Curie, <u>a woman chemist</u>, discovered radium.

Revised   Marie Curie, a chemist, discovered radium.

Sexist   The patients were tended by <u>a male nurse</u>.

Revised   The patients were tended by a nurse.

■ **Avoid using *man* or words containing *man* to refer to all human beings.** Here are a few alternatives:

businessman	businessperson
chairman	chair, chairperson
congressman	representative in Congress, legislator
craftsman	craftsperson, artisan
layman	layperson
mankind	humankind, humanity, human beings, humans
manmade	handmade, manufactured, synthetic, artificial
manpower	personnel, human resources
policeman	police officer
salesman	salesperson

Sexist   <u>Man</u> has not reached the limits of social justice.

Revised   Humankind [or Humanity] has not reached the limits of social justice.

Sexist   The furniture consists of <u>manmade</u> materials.

Revised   The furniture consists of synthetic materials.

(continued)

Eliminating sexist language
(continued)

▪ **Avoid the generic *he,*** the male pronoun used to refer to both genders. (See also **4** pp. 217–18.)

Sexist The newborn child explores his world.

Revised Newborn children explore their world. [Use the plural for the pronoun and the word it refers to.]

Revised The newborn child explores the world. [Avoid the pronoun altogether.]

Revised The newborn child explores his or her world. [Substitute male and female pronouns.]

Use the last option sparingly—only once in a group of sentences and only to stress the singular individual.

Appropriate labels

We often need to label groups: *swimmers, politicians, mothers, Christians, Westerners, students.* But labels can be shorthand stereotypes, slighting the person labeled and ignoring the preferences of the group members themselves. Although sometimes dismissed as "political correctness," showing sensitivity about labels hurts no one and helps gain your readers' trust and respect.

▪ **Avoid labels that (intentionally or not) disparage the person or group you refer to.** A person with emotional problems is not a *mental patient.* A person with cancer is not a *cancer victim.* A person using a wheelchair is not *wheelchair-bound.*

▪ **Use names for racial, ethnic, and other groups that reflect the preferences of each group's members,** or at least many of them. Examples of current preferences include *African American* or *black, latino/latina* (for Americans and American immigrants of Spanish-speaking descent), and *people with disabilities* (rather than *the disabled* or *the handicapped*). But labels change often. To learn how a group's members wish to be labeled, ask them directly, attend to usage in reputable periodicals, or check a recent dictionary.

▪ **Identify a person's group only when it is relevant to the point you're making.** Consider the context of the label: Is it a necessary piece of information? If not, don't use it.

A helpful reference for appropriate labels is *Guidelines for Bias-Free Writing,* by Marilyn Schwartz and the Task Force on Bias-Free Language of the Association of American University Presses.

18b Choosing exact language

To write clearly and effectively, you will want to find the words that fit your meaning exactly and convey your attitude precisely.

Grammar checkers A grammar checker can provide some help with inexact language. For instance, you can set it to flag commonly confused words (such as *continuous/continual*), misused prepositions in idioms (such as *accuse for* instead of *accuse of*), and clichés. But a checker can't help you at all with inappropriate connotation, excessive abstraction, or other problems discussed in this section.

1 Word meanings and synonyms

For writing exactly, a dictionary is essential and a thesaurus can be helpful.

Desk dictionaries

A desk dictionary defines about 150,000 to 200,000 words and provides pronunciation, grammatical functions, etymology (word history), and other information. The sample below is from *Merriam-Webster's Collegiate Dictionary.*

Dictionary entry for *reckon*

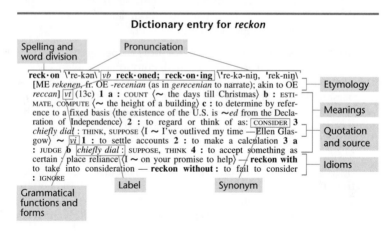

Good desk dictionaries, in addition to *Merriam-Webster's,* include the *American Heritage College Dictionary,* the *Random House Webster's College Dictionary,* and *Webster's New World Dictionary.* Most of these are available in both print and electronic form (CD-ROM or online). In addition, several Web sites provide online dictionaries or links to online dictionaries.

CULTURE LANGUAGE If English is not your native language, you may want a dictionary prepared especially for students using English as a second language (ESL). Such a dictionary contains special information on prepositions, count versus noncount nouns, and many other matters. Reliable ESL dictionaries include *COBUILD English Language Dictionary, Longman Dictionary of Contemporary English,* and *Oxford Advanced Learner's Dictionary.*

Thesauruses

To find a word with the exact shade of meaning you intend, you may want to consult a thesaurus, or book of **synonyms**—words with approximately the same meaning. A thesaurus such as *Roget's International Thesaurus* lists most imaginable synonyms for thousands of words. The word *news,* for instance, has half a page of synonyms in *Roget's International,* including *tidings, gossip,* and *journalism.*

Since a thesaurus aims to open up possibilities, its lists of synonyms include approximate as well as precise matches. The thesaurus does not define synonyms or distinguish among them, however, so you need a dictionary to discover exact meanings. In general, don't use a word from a thesaurus—even one you like the sound of—until you know it is appropriate for your meaning.

Note Your word processor may also include a thesaurus, making it easy to look up synonyms and insert the chosen word into your text. But still you should consult a dictionary unless you are certain of the word's meaning.

2 The right word for your meaning

All words have one or more basic meanings, called **denotations**—the meanings listed in the dictionary, without reference to emotional associations. If readers are to understand you, you must use words according to their established meanings.

- Consult a dictionary whenever you are unsure of a word's meaning.
- Distinguish between similar-sounding words that have widely different denotations:

Inexact	Older people often suffer infirmaries [places for the sick].
Exact	Older people often suffer infirmities [disabilities].

Some words, called **homonyms,** sound exactly alike but differ in meaning: for example, *principal/principle* and *rain/reign/rein.* (See **6** pp. 282–83 for a list of commonly confused homonyms.)

- Distinguish between words with related but distinct meanings:

Inexact	Television commercials continuously [unceasingly] interrupt programming.

Exact   Television commercials <u>continually</u> [regularly] interrupt pro-
gramming.

In addition to their emotion-free meanings, many words carry
related meanings that evoke specific feelings. These **connotations**
can shape readers' responses and are thus a powerful tool for writers. The following word pairs have related denotations but very
different connotations:

pride: sense of self-worth
vanity: excessive regard for oneself

firm: steady, unchanging, unyielding
stubborn: unreasonable, bullheaded

enthusiasm: excitement
mania: excessive interest or desire

A dictionary can help you track down words with the exact connotations you want. Besides providing meanings, your dictionary
may also list and distinguish synonyms to guide your choices. A thesaurus can also help if you use it carefully, as discussed on the previous page.

3 Concrete and specific words

Clear, exact writing balances abstract and general words, which
outline ideas and objects, with concrete and specific words, which
sharpen and solidify.

- **Abstract words** name ideas: *beauty, inflation, management, culture, liberal.* **Concrete words** name qualities and things we can
know by our five senses of sight, hearing, touch, taste, and
smell: *sleek, humming, rough, salty, musty.*
- **General words** name classes or groups of things, such as *birds,
weather,* and *buildings,* and include all the varieties of the
class. **Specific words** limit a general class, such as *buildings,* by
naming a variety, such as *skyscraper, Victorian courthouse,* or
hut.

Abstract and general words are useful in the broad statements
that set the course for your writing.

The wild horse in America has a <u>romantic</u> history.

Relations between the sexes today are more <u>relaxed</u> than they were in
the past.

But such statements need development with concrete and specific
detail. Detail can turn a vague sentence into an exact one:

Vague   The size of his hands made his smallness real. [How big were his
hands? How small was he?]

Exact Not until I saw his delicate, doll-like hands did I realize that he stood a full head shorter than most other men.

Note You can use your computer's Find function to help you find and revise abstract and general words that you tend to overuse. Examples of such words include *nice, interesting, things, very, good, a lot, a little,* and *some.*

4 Idioms

Idioms are expressions in any language that do not fit the rules for meaning or grammar—for instance, *put up with, plug away at, make off with.*

Idioms that involve prepositions can be especially confusing for both native and nonnative speakers of English. Some idioms with prepositions are listed in the following box. (More appear in **4** pp. 193–94.)

Idioms with prepositions

abide by a rule
    in a place or state
according to
accords with
accuse of a crime
accustomed to
adapt from a source
    to a situation
afraid of
agree on a plan as a group
    to someone else's plan
    with a person
angry with
aware of
based on
belong in or on a place
    to a group
capable of
certain of
charge for a purchase
    with a crime
concur in an opinion
    with a person
contend for a principle
    with a person

dependent on
differ about or over a question
    from in some quality
    with a person
disappointed by or in a person
    in or with a thing
familiar with
identical with or to
impatient for a raise
    with a person
independent of
infer from
inferior to
involved in a task
    with a person
oblivious of or to one's surroundings
    of something forgotten
occupied by a person
    in study
    with a thing
opposed to
part from a person
    with a possession
prior to
proud of

related <u>to</u>	superior <u>to</u>
rewarded <u>by</u> the judge	wait <u>at</u> a place
<u>for</u> something done	<u>for</u> a train, a person
<u>with</u> a gift	<u>in</u> a room
similar <u>to</u>	<u>on</u> a customer
sorry <u>about</u> an error	
<u>for</u> a person	

CULTURE LANGUAGE If you are learning standard American English, you are justified in stumbling over its prepositions: their meanings can shift depending on context, and they have many idiomatic uses. In mastering the prepositions of standard English, you probably can't avoid memorization. But you can help yourself by memorizing related groups, such as *at/in/on* and *for/since*.

At, in, or *on* in expressions of time

- Use *at* before actual clock time: *at 8:30.*
- Use *in* before a month, year, century, or period: *in April, in 2007, in the twenty-first century, in the next month.*
- Use *on* before a day or date: *on Tuesday, on May 3, on Labor Day.*

At, in, or *on* in expressions of place

- Use *at* before a specific place or address: *at the school, at 511 Iris Street.*
- Use *in* before a place with limits or before a city, state, country, or continent: *in the house, in a box, in Oklahoma City, in China, in Asia.*
- Use *on* to mean "supported by" or "touching the surface of": *on the table, on Iris Street, on page 150.*

For or *since* in expressions of time

- Use *for* before a period of time: *for an hour, for two years.*
- Use *since* before a specific point in time: *since 1999, since Friday.*

A dictionary of English as a second language is the best source for the meanings of prepositions; see the suggestions on p. 153.

5 | Figurative language

Figurative language (or a **figure of speech**) departs from the literal meanings of words, usually by comparing very different ideas or objects:

Literal   As I try to write, I can think of nothing to say.
Figurative   As I try to write, <u>my mind is a slab of black slate.</u>

Imaginatively and carefully used, figurative language can capture meaning more precisely and emotionally than literal language. Here is a figure of speech at work in technical writing (paraphrasing the physicist Edward Andrade):

> The molecules in a liquid move continuously like couples on an overcrowded dance floor, jostling each other.

The two most common figures of speech are the simile and the metaphor. Both compare two things of different classes, often one abstract and the other concrete. A **simile** makes the comparison explicit and usually begins with *like* or *as:*

> Whenever we grow, we tend to feel it, as a young seed must feel the weight and inertia of the earth when it seeks to break out of its shell on its way to becoming a plant. —Alice Walker

A **metaphor** claims that the two things are identical, omitting such words as *like* and *as:*

> A school is a hopper into which children are heaved while they are young and tender; therein they are pressed into certain standard shapes and covered from head to heels with official rubber stamps.
> —H. L. Mencken

To be successful, figurative language must be fresh and unstrained, calling attention not to itself but to the writer's meaning. Be especially wary of mixed metaphors, which combine two or more incompatible figures:

Mixed   Various thorny problems that we try to sweep under the rug continue to bob up all the same.

Improved   Various thorny problems that we try to weed out continue to thrive all the same.

6 Trite expressions

Trite expressions, or **clichés,** are phrases so old and so often repeated that they have become stale. They include the following:

add insult to injury	easier said than done
better late than never	face the music
crushing blow	few and far between
green with envy	ripe old age
hard as a rock	rude awakening
heavy as lead	shoulder the burden
hit the nail on the head	shoulder to cry on
hour of need	sneaking suspicion
ladder of success	stand in awe
moving experience	strong as an ox
a needle in a haystack	thin as a rail
point with pride	tried and true
pride and joy	wise as an owl

To edit clichés, listen to your writing for any expressions that you have heard or used before. You can also supplement your efforts with a style checker, which may include a cliché detector. When you find a cliché, substitute fresh words of your own or restate the idea in plain language.

19 Completeness

The most serious kind of incomplete sentence is the grammatical fragment (see **4** pp. 236–39). But sentences are also incomplete when they omit one or more words needed for clarity.

Grammar checkers A grammar checker will not flag most kinds of incomplete sentences discussed in this chapter.

19a Writing complete compounds

You may omit words from a compound construction when the omission will not confuse readers:

> Environmentalists have hopes for alternative fuels and [for] public transportation.

> Some cars will run on electricity, some [will run] on ethanol, and some [will run] on hydrogen.

Such omissions are possible only when the words omitted are common to all the parts of a compound construction. When the parts differ in any way, all words must be included in all parts.

> One new car <u>gets</u> eighty miles per gallon; some old cars <u>get</u> as little as five miles per gallon. [One verb is singular, the other plural.]

> Environmentalists believe <u>in</u> and work <u>for</u> fuel conservation. [Idiom requires different prepositions with *believe* and *work*.]

┌─ **Key term** ───

compound construction Two or more elements (words, phrases, clauses) that are equal in importance and that function as a unit: *Rain fell, and streams overflowed* (clauses); *dogs and cats* (words).

└──

---

mycomplab

Visit *mycomplab.com* for more resources on complete sentences.

19b Adding needed words

In haste or carelessness, do not omit small words that are needed for clarity:

Incomplete   Regular payroll deductions are a type painless savings. You hardly notice missing amounts, and after period of years the contributions can add a large total.

Revised   Regular payroll deductions are a type of painless savings. You hardly notice the missing amounts, and after a period of years the contributions can add up to a large total.

Attentive proofreading is the only insurance against this kind of omission. *Proofread all your papers carefully.* See **1** p. 29 for tips.

CULTURE LANGUAGE   If your native language or dialect is not standard American English, you may have difficulty knowing when to use the English articles *a, an,* and *the.* For guidelines see **4** pp. 226–30.

20 Conciseness

Concise writing makes every word count. Conciseness is not the same as mere brevity: detail and originality should not be cut with needless words. Rather, the length of an expression should be appropriate to the thought.

You may find yourself writing wordily when you are unsure of your subject or when your thoughts are tangled. It's fine, even necessary, to grope while drafting. But you should straighten out your ideas and eliminate wordiness during revision and editing.

Grammar checkers A grammar checker will identify at least some wordy structures, such as repeated words, weak verbs, passive voice, and *there is* and *it is* constructions. But a checker can't identify all potentially wordy structures, nor can it tell you whether a structure is appropriate for your ideas.

CULTURE LANGUAGE   As you'll see in the examples that follow, wordiness is not a problem of incorrect grammar. A sentence may be perfectly grammatical but still contain unneeded words that interfere with the clarity and force of your idea.

my**comp**lab

Visit *mycomplab.com* for more resources as well as exercises on writing concisely.

Ways to achieve conciseness

Wordy (87 words)

The highly pressured <u>nature</u> of critical-care nursing is <u>due to the fact that</u> the patients have life-threatening illnesses. Critical-care nurses must <u>have possession of</u> steady nerves to <u>care for patients who are critically ill and very sick.</u> The nurses must also have possession of interpersonal skills. They must also have medical skills. <u>It is considered by most health-care professionals</u> that these nurses are essential <u>if there is to be improvement of patients</u> who are now in critical care from that status to the status of intermediate care.

— Focus on subject and verb, and cut or shorten empty words and phrases.

— Avoid nouns made from verbs.

— Cut unneeded repetition.

— Combine sentences.

— Change passive voice to active voice.

— Revise *there is* constructions.

— Cut unneeded repetition, and reduce clauses and phrases.

Concise (37 words)

Critical-care nursing is highly pressured because the patients have life-threatening illnesses. Critical-care nurses must possess steady nerves and interpersonal and medical skills. Most health-care professionals consider these nurses essential if patients are to improve to intermediate care.

20a Focusing on the subject and verb

Using the subjects and verbs of your sentences for the key actors and actions will reduce words and emphasize important ideas. (See pp. 130–32 for more on this topic.)

Wordy	The <u>reason</u> why most of the country shifts to daylight time <u>is</u> that winter days are much shorter than summer days.
Concise	Most of the <u>country shifts</u> to daylight time because winter days are much shorter than summer days.

Focusing on subjects and verbs will also help you avoid several other causes of wordiness discussed further on pp. 131–32:

Nouns made from verbs

Wordy	The <u>occurrence</u> of the winter solstice, the shortest day of the year, <u>is</u> an event occurring about December 22.
Concise	The winter <u>solstice</u>, the shortest day of the year, <u>occurs</u> about December 22.

Weak verbs

Wordy	The earth's axis has a tilt as the planet is in orbit around the sun so that the northern and southern hemispheres are alternately in alignment toward the sun.
Concise	The earth's axis tilts as the planet orbits the sun so that the northern and southern hemispheres alternately align toward the sun.

Passive voice

Wordy	During its winter the northern hemisphere is tilted farthest away from the sun, so the nights are made longer and the days are made shorter.
Concise	During its winter the northern hemisphere tilts away from the sun, making the nights longer and the days shorter.

See also **4** pp. 202–03 on changing the passive voice to the active voice, as in the example above.

20b Cutting empty words

Empty words walk in place, gaining little or nothing in meaning. Many can be cut entirely. The following are just a few examples:

all things considered	in a manner of speaking
as far as I'm concerned	in my opinion
for all intents and purposes	last but not least
for the most part	more or less

Other empty words can also be cut, usually along with some of the words around them.

area	case	factor	kind	nature	thing
aspect	element	field	manner	situation	type

Still others can be reduced from several words to a single word:

For	Substitute
at the present time	now, yet
because of the fact that	because
due to the fact that	because
for the purpose of	for
in order to	to
For	**Substitute**
in the event that	if
in the final analysis	finally

Key terms

passive voice The verb form when the subject names the *receiver* of the verb's action: *The house was destroyed by the tornado.* (See **4** p. 202.)

active voice The verb form when the subject names the *performer* of the verb's action: *The tornado destroyed the house.* (See **4** p. 202.)

Cutting or reducing such words and phrases will make your writing move faster and work harder:

> **Wordy** In my opinion, the council's proposal to improve the city center is inadequate, all things considered.
>
> **Revised** The council's proposal to improve the city center is inadequate.

20c Cutting unneeded repetition

Unnecessary repetition weakens sentences:

> **Wordy** Many unskilled workers without training in a particular job are unemployed and do not have any work.
>
> **Concise** Many unskilled workers are unemployed.

Be especially alert to phrases that say the same thing twice. In the examples below, the unneeded words are underlined:

circle around	important [basic] essentials
consensus of opinion	puzzling in nature
cooperate together	repeat again
final completion	return again
frank and honest exchange	square [round] in shape
the future to come	surrounding circumstances

CULTURE LANGUAGE The preceding phrases are redundant because the main word already implies the underlined word or words. A dictionary will tell you what meanings a word implies. *Assassinate,* for instance, means "murder someone well known," so the following sentence is redundant: *Julius Caesar was assassinated and killed.*

20d Reducing clauses and phrases

Modifiers can be expanded or contracted depending on the emphasis you want to achieve. (Generally, the longer a construction, the more emphatic it is.) When editing sentences, consider whether any modifiers can be reduced without loss of emphasis or clarity.

> **Wordy** The Channel Tunnel, which runs between Britain and France, bores through a bed of solid chalk that is twenty-three miles across.
>
> **Concise** The Channel Tunnel between Britain and France bores through twenty-three miles of solid chalk.

Key term

modifier A word or word group that limits or qualifies another word: *slippery* road, cars *with tire chains.*

20e Revising *there is, here is,* or *it is*

You can postpone the sentence subject with the words *there, here,* and *it: There are three tests. Here is the main problem. It was not fair that only seniors could vote.* These **expletive constructions** can be useful to emphasize the subject (as when introducing it for the first time) or to indicate a change in direction. But often they just add words and create limp substitutes for more vigorous sentences:

| Wordy | There were delays and cost overruns that plagued construction of the Channel Tunnel. It had been the hope of investors that they would see earnings soon after there were trains passing through the tunnel, but profits took years to come. |
| Concise | Delays and cost overruns plagued construction of the Channel Tunnel. Investors had hoped to see earnings soon after trains began passing through the tunnel, but profits took years to come. |

CULTURE LANGUAGE When you must use an expletive construction, be careful to include *there, here,* or *it.* Only commands and some questions can begin with verbs.

20f Combining sentences

Often the information in two or more sentences can be combined into one tight sentence:

| Wordy | An unexpected problem with the Channel Tunnel is stowaways. The stowaways are mostly illegal immigrants. They are trying to smuggle themselves into England. |
| Concise | An unexpected problem with the Channel Tunnel is stowaways, mostly illegal immigrants who are trying to smuggle themselves into England. |

20g Rewriting jargon

Jargon can refer to the special vocabulary of any discipline or profession. But it has also come to describe vague, inflated language that is overcomplicated, even incomprehensible. When it comes from government or business, we call it **bureaucratese.**

Jargon   The necessity for individuals to become separate entities in their own right may impel children to engage in open rebelliousness against parental authority or against sibling influence, with resultant bewilderment of those being re-belled against.

Translation   Children's natural desire to become themselves may make them rebel against bewildered parents or siblings.

MICHIGAN STATE
UNIVERSITY

Basic Grammar

Grammar describes how language works, and understanding it can help you create clear and accurate sentences. This section explains the kinds of words in sentences (Chapter 21) and how to build basic sentences (22), expand them (23), and classify them (24).

Grammar checkers A grammar checker can both offer assistance and cause problems as you compose sentences. Look for the cautions and tips for using a checker in this and the next part of this book. For more information about grammar checkers, see **1** p. 28.

21 | Parts of Speech

All English words fall into eight groups, called **parts of speech:** nouns, pronouns, verbs, adjectives, adverbs, prepositions, conjunctions, and interjections.

Note In different sentences a word may serve as different parts of speech. For example:

> The government sent <u>aid</u> to the city. [*Aid* is a noun.]
> Governments <u>aid</u> citizens. [*Aid* is a verb.]

The *function* of a word in a sentence always determines its part of speech in that sentence.

21a | Recognizing nouns

Nouns name. They may name a person (*Helen Mirren, Jesse Jackson, astronaut*), a thing (*chair, book, Mt. Rainier*), a quality (*pain, mystery, simplicity*), a place (*city, Washington, ocean, Red Sea*), or an idea (*reality, peace, success*).

The forms of nouns depend partly on where they fit in certain groups. As the following examples indicate, the same noun may appear in more than one group.

> ■ A *common noun* names a general class of things and does not begin with a capital letter: *earthquake, citizen, earth, fortitude, army.*

Visit *mycomplab.com* for more resources as well as exercises on the parts of speech.

- A *proper noun* names a specific person, place, or thing and begins with a capital letter: *Angelina Jolie, Washington Monument, El Paso, US Congress.*
- A *count noun* names a thing considered countable in English. Most count nouns add *-s* or *-es* to distinguish between singular (one) and plural (more than one): *citizen, citizens; city, cities.* Some count nouns form irregular plurals: *woman, women; child, children.*
- A *noncount noun* names things or qualities that aren't considered countable in English: *earth, sugar, chaos, fortitude.* Noncount nouns do not form plurals.
- A *collective noun* is singular in form but names a group: *army, family, herd, US Congress.*

In addition, most nouns form the **possessive** by adding *-'s* to show ownership (*Nadia's books, citizen's rights*), source (*Auden's poems*), and some other relationships.

21b Recognizing pronouns

Most **pronouns** substitute for nouns and function in sentences as nouns do: *Susanne Ling enlisted in the Air Force when she graduated.* Pronouns fall into groups depending on their form or function:

- A *personal pronoun* refers to a specific individual or to individuals: *I, you, he, she, it, we,* and *they.*
- An *indefinite pronoun* does not refer to a specific noun: *anyone, everything, no one, somebody,* and so on. *No one came. Nothing moves. Everybody speaks.*
- A *relative pronoun* relates a group of words to a noun or another pronoun: *who, whoever, which, that. Everyone who attended received a prize. The book that won is a novel.*
- An *interrogative pronoun* introduces a question: *who, whom, whose, which, what. What song is that? Who will contribute?*
- A *demonstrative pronoun* identifies or points to a noun: *this, these, that, those,* and so on. *Those berries are ripe. This is the site.*
- An *intensive pronoun* emphasizes a noun or another pronoun: *myself, himself, itself, themselves,* and so on. *I myself asked that question. The price itself is in doubt.*
- A *reflexive pronoun* indicates that the sentence subject also receives the action of the verb: *myself, himself, itself, themselves,* and so on. *He perjured himself. They injured themselves.*

The personal pronouns *I, he, she, we,* and *they* and the relative pronouns *who* and *whoever* change form depending on their function in the sentence. (See Chapter 30.)

21c Recognizing verbs

Verbs express an action (*bring, change, grow, consider*), an occurrence (*become, happen, occur*), or a state of being (*be, seem, remain*).

1 Forms of verbs

Verbs have five distinctive forms. If the form can change as described here, the word is a verb:

- The *plain form* **is the dictionary form of the verb.** When the subject is a plural noun or the pronoun *I, we, you,* or *they,* the plain form indicates action that occurs in the present, occurs habitually, or is generally true.

  A few artists <u>live</u> in town today.
  They <u>hold</u> classes downtown.

- The *-s form* **ends in *-s* or *-es*.** When the subject is a singular noun, a pronoun such as *everyone,* or the personal pronoun *he, she,* or *it,* the *-s* form indicates action that occurs in the present, occurs habitually, or is generally true.

  The artist <u>lives</u> in town today.
  She <u>holds</u> classes downtown.

- The *past-tense form* **indicates that the action of the verb occurred before now.** It usually adds *-d* or *-ed* to the plain form, although most irregular verbs create it in different ways (see pp. 182–84).

  Many artists <u>lived</u> in town before this year.
  They <u>held</u> classes downtown. [Irregular verb.]

- The *past participle* **is usually the same as the past-tense form, except in most irregular verbs.** It combines with forms of *have* or *be* (*has <u>climbed</u>, was <u>created</u>*), or by itself it modifies nouns and pronouns (*the <u>sliced</u> apples*).

  Artists have <u>lived</u> in town for decades.
  They have <u>held</u> classes downtown. [Irregular verb.]

- The *present participle* **adds *-ing* to the verb's plain form.** It combines with forms of *be* (*is <u>buying</u>*), modifies nouns and pronouns (*the <u>boiling</u> water*), or functions as a noun (<u>*Running*</u> *exhausts me*).

  A few artists are <u>living</u> in town today.
  They are <u>holding</u> classes downtown.

The verb *be* has eight forms rather than the five forms of most other verbs:

Plain form	be		
Present participle	being		
Past participle	been		

	I	*he, she, it*	*we, you, they*
Present tense	am	is	are
Past tense	was	was	were

2 Helping verbs

Some verb forms combine with **helping verbs** to indicate time, possibility, obligation, necessity, and other kinds of meaning: *can run, was sleeping, had been working.* In these **verb phrases** *run, sleeping,* and *working* are **main verbs**—they carry the principal meaning.

Verb phrase

Helping   Main

Artists <u>can</u>   <u>train</u> others to draw.
The techniques <u>have</u>   <u>changed</u> little.

The most common helping verbs are listed in the box below. See pp. 186–91 for more on helping verbs.

Common helping verbs

Forms of *be:* be, am, is, are, was, were, been, being
Forms of *have:* have, has, had, having
Forms of *do:* do, does, did

be able to	could	may	ought to	used to
be supposed to	had better	might	shall	will
can	have to	must	should	would

21d Recognizing adjectives and adverbs

Adjectives describe or modify nouns and pronouns. They specify which one, what quality, or how many.

old   city   generous one   two pears
adjective noun   adjective pronoun   adjective noun

Adverbs describe or modify verbs, adjectives, other adverbs, and whole groups of words. They specify when, where, how, and to what extent.

nearly destroyed   too quickly
adverb verb   adverb adverb

very generous   Unfortunately, taxes will rise.
adverb adjective   adverb   word group

An *-ly* ending often signals an adverb, but not always: *friendly* is an adjective; *never* and *not* are adverbs. The only way to tell whether a word is an adjective or an adverb is to determine what part of speech it modifies.

Adjectives and adverbs appear in three forms: **positive** (*green, angrily*), **comparative** (*greener, more angrily*), and **superlative** (*greenest, most angrily*).

See Chapter 33 for more on adjectives and adverbs.

21e   Recognizing connecting words: Prepositions and conjunctions

Connecting words are mostly small words that link parts of sentences. They never change form.

1   Prepositions

Prepositions form nouns or pronouns (plus any modifiers) into word groups called **prepositional phrases**: *about love, down the stairs*. These phrases usually serve as modifiers in sentences, as in *The plants trailed down the stairs.* (See p. 177.)

Common prepositions

about	before	except for	of	throughout
above	behind	excepting	off	till
according to	below	for	on	to
across	beneath	from	onto	toward
after	beside	in	on top of	under
against	between	in addition to	out	underneath
along	beyond	inside	out of	unlike
along with	by	inside of	outside	until
among	concerning	in spite of	over	up
around	despite	instead of	past	upon
as	down	into	regarding	up to
aside from	due to	like	round	with
at	during	near	since	within
because of	except	next to	through	without

 The meanings and uses of English prepositions can be difficult to master. See **3** pp. 155–56 for a discussion of prepositions in idioms. See pp. 193–94 for uses of prepositions in two-word verbs such as *look after* or *look up.*

2 Subordinating conjunctions

Subordinating conjunctions form sentences into word groups called **subordinate clauses,** such as *when the meeting ended* or *that she knew.* These clauses serve as parts of sentences: *Everyone was relieved when the meeting ended. She said that she knew.* (See pp. 179–80.)

Common subordinating conjunctions			
after	even if	rather than	until
although	even though	since	when
as	if	so that	whenever
as if	if only	than	where
as long as	in order that	that	whereas
as though	now that	though	wherever
because	once	till	whether
before	provided	unless	while

CULTURE LANGUAGE Subordinating conjunctions convey meaning without help from other function words, such as the coordinating conjunctions *and, but, for,* or *so:*

Faulty <u>Even though</u> the parents are illiterate, <u>but</u> their children may read well. [*Even though* and *but* have the same meaning, so both are not needed.]

Revised <u>Even though</u> the parents are illiterate, their children may read well.

3 Coordinating and correlative conjunctions

Coordinating and **correlative conjunctions** connect words or word groups of the same kind, such as nouns or sentences.

Coordinating conjunctions consist of a single word:

Coordinating conjunctions			
and	nor	for	yet
but	or	so	

Biofeedback <u>or</u> simple relaxation can relieve headaches.
Relaxation works well, <u>and</u> it is inexpensive.

Correlative conjunctions are combinations of coordinating conjunctions and other words:

> ## Common correlative conjunctions
>
> both . . . and   neither . . . nor
> not only . . . but also   whether . . . or
> not . . . but   as . . . as
> either . . . or

<u>Both</u> biofeedback <u>and</u> relaxation can relieve headaches.

The headache sufferer learns <u>not only</u> to recognize the causes of headaches <u>but also</u> to control those causes.

21f   Recognizing interjections

Interjections express feeling or command attention. They are rarely used in academic or business writing.

<u>Oh</u>, the meeting went fine.
They won seven thousand dollars! <u>Wow!</u>

22   The Sentence

The **sentence** is the basic unit of expression. It is grammatically complete and independent: it does not serve as an adjective, adverb, or other single part of speech.

22a   Recognizing subjects and predicates

Most sentences make statements. First the **subject** names something; then the **predicate** makes an assertion about the subject or describes an action by the subject.

Subject	Predicate
Art	thrives.

Visit *mycomplab.com* for more resources as well as exercises on the sentence.

The **simple subject** consists of one or more nouns or pronouns, whereas the **complete subject** also includes any modifiers. The **simple predicate** consists of one or more verbs, whereas the **complete predicate** adds any words needed to complete the meaning of the verb plus any modifiers.

Sometimes, as in *Art thrives*, the simple and complete subject and predicate are the same. More often, they are different:

In the second example, the simple subject and simple predicate are both **compound:** in each, two words joined by a coordinating conjunction (*and*) serve the same function.

Tests to find subjects and predicates

The tests below use the following example:

> Art that makes it into museums has often survived controversy.

Identify the subject.

- Ask *who* or *what* is acting or being described in the sentence.

    Complete subject   art that makes it into museums

- Isolate the simple subject by deleting modifiers—words or word groups that don't name the actor of the sentence but give information about it. In the example, the word group *that makes it into museums* does not name the actor but modifies it.

    Simple subject   art

Identify the predicate.

- Ask what the sentence asserts about the subject: what is its action, or what state is it in? In the example, the assertion about *art* is that it *has often survived controversy.*

    Complete predicate has often survived controversy

- Isolate the verb, the simple predicate, by changing the time of the subject's action. The simple predicate is the word or words that change as a result.

Example	Art . . . has often survived controversy.
Present	Art . . . often survives controversy.
Future	Art . . . will often survive controversy.
Simple predicate	has survived

Note If a sentence contains a word group such as *that makes it into museums* or *because viewers agree about its quality*, you may be tempted to mark the subject and verb in the word group as the subject and verb of the sentence. But these word groups are subordinate clauses, made into modifiers by the words they begin with: *that* and *because*. See pp. 179–80 for more on subordinate clauses.

⟨CULTURE LANGUAGE⟩ The subject of a sentence in standard American English may be a noun (*art*) or a pronoun that refers to the noun (*it*), but not both. (See p. 246.)

Faulty   Some <u>art it</u> stirs controversy.
Revised Some <u>art</u> stirs controversy.

22b   Recognizing predicate patterns

All English sentences are based on five patterns, each differing in the complete predicate (the verb and any words following it).

⟨CULTURE LANGUAGE⟩ Word order in English sentences may not correspond to word order in the sentences of your native language or dialect. English, for instance, strongly prefers subject first, then verb, whereas some other languages prefer the verb first.

Pattern 1: The earth trembled.

In the simplest pattern the predicate consists only of an **intransitive verb,** a verb that does not require a following word to complete its meaning.

Subject	Predicate
	Intransitive verb
The earth	trembled.
The hospital	may close.

Pattern 2: The earthquake destroyed the city.

In pattern 2 the verb is followed by a **direct object**, a noun or pronoun that identifies who or what receives the action of the verb. A verb that requires a direct object to complete its meaning is called **transitive.**

Subject	Predicate	
	Transitive verb	*Direct object*
The earthquake	destroyed	the city.
Education	opens	doors.

⟨CULTURE LANGUAGE⟩ Only transitive verbs may be used in the passive voice: *The city <u>was destroyed</u>*. Your dictionary will

The five basic sentence patterns

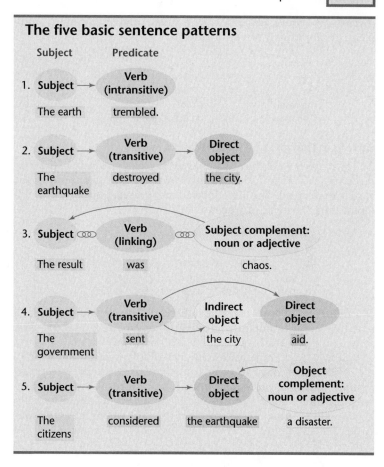

Subject	Predicate

1. Subject → Verb (intransitive)

   The earth trembled.

2. Subject → Verb (transitive) → Direct object

   The earthquake destroyed the city.

3. Subject ⟶ Verb (linking) ⟶ Subject complement: noun or adjective

   The result was chaos.

4. Subject → Verb (transitive) Indirect object Direct object

   The government sent the city aid.

5. Subject → Verb (transitive) → Direct object Object complement: noun or adjective

   The citizens considered the earthquake a disaster.

indicate whether a verb is transitive or intransitive. For some verbs (*begin, learn, read, write,* and others), it will indicate both uses.

Pattern 3: The result was chaos.

In pattern 3 the verb is followed by a **subject complement,** a word that renames or describes the subject. A verb in this pattern is called a **linking verb** because it links its subject to the description following. The linking verbs include *be, seem, appear, become, grow,*

┌─ **Key term** ───

passive voice The verb form when the subject names the receiver of the verb's action: *Bad weather was predicted.* (See p. 202.)

└──

remain, stay, prove, feel, look, smell, sound, and *taste.* Subject complements are usually nouns or adjectives.

Subject	Predicate	
	Linking verb	*Subject complement*
The result	was	chaos.
The man	became	an accountant.

Pattern 4: The government sent the city aid.

In pattern 4 the verb is followed by a direct object and an **indirect object,** a word identifying to or for whom the action of the verb is performed. The direct object and indirect object refer to different things, people, or places.

Subject	Predicate		
	Transitive verb	*Indirect object*	*Direct object*
The government	sent	the city	aid.
One company	offered	its employees	bonuses.

A number of verbs can take indirect objects, including *send* and *offer* (preceding examples) and *allow, bring, buy, deny, find, get, give, leave, make, pay, read, sell, show, teach,* and *write.*

CULTURE LANGUAGE Some verbs are never followed by an indirect object—*admit, announce, demonstrate, explain, intro-duce, mention, prove, recommend, say,* and some others. However, the direct objects of these verbs may be followed by *to* or *for* and a noun or pronoun that specifies to or for whom the action was done: *The manual explains the new procedure <u>to workers</u>. A video demonstrates the procedure <u>for us</u>.*

Pattern 5: The citizens considered the earthquake a disaster.

In pattern 5 the verb is followed by a direct object and an **object complement,** a word that renames or describes the direct object. Object complements may be nouns or adjectives.

Subject	Predicate		
	Transitive verb	*Direct object*	*Object complement*
The citizens	considered	the earthquake	a disaster.
Success	makes	some people	nervous.

23 Phrases and Subordinate Clauses

Most sentences contain word groups that serve as adjectives, adverbs, or nouns and thus cannot stand alone as sentences.

- A *phrase* lacks either a subject or a predicate or both: *fearing an accident; in a panic.*
- A *subordinate clause* contains a subject and a predicate but begins with a subordinating word: <u>when</u> *prices rise;* <u>whoever</u> *laughs.*

23a Recognizing phrases

1 Prepositional phrases

A **prepositional phrase** consists of a preposition plus a noun, a pronoun, or a word group serving as a noun, called the **object of the preposition.** A list of prepositions appears on p. 170.

Preposition	Object
of	spaghetti
on	the surface
with	great satisfaction
upon	entering the room
from	where you are standing

Prepositional phrases usually function as adjectives or adverbs.

Life on a raft was an opportunity for adventure.
   adjective phrase   adjective phrase

Huck Finn rode the raft by choice.
               adverb phrase

With his companion, Jim, Huck met many types of people.
  adverb phrase   adjective phrase

2 Verbal phrases

Certain forms of verbs, called **verbals,** can serve as modifiers or nouns. Often these verbals appear with their own modifiers and objects in **verbal phrases.**

Note Verbals cannot serve as verbs in sentences. *The sun <u>rises</u> over the dump* is a sentence; *The sun <u>rising</u> over the dump* is a sentence fragment. (See p. 236.)

Visit *mycomplab.com* for more resources as well as exercises on phrases and subordinate clauses.

Participial phrases

A **participle** is a verb form ending in *-ing* (*walking*) or, often, *-d* or *-ed* (*walked*). Participles and participial phrases serve as adjectives.

Strolling shoppers fill the malls.
adjective

They make selections determined by personal taste.
adjective phrase

Note With irregular verbs, the past participle may have a different ending—for instance, *hidden funds*. (See pp. 182–84.)

CULTURE LANGUAGE For verbs expressing feeling, the present and past participles have different meanings: *It was a boring lecture. The bored students slept.* (See p. 226.)

Gerund phrases

A **gerund** is the *-ing* form of a verb when it serves as a noun. Gerunds and gerund phrases can do whatever nouns can do.

sentence
subject
Shopping satisfies personal needs.
noun

object of preposition
Malls are good at creating such needs.
noun phrase

Infinitive phrases

An **infinitive** is the plain form of a verb plus *to: to hide*. Infinitives and infinitive phrases serve as adjectives, adverbs, or nouns.

sentence
subject   subject complement
To design a mall is to create an artificial environment.
noun phrase   noun phrase

Malls are designed to make shoppers feel safe.
adverb phrase

The environment supports the impulse to shop.
adjective

CULTURE LANGUAGE Infinitives and gerunds may follow some verbs and not others and may differ in meaning after a verb: *The cowboy stopped to sing. The cowboy stopped singing.* (See pp. 191–93.)

3 Absolute phrases

An **absolute phrase** consists of a noun or pronoun and a participle, plus any modifiers. It modifies the entire rest of the sentence it appears in.

```
  ┌──────── absolute phrase ────────┐ ┌──────────→
```
Their own place established, many ethnic groups are making way for
new arrivals.

Unlike a participial phrase (opposite), an absolute phrase always contains a noun that serves as a subject.

```
      participial
  ┌──── phrase ────┐
```
Learning English, many immigrants discover American culture.

```
  ┌──────────── absolute phrase ────────────┐
```
Immigrants having learned English, their opportunities widen.

4 Appositive phrases

An **appositive** is usually a noun that renames another noun. An appositive phrase includes modifiers as well.

```
          ┌─appositive phrase ┐
```
Bizen ware, a dark stoneware, is produced in Japan.

Appositives and appositive phrases sometimes begin with *that is, such as, for example,* or *in other words.*

```
                              ┌──── appositive phrase ────
```
Bizen ware is used in the Japanese tea ceremony, that is, the Zen Buddhist
observance that links meditation and art.

23b Recognizing subordinate clauses

A **clause** is any group of words that contains both a subject and a predicate. There are two kinds of clauses, and the distinction between them is important.

- A *main clause* makes a complete statement and can stand alone as a sentence: *The sky darkened.*
- A *subordinate clause* is just like a main clause *except* that it begins with a subordinating word: *when the sky darkened; whoever calls.* The subordinating word reduces the clause from a complete statement to a single part of speech: an adjective, adverb, or noun. Use subordinate clauses to support the ideas in main clauses, as described in **3** pp. 136–37.

Note A subordinate clause punctuated as a sentence is a sentence fragment. (See p. 238.)

Adjective clauses

An **adjective clause** modifies a noun or pronoun. It usually begins with the relative pronoun *who, whom, whose, which,* or *that.*

The relative pronoun is the subject or object of the clause it begins. The clause ordinarily falls immediately after the word it modifies.

── adjective clause ──
Parents who cannot read may have bad memories of school.

──── adjective clause ────
One school, which is open year-round, helps parents learn to read.

Adverb clauses

An **adverb clause** modifies a verb, an adjective, another adverb, or a whole word group. It always begins with a subordinating conjunction, such as *although, because, if,* or *when* (see p. 185 for a list).

──────── adverb clause ────────
The school began teaching parents when adult illiteracy gained national attention.

──── adverb clause ──── ── main clause ──
Because it was directed at people who could not read, advertising had to be inventive.

Noun clauses

A **noun clause** replaces a noun in a sentence and serves as a subject, object, or complement. It begins with *that, what, whatever, who, whom, whoever, whomever, when, where, whether, why,* or *how.*

──── sentence subject ────
Whether the program would succeed depended on door-to-door advertising.
  noun clause

──── object of verb ────
Teachers explained in person how the program would work.
  noun clause

24 Sentence Types

The four basic sentence structures vary in the number of main and subordinate clauses. Each structure gives different emphasis to the main and supporting information in a sentence.

Visit *mycomplab.com* for more resources as well as exercises on sentence types.

24a Recognizing simple sentences

A **simple sentence** consists of a single main clause and no subordinate clause.

```
┌─────── main clause ───────┐
Last summer was unusually hot.
```

```
┌──────────────────── main clause ────────────────────
The summer made many farmers leave the area for good or reduced them

──────────┐
to bare existence.
```

24b Recognizing compound sentences

A **compound sentence** consists of two or more main clauses and no subordinate clause.

```
┌─ main clause ─┐        ┌─── main clause ───┐
Last July was hot, but August was even hotter.
```

```
┌─────────── main clause ───────────┐    ┌───────── main clause ─────────┐
The hot sun scorched the earth, and the lack of rain killed many crops.
```

24c Recognizing complex sentences

A **complex sentence** consists of one main clause and one or more subordinate clauses.

```
┌── main clause ──┐ ┌───────── subordinate clause ─────────┐
Rain finally came, although many had left the area by then.
```

```
┌───────────────── main clause ─────────────────┐ ┌── subordinate clause ──
Those who remained were able to start anew because the government
        subordinate clause
──────────────────┐
came to their aid.
```

24d Recognizing compound-complex sentences

A **compound-complex sentence** has the characteristics of both the compound sentence (two or more main clauses) and the complex sentence (at least one subordinate clause).

```
┌──────── subordinate clause ────────┐ ┌──────── main clause ────────
When government aid finally came, many people had already been reduced

──────────┐ ┌──────── main clause ────────┐
to poverty and others had been forced to move.
```

Verbs

Verbs express actions, conditions, and states of being. The basic uses and forms of verbs are described on pp. 168–169. This section explains and solves the most common problems with verbs' forms (Chapter 25), tenses (26), mood (27), and voice (28) and shows how to make verbs match their subjects (29).

25 Verb Forms

25a Use the correct forms of *sing/sang/sung* and other irregular verbs.

Most verbs are **regular:** they form their past tense and past participle by adding *-d* or *-ed* to the plain form.

Plain form	Past tense	Past participle
live	lived	lived
act	acted	acted

About two hundred English verbs are **irregular:** they form their past tense and past participle in some irregular way. Check a dictionary under the verb's plain form if you have any doubt about its other forms. If the verb is irregular, the dictionary will list the plain form, the past tense, and the past participle in that order (*go, went, gone*). If the dictionary gives only two forms (as in *think, thought*), then the past tense and the past participle are the same.

Grammar checkers A grammar checker may not flag incorrect forms of irregular verbs. For example, a checker flagged *The runner*

Key terms

plain form The dictionary form of the verb: *I walk. You forget.* (See p. 168.)

past-tense form The verb form indicating action that occurred in the past: *I walked. You forgot.* (See p. 168.)

past participle The verb form used with *have, has,* or *had: I have walked.* It may serve as a modifier: *It is a forgotten book.* (See p. 168.)

---

my**comp**lab

Visit *mycomplab.com* for more resources as well as exercises on verb forms.

Common irregular verbs

Plain form	Past tense	Past participle
be	was, were	been
become	became	become
begin	began	begun
bid	bid	bid
bite	bit	bitten, bit
blow	blew	blown
break	broke	broken
bring	brought	brought
burst	burst	burst
buy	bought	bought
catch	caught	caught
choose	chose	chosen
come	came	come
cut	cut	cut
dive	dived, dove	dived
do	did	done
dream	dreamed, dreamt	dreamed, dreamt
drink	drank	drunk
drive	drove	driven
eat	ate	eaten
fall	fell	fallen
find	found	found
flee	fled	fled
fly	flew	flown
forget	forgot	forgotten, forgot
freeze	froze	frozen
get	got	got, gotten
give	gave	given
go	went	gone
grow	grew	grown
hang (suspend)	hung	hung
have	had	had
hear	heard	heard
hide	hid	hidden
hold	held	held
keep	kept	kept
know	knew	known
lead	led	led
leave	left	left
lend	lent	lent
let	let	let
lose	lost	lost
pay	paid	paid
ride	rode	ridden
ring	rang	rung

(continued)

Common irregular verbs
(continued)

Plain form	Past tense	Past participle
run	ran	run
say	said	said
see	saw	seen
shake	shook	shaken
shrink	shrank, shrunk	shrunk, shrunken
sing	sang, sung	sung
sink	sank, sunk	sunk
sleep	slept	slept
slide	slid	slid
speak	spoke	spoken
spring	sprang, sprung	sprung
stand	stood	stood
steal	stole	stolen
swim	swam	swum
swing	swung	swung
take	took	taken
tear	tore	torn
throw	threw	thrown
wear	wore	worn
write	wrote	written

stealed second base (*stole* is correct) but not *The runner had steal second base* (*stolen* is correct). When in doubt about the forms of irregular verbs, refer to the preceding list or consult a dictionary.

⟨CULTURE LANGUAGE⟩ Some English dialects use distinctive verb forms that differ from those of standard American English: for instance, *drug* for *dragged*, *growed* for *grew*, *come* for *came*, or *went* for *gone*. In situations requiring standard American English, use the forms in the list here or in a dictionary.

25b Distinguish between *sit* and *set, lie* and *lay,* and *rise* and *raise.*

The forms of *sit* and *set, lie* and *lay,* and *rise* and *raise* are easy to confuse.

Plain form	Past tense	Past participle
sit	sat	sat
set	set	set
lie	lay	lain
lay	laid	laid
rise	rose	risen
raise	raised	raised

In each of these confusing pairs, one verb is intransitive (it does not take an object) and one is transitive (it does take an object). (See pp. 174–75 for more on this distinction.)

Intransitive

The patients lie in their beds. [*Lie* means "recline" and takes no object.]

Visitors sit with them. [*Sit* means "be seated" or "be located" and takes no object.]

Patients' temperatures rise. [*Rise* means "increase" or "get up" and takes no object.]

Transitive

Orderlies lay the dinner trays on tables. [*Lay* means "place" and takes an object, here *trays*.]

Orderlies set the trays down. [*Set* means "place" and takes an object, here *trays*.]

Nursing aides raise the shades. [*Raise* means "lift" or "bring up" and takes an object, here *shades*.]

25c Use the *-s* and *-ed* forms of the verb when they are required.

Speakers of some English dialects and nonnative speakers of English sometimes omit the *-s* and *-ed* verb endings when they are required in standard American English.

Grammar checkers A grammar checker will flag many omitted *-s* and *-ed* endings from verbs, as in *he ask* and *was ask*. But it will miss many omissions, too.

1 Required *-s* ending

Use the *-s* form of a verb when *both* of these situations hold:

■ **The subject is a singular noun** (*boy*), **an indefinite pronoun** (*everyone*), **or** *he, she,* **or** *it*. These subjects are **third person,** used when someone or something is being spoken about.

■ **The verb's action occurs in the present.**

The letter asks [not ask] for a quick response.
Delay costs [not cost] money.

Be especially careful with the *-s* forms of *be* (*is*), *have* (*has*), and *do* (*does, doesn't*). These forms should always be used to indicate present time with third-person singular subjects.

The company is [not be] late in responding.
It has [not have] problems.
It doesn't [not don't] have the needed data.
The contract does [not do] depend on the response.

In addition, *be* has an *-s* form in the past tense with *I* and third-person singular subjects:

> The company <u>was</u> [not <u>were</u>] in trouble before.

I, you, and plural subjects do *not* take the *-s* form of verbs:

> I <u>am</u> [not <u>is</u>] a student.
> You <u>are</u> [not <u>is</u>] also a student.
> They <u>are</u> [not <u>is</u>] students, too.

2 Required *-ed* or *-d* ending

The *-ed* or *-d* verb form is required in *any* of these situations:

■ **The verb's action occurred in the past:**

> The company <u>asked</u> [not <u>ask</u>] for more time.

■ **The verb form functions as a modifier:**

> The data <u>concerned</u> [not <u>concern</u>] should be retrievable.

■ **The verb form combines with a form of *be* or *have*:**

> The company is <u>supposed</u> [not <u>suppose</u>] to be the best.
> It has <u>developed</u> [not <u>develop</u>] an excellent reputation.

Watch especially for a needed *-ed* or *-d* ending when it isn't pronounced clearly in speech, as in *asked, discussed, mixed, supposed, walked,* and *used.*

25d Use helping verbs with main verbs appropriately.

Helping verbs combine with main verbs in verb phrases: *The line <u>should have been cut</u>. Who <u>was calling</u>?*

Grammar checkers A grammar checker often spots omitted helping verbs and incorrect main verbs with helping verbs, but sometimes it does not. A checker flagged *Many been fortunate* and *She working* but overlooked other errors, such as *The conference will be occurred.*

Key terms

helping verb A word such as *can, may, be, have,* or *do* that forms a verb phrase with another verb to show time, permission, and other meanings. (See p. 169.)

main verb The verb that carries the principal meaning in a verb phrase: *has <u>walked</u>, could be <u>happening</u>.* (See p. 169.)

verb phrase A helping verb plus a main verb: *will be singing, would speak.* (See p. 169.)

1 Required helping verbs

Standard American English requires helping verbs in certain situations:

- **The main verb ends in -*ing*:**

  Researchers <u>are</u> conducting fieldwork all over the world. [Not <u>Researchers conducting</u>. . . .]

- **The main verb is *been* or *be*:**

  Many <u>have</u> been fortunate in their discoveries. [Not <u>Many been</u>. . . .]
  Some <u>could</u> be real-life Indiana Joneses. [Not <u>Some be</u>. . . .]

- **The main verb is a past participle,** such as *talked, begun,* or *thrown.*

  Their discoveries <u>were</u> covered in newspapers and magazines. [Not <u>Their discoveries covered</u>. . . .]
  The researchers <u>have</u> given interviews on TV. [Not <u>The researchers given</u>. . . .]

The omission of a helping verb may create an incomplete sentence, or **sentence fragment,** because a present participle (*conducting*), an irregular past participle (*been*), or the infinitive *be* cannot stand alone as the only verb in a sentence (see p. 236). To work as sentence verbs, these verb forms need helping verbs.

2 Combination of helping verb + main verb

Helping verbs and main verbs combine into verb phrases in specific ways.

Note The main verb in a verb phrase (the one carrying the main meaning) does not change to show a change in subject or time: *she has <u>sung</u>, you had <u>sung</u>.* Only the helping verb may change.

Form of *be* + present participle

The **progressive tenses** indicate action in progress. Create them with *be, am, is, are, was, were,* or *been* followed by the main verb's present participle:

  She <u>is working</u> on a new book.

Key terms

present participle The -*ing* form of a verb: *flying, playing.* (See p. 168.)

progressive tenses Verb tenses expressing action in progress—for instance, *I am flying. I was flying. I will be flying.* (See p. 197.)

Be and *been* always require additional helping verbs to form progressive tenses:

can	might	should			have		
could	must	will	}	be working	has	}	been working
may	shall	would			had		

When forming the progressive tenses, be sure to use the *-ing* form of the main verb.

Faulty	Her ideas are <u>grow</u> more complex. She is <u>developed</u> a new approach to ethics.
Revised	Her ideas are <u>growing</u> more complex. She is <u>developing</u> a new approach to ethics.

Form of *be* + past participle

The **passive voice** of the verb indicates that the subject *receives* the action of the verb. Create the passive voice with a form of *be* (*be, am, is, are, was, were, being,* or *been*) followed by the main verb's past participle:

Her latest book <u>was completed</u> in four months.

Be, being, and *been* always require additional helping verbs to form the passive voice:

have			am	was		
has	}	<u>been</u> completed	is	were	}	<u>being</u> completed
had			are			

will <u>be</u> completed

Be sure to use the main verb's past participle for the passive voice:

Faulty	Her next book will be <u>publish</u> soon.
Revised	Her next book will be <u>published</u> soon.

Note Only transitive verbs may form the passive voice:

Faulty	A philosophy conference <u>will be occurred</u> in the same week. [*Occur* is not a transitive verb.]
Revised	A philosophy conference <u>will occur</u> in the same week.

Key terms

past participle The *-d* or *-ed* form of a regular verb: *hedged, walked.* Most irregular verbs have distinctive past participles: *eaten, swum.* (See p. 168.)

passive voice The verb form when the subject names the receiver of the verb's action: *An essay <u>was written</u> by every student.* (See p. 202.)

See pp. 202–03 for advice on when to use and when to avoid the passive voice.

Forms of *have*

Four forms of *have* serve as helping verbs: *have, has, had, having.* One of these forms plus the main verb's past participle creates one of the **perfect tenses,** those expressing action completed before another specific time or action:

Some students have complained about the laboratory.
Others had complained before.

Will and other helping verbs sometimes accompany forms of *have* in the perfect tenses:

Several more students will have complained by the end of the week.

Forms of *do*

Do, does, and *did* have three uses as helping verbs, always with the plain form of the main verb:

- **To pose a question:** *How did the trial end?*
- **To emphasize the main verb:** *It did end eventually.*
- **To negate the main verb, along with *not* or *never:* The judge did not withdraw.**

Be sure to use the main verb's plain form with any form of *do:*

Faulty   The judge did remained in court.
Revised The judge did remain in court.

Modals

The modal helping verbs include *can, could, may,* and *might,* along with several two- and three-word combinations, such as *have to* and *be able to.* (See p. 169 for a list of helping verbs.) Use the plain form of the main verb with a modal unless the modal combines with another helping verb (usually *have*):

Faulty   The equipment can detects small vibrations. It should have detect the change.
Revised The equipment can detect small vibrations. It should have detected the change.

┌─ **Key terms** ───

transitive verb A verb that requires an object to complete its meaning: *Every student completed an essay* (*essay* is the object of *completed*). (See p. 174.)

perfect tenses Verb tenses expressing an action completed before another specific time or action: *We have eaten. We had eaten. We will have eaten.* (See p. 198.)

Modals convey various meanings, with these being most common:

■ **Ability:** *can, could, be able to*

The equipment <u>can detect</u> small vibrations. [Present.]
The equipment <u>could detect</u> small vibrations. [Past.]
The equipment <u>is able to detect</u> small vibrations. [Present. Past: *was able to.* Future: *will be able to.*]

■ **Possibility:** *could, may, might; could/may/might have + past participle*

The equipment <u>could fail</u>. [Present.]
The equipment <u>may fail</u>. [Present or future.]
The equipment <u>might fail</u>. [Present or future.]
The equipment <u>may have failed</u>. [Past.]

■ **Necessity or obligation:** *must, have to, be supposed to*

The lab <u>must purchase</u> a backup. [Present or future.]
The lab <u>has to purchase</u> a backup. [Present or future. Past: *had to.*]
The lab <u>will have to purchase</u> a backup. [Future.]
The lab <u>is supposed to purchase</u> a backup. [Present. Past: *was supposed to.*]

■ **Permission:** *may, can, could*

The lab <u>may spend</u> the money. [Present or future.]
The lab <u>can spend</u> the money. [Present or future.]
The lab <u>could spend</u> the money. [Present or future, more tentative.]
The lab <u>could have spent</u> the money. [Past.]

■ **Intention:** *will, shall, would*

The lab <u>will spend</u> the money. [Future.]
Shall we <u>offer</u> advice? [Future. Use *shall* for questions requesting opinion or consent.]
We <u>would have offered</u> advice. [Past.]

■ **Request:** *could, can, would*

<u>Could</u> [or <u>Can</u> or <u>Would</u>] you please <u>obtain</u> a bid? [Present or future.]

■ **Advisability:** *should, had better, ought to; should have + past participle*

You <u>should obtain</u> three bids. [Present or future.]
You <u>had better obtain</u> three bids. [Present or future.]
You <u>ought to obtain</u> three bids. [Present or future.]
You <u>should have obtained</u> three bids. [Past.]

■ **Past habit:** *would, used to*

In years past we <u>would obtain</u> five bids.
We <u>used to obtain</u> five bids.

| **25e** | Use a gerund or an infinitive after a verb as appropriate. | |

Nonnative speakers of English sometimes stumble over whether to use a gerund or an infinitive after a verb. Gerunds and infinitives may follow certain verbs but not others. And sometimes the use of a gerund or infinitive with the same verb changes the meaning.

Grammar checkers A grammar checker will spot some but not all errors in matching gerunds or infinitives with verbs. For example, a checker failed to flag *I practice to swim* and *I promise helping out.* Use the lists given here and a dictionary of English as a second language to determine whether an infinitive or a gerund is appropriate. (See **3** p. 153 for a list of ESL dictionaries.)

1 Either gerund or infinitive

A gerund or an infinitive may come after the following verbs with no significant difference in meaning.

begin	continue	intend	prefer
can't bear	hate	like	start
can't stand	hesitate	love	

The pump began <u>working</u>.
The pump began <u>to work</u>.

2 Meaning change with gerund or infinitive

With four verbs, a gerund has quite a different meaning from an infinitive:

forget	stop
remember	try

The engineer stopped <u>eating</u>. [He no longer ate.]
The engineer stopped <u>to eat</u>. [He stopped in order to eat.]

> ┌─ **Key terms** ─────────────────────────────────
> **gerund** The *-ing* form of the verb used as a noun: *Smoking is unhealthful.* (See p. 178.)
>
> **infinitive** The plain form of the verb usually preceded by *to: to smoke.* An infinitive may serve as an adjective, adverb, or noun. (See p. 178.)

3 Gerund, not infinitive

Do not use an infinitive after these verbs:

admit	discuss	mind	recollect
adore	dislike	miss	resent
appreciate	enjoy	postpone	resist
avoid	escape	practice	risk
consider	finish	put off	suggest
deny	imagine	quit	tolerate
detest	keep	recall	understand

Faulty He finished to eat lunch.
Revised He finished eating lunch.

4 Infinitive, not gerund

Do not use a gerund after these verbs:

agree	claim	manage	promise
appear	consent	mean	refuse
arrange	decide	offer	say
ask	expect	plan	wait
assent	have	prepare	want
beg	hope	pretend	wish

Faulty He decided checking the pump.
Revised He decided to check the pump.

5 Noun or pronoun + infinitive

Some verbs may be followed by an infinitive alone or by a noun or pronoun and an infinitive. The presence of a noun or pronoun changes the meaning.

ask	dare	need	wish
beg	expect	promise	would like
choose	help	want	

He expected to watch.
He expected his workers to watch.

Some verbs *must* be followed by a noun or pronoun before an infinitive:

advise	encourage	oblige	require
allow	forbid	order	teach
cause	force	permit	tell
challenge	hire	persuade	train
command	instruct	remind	urge
convince	invite	request	warn

He instructed his workers to watch.

Do not use *to* before the infinitive when it follows one of these verbs and a noun or pronoun:

feel	hear	make ("force")	watch
have	let	see	

He let his workers <u>learn</u> by observation.

25f Use the appropriate particles with two-word verbs.

Standard American English includes some verbs that consist of two words: the verb itself and a **particle,** a preposition or adverb that affects the meaning of the verb.

<u>Look up</u> the answer. [Research the answer.]
<u>Look over</u> the answer. [Examine the answer.]

The meanings of these two-word verbs are often quite different from the meanings of the individual words that make them up. (There are some three-word verbs, too, such as *put up with* and *run out of.*) A dictionary of English as a second language will define two-word verbs and say whether the verbs may be separated in a sentence, as explained below and on the next page. (See **3** p. 153 for a list of ESL dictionaries.) A grammar checker will recognize few if any misuses of two-word verbs.

Note Many two-word verbs are more common in speech than in more formal academic or business writing. For formal writing, consider using *research* instead of *look up, examine* or *inspect* instead of *look over.*

1 Inseparable two-word verbs

Verbs and particles that may not be separated by any other words include the following:

catch on	go over	play around	stay away
come across	grow up	run into	stay up
get along	keep on	run out of	take care of
give in	look into	speak up	turn up at

Faulty Children <u>grow</u> quickly <u>up</u>.
Revised Children <u>grow up</u> quickly.

Key terms

preposition A word such as *about, for,* or *to* that takes a noun or pronoun as its object: *at the house, in the woods.* (See p. 170 for a list of prepositions.)

adverb A word that modifies a verb, adjective, other adverb, or whole word group. (See pp. 169–70.)

---

2 Separable two-word verbs

Most two-word verbs that take direct objects may be separated by the object.

> Parents <u>help out</u> their children.
> Parents <u>help</u> their children <u>out</u>.

If the direct object is a pronoun, the pronoun *must* separate the verb from the particle.

> **Faulty** Parents <u>help out</u> them.
> **Revised** Parents <u>help</u> them <u>out</u>.

The separable two-word verbs include the following:

bring up	give back	make up	throw out
call off	hand in	point out	try on
call up	hand out	put away	try out
drop off	help out	put back	turn down
fill out	leave out	put off	turn on
fill up	look over	take out	turn up
give away	look up	take over	wrap up

26 Verb Tenses

Tense shows the time of a verb's action. The box on the next page illustrates the tense forms for a regular verb. (Irregular verbs have different past-tense and past-participle forms. See pp. 182–84.)

Grammar checkers A grammar checker can provide little help with incorrect verb tenses and tense sequences because correctness usually depends on meaning.

CULTURE LANGUAGE In standard American English, a verb conveys time and sequence through its form. In some other languages and English dialects, various markers besides verb form may indicate the time of a verb. For instance, in African American dialect *I be attending class on Friday* means that the speaker attends class every Friday. To a speaker of standard American English,

my**comp**lab

Visit *mycomplab.com* for more resources as well as exercises on verb tenses.

Tenses of a regular verb (active voice)

Present Action that is occurring now, occurs habitually, or is generally true

Simple present Plain form or *-s* form

I walk.
You/we/they walk.
He/she/it walks.

Present progressive *Am, is,* or *are* plus *-ing* form

I am walking.
You/we/they are walking.
He/she/it is walking.

Past Action that occurred before now

Simple past Past-tense form (*-d* or *-ed*)

I/he/she/it walked.
You/we/they walked.

Past progressive *Was* or *were* plus *-ing* form

I/he/she/it was walking.
You/we/they were walking.

Future Action that will occur in the future

Simple future Plain form plus *will*

I/you/he/she/it/we/they will walk.

Future progressive *Will be* plus *-ing* form

I/you/he/she/it/we/they will be walking.

Present perfect Action that began in the past and is linked to the present

Present perfect *Have* or *has* plus past participle (*-d* or *-ed*)

I/you/we/they have walked.
He/she/it has walked.

Present perfect progressive *Have been* or *has been* plus *-ing* form

I/you/we/they have been walking.
He/she/it has been walking.

Past perfect Action that was completed before another past action

Past perfect *Had* plus past participle (*-d* or *-ed*)

I/you/he/she/it/we/they had walked.

Past perfect progressive *Had been* plus *-ing* form

I/you/he/she/it/we/they had been walking.

Future perfect Action that will be completed before another future action

Future perfect *Will have* plus past participle (*-d* or *-ed*)

I/you/he/she/it/we/they will have walked.

Future perfect progressive *Will have been* plus *-ing* form

I/you/he/she/it/we/they will have been walking.

however, the sentence may be unclear: last Friday? this Friday? every Friday? The intended meaning must be indicated by verb tense. *I attended class on Friday. I will attend class on Friday. I attend class on Friday.*

26a Observe the special uses of the present tense (*sing*).

The present tense has several distinctive uses.

Action occurring now
She understands the problem.
We define the problem differently.

Habitual or recurring action
Banks regularly undergo audits.
The audits monitor the banks' activities.

A general truth
The mills of the gods grind slowly.
The earth is round.

Discussion of literature, film, and so on
Huckleberry Finn has adventures we all envy.
In that article the author examines several causes of crime.

Future time
Next week we draft a new budget.
Funding ends in less than a year.

(The present tense shows future time with expressions like those in the examples above: *next week, in less than a year.*)

26b Observe the uses of the perfect tenses (*have/had/will have sung*).

The **perfect tenses** consist of a form of *have* plus the verb's past participle (*closed, hidden*). They indicate an action completed before another specific time or action. The present perfect tense also indicates action begun in the past and continued into the present.

present perfect
The dancer has performed here only once. [The action is completed at the time of the statement.]

present perfect
Critics have written about the performance ever since. [The action began in the past and continues now.]

past perfect
The dancer had trained in Asia before his performance. [The action was completed before another past action.]

future perfect
He will have danced here again by the end of the year. [The action begins now or in the future and will be completed by a specific time in the future.]

CULTURE LANGUAGE With the present perfect tense, the words *since* and *for* are followed by different information. After *since,* give a specific point in time: *The play has run since 1989.* After *for,* give a span of time: *It has run for decades.*

26c Observe the uses of the progressive tenses (*is/was/will be singing*).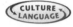

The **progressive tenses** indicate continuing (therefore progressive) action. In standard American English the progressive tenses consist of a form of *be* plus the verb's *-ing* form (present participle). (The words *be* and *been* must be combined with other helping verbs. See pp. 187–88.)

present progressive
The economy is improving.

past progressive
Last year the economy was stagnating.

future progressive
Economists will be watching for signs of growth.

present perfect progressive
The government has been expecting an upturn.

past perfect progressive
Various indicators had been suggesting improvement.

future perfect progressive
By the end of this year, investors will have been watching interest rates nervously for nearly a decade.

Note Verbs that express unchanging states (especially mental states) rather than physical actions do not usually appear in the progressive tenses. These verbs include *adore, appear, believe, belong, care, hate, have, hear, know, like, love, mean, need, own, prefer, remember, see, sound, taste, think, understand,* and *want.*

| Faulty | She is wanting to study ethics. |
| Revised | She wants to study ethics. |

26d Keep tenses consistent.

Within a sentence, the tenses of verbs and verb forms need not be identical as long as they reflect actual changes in time: *Ramon will graduate from college thirty years after his father arrived in America.* But needless shifts in tense will confuse or distract readers:

| Inconsistent | Immediately after Booth shot Lincoln, Major Rathbone threw himself upon the assassin. But Booth pulls a knife and plunges it into the major's arm. |

Revised	Immediately after Booth <u>shot</u> Lincoln, Major Rathbone <u>threw</u> himself upon the assassin. But Booth <u>pulled</u> a knife and <u>plunged</u> it into the major's arm.
Inconsistent	The main character in the novel <u>suffers</u> psychologically because he <u>has</u> a clubfoot, but he eventually <u>triumphed</u> over his disability.
Revised	The main character in the novel <u>suffers</u> psychologically because he <u>has</u> a clubfoot, but he eventually <u>triumphs</u> over his disability. [Use the present tense to discuss the content of literature, film, and so on.]

26e Use the appropriate sequence of verb tenses.

The **sequence of tenses** is the relation between the verb tense in a main clause and the verb tense in a subordinate clause. The tenses should change when necessary to reflect changes in actual or relative time. The main difficulties with tense sequence are discussed on these pages.

1 Past or past perfect tense in main clause

When the verb in the main clause is in the past or past perfect tense, the verb in the subordinate clause must also be past or past perfect:

main clause: subordinate clause:
past   past

The researchers <u>discovered</u> that people <u>varied</u> widely in their knowledge of public events.

main clause: subordinate clause:
past   past perfect

The variation <u>occurred</u> because respondents <u>had been born</u> in different decades.

main clause: subordinate clause:
past perfect   past

None of them <u>had been born</u> when Dwight Eisenhower <u>was</u> President.

Key terms

main clause A word group that can stand alone as a sentence because it contains a subject and a predicate and does not begin with a subordinating word. *Books are valuable.* (See p. 179.)

subordinate clause A word group that contains a subject and a predicate, begins with a subordinating word such as *because* or *who,* and is not a question: *Books are valuable when they enlighten.* (See p. 179.)

Exception Always use the present tense for a general truth, such as *The earth is round:*

> main clause:
> past   subordinate clause:
> present
>
> Most <u>understood</u> that popular Presidents <u>are</u> not necessarily good Presidents.

2 Conditional sentences

A **conditional sentence** states a factual relation between cause and effect, makes a prediction, or speculates about what might happen. Such a sentence usually contains a subordinate clause beginning with *if, when,* or *unless* and a main clause stating the result. The three kinds of conditional sentences use distinctive verbs.

Factual relation

Statements linking factual causes and effects use matched tenses in the subordinate and main clauses:

> subordinate clause:
> present   main clause:
> present
>
> When a voter <u>casts</u> a ballot, he or she <u>has</u> complete privacy.

> subordinate clause:
> past   main clause:
> past
>
> When voters <u>registered</u> in some states, they <u>had</u> to pay a poll tax.

Prediction

Predictions generally use the present tense in the subordinate clause and the future tense in the main clause:

> subordinate clause:
> present   main clause:
> future
>
> Unless citizens <u>regain</u> faith in politics, they <u>will</u> not <u>vote</u>.

Sometimes the verb in the main clause consists of *may, can, should,* or *might* plus the verb's plain form: *If citizens <u>regain</u> faith, they <u>may vote</u>.*

Speculation

The verbs in speculations depend on whether the linked events are possible or impossible. For possible events in the present, use the past tense in the subordinate clause and *would, could,* or *might* plus the verb's plain form in the main clause:

> subordinate clause:
> past   main clause:
> *would* + verb
>
> If voters <u>had</u> more confidence, they <u>would vote</u> more often.

Use *were* instead of *was* in the subordinate clause, even when the subject is *I, he, she, it,* or a singular noun. (See pp. 200–01 for more on this distinctive verb form.)

subordinate clause:
past

main clause:
would + verb

If the voter <u>were</u> more confident, he or she <u>would vote</u> more often.

For impossible events in the present—events that are contrary to fact—use the same forms as above (including the distinctive *were* when applicable):

subordinate clause:
past

main clause:
might + verb

If Lincoln <u>were</u> alive, he <u>might inspire</u> confidence.

For impossible events in the past, use the past perfect tense in the subordinate clause and *would, could,* or *might* plus the present perfect tense in the main clause:

subordinate clause:
past perfect

main clause:
might + present perfect

If Lincoln <u>had lived</u> past the Civil War, he <u>might have helped</u> stabilize the country.

27 Verb Mood

Mood in grammar is a verb form that indicates the writer's or speaker's attitude toward what he or she is saying. The **indicative mood** states a fact or opinion or asks a question: *The theater needs help.* The **imperative mood** expresses a command or gives a direction. It omits the subject of the sentence, *you: Help the theater.*

The **subjunctive mood** is trickier and requires distinctive verb forms described below and opposite.

Grammar checkers A grammar checker may spot some errors in the subjunctive mood, but it may miss others. For example, a checker flagged *I wish I <u>was</u> home* (should be *<u>were</u> home*) but not *If I <u>were</u> home, I <u>will</u> not leave* (should be *<u>would</u> not leave*).

27a Use the subjunctive verb forms appropriately, as in *I wish I were.*

The subjunctive mood expresses a suggestion, requirement, or desire, or it states a condition that is contrary to fact (that is, imaginary or hypothetical).

my**comp**lab

Visit *mycomplab.com* for more resources as well as exercises on verb mood.

■ Verbs such as *ask, insist, urge, require, recommend,* and *suggest* indicate **request or requirement.** They often precede a subordinate clause beginning with *that* and containing the substance of the request or requirement. For all subjects, the verb in the *that* clause is the plain form:

plain form

Rules require that every donation <u>be</u> mailed.

■ **Contrary-to-fact clauses** state imaginary or hypothetical conditions and usually begin with *if* or *unless* or follow *wish.* For present contrary-to-fact clauses, use the verb's past-tense form (for *be,* use the past-tense form *were*):

past   past

If the theater <u>were</u> in better shape and <u>had</u> more money, its future would be assured.

past

I wish I <u>were</u> able to donate money.

For past contrary-to-fact clauses, use the verb's past perfect form (*had* + past participle):

past perfect

The theater would be better funded if it <u>had been</u> better managed.

Note Do not use the helping verb *would* or *could* in a contrary-to-fact clause beginning with *if:*

Not	Many people would have helped if they <u>would have</u> known.
But	Many people would have helped if they <u>had</u> known.

See also pp. 199–200 on verb tenses in sentences like these.

27b Keep mood consistent.

Shifts in mood within a sentence or among related sentences can be confusing. Such shifts occur most frequently in directions.

Inconsistent	<u>Cook</u> the mixture slowly, and <u>you should stir</u> it until the sugar is dissolved. [Mood shifts from imperative to indicative.]
Revised	<u>Cook</u> the mixture slowly, and <u>stir</u> it until the sugar is dissolved. [Consistently imperative.]

28 Verb Voice

The **voice** of a verb tells whether the subject of the sentence performs the action (**active**) or is acted upon (**passive**). The actor in a passive sentence may be named in a prepositional phrase (as in *Rents are controlled by the city*), or the actor may be omitted (as in *Rents are controlled*).

Active and passive voice

Active voice   The subject acts.

Subject = actor → Transitive verb in active voice → Direct object

The city   controls   rents.

Passive voice The subject is acted upon.

Subject = object of action ← Transitive verb in passive voice   (optional) by actor

Rents   are controlled   by the city.
Rents   are controlled.

CULTURE LANGUAGE A passive verb always consists of a form of *be* plus the past participle of the main verb: *rents are controlled, people were inspired*. Other helping verbs must also be used with the words *be, being,* and *been: rents have been controlled, people would have been inspired*. Only a transitive verb (one that takes an object) may be used in the passive voice. (See p. 174.)

28a Generally, prefer the active voice. Use the passive voice when the actor is unknown or unimportant.

The active voice is usually clearer, more concise, and more forthright than the passive voice.

mycomplab

Visit *mycomplab.com* for more resources as well as exercises on verb voice.

| Weak passive | The library is used by both students and teachers for studying and research, and the plan to expand it has been praised by many. |
| Strong active | Both students and teachers use the library for studying and research, and many have praised the plan to expand it. |

The passive voice is useful in two situations: when the actor is unknown and when the actor is unimportant or less important than the object of the action.

> The Internet was established in 1969 by the US Department of Defense. The network has been extended internationally to governments, universities, foundations, corporations, and private individuals. [In the first sentence the writer wishes to stress the Internet rather than the Department of Defense. In the second sentence the actor is unknown or too complicated to name.]

> After the solution had been cooled to 10°C, the acid was added. [The person who cooled and added, perhaps the writer, is less important than the facts that the solution was cooled and acid was added. Passive sentences are common in scientific writing.]

Grammar checkers Most grammar checkers can be set to spot the passive voice. But they will also flag appropriate uses of the passive voice (such as when the actor is unknown).

28b Keep voice consistent.

Shifts in voice that involve shifts in subject are usually unnecessary and confusing.

| Inconsistent | Internet blogs cover an enormous range of topics. Opportunities for people to discuss pet issues are provided on these sites. |
| Revised | Internet blogs cover an enormous range of topics and provide opportunities for people to discuss pet issues. |

A shift in voice is appropriate when it helps focus the reader's attention on a single subject, as in *The candidate campaigned vigorously and was nominated on the first ballot.*

29 Agreement of Subject and Verb

A subject and its verb should agree in number and person.

More Japanese Americans live in Hawaii and California than elsewhere.
subject   verb

Daniel Inouye was the first Japanese American in Congress.
subject   verb

Most problems of subject-verb agreement arise when endings are omitted from subjects or verbs or when the relation between sentence parts is uncertain.

Grammar checkers A grammar checker will catch many simple errors in subject-verb agreement, such as *Addie and John is late,* and some more complicated errors, such as *Is Margaret and Tom going with us?* (should be *are* in both cases). But a checker failed to flag *The old group has gone their separate ways* (should be *have*) and offered a wrong correction for *The old group have gone their separate ways,* which is already correct.

29a | The -s and -es endings work differently for nouns and verbs.

An *-s* or *-es* ending does opposite things to nouns and verbs: it usually makes a noun *plural,* but it always makes a present-tense verb *singular.* Thus a singular-noun subject will not end in *-s,* but its verb will. A plural-noun subject will end in *-s,* but its verb will not. Between them, subject and verb use only one *-s* ending.

Singular subject	Plural subject
The boy plays.	The boys play.
The bird soars.	The birds soar.

Key terms

Person	Number	
	Singular	**Plural**
First	I eat.	We eat.
Second	You eat.	You eat.
Third	He/she/it eats.	They eat.
	The bird eats.	Birds eat.

The only exceptions to these rules involve the nouns that form irregular plurals, such as *child/children, woman/women*. The irregular plural still requires a plural verb: *The children play. The women read.*

CULTURE LANGUAGE If your first language or dialect is not standard American English, subject-verb agreement may be problematic, especially for the following reasons:

■ **Some English dialects follow different rules for subject-verb agreement,** such as omitting the -*s* ending for singular verbs or using the -*s* ending for plural verbs.

Nonstandard	The voter resist change.
Standard	The voter resists change.
Standard	The voters resist change.

The verb *be* changes spelling for singular and plural in both present and past tense. (See also pp. 168–69.)

| Nonstandard | Taxes is high. They was raised just last year. |
| Standard | Taxes are high. They were raised just last year. |

Have also has a distinctive -*s* form, *has:*

| Nonstandard | The new tax have little chance of passing. |
| Standard | The new tax has little chance of passing. |

■ **Some other languages change all parts of verb phrases to match their subjects.** In English verb phrases, however, only the helping verbs *be, have,* and *do* change for different subjects. The modal helping verbs—*can, may, should, will,* and others—do not change:

| Nonstandard | The tax mays pass next year. |
| Standard | The tax may pass next year. |

The main verb in a verb phrase also does not change for different subjects:

| Nonstandard | The tax may passes next year. |
| Standard | The tax may pass next year. |

29b Subject and verb should agree even when other words come between them.

The catalog of course requirements often baffles [not baffle] students.

The requirements stated in the catalog are [not is] unclear.

Note Phrases beginning with *as well as, together with, along with,* and *in addition to* do not change a singular subject to plural:

The president, as well as the deans, has [not have] agreed.

29c Subjects joined by *and* usually take plural verbs.

Frost and Roethke were contemporaries.

Exceptions When the parts of the subject form a single idea or refer to a single person or thing, they take a singular verb:

Avocado and bean sprouts is a California sandwich.

When a compound subject is preceded by the adjective *each* or *every,* the verb is usually singular:

Each man, woman, and child has a right to be heard.

29d When parts of a subject are joined by *or* or *nor,* the verb agrees with the nearer part.

Either the painter or the carpenter knows the cost.

The cabinets or the bookcases are too costly.

When one part of the subject is singular and the other plural, avoid awkwardness by placing the plural part closer to the verb so that the verb is plural:

Awkward   Neither the owners nor the contractor agrees.

Revised   Neither the contractor nor the owners agree.

29e With *everyone* and other indefinite pronouns, use a singular or plural verb as appropriate.

Most indefinite pronouns are singular in meaning (they refer to a single unspecified person or thing), and they take a singular verb:

Something smells.   Neither is right.

The plural indefinite pronouns refer to more than one unspecified thing, and they take a plural verb:

Both are correct.   Several were invited.

The other indefinite pronouns take a singular or a plural verb depending on whether the word they refer to is singular or plural:

All of the money is reserved for emergencies.

All of the funds are reserved for emergencies.

> **CULTURE LANGUAGE** See p. 230 for the distinction between *few* ("not many") and *a few* ("some").

29f Collective nouns such as *team* take singular or plural verbs depending on meaning.

Use a singular verb with a collective noun when the group acts as a unit:

The team has won five of the last six meets.

But when the group's members act separately, not together, use a plural verb:

The old team have gone their separate ways.

The collective noun *number* may be singular or plural. Preceded by *a,* it is plural; preceded by *the,* it is singular:

A number of people are in debt.

The number of people in debt is very large.

> **CULTURE LANGUAGE** Some noncount nouns (nouns that don't form plurals) are collective nouns because they name groups: for instance, *furniture, clothing, mail, machinery, equipment, military, police.* These noncount nouns usually take singular verbs: *Mail arrives daily.* But some of these nouns take plural verbs,

---

Key terms

indefinite pronoun A pronoun that does not refer to a specific person or thing:

Singular			*Singular or plural*	*Plural*
anybody	everyone	nothing	all	both
anyone	everything	one	any	few
anything	much	somebody	more	many
each	neither	someone	most	several
either	nobody	something	none	
everybody	no one		some	

collective noun A noun with singular form that names a group of individuals or things—for instance, *army, audience, committee, crowd, family.*

including *clergy, military, people, police,* and any collective noun that comes from an adjective, such as *the poor, the rich, the young, the elderly.* If you mean one representative of the group, use a singular noun such as *police officer* or *poor person.*

29g   *Who, which,* and *that* take verbs that agree with their antecedents.

When used as subjects, *who, which,* and *that* refer to another word in the sentence, called the **antecedent.** The verb agrees with the antecedent:

Mayor Garber ought to listen to the people who work for her.

Bardini is the only aide who has her ear.

Agreement problems often occur with *who* and *that* when the sentence includes *one of the* or *the only one of the:*

Bardini is one of the aides who work unpaid. [Of the aides who work unpaid, Bardini is one.]

Bardini is the only one of the aides who knows the community. [Of the aides, only one, Bardini, knows the community.]

⟨CULTURE / LANGUAGE⟩ In phrases beginning with *one of the,* be sure the noun is plural: *Bardini is one of the aides* [not *aide*] *who work unpaid.*

29h   *News* and other singular nouns ending in -*s* take singular verbs.

Singular nouns ending in -*s* include *athletics, economics, mathematics, measles, mumps, news, physics, politics,* and *statistics,* as well as place names such as *Athens, Wales,* and *United States.*

After so long a wait, the news has to be good.

Statistics is required of psychology majors.

A few of these words also take plural verbs, but only when they describe individual items rather than whole bodies of activity or knowledge: *The statistics prove him wrong.*

Measurements and figures ending in -*s* may also be singular when the quantity they refer to is a unit:

Three years is a long time to wait.

Three-fourths of the library consists of reference books.

29i The verb agrees with the subject even when it precedes the subject.

The verb precedes the subject mainly in questions and in constructions beginning with *there* or *here* and a form of *be:*

Is voting a right or a privilege?

Are a right and a privilege the same thing?

There are differences between them.

29j *Is, are,* and other linking verbs agree with their subjects, not subject complements.

Make a linking verb agree with its subject, usually the first element in the sentence, not with the noun or pronoun serving as a subject complement.

The child's sole support is her court-appointed guardians.

Her court-appointed guardians are the child's sole support.

29k Use singular verbs with titles and with words being defined.

Hakada Associates is a new firm.

Dream Days remains a favorite book.

Folks is a down-home word for *people.*

Key terms

linking verb A verb that connects or equates the subject and subject complement: for example, *seem, become, appear,* and forms of *be.* (See p. 175.)

subject complement A word that describes or renames the subject: *They became chemists.* (See p. 175.)

Pronouns

Pronouns—words such as *she* and *who* that refer to nouns—merit special care because all their meaning comes from the other words they refer to. This section discusses pronoun case (Chapter 30), matching pronouns and the words they refer to (31), and making sure pronouns refer to the right nouns (32).

30 Pronoun Case

Case is the form of a noun or pronoun that shows the reader how it functions in a sentence.

- ■ **The subjective case** indicates that the word is a subject or subject complement.
- ■ **The objective case** indicates that the word is an object of a verb or preposition.
- ■ **The possessive case** indicates that the word owns or is the source of a noun in the sentence.

Nouns change form only to show possession: *teacher's* (see **5** pp. 267–70). Most of the pronouns listed on the next page change more frequently.

Key terms

subject Who or what a sentence is about: *Biologists often study animals. They often work in laboratories.* (See pp. 172–73.)

subject complement A word or words that rename or describe the sentence subject: *Biologists are scientists. The best biologists are she and Scoggins.* (See p. 175.)

object of verb The receiver of the verb's action (**direct object**): *Many biologists study animals. The animals teach them.* Or the person or thing the action is performed for (**indirect object**): *Some biologists give animals homes. The animals give them pleasure.* (See pp. 174–76.)

object of preposition The word linked by *with, for,* or another preposition to the rest of the sentence: *Many biologists work in a laboratory. For them the lab often provides a second home.* (See p. 177.)

Visit *mycomplab.com* for more resources as well as exercises on pronoun case.

Subjective	Objective	Possessive
I	me	my, mine
you	you	your, yours
he	him	his
she	her	her, hers
it	it	its
we	us	our, ours
you	you	your, yours
they	them	their, theirs
who	whom	whose
whoever	whomever	—

Grammar checkers A grammar checker may flag some problems with pronoun case, but it will also miss a lot. For instance, one checker spotted the error in *We asked <u>whom</u> would come* (should be <u>*who*</u> *would come*), but it overlooked *We dreaded <u>them</u> coming* (should be <u>*their*</u> *coming*).

(CULTURE LANGUAGE) In standard American English, *-self* pronouns do not change form to show function. Their only forms are *myself, yourself, himself, herself, itself, ourselves, yourselves, themselves.* Avoid nonstandard forms such as *hisself, ourself,* and *theirselves.*

30a | Distinguish between compound subjects and compound objects: *she and I* vs. *her and me.*

Compound subjects or objects—those consisting of two or more nouns or pronouns—have the same case forms as they would if one noun or pronoun stood alone:

> compound
> subject
> <u>She and Novick</u> discussed the proposal.

> compound
> object
> The proposal disappointed <u>her and him</u>.

If you are in doubt about the correct form, try the test in the following box:

A test for case forms in compound constructions

1. **Identify a compound construction** (one connected by *and, but, or, nor*).

   [He, Him] and [I, me] won the prize.
   The prize went to [he, him] and [I, me].

(continued)

A test for case forms in compound constructions

(continued)

2. **Write a separate sentence for each part of the compound:**

   [He, Him] won the prize. [I, Me] won the prize.
   The prize went to [he, him]. The prize went to [I, me].

3. **Choose the pronouns that sound correct.**

   He won the prize. I won the prize. [Subjective.]
   The prize went to him. The prize went to me. [Objective.]

4. **Put the separate sentences back together.**

   He and I won the prize.
   The prize went to him and me.

30b Use the subjective case for subject complements: *It was she.*

After a linking verb, a pronoun renaming the subject (a subject complement) should be in the subjective case:

subject complement
The ones who care most are she and Novick.

subject
complement
It was they whom the mayor appointed.

If this construction sounds stilted to you, use the more natural order: *She and Novick are the ones who care most. The mayor appointed them.*

30c The use of *who* vs. *whom* depends on the pronoun's function in its clause.

Use *who* where you would use *he* or *she*—all ending in vowels. Use *whom* where you would use *him* or *her*—all ending in consonants.

1 Questions

At the beginning of a question, use *who* for a subject and *whom* for an object:

subject
Who wrote the policy?   object
Whom does it affect?

┌─ **Key term** ───

linking verb A verb, such as a form of *be*, that connects a subject and a word that renames or describes the subject (subject complement): *They are biologists.* (See p. 175.)

To find the correct case of *who* in a question, use the following test:

1. **Pose the question:**

   [Who, Whom] makes that decision?
   [Who, Whom] does one ask?

2. **Answer the question, using a personal pronoun.** Choose the pronoun that sounds correct, and note its case:

   [She, Her] makes that decision. She makes that decision. [Subjective.]
   One asks [she, her]. One asks her. [Objective.]

3. **Use the same case (*who* or *whom*) in the question:**

   Who makes that decision? [Subjective.]
   Whom does one ask? [Objective.]

2 Subordinate clauses

In a subordinate clause, use *who* or *whoever* for a subject, *whom* or *whomever* for an object.

    subject ⟶
Give old clothes to whoever needs them.

    object ⟵
I don't know whom the mayor appointed.

To determine which form to use, try the following test:

1. **Locate the subordinate clause:**

   Few people know [who, whom] they should ask.
   They are unsure [who, whom] makes the decision.

2. **Rewrite the subordinate clause as a separate sentence, substituting a personal pronoun for *who, whom*.** Choose the pronoun that sounds correct, and note its case:

   They should ask [she, her]. They should ask her. [Objective.]
   [She, her] makes the decision. She makes the decision. [Subjective.]

3. **Use the same case (*who* or *whom*) in the subordinate clause:**

   Few people know whom they should ask. [Objective.]
   They are unsure who makes the decision. [Subjective.]

┌─ **Key term** ───

subordinate clause A word group that contains a subject and a predicate and also begins with a subordinating word, such as *who, whom,* or *because.* (See p. 179.)

└──

Note Don't let expressions such as *I think* and *she says* mislead you into using *whom* rather than *who* for the subject of a clause.

subject ⟶
He is the one who I think is best qualified.

To choose between *who* and *whom* in such constructions, delete the interrupting phrase so that you can see the true relation between parts: *He is the one who is best qualified.*

30d Use the appropriate case in other constructions.

1 *We* or *us* with a noun

The choice of *we* or *us* before a noun depends on the use of the noun:

object of
preposition
Freezing weather is welcomed by us skaters.

subject ⟶
We skaters welcome freezing weather.

2 Pronoun in an appositive

In an appositive the case of a pronoun depends on the function of the word the appositive describes or identifies:

appositive
identifies object
The class elected two representatives, DeShawn and me.

appositive
identifies subject
Two representatives, DeShawn and I, were elected.

3 Pronoun after *than* or *as*

When a pronoun follows *than* or *as* in a comparison, the case of the pronoun indicates what words may have been omitted. A subjective pronoun must be the subject of the omitted verb:

subject
Some critics like Glass more than he [does].

An objective pronoun must be the object of the omitted verb:

object
Some critics like Glass more than [they like] him.

Key term

appositive A noun or noun substitute that renames another noun immediately before it. (See p. 179.)

4 Subject and object of infinitive

Both the object *and* the subject of an infinitive are in the objective case:

subject
of infinitive
The school asked <u>him</u> to speak.

object
of infinitive
Students chose to invite <u>him</u>.

5 Case before a gerund

Ordinarily, use the possessive form of a pronoun or noun immediately before a gerund:

The coach disapproved of <u>their</u> lifting weights.

The <u>coach's</u> disapproving was a surprise.

31 Agreement of Pronoun and Antecedent

The **antecedent** of a pronoun is the noun or other pronoun to which the pronoun refers:

<u>Homeowners</u> fret over <u>their</u> tax bills.
antecedent   pronoun

<u>Its</u> constant increases make the tax <u>bill</u> a dreaded document.
pronoun   antecedent

For clarity, a pronoun should agree with its antecedent in person, number, and gender.

Grammar checkers A grammar checker cannot help you with agreement between pronoun and antecedent because it cannot recognize the intended relation between the two.

Key terms

infinitive The plain form of the verb plus *to: to run.* (See p. 178.)

gerund The *-ing* form of a verb used as a noun: *Running is fun.* (See p. 178.)

---

mycomplab

Visit *mycomplab.com* for more resources as well as exercises on pronoun-antecedent agreement.

CULTURE
LANGUAGE
The gender of a pronoun should match its antecedent, not a noun that the pronoun may modify: *Sara Young invited her* [not *his*] *son.* Also, English nouns have only neuter gender unless they specifically refer to males or females. Thus nouns such as *book, table, sun,* and *earth* take the pronoun *it.*

31a Antecedents joined by *and* usually take plural pronouns.

Mr. Bartos and I cannot settle our dispute.

The dean and my adviser have offered their help.

Exceptions When the compound antecedent refers to a single idea, person, or thing, then the pronoun is singular:

My friend and adviser offered her help.

When the compound antecedent follows *each* or *every,* the pronoun is singular:

Every girl and woman took her seat.

31b When parts of an antecedent are joined by *or* or *nor,* the pronoun agrees with the nearer part.

Tenants or owners must present their grievances.

Either the tenant or the owner will have her way.

When one subject is plural and the other singular, the sentence will be awkward unless you put the plural subject second:

Awkward Neither the tenants nor the owner has yet made her case.

Revised Neither the owner nor the tenants have yet made their case.

┌─ **Key terms** ─────────────────────────────────────

	Number	
Person	**Singular**	**Plural**
First	*I*	*we*
Second	*you*	*you*
Third	*he, she, it,*	*they,*
	indefinite pronouns,	plural nouns
	singular nouns	
Gender		
Masculine	*he,* nouns naming males	
Feminine	*she,* nouns naming females	
Neuter	*it,* all other nouns	

└───

31c With *everyone, person,* and other indefinite words, use a singular or plural pronoun as appropriate.

Indefinite words—indefinite pronouns and generic nouns—do not refer to any specific person or thing. Most indefinite pronouns and all generic nouns are singular in meaning. When they serve as antecedents of pronouns, the pronouns should be singular:

Everyone on the women's team now has her own locker.
indefinite
pronoun

Every person on the women's team now has her own locker.
generic noun

Five indefinite pronouns—*all, any, more, most, some*—may be singular or plural in meaning depending on what they refer to:

Few women athletes had changing spaces, so most had to change in their rooms.

Most of the changing space was dismal, its color a drab olive green.

Four indefinite pronouns—*both, few, many, several*—are always plural in meaning:

Few realize how their athletic facilities have changed.

Most agreement problems arise with the singular indefinite words. We often use these words to mean "many" or "all" rather than "one" and then refer to them with plural pronouns, as in *Everyone has their own locker.* Often, too, we mean indefinite words to include both masculine and feminine genders and thus resort to *they* instead of the **generic** *he*—the masculine pronoun referring to both genders, as in *Everyone deserves his privacy.* (For more on the

---

Key terms

indefinite pronoun A pronoun that does not refer to a specific person or thing:

Singular			*Singular or plural*	*Plural*
anybody	everyone	nothing	all	both
anyone	everything	one	any	few
anything	much	somebody	more	many
each	neither	someone	most	several
either	nobody	something	none	
everybody	no one		some	

generic noun A singular noun such as *person* and *student* when it refers to a typical member of a group, not to a particular individual.

generic *he,* which many readers view as sexist, see **3** p. 150.) To achieve agreement in such cases, you have the following options.

Ways to correct agreement with indefinite words

■ **Change the indefinite word to a plural, and use a plural pronoun to match:**

Faulty   Every <u>athlete</u> deserves <u>their</u> privacy.
Revised   **Athletes** deserve their privacy.

■ **Rewrite the sentence to omit the pronoun:**

Faulty   <u>Everyone</u> is entitled to <u>their</u> own locker.
Revised   Everyone is entitled to **a** locker.

■ **Use *he or she* (*him or her, his or her*) to refer to the indefinite word:**

Faulty   Now <u>everyone</u> has <u>their</u> private space.
Revised   Now everyone has **his or her** private space.

However, used more than once in several sentences, *he or she* quickly becomes awkward. (Many readers do not accept the alternative *he/she.*) Using the plural or omitting the pronoun will usually correct agreement problems and create more readable sentences.

31d Collective nouns such as *team* take singular or plural pronouns depending on meaning.

Use a singular pronoun with a collective noun when referring to the group as a unit:

The committee voted to disband <u>itself</u>.

When referring to the individual members of the group, use a plural pronoun:

The old team have gone <u>their</u> separate ways.

(CULTURE LANGUAGE) In standard American English, collective nouns that are noncount nouns (they don't form plurals) usually take singular pronouns: *The mail sits in <u>its</u> own basket.* A few noncount nouns take plural pronouns, including *clergy, military, police, the rich,* and *the poor: The police support <u>their</u> unions.*

Key term

collective noun A noun with singular form that names a group of individuals or things—for instance, *army, audience, committee, crowd, family, group, team.*

---

32 Reference of Pronoun to Antecedent

A **pronoun** should refer clearly to its **antecedent,** the noun it substitutes for. Otherwise, readers will have difficulty grasping the pronoun's meaning.

Grammar checkers A grammar checker cannot recognize unclear pronoun reference. For instance, a checker did not flag any of the confusing examples in this chapter.

CULTURE LANGUAGE In standard American English, a pronoun needs a clear antecedent nearby, but don't use both a pronoun and its antecedent as the subject of the same clause: *Jim* [not *Jim he*] *told Mark to go alone.* (See also p. 246.)

32a Make a pronoun refer clearly to one antecedent.

When either of two nouns can be a pronoun's antecedent, the reference will not be clear.

Confusing   Emily Dickinson is sometimes compared with Jane Austen, but she was quite different.

Revise such a sentence in one of two ways:

■ **Replace the pronoun with the appropriate noun.**

Clear   Emily Dickinson is sometimes compared with Jane Austen, but Dickinson [or Austen] was quite different.

■ **Avoid repetition by rewriting the sentence.** If you use the pronoun, make sure it has only one possible antecedent.

Clear   Despite occasional comparison, Emily Dickinson and Jane Austen were quite different.

Clear   Though sometimes compared with her, Emily Dickinson was quite different from Jane Austen.

32b Place a pronoun close enough to its antecedent to ensure clarity.

A clause beginning with *who, which,* or *that* should generally fall immediately after the word to which it refers.

my**comp**lab

Visit *mycomplab.com* for more resources as well as exercises on pronoun reference.   **219**

| Confusing | Jody found a lamp in the attic that her aunt had used. |
| Clear | In the attic Jody found a lamp that her aunt had used. |

32c Make a pronoun refer to a specific antecedent, not an implied one.

A pronoun should refer to a specific noun or other pronoun. A reader can only guess at the meaning of a pronoun when its antecedent is implied by the context, not stated outright.

1 Vague *this, that, which,* or *it*

This, that, which, or *it* should refer to a specific noun, not to a whole word group expressing an idea or situation.

| Confusing | The British knew little of the American countryside, and they had no experience with the colonists' guerrilla tactics. This gave the colonists an advantage. |
| Clear | The British knew little of the American countryside, and they had no experience with the colonists' guerrilla tactics. This ignorance and inexperience gave the colonists an advantage. |

2 Indefinite antecedents with *it* and *they*

It and *they* should have definite noun antecedents. Rewrite the sentence if the antecedent is missing.

| Confusing | In Chapter 4 of this book it describes the early flights of the Wright brothers. |
| Clear | Chapter 4 of this book describes the early flights of the Wright brothers. |

| Confusing | Even in reality TV shows, they present a false picture of life. |
| Clear | Even reality TV shows present a false picture of life. |

3 Implied nouns

A noun may be implied in some other word or phrase, as *happiness* is implied in *happy, driver* is implied in *drive,* and *mother* is implied in *mother's*. But a pronoun cannot refer clearly to an implied noun, only to a specific, stated one.

| Confusing | Cohen's report brought her a lawsuit. |
| Clear | Cohen was sued over her report. |

| Confusing | Her reports on psychological development generally go unnoticed outside it.⊘ |
| Clear | Her reports on psychological development generally go unnoticed outside the field. |

32d Use *you* only to mean "you, the reader."

You should clearly mean "you, the reader." The context must be appropriate for such a meaning:

| Inappropriate | In the fourteenth century you had to struggle simply to survive. |
| Revised | In the fourteenth century one [or a person] had to struggle simply to survive. |

Writers sometimes drift into *you* because *one, a person,* or a similar indefinite word can be difficult to sustain. Sentence after sentence, the indefinite word may sound stuffy, and it requires *he* or *he or she* for pronoun-antecedent agreement (see pp. 217–18). To avoid these problems, try using plural nouns and pronouns:

| Original | In the fourteenth century one had to struggle simply to survive. |
| Revised | In the fourteenth century people had to struggle simply to survive. |

32e Keep pronouns consistent.

Within a sentence or a group of related sentences, pronouns should be consistent. Partly, consistency comes from making pronouns and their antecedents agree (see Chapter 31). In addition, the pronouns within a passage should match each other.

| Inconsistent | One finds when reading that your concentration improves with practice, so that I now comprehend more in less time. |
| Revised | I find when reading that my concentration improves with practice, so that I now comprehend more in less time. |

——————— Modifiers ———————

Modifiers describe or limit other words in a sentence. They are adjectives, adverbs, or word groups serving as adjectives or adverbs. This section shows how to solve problems in the forms of modifiers (Chapter 33) and in their relation to the rest of the sentence (34).

33 Adjectives and Adverbs

Adjectives modify nouns (*happy child*) and pronouns (*special someone*). **Adverbs** modify verbs (*almost see*), adjectives (*very happy*), other adverbs (*not very*), and whole word groups (*Otherwise, I'll go*). The only way to tell whether a modifier should be an adjective or an adverb is to determine its function in the sentence.

Grammar checkers A grammar checker will spot some but not all problems with misused adjectives and adverbs. For instance, a checker flagged *Some children suffer bad* and *Jenny did not feel nothing*. But it did not flag *Educating children good should be everyone's focus.*

CULTURE LANGUAGE In standard American English, an adjective does not change along with the noun it modifies to show plural number: *square* [not *squares*] *spaces*. Only nouns form plurals.

33a Use adjectives only to modify nouns and pronouns.

Do not use adjectives instead of adverbs to modify verbs, adverbs, or other adjectives:

Faulty	Educating children good should be everyone's focus.
Revised	Educating children well should be everyone's focus.
Faulty	Some children suffer bad.
Revised	Some children suffer badly.

CULTURE LANGUAGE To negate a verb or an adjective, use the adverb *not*.

They are not learning. They are not stupid.

---

mycomplab

Visit *mycomplab.com* for more resources as well as exercises on adjectives and adverbs.

To negate a noun, use the adjective *no.*

No child should fail to read.

33b	Use an adjective after a linking verb to modify the subject. Use an adverb to modify a verb.

Some verbs may or may not be linking verbs, depending on their meaning in the sentence. When the word after the verb modifies the subject, the verb is linking and the word should be an adjective: *He looked happy.* When the word modifies the verb, however, it should be an adverb: *He looked carefully.*

Two word pairs are especially tricky. One is *bad* and *badly:*

The weather grew **bad.**
      linking adjective
      verb

She felt **bad.**
   linking adjective
   verb

Flowers grow **badly** in such soil.
  verb adverb

The other pair is *good* and *well. Good* serves only as an adjective. *Well* may serve as an adverb with a host of meanings or as an adjective meaning only "fit" or "healthy."

Decker trained **well.**
    verb adverb

She felt **well.**
  linking adjective
  verb

Her health was **good.**
    linking adjective
    verb

33c	Use the comparative and superlative forms of adjectives and adverbs appropriately.

Adjectives and adverbs can show degrees of quality or amount with the endings *-er* and *-est* or with the words *more* and *most* or *less* and *least.* Most modifiers have three forms:

Positive The basic form listed in the dictionary	**Comparative** A greater or lesser degree of the quality	**Superlative** The greatest or least degree of the quality
Adjectives		
red	redder	reddest
awful	more/less awful	most/least awful
Adverbs		
soon	sooner	soonest
quickly	more/less quickly	most/least quickly

> **Key term**
>
> **linking verb** A verb that connects a subject and a word that describes the subject: *They are golfers.* Linking verbs include *look, sound, feel, appear, seem, become,* and forms of *be.* (See p. 175.)

If sound alone does not tell you whether to use *-er/-est* or *more/most*, consult a dictionary. If the endings can be used, the dictionary will list them. Otherwise, use *more* or *most*.

1 Irregular adjectives and adverbs

Irregular modifiers change the spelling of their positive form to show comparative and superlative degrees.

Positive	Comparative	Superlative
Adjectives		
good	better	best
bad	worse	worst
little	littler, less	littlest, least
many		
some	more	most
much		
Adverbs		
well	better	best
badly	worse	worst

2 Double comparisons

A double comparative or double superlative combines the *-er* or *-est* ending with the word *more* or *most*. It is redundant.

Chang was the <u>wisest</u> [not <u>most wisest</u>] person in town.
He was <u>smarter</u> [not <u>more smarter</u>] than anyone else.

3 Logical comparisons

Absolute modifiers

Some adjectives and adverbs cannot logically be compared—for instance, *perfect, unique, dead, impossible, infinite.* These absolute words can be preceded by adverbs like *nearly* or *almost* that mean "approaching," but they cannot logically be modified by *more* or *most* (as in *most perfect*).

| Not | He was the <u>most unique</u> teacher we had. |
| But | He was a <u>unique</u> teacher. |

Completeness

To be logical, a comparison must also be complete in the following ways:

■ **The comparison must state a relation fully enough for clarity.**

Unclear	Carmakers worry about their industry more than environmentalists.
Clear	Carmakers worry about their industry more than environmentalists <u>do</u>.
Clear	Carmakers worry about their industry more than <u>they worry about</u> environmentalists.

■ **The items being compared should in fact be comparable.**

Illogical	The cost of a hybrid car can be greater than a gasoline-powered car. [Illogically compares a cost and a car.]
Revised	The cost of a hybrid car can be greater than <u>the cost of</u> [or that of] a gasoline-powered car.

See also **3** p. 140 on parallelism with comparisons.

Any versus *any other*

Use *any other* when comparing something with others in the same group. Use *any* when comparing something with others in a different group.

Illogical	Los Angeles is larger than <u>any</u> city in California. [Since Los Angeles is itself a city in California, the sentence seems to say that Los Angeles is larger than itself.]
Revised	Los Angeles is larger than <u>any other</u> city in California.
Illogical	Los Angeles is larger than <u>any other</u> city in Canada. [The cities in Canada constitute a group to which Los Angeles does not belong.]
Revised	Los Angeles is larger than <u>any</u> city in Canada.

33d Watch for double negatives.

In a **double negative** two negative words such as *no, not, none, neither, barely, hardly,* or *scarcely* cancel each other out. Some double negatives are intentional: for instance, *She was not unhappy* indicates with understatement that she was indeed happy. But most double negatives say the opposite of what is intended: *Jenny did not feel nothing* asserts that Jenny felt other than nothing, or something. For the opposite meaning, one of the negatives must be eliminated (*She felt nothing*) or one of them must be changed to a positive (*She did not feel anything*).

Faulty	The IRS <u>cannot hardly</u> audit all tax returns. <u>None</u> of its audits <u>never</u> touch many cheaters.

Revised   The IRS <u>cannot</u> audit all tax returns. Its audits <u>never</u> touch many cheaters.

33e Distinguish between present and past participles as adjectives.

Both present participles and past participles may serve as adjectives: *a burning building, a burned building.* As in the examples, the two participles usually differ in the time they indicate.

But some present and past participles—those derived from verbs expressing feeling—can have altogether different meanings. The present participle modifies something that causes the feeling: *That was a frightening storm* (the storm frightens). The past participle modifies something that experiences the feeling: *They quieted the frightened horses* (the horses feel fright).

The following participles are among those likely to be confused:

amazing/amazed	fascinating/fascinated
amusing/amused	frightening/frightened
annoying/annoyed	frustrating/frustrated
astonishing/astonished	interesting/interested
boring/bored	pleasing/pleased
confusing/confused	satisfying/satisfied
depressing/depressed	shocking/shocked
embarrassing/embarrassed	surprising/surprised
exciting/excited	tiring/tired
exhausting/exhausted	worrying/worried

33f Use *a, an, the,* and other determiners appropriately.

Determiners are special kinds of adjectives that mark nouns because they always precede nouns. Some common determiners are *a, an,* and *the* (called **articles**) and *my, their, whose, this, these, those, one, some,* and *any.*

Native speakers of standard American English can rely on their intuition when using determiners, but speakers of other languages

---

Key terms

present participle The *-ing* form of a verb: *flying, writing.* (See p. 168.)

past participle The *-d* or *-ed* form of a regular verb: *slipped, walked.* Most irregular verbs have distinctive past participles, such as *eaten* or *swum.* (See p. 168.)

and dialects often have difficulty with them. In standard American English, the use of determiners depends on the context they appear in and the kind of noun they precede:

- A *proper noun* names a particular person, place, or thing and begins with a capital letter: *February, Joe Allen, Red River.* Most proper nouns are not preceded by determiners.
- A *count noun* names something that is countable in English and can form a plural: *girl/girls, apple/apples, child/children.* A singular count noun is always preceded by a determiner; a plural count noun sometimes is.
- A *noncount noun* names something not usually considered countable in English, and so it does not form a plural. A noncount noun is sometimes preceded by a determiner. Here is a sample of noncount nouns, sorted into groups by meaning:

Abstractions: confidence, democracy, education, equality, evidence, health, information, intelligence, knowledge, luxury, peace, pollution, research, success, supervision, truth, wealth, work

Food and drink: bread, candy, cereal, flour, meat, milk, salt, water, wine

Emotions: anger, courage, happiness, hate, joy, love, respect, satisfaction

Natural events and substances: air, blood, dirt, gasoline, gold, hair, heat, ice, oil, oxygen, rain, silver, smoke, weather, wood

Groups: clergy, clothing, equipment, furniture, garbage, jewelry, junk, legislation, machinery, mail, military, money, police, vocabulary

Fields of study: architecture, accounting, biology, business, chemistry, engineering, literature, psychology, science

A dictionary of English as a second language will tell you whether a noun is a count noun, a noncount noun, or both. (See **3** p. 153 for recommended dictionaries.)

Note Many nouns are sometimes count nouns and sometimes noncount nouns:

The library has <u>a room</u> for readers. [*Room* is a count noun meaning "walled area."]

The library has <u>room</u> for reading. [*Room* is a noncount noun meaning "space."]

Grammar checkers Partly because the same noun may fall into different groups, a grammar checker is an unreliable guide to missing or misused articles and other determiners. For instance, a checker flagged the omitted *a* before *Scientist* in *Scientist developed new processes;* it did not flag the omitted *a* before *new* in *A scientist developed new process;* and it mistakenly flagged the correctly omitted article *the* before *Vegetation* in *Vegetation suffers from drought.*

1 | *A, an,* and *the*

With singular count nouns

A or *an* precedes a singular count noun when the reader does not already know its identity, usually because you have not mentioned it before:

> A scientist in our chemistry department developed a process to strengthen metals. [*Scientist* and *process* are being introduced for the first time.]

The precedes a singular count noun that has a specific identity for the reader, for one of the following reasons:

- ■ **You have mentioned the noun before:**

> A scientist in our chemistry department developed a process to strengthen metals. The scientist patented the process. [*Scientist* and *process* were identified in the preceding sentence.]

- ■ **You identify the noun immediately before or after you state it:**

> The most productive laboratory is the research center in the chemistry department. [*Most productive* identifies *laboratory. In the chemistry department* identifies *research center.* And *chemistry department* is a shared facility—see below.]

- ■ **The noun names something unique—the only one in existence:**

> The sun rises in the east. [*Sun* and *east* are unique.]

- ■ **The noun names an institution or facility that is shared by the community of readers:**

> Many men and women aspire to the presidency. [*Presidency* is a shared institution.]

> The cell phone has changed business communication. [*Cell phone* is a shared facility.]

The is not used before a singular noun that names a general category:

> Wordsworth's poetry shows his love of nature [not the nature].
> General Sherman said that war is hell. [*War* names a general category.]
> The war in Iraq left many wounded. [*War* names a specific war.]

With plural count nouns

A or *an* never precedes a plural noun. *The* does not precede a plural noun that names a general category. *The* does precede a plural noun that names specific representatives of a category.

Men and women are different. [*Men* and *women* name general categories.]

The women formed a team. [*Women* refers to specific people.]

With noncount nouns

A or *an* never precedes a noncount noun. *The* does precede a noncount noun that names specific representatives of a general category.

Vegetation suffers from drought. [*Vegetation* names a general category.]

The vegetation in the park withered or died. [*Vegetation* refers to specific plants.]

With proper nouns

A or *an* never precedes a proper noun. *The* generally does not precede proper nouns.

Garcia lives in Boulder.

There are exceptions, however. For instance, we generally use *the* before plural proper nouns (*the Murphys, the Boston Celtics*) and before the names of groups and organizations (*the Department of Justice, the Sierra Club*), ships (*the Lusitania*), oceans (*the Pacific*), mountain ranges (*the Alps*), regions (*the Middle East*), rivers (*the Mississippi*), and some countries (*the United States, the Netherlands*).

2 Other determiners

The uses of English determiners besides articles also depend on context and kind of noun. The following determiners may be used as indicated with singular count nouns, plural count nouns, or noncount nouns.

With any kind of noun (singular count, plural count, noncount)

my, our, your, his, her, its, their, possessive nouns (*boy's, boys'*)
whose, which(ever), what(ever)
some, any, the other
no

Their account is overdrawn. [Singular count.]
Their funds are low. [Plural count.]
Their money is running out. [Noncount.]

Only with singular nouns (count and noncount)

this, that

This account has some money. [Count.]
That information may help. [Noncount.]

Only with noncount nouns and plural count nouns

most, enough, other, such, all, all of the, a lot of

<u>Most</u> funds are committed. [Plural count.]
<u>Most</u> money is needed elsewhere. [Noncount.]

Only with singular count nouns

one, every, each, either, neither, another

<u>One</u> car must be sold. [Singular count.]

Only with plural count nouns

these, those
both, many, few, a few, fewer, fewest, several
two, three, and so forth

<u>Two</u> cars are unnecessary. [Plural count.]

Note *Few* means "not many" or "not enough." *A few* means "some" or "a small but sufficient quantity."

<u>Few</u> committee members came to the meeting.
<u>A few</u> members can keep the committee going.

Do not use *much* with a plural count noun.

<u>Many</u> [not <u>Much</u>] members want to help.

Only with noncount nouns

much, more, little, a little, less, least, a large amount of

<u>Less</u> luxury is in order. [Noncount.]

Note *Little* means "not many" or "not enough." *A little* means "some" or "a small but sufficient quantity."

<u>Little</u> time remains before the conference.
The members need <u>a little</u> help from their colleagues.

Do not use *many* with a noncount noun.

<u>Much</u> [not <u>Many</u>] work remains.

34 Misplaced and Dangling Modifiers

The arrangement of words in a sentence is an important clue to their relationships. Modifiers will be unclear if readers can't connect them to the words they modify.

Grammar checkers A grammar checker cannot recognize most problems with modifiers. For instance, a checker failed to flag the misplaced modifiers in *Gasoline high prices affect usually car sales* or the dangling modifier in *The vandalism was visible passing the building.*

34a Reposition misplaced modifiers.

A **misplaced modifier** falls in the wrong place in a sentence. It is usually awkward or confusing. It may even be unintentionally funny.

1 Clear placement

Readers tend to link a modifier to the nearest word it could modify. Any other placement can link the modifier to the wrong word.

| Confusing | He served steak to the men on paper plates. |
| Clear | He served the men steak on paper plates. |

| Confusing | According to the police, many dogs are killed by automobiles and trucks roaming unleashed. |
| Clear | According to the police, many dogs roaming unleashed are killed by automobiles and trucks. |

2 *Only* and other limiting modifiers

Limiting modifiers include *almost, even, exactly, hardly, just, merely, nearly, only, scarcely,* and *simply.* For clarity place such a modifier immediately before the word or word group you intend it to limit.

Unclear	The archaeologist only found the skull on her last dig.
Clear	The archaeologist found only the skull on her last dig.
Clear	The archaeologist found the skull only on her last dig.

mycomplab

Visit *mycomplab.com* for more resources as well as exercises on misplaced and dangling modifiers.

3 | Adverbs with grammatical units

Adverbs can often move around in sentences, but some will be awkward if they interrupt certain grammatical units:

- **A long adverb stops the flow from subject to verb.**

- **Any adverb is awkward between a verb and its direct object.**

	verb ──── adverb object
Awkward	The hurricane had damaged <u>badly</u> many homes in the city.

	── verb ── object
Revised	The hurricane had <u>badly</u> damaged many homes in the city.
	adverb

- **A *split infinitive*—an adverb placed between *to* and the verb— annoys many readers.**

	▾ infinitive ▾
Awkward	The weather service expected temperatures to <u>not</u> rise.

	infinitive
Revised	The weather service expected temperatures <u>not</u> to rise.

A split infinitive may sometimes be natural and preferable, though it may still bother some readers.

              ─infinitive ─
Several US industries expect to <u>more than</u> triple their use of robots.

Here the split infinitive is more economical than the alternatives, such as *Several US industries expect to increase their use of robots by more than three times.*

- **A long adverb is usually awkward inside a verb phrase.**

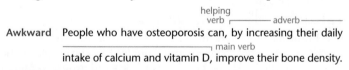

┌─ **Key terms** ───

adverb A word or word group that describes a verb, adjective, other adverb, or whole word group, specifying how, when, where, or to what extent: *quickly see, solid like a boulder.*

direct object The receiver of the verb's action: *The car hit a tree.* (See p. 174.)

infinitive A verb form consisting of *to* plus the verb's plain (or dictionary) form: *to produce, to enjoy.* (See p. 178.)
└──

Revised   By increasing their daily intake of calcium and vitamin D,
                                                                verb phrase
        people who have osteoporosis can improve their bone density.

 In a question, place a one-word adverb after the first helping verb and subject:

helping
verb   subject   adverb   rest of
                          verb phrase
Will spacecraft ever be able to leave the solar system?

4 Other adverb positions

Placements of a few adverbs can be difficult for nonnative speakers of English:

■ **Adverbs of frequency** include *always, never, often, rarely, seldom, sometimes,* and *usually.* They generally appear at the beginning of a sentence, before a one-word verb, or after the helping verb in a verb phrase.

helping   main
verb   adverb   verb
Robots have sometimes put humans out of work.

adverb   verb phrase
Sometimes robots have put humans out of work.

Adverbs of frequency always follow the verb *be.*

verb adverb
Robots are often helpful to workers.

verb adverb
Robots are seldom useful around the house.

■ **Adverbs of degree** include *absolutely, almost, certainly, completely, definitely, especially, extremely, hardly,* and *only.* They fall just before the word modified (an adjective, another adverb, sometimes a verb).

adverb   adjective
Robots have been especially useful in making cars.

■ **Adverbs of manner** include *badly, beautifully, openly, sweetly, tightly, well,* and others that describe how something is done. They usually fall after the verb.

verb   adverb
Robots work smoothly on assembly lines.

Key term

verb phrase A verb consisting of a helping verb and a main verb that carries the principal meaning: *will have begun, can see.* (See p. 169.)

■ **The adverb** *not* changes position depending on what it modifies. When it modifies a verb, place it after the helping verb (or the first helping verb if more than one).

helping   main
 verb   verb
Robots do <u>not</u> think.

When *not* modifies another adverb or an adjective, place it before the other modifier.

adjective
Robots are <u>not</u> sleek machines.

5 Order of adjectives   ⟨CULTURE · LANGUAGE⟩

English follows distinctive rules for arranging two or three adjectives before a noun. (A string of more than three adjectives before a noun is rare.) The order is shown in the chart below.

Determiner	Opinion	Size or shape	Color	Origin	Material	Noun used as adjective	Noun
many						state	**laws**
	lovely		green	Thai			**birds**
a	fine			German			**camera**
this		square			wooden		**table**
all						business	**reports**
the			blue		litmus		**paper**

See **5** pp. 261–62 on punctuating adjectives before a noun.

34b Connect dangling modifiers to their sentences.

A **dangling modifier** does not sensibly modify anything in its sentence.

Dangling   Passing the building, the vandalism became visible.

Dangling modifiers usually introduce sentences, contain a verb form, and imply but do not name a subject. In the example above, the implied subject is the someone or something passing the building.

┌─ **Key term** ─────────────────────────────────
adjective A word that describes a noun or pronoun, specifying which one, what quality, or how many: <u>*good*</u> *one,* <u>*three*</u> *cars.* (See p. 169.)
└──

Identifying and revising dangling modifiers

- **Find a subject.** If the modifier lacks a subject of its own (e.g., *when in diapers*), identify what it describes.
- **Connect the subject and modifier.** Verify that what the modifier describes is in fact the subject of the main clause. If it is not, the modifier is probably dangling:

     ⌐——— modifier———⌐ subject

  Dangling When in diapers, my mother remarried.

- **Revise as needed.** Revise a dangling modifier (*a*) by recasting it with a subject of its own or (*b*) by changing the subject of the main clause:

  Revision *a* When I was in diapers, my mother remarried.

  Revision *b* When in diapers, I attended my mother's second wedding.

Readers assume that this implied subject is the same as the subject of the sentence (*vandalism* in the example), but vandalism does not pass buildings. The modifier "dangles" because it does not connect sensibly to the rest of the sentence. Here is another example:

Dangling Although intact, graffiti covered every inch of the walls and windows. [The walls and windows, not the graffiti, were intact.]

To revise a dangling modifier, you have to recast the sentence it appears in. (Revising just by moving the modifier will leave it dangling: *The vandalism became visible passing the building.*) Choose a revision method depending on what you want to emphasize in the sentence.

- **Rewrite the dangling modifier as a complete clause with its own stated subject and verb.** Readers can accept that the new subject and the sentence subject are different.

  Dangling Passing the building, the vandalism became visible.

  Revised As we passed the building, the vandalism became visible.

- **Change the subject of the sentence to a word the modifier properly describes.**

  Dangling Trying to understand the causes, vandalism has been extensively studied.

  Revised Trying to understand the causes, researchers have extensively studied vandalism.

Sentence Faults

A word group punctuated as a sentence will confuse or annoy readers if it lacks needed parts, has too many parts, or has parts that don't fit together.

35 Sentence Fragments

A **sentence fragment** is part of a sentence that is set off as if it were a whole sentence by an initial capital letter and a final period or other end punctuation. Although writers occasionally use fragments deliberately and effectively (see pp. 238–39), readers perceive most fragments as serious errors.

Grammar checkers A grammar checker can spot many but not all sentence fragments, and it may flag sentences that are actually commands, such as *Continue reading.*

35a Test your sentences for completeness.

A word group punctuated as a sentence should pass *all three* of the following tests. If it does not, it is a fragment and needs revision.

Complete sentence versus sentence fragment

A complete sentence or main clause
1. contains a subject and a predicate verb (The wind blows)
2. and is not a subordinate clause (beginning with a word such as *because* or *who*).

A sentence fragment
1. lacks a predicate verb (*The wind blowing*),
2. or lacks a subject (*And blows*),
3. or is a subordinate clause not attached to a complete sentence (*Because the wind blows*).

Test 1: Find the predicate verb.

Look for a verb that can serve as the predicate of a sentence. Some fragments lack any verb at all.

---

mycomplab

Visit *mycomplab.com* for more resources as well as exercises on sentence fragments.

236

Fragment	Uncountable numbers of sites on the Web.
Revised	Uncountable numbers of sites <u>make up</u> the Web.

Other fragments may include a verb form but not a **finite verb**, one that changes form as indicated below. A verbal does not change; it cannot serve as a predicate verb without the aid of a helping verb.

	Finite verbs in complete sentences	Verbals in sentence fragments
Singular	The network <u>grows</u>.	The network <u>growing</u>.
Plural	Networks <u>grow</u>.	Networks <u>growing</u>.
Present	The network <u>grows</u>.	
Past	The network <u>grew</u>.	The network <u>growing</u>.
Future	The network <u>will grow</u>.	

CULTURE LANGUAGE Some languages allow forms of *be* to be omitted as helping verbs or linking verbs. But English requires stating forms of *be,* as shown in the following revised example.

Fragments	The network growing. It much larger than its developers anticipated.
Revised	The network <u>is</u> growing. It <u>is</u> much larger than its developers anticipated.

Test 2: Find the subject.

The subject of the sentence will usually come before the verb. If there is no subject, the word group is probably a fragment:

Fragment	And has enormous popular appeal.
Revised	And <u>the Web</u> has enormous popular appeal.

In one kind of complete sentence, a command, the subject *you* is understood: [*You*] *Experiment with the Web.*

CULTURE LANGUAGE Some languages allow the omission of the sentence subject, especially when it is a pronoun. But in English, except in commands, the subject is always stated.

Key terms

predicate The part of a sentence containing a verb that asserts something about the subject: *Ducks <u>swim</u>.* (See pp. 172–73.)

verbal A verb form that can serve as a noun, a modifier, or a part of a sentence verb, but not alone as the only verb of a sentence: *drawing, to draw, drawn.* (See p. 177.)

helping verb A verb such as *is, were, have, might,* and *could* that combines with various verb forms to indicate time and other kinds of meaning: for instance, *<u>were</u> drawing, <u>might</u> draw.* (See p. 169.)

subject The part of a sentence that names who or what performs the action or makes the assertion of the predicate: *<u>Ducks</u> swim.* (See pp. 172–73.)

Fragment	Web commerce has expanded. Has hurt traditional stores.
Revised	Web commerce has expanded. <u>It</u> has hurt traditional stores.

Test 3: Make sure the clause is not subordinate.

A subordinate clause usually begins with a subordinating word, such as one of the following:

Subordinating conjunctions			Relative pronouns	
after	once	until	that	who/whom
although	since	when	which	whoever/whomever
as	than	where		whose
because	that	whereas		
if	unless	while		

Subordinate clauses serve as parts of sentences (as nouns or modifiers), not as whole sentences:

Fragment	When the government devised the Internet.
Revised	The government devised the Internet.
Revised	When the government devised the Internet, <u>no expansive computer network existed.</u>
Fragment	The reason that the government devised the Internet.
Revised	The reason that the government devised the Internet <u>was to link departments and defense contractors.</u>

Note Questions beginning with *how, what, when, where, which, who, whom, whose,* and *why* are not sentence fragments: *Who was responsible? When did it happen?*

35b Revise sentence fragments.

Almost all sentence fragments can be corrected in one of the two ways shown in the box on the facing page. The choice depends on the importance of the information in the fragment and thus how much you want to stress it.

35c Be aware of the acceptable uses of incomplete sentences.

A few word groups lacking the usual subject-predicate combination are incomplete sentences, but they are not fragments because they conform to the expectations of most readers. They include commands (*Move along. Shut the window.*); exclamations (*Oh*

Key term

subordinate clause A word group that contains a subject and a predicate, begins with a subordinating word such as *because* or *who,* and is not a question: *Ducks can swim <u>when they are young</u>.* A subordinate clause may serve as a modifier or as a noun. (See p. 179.)

Revision of sentence fragments

Option 1

Rewrite the fragment as a complete sentence. This revision gives the information in the fragment the same importance as that in other complete sentences.

Fragment	A major improvement in public health occurred with the widespread use of vaccines. <u>Which protected children against life-threatening diseases.</u>
Revised	A major improvement in public health occurred with the widespread use of vaccines. They protected children against life-threatening diseases.

Two main clauses may be separated by a semicolon instead of a period (see **5** p. 262).

Option 2

Combine the fragment with a main clause. This revision subordinates the information in the fragment to the information in the main clause.

Fragment	The polio vaccine eradicated the disease from most of the globe. <u>The first vaccine to be used widely.</u>
Revised	The polio vaccine**,** the first to be used widely**,** eradicated the disease from most of the globe.

no!); questions and answers (*Where next? To Kansas.*); and descriptions in employment résumés (*Weekly volunteer in soup kitchen.*)

Experienced writers sometimes use sentence fragments when they want to achieve a special effect. Such fragments appear more in informal than in formal writing. Unless you are experienced and thoroughly secure in your own writing, you should avoid all fragments and concentrate on writing clear, well-formed sentences.

36 Comma Splices and Fused Sentences

When two main clauses fall in a row, readers need a signal that one main clause is ending and another is beginning. The four ways to provide this signal appear in the box on the next page.

mycomplab

Visit *mycomplab.com* for more resources as well as exercises on comma splices and fused sentences.

Punctuation of two or more main clauses

■ **Separate main clauses with periods.**

Main clause **.** Main clause **.**

Hybrid cars are popular with consumers **.** Automakers are releasing new models.

■ **Link main clauses with a coordinating conjunction and a comma.**

Main clause **,** *for and or*
so but nor main clause **.**
yet

Hybrid cars are popular with consumers **,** and automakers are releasing new models.

■ **Link main clauses with a semicolon.**

Main clause **;** main clause **.**

Hybrid cars are popular with consumers **;** automakers are releasing new models.

■ **Relate main clauses with a semicolon and a conjunctive adverb or transitional expression.**

Main clause **;** *however,*
for example, **,** main clause **.**
etc.

Hybrid cars are popular with consumers **;** as a result **,** automakers are releasing new models.

Two problems in punctuating main clauses fail to signal the break between main clauses. One is the **comma splice**, in which the clauses are joined (or spliced) *only* with a comma.

┌─ **Key terms** ───

main clause A word group that can stand alone as a sentence because it contains a subject and a predicate and does not begin with a subordinating word: *A dictionary is essential.*

coordinating conjunction *And, but, or, nor, for, so, yet.* (See p. 171.)

conjunctive adverb A modifier that describes the relation of the ideas in two clauses, such as *consequently, however, indeed,* and *therefore.* (See p. 243.)

Comma splice   The ship was huge, its mast stood eighty feet high.

The other is the **fused sentence** (or **run-on sentence**), in which no punctuation or conjunction appears between the clauses.

Fused sentence   The ship was huge its mast stood eighty feet high.

Grammar checkers A grammar checker can detect many comma splices, but it will miss most fused sentences. For example, a checker flagged *Money is tight, we need to spend carefully* but not *Money is tight we need to spend carefully*. A checker may also question sentences that are actually correct, such as *Money being tighter now than before, we need to spend carefully*.

(CULTURE LANGUAGE) In standard American English, a sentence may not include more than one main clause unless the clauses are separated by a comma and a coordinating conjunction or by a semicolon. If your native language does not have such a rule or has accustomed you to writing long sentences, you may need to edit your English writing especially for comma splices and fused sentences.

36a | Separate main clauses not joined by *and, but,* or another coordinating conjunction.

If your readers point out comma splices or fused sentences in your writing, you're not creating enough separation between main clauses in your sentences. Punctuate consecutive main clauses in the following ways.

Separate sentences

Make the clauses into separate sentences when the ideas expressed are only loosely related:

Comma splice   Chemistry has contributed much to our understanding of foods, many foods such as wheat and beans can be produced in the laboratory.

Revised   Chemistry has contributed much to our understanding of foods. Many foods such as wheat and beans can be produced in the laboratory.

Coordinating conjunction

Insert a coordinating conjunction in a comma splice when the ideas in the main clauses are closely related and equally important:

Comma splice   Some laboratory-grown foods taste good, they are nutritious.

| Revised | Some laboratory-grown foods taste good, <u>and</u> they are nutritious. |

In a fused sentence insert a comma and a coordinating conjunction:

| Fused sentence | Chemists have made much progress they still have a way to go. |
| Revised | Chemists have made much progress<u>,</u> <u>but</u> they still have a way to go. |

Semicolon

Insert a semicolon between clauses if the relation between the ideas is very close and obvious without a conjunction:

| Comma splice | Good taste is rare in laboratory-grown vegetables, they are usually bland. |
| Revised | Good taste is rare in laboratory-grown vegetables<u>;</u> they are usually bland. |

Subordination

When one idea is less important than the other, express the less important idea in a subordinate clause:

| Comma splice | The vitamins are adequate, the flavor is deficient. |
| Revised | <u>Even though</u> the vitamins are adequate, the flavor is deficient. |

36b Separate main clauses related by *however, for example,* and so on.

Two groups of words, shown in the box opposite, describe how one main clause relates to another: **conjunctive adverbs** and other **transitional expressions**. (See **1** pp. 36–37 for a longer list of transitional expressions.)

When two main clauses are related by a conjunctive adverb or another transitional expression, they must be separated by a period or by a semicolon. The adverb or expression is also generally set off by a comma or commas.

Key term

subordinate clause A word group that contains a subject and a predicate, begins with a subordinating word such as *because* or *who,* and is not a question: *Ducks can swim <u>when they are young</u>.* A subordinate clause may serve as a modifier or as a noun. (See p. 179.)

Common conjunctive adverbs and transitional expressions

accordingly	for instance	instead	on the contrary
anyway	further	in the meantime	otherwise
as a result	furthermore	in the past	similarly
at last	hence	likewise	still
besides	however	meanwhile	that is
certainly	incidentally	moreover	then
consequently	in contrast	namely	thereafter
even so	indeed	nevertheless	therefore
finally	in fact	nonetheless	thus
for all that	in other words	now	undoubtedly
for example	in short	of course	until now

Comma splice	Healthcare costs are higher in the United States than in many other countries, <u>consequently</u> health insurance is also more costly.
Revised	Healthcare costs are higher in the United States than in many other countries. <u>Consequently,</u> health insurance is also more costly.
Revised	Healthcare costs are higher in the United States than in many other countries; <u>consequently,</u> health insurance is also more costly.

Conjunctive adverbs and transitional expressions are different from coordinating conjunctions (*and, but,* and so on) and subordinating conjunctions (*although, because,* and so on):

- Unlike conjunctions, conjunctive adverbs and transitional expressions do not join two clauses into a grammatical unit. They merely describe the way two clauses relate in meaning.

- Unlike conjunctions, conjunctive adverbs and transitional expressions can be moved within a clause. No matter where in the clause an adverb or expression falls, though, the clause must be separated from another main clause by a period or semicolon:

Most Americans refuse to give up unhealthful habits; our medical costs, <u>consequently,</u> are higher than those of many other countries.

37 Mixed Sentences

A **mixed sentence** contains parts that do not fit together. The misfit may be in meaning or in grammar.

Grammar checkers A grammar checker may recognize a simple mixed construction such as *reason is because,* but it will fail to flag most mixed sentences.

37a Match subjects and predicates in meaning.

In a sentence with mixed meaning, the subject is said to do or be something illogical. Such a mixture is sometimes called **faulty predication** because the predicate conflicts with the subject.

1 Illogical equation with *be*

When a form of *be* connects a subject and a word that describes the subject (a complement), the subject and complement must be logically related:

> **Mixed** A compromise between the city and the country would be the ideal place to live.

> **Revised** A community that offered the best qualities of both city and country would be the ideal place to live.

2 *Is when, is where*

Definitions require nouns on both sides of *be.* Clauses that define and begin with *when* or *where* are common in speech but should be avoided in writing:

> **Mixed** An examination is when you are tested on what you know.

> **Revised** An examination is a test of what you know.

Key terms

subject The part of a sentence that names who or what performs the action or makes the assertion of the predicate: <u>Geese</u> fly. (See pp. 172–73.)

predicate The part of a sentence containing a verb that asserts something about the subject: Geese <u>fly</u>. (See pp. 172–73.)

Visit *mycomplab.com* for more resources on mixed sentences.

3 *Reason is because*

The commonly heard construction *reason is because* is redundant since *because* means "for the reason that":

Mixed	The <u>reason</u> the temple requests donations <u>is because</u> the school needs expansion.
Revised	The <u>reason</u> the temple requests donations <u>is that</u> the school needs expansion.
Revised	The temple requests donations <u>because</u> the school needs expansion.

4 Other mixed meanings

Faulty predications are not confined to sentences with *be:*

Mixed	The <u>use</u> of emission controls <u>was created</u> to reduce air pollution.
Revised	Emission <u>controls were created</u> to reduce air pollution.

37b Untangle sentences that are mixed in grammar.

Many mixed sentences start with one grammatical plan or construction but end with a different one:

Mixed	— modifier (prepositional phrase) — verb By paying more attention to impressions than facts leads us to misjudge others.
Revised	— modifier (prepositional phrase) — subject By paying more attention to impressions than facts, <u>we</u> verb <u>misjudge</u> others.

Constructions that use *Just because* clauses as subjects are common in speech but should be avoided in writing:

Mixed	— modifier (subordinate clause) — verb — Just because no one is watching doesn't mean we have license to break the law.
Revised	— modifier (subordinate clause) — subject + verb Even when no one is watching, <u>we don't have</u> license to break the law.

A mixed sentence is especially likely when you are working on a computer and connect parts of two sentences or rewrite half a sentence but not the other half. A mixed sentence may also occur when you don't make the subject and predicate verb carry the principal meaning. (See **3** p. 130.)

37c State parts of sentences, such as subjects, only once.

In some languages other than English, certain parts of sentences may be repeated. These include the subject in any kind of clause or an object or adverb in an adjective clause. In English, however, these parts are stated only once in a clause.

1 Repetition of subject

You may be tempted to restate a subject as a pronoun before the verb. But the subject needs stating only once in its clause:

Faulty   The liquid it reached a temperature of 180°F.
Revised   The liquid reached a temperature of 180°F.

Faulty   Gases in the liquid they escaped.
Revised   Gases in the liquid escaped.

2 Repetition in an adjective clause

Adjective clauses begin with *who, whom, whose, which, that, where,* and *when* (see also pp. 193–94). The beginning word replaces another word: the subject (*He is the person who called*), an object of a verb or preposition (*He is the person whom I mentioned*), or a preposition and pronoun (*He knows the office where [in which] the conference will occur*).
Do not state the word being replaced in an adjective clause:

Faulty   The technician whom the test depended on her was burned. [*Whom* should replace *her.*]
Revised   The technician whom the test depended on was burned.

Adjective clauses beginning with *where* or *when* do not need an adverb such as *there* or *then:*

Faulty   Gases escaped at a moment when the technician was unprepared then.
Revised   Gases escaped at a moment when the technician was unprepared.

Note *Whom, which,* and similar words are sometimes omitted but are still understood by the reader. Thus the word being replaced should not be stated.

Faulty   Accidents rarely happen to technicians the lab has trained *them.* [*Whom* is understood: . . . *technicians whom the lab has trained.*]
Revised   Accidents rarely happen to technicians the lab has trained.

Punctuation

MICHIGAN STATE
U N I V E R S I T Y

38 End Punctuation

End a sentence with one of three punctuation marks: a period (.), a question mark (?), or an exclamation point (!).

Grammar checkers A grammar checker may flag missing question marks after direct questions or incorrect combinations of marks (such as a question mark and a period at the end of a sentence), but it cannot do much else.

38a Use a period after most sentences and with some abbreviations.

1 Statements, mild commands, and indirect questions

Statement

The airline went bankrupt.   It no longer flies.

Mild command

Think of the possibilities.   Please consider others.

Indirect question

An **indirect question** reports what someone asked but not in the exact form or words of the original question:

The judge asked why I had been driving with my lights off.
No one asked how we got home.

 In standard American English, an indirect question uses the wording and subject-verb order of a statement: *The reporter asked why the negotiations failed* [not *why did the negotiations fail*].

2 Abbreviations

Use periods with abbreviations that consist of or end in small letters. Otherwise, omit periods from abbreviations.

Dr.	Mr., Mrs.	e.g.	Feb.	ft.
St.	Ms.	i.e.	p.	a.m., p.m.
PhD	BC, BCE	USA	IBM	AM, PM
BA	AD, CE	US	USMC	AIDS

Note When a sentence ends in an abbreviation with a period, don't add a second period: *My first class is at 8 a.m.*

Visit *mycomplab.com* for more resources as well as exercises on end eunctuation.

38b Use a question mark after a direct question and sometimes to indicate doubt.

1 Direct questions

Who will follow her**?**
What is the difference between these two people**?**

After indirect questions, use a period: *We wondered who would follow her.* (See the preceding page.)

Questions in a series are each followed by a question mark:

The officer asked how many times the suspect had been arrested. Three times**?** Four times**?** More than that**?**

Note Do not combine question marks with other question marks, periods, commas, or other punctuation.

2 Doubt

A question mark within parentheses can indicate doubt about a number or date.

The Greek philosopher Socrates was born in 470 **(?)** BC and died in 399 BC from drinking poison. [Socrates's birthdate is not known for sure.]

Use sentence structure and words, not a question mark, to express sarcasm or irony.

Not   Stern's friendliness (?) bothered Crane.
But   Stern's <u>insincerity</u> bothered Crane.

38c Use an exclamation point after an emphatic statement, interjection, or command.

No**!** We must not lose this election**!**
Come here immediately**!**

Follow mild interjections and commands with commas or periods, as appropriate: *Oh, call whenever you can.*

Note Do not combine exclamation points with periods, commas, or other punctuation marks. And use exclamation points sparingly, even in informal writing. Overused, they'll fail to impress readers, and they may make you sound overemotional.

Key term

interjection A word that expresses feeling or commands attention, either alone or within a sentence: *Oh! Hey! Wow!*

39 The Comma

The comma (,) is the most common punctuation mark inside sentences. Its main uses are shown in the box on the next page.

Grammar checkers A grammar checker will ignore many comma errors. For example, a checker failed to catch the missing commas in *We cooked lasagna_spinach_and apple pie* and the misused commas in *The trip was short but, the weather was perfect* and *The travelers were tempted by, the many shops.*

39a | Use a comma before *and, but,* or another coordinating conjunction linking main clauses.

When a coordinating conjunction links words or phrases, do not use a comma: *Dugain plays_and sings Irish_and English folk songs.* However, *do* use a comma when a coordinating conjunction joins main clauses, as in the next examples.

> Caffeine can keep coffee drinkers alert, and it may elevate their mood.
>
> Caffeine was once thought to be safe, but now researchers warn of harmful effects.
>
> Coffee drinkers may suffer sleeplessness, for the drug acts as a stimulant to the nervous system.

Note The comma goes *before*, not after, a coordinating conjunction that links main clauses: *Caffeine increases heart rate, and it* [not *and, it*] *constricts blood vessels.*

Exception Some writers omit the comma between main clauses that are very short and closely related in meaning: *Caffeine helps but it also hurts.* If you are in doubt about whether to use the comma in such a sentence, use it. It will always be correct.

┌─ **Key terms** ───

coordinating conjunctions *And, but, or, nor,* and sometimes *for, so, yet.* (See **4** p. 171.)

main clause A word group that can stand alone as a sentence because it contains a subject and a predicate and does not begin with a subordinating word: *Water freezes at temperatures below 32°F.* (See **4** p. 179.)

└──

Visit *mycomplab.com* for more resources as well as exercises on the comma.

250

Principal uses of the comma

■ **Separate main clauses linked by a coordinating conjunction** (previous page):

| Main clause | , | for and or
so but nor
yet | main clause | • |

The building is finished , but it has no tenants.

■ **Set off most introductory elements** (opposite):

| Introductory
element | , | main clause | • |

Unfortunately , the only tenant pulled out.

■ **Set off nonessential elements** (p. 253):

| Main clause | , | nonessential
element | • |

The empty building symbolizes a weak local economy , which affects everyone.

| Beginning of
main clause | , | nonessential
element | , | end of
main clause | • |

The primary cause , the decline of local industry , is not news.

■ **Separate items in a series** (p. 257):

| . . . | item 1 | , | item 2 | , | and
or | item 3 | . . . |

The city needs healthier businesses , new schools , and improved housing.

■ **Separate coordinate adjectives** (p. 257):

| . . . | first
adjective | , | second
adjective | word
modified | . . . |

A tall , sleek skyscraper is not needed.

Other uses of the comma:

Separate parts of dates, addresses, long numbers (p. 258).
Separate quotations and signal phrases (p. 258).

See also p. 259 for when *not* to use the comma.

39b Use a comma to set off most introductory elements.

An **introductory element** begins a sentence and modifies a word or words in the main clause. It is usually followed by a comma.

Subordinate clause

Even when identical twins are raised apart, they grow up very like each other.

Verbal or verbal phrase

Explaining the similarity, some researchers claim that one's genes are one's destiny.

Concerned, other researchers deny the claim.

Prepositional phrase

In a debate that has lasted centuries, scientists use identical twins to argue for or against genetic destiny.

Transitional expression

Of course, scientists can now look directly at the genes themselves to answer questions.

You may omit the comma after a short subordinate clause or prepositional phrase if its omission does not create confusion: *When snow falls the city collapses. By the year 2000 the world population had topped 6 billion.* You may also omit the comma after some transitional expressions when they start sentences: *Thus the debate continues* (see p. 256). However, in both situations the comma is never wrong.

Note Take care to distinguish *-ing* words used as modifiers from *-ing* words used as subjects. The former almost always take a comma; the latter never do.

Key terms

subordinate clause A word group that contains a subject and a predicate, begins with a subordinating word such as *because* or *who,* and is not a question: *When water freezes, crystals form.* (See **4** p. 179.)

verbal A verb form used as an adjective, adverb, or noun. A verbal plus any object or modifier is a **verbal phrase:** *frozen water, ready to freeze, rapid freezing.* (See **4** p. 177.)

prepositional phrase A word group consisting of a preposition, such as *for* or *in,* followed by a noun or pronoun plus any modifiers: *in a jar, with a spoon.* (See **4** p. 177.)

transitional expression A word or phrase that shows the relationship between sentences: *for example, however, in fact, of course.* (See **1** pp. 36–37.)

┌───── modifier ─────┐   subject   verb
Studying identical twins, geneticists learn about inheritance.
┌───── subject ─────┐ verb
Studying identical twins helps geneticists learn about inheritance.

39c Use a comma or commas to set off nonessential elements.

Commas around part of a sentence often signal that the element is not necessary to the meaning. This **nonessential element** may modify or rename the word it refers to, but it does not limit the word to a particular individual or group. The meaning of the word would still be clear if the element were deleted:

Nonessential element

The company, which is located in Oklahoma, has a good reputation.

(Because it does not restrict meaning, a nonessential element is also called a **nonrestrictive element**.)

In contrast, an **essential** (or **restrictive**) **element** *does* limit the word it refers to: the element cannot be omitted without leaving the meaning too general. Because it is essential, such an element is *not* set off with a comma or commas.

Essential element

The company rewards employees who work hard.

Omitting the underlined words would distort the meaning: the company doesn't necessarily reward *all* employees, only the hardworking ones.

The same element in the same sentence may be essential or nonessential depending on your meaning and the context:

Essential

Not all the bands were equally well received, however. The band playing old music held the audience's attention. The other groups created much less excitement. [*Playing old music* identifies a particular band.]

Nonessential

A new band called Fats made its debut on Saturday night. The band, playing old music, held the audience's attention. If this performance is typical, the group has a bright future. [*Playing old music* adds information about a band already named.]

Note When a nonessential element falls in the middle of a sentence, be sure to set it off with a pair of commas, one *before* and one *after* the element.

A test for nonessential and essential elements

1. Identify the element:

Hai Nguyen who emigrated from Vietnam lives in Dallas.
Those who emigrated with him live elsewhere.

2. Remove the element. Does the fundamental meaning of the sentence change?

Hai Nguyen lives in Dallas. *No.*
Those live elsewhere. *Yes.* [Who are *Those?*]

3. If *no,* the element is *nonessential* and *should* be set off with punctuation:

Hai Nguyen, who emigrated from Vietnam, lives in Dallas.

If *yes,* the element is *essential* and should *not* be set off with punctuation:

Those who emigrated with him live elsewhere.

---

1 Nonessential phrases and clauses

Most nonessential phrases and subordinate clauses function as adjectives or, less commonly, as adverbs. In each of the following examples, the underlined words could be omitted with no loss of clarity.

> Elizabeth Blackwell was the first woman to graduate from an American medical school, in 1849. [Phrase.]
>
> She was a medical pioneer, helping to found the first medical college for women. [Phrase.]
>
> She taught at the school, which was affiliated with the New York Infirmary. [Clause.]
>
> Blackwell, who published books and papers on medicine, practiced pediatrics and gynecology. [Clause.]

Note Use *that* only in an essential clause, never in a nonessential clause: *. . . school, which* [not *that*] *was affiliated. . . .* Many writers reserve *which* for nonessential clauses.

Key terms

phrase A word group lacking a subject or a verb or both: *in Duluth, carrying water.* (See **4** p. 177.)

subordinate clause A word group that contains a subject and a predicate, begins with a subordinating word such as *who* or *although,* and is not a question: *Samson, who won a gold medal, coaches in Utah.* (See **4** p. 179.)

2 Nonessential appositives

A nonessential appositive merely adds information about the word it refers to.

Toni Morrison's fifth novel, _Beloved_, won the Pulitzer Prize in 1988. [The word _fifth_ identifies the novel, while the title adds a detail.]

In contrast, an essential appositive limits or defines the word it refers to:

Morrison's novel _The Bluest Eye_ is about an African American girl who longs for blue eyes. [Morrison has written more than one novel, so the title is essential to identify the intended one.]

3 Other nonessential elements

Like nonessential modifiers or appositives, many other elements contribute to texture, tone, or overall clarity but are not essential to the meaning. Unlike nonessential modifiers or appositives, these other nonessential elements generally do not refer to any specific word in the sentence.

Note Use a pair of commas—one before, one after—when any of these elements falls in the middle of a sentence.

Absolute phrases

Household recycling having succeeded, the city now wants to extend the program to businesses.

Many businesses, their profits already squeezed, resist recycling.

Parenthetical and transitional expressions

Generally, set off parenthetical and transitional expressions with commas:

The world's most celebrated holiday is, perhaps surprisingly, New Year's Day. [Parenthetical expression.]

Interestingly, Americans have relatively few holidays. [Parenthetical expression.]

Key terms

appositive A noun that renames another noun immediately before it: _His wife, Kyra Sedgwick, is also an actor._ (See **4** p. 179.)

absolute phrase A phrase modifying a whole main clause and consisting of a participle and its subject: _Their homework completed, the children watched TV._ (See **4** p. 178.)

parenthetical expression An explanatory or supplemental word or phrase, such as _all things considered, to be frank,_ or a brief example. (See p. 276.)

transitional expression A word or phrase that shows the relationship between sentences: _for example, however, in fact, of course._ (See **1** pp. 36–37.)

US workers **,** for example **,** receive fewer holidays than European workers do. [Transitional expression.]

(Dashes and parentheses may also set off parenthetical expressions. See pp. 275–76.)

When a transitional expression links main clauses, precede it with a semicolon and follow it with a comma (see pp. 262–63):

European workers often have long paid vacations **;** indeed **,** they may receive a full month after just a few years with a company.

Exception The conjunctions *and* and *but*, sometimes used as transitional expressions, are never followed by commas (see p. 252). Usage varies with some other transitional expressions, depending on the expression and the writer's judgment. Many writers omit commas with expressions that we read without pauses, such as *also, hence, next, now, then,* and *thus.* The same applies to *therefore* and *instead* when they fall inside or at the ends of clauses.

US workers therefore put in more work days. But the days themselves may be shorter.

Then the total hours worked would come out roughly the same.

Phrases of contrast

The substance **,** not the style **,** is important.

Substance **,** unlike style **,** cannot be faked.

Tag questions

They don't stop to consider others **,** do they?

Jones should be allowed to vote **,** shouldn't he?

Yes **and** *no*

Yes **,** the editorial did have a point.

No **,** that can never be.

Words of direct address

Cody **,** please bring me the newspaper.

With all due respect **,** sir **,** I will not.

Mild interjections

Well **,** you will never know who did it.

Oh **,** they forgot all about the baby.

Key terms

tag question A question at the end of a statement, consisting of a pronoun, a helping verb, and sometimes *not: It isn't wet, is it?*

interjection A word that expresses feeling or commands attention: *Oh, must we?*

39d Use commas between items in a series.

A **series** consists of three or more items of equal importance. The items may be words, phrases, or clauses.

> Anna Spingle married at the age of seventeen, had three children by twenty-one, and divorced at twenty-two.
> She worked as a cook, a baby-sitter, and a crossing guard.

Some writers omit the comma before the coordinating conjunction in a series (*Breakfast consisted of coffee, eggs and kippers*). But the final comma is never wrong, and it always helps the reader see the last two items as separate.

39e Use commas between two or more adjectives that equally modify the same word.

Adjectives that equally modify the same word—**coordinate adjectives**—may be separated either by *and* or by a comma.

> Spingle's scratched and dented car is old, but it gets her to work.
> She has dreams of a sleek, shiny car.

Adjectives are not coordinate—and should not be separated by commas—when the one nearer the noun is more closely related to the noun in meaning.

> Spingle's children work at various part-time jobs.
> They all expect to go to a nearby community college.

Tests for commas with adjectives

1. **Identify the adjectives.**

   She was a faithful sincere friend.
   They are dedicated medical students.

2. **Can the adjectives be reversed without changing meaning?**

   She was a sincere faithful friend. *Yes.*
   They are medical dedicated students. *No.*

3. **Can the word *and* be sensibly inserted between the adjectives?**

   She was a faithful and sincere friend. *Yes.*
   They are dedicated and medical students. *No.*

4. If *yes* to both questions, the adjectives *are* coordinate and *should* be separated by a comma.

She was a faithful, sincere friend.

If *no* to both questions, the adjectives are *not* coordinate and should *not* be separated by a comma.

They are dedicated medical students.

39f Use commas in dates, addresses, place names, and long numbers.

Within a sentence, any date, address, or place name that contains a comma should also end with a comma.

Dates

July 4, 1776, is the date the Declaration was signed.

The bombing of Pearl Harbor on Sunday, December 7, 1941, prompted American entry into World War II.

Do not use commas between the parts of a date in inverted order (*15 December 1992*) or in dates consisting of a month or season and a year (*December 1941*).

Addresses and place names

Use the address 220 Cornell Road, Woodside, California 94062, for all letters. [Do not use a comma between a state name and a zip code.]

Columbus, Ohio, is the location of Ohio State University.

Long numbers

Use the comma to separate the figures in long numbers into groups of three, counting from the right. With numbers of four digits, the comma is optional.

The new assembly plant cost $7,525,000.

A kilometer is 3,281 feet [*or* 3281 feet].

CULTURE LANGUAGE Usage in standard American English differs from that in some other languages and dialects, which use a period, not a comma, to separate the figures in long numbers.

39g Use commas with quotations according to standard practice.

The words *she said, he writes,* and so on identify the source of a quotation. These **signal phrases** should be separated from the quotation by punctuation, usually a comma or commas.

"Knowledge is power," writes Francis Bacon.

"The shore has a dual nature," observes Rachel Carson, "changing with the swing of the tides." [The signal phrase interrupts the quotation at a comma and thus ends with a comma.]

Exceptions When a signal phrase interrupts a quotation between main clauses, follow the signal phrase with a semicolon or a period. The choice depends on the punctuation of the original.

Not   "That part of my life was over," she wrote, "his words had sealed it shut."

But   "That part of my life was over," she wrote. "His words had sealed it shut." [*She wrote* interrupts the quotation at a period.]

Or   "That part of my life was over," she wrote; "his words had sealed it shut." [*She wrote* interrupts the quotation at a semicolon.]

Do not use a comma when a signal phrase follows a quotation ending in an exclamation point or a question mark:

"Claude!" Mrs. Harrison called.
"Why must I come home?" he asked.

Do not use a comma with a quotation that is integrated into your sentence structure, including one introduced by *that:*

James Baldwin insists that "one must never, in one's life, accept . . . injustices as commonplace."

Baldwin thought that the violence of a riot "had been devised as a corrective" to his own violence.

Do not use a comma with a quoted title unless it is a nonessential appositive:

The Beatles recorded "She Loves You" in 1963.

The Beatles' first huge US hit, "She Loves You," appeared in 1963.

39h Delete commas where they are not required.

Commas can make sentences choppy and even confusing if they are used more often than needed.

Key term

nonessential appositive A word or words that rename an immediately preceding noun but do not limit or define the noun: *The author's first story, "Biloxi," won a prize.* (See p. 255.)

1 No comma between subject and verb, verb and object, or preposition and object

Not The returning <u>soldiers, received</u> a warm welcome. [Separated subject and verb.]

But The returning <u>soldiers received</u> a warm welcome.

Not They had <u>chosen, to fight</u> for their country <u>despite, the risks</u>. [Separated verb *chosen* and its object; separated preposition *despite* and its object.]

But They had <u>chosen to fight</u> for their country <u>despite the risks</u>.

2 No comma in most compound constructions

Compound constructions consisting of two elements almost never require a comma. The only exception is the sentence consisting of two main clauses linked by a coordinating conjunction: *The computer failed, but employees kept working* (see p. 250).

compound subject

Not <u>Banks, and other financial institutions</u> have helped older people

compound object of preposition

with <u>money management, and investment</u>.

But <u>Banks and other financial institutions</u> have helped older people with <u>money management and investment</u>.

compound predicate

Not One bank <u>created</u> special accounts for older people, and held

compound object of verb

<u>classes, and workshops</u>.

But One bank <u>created</u> special accounts for older people and held <u>classes and workshops</u>.

3 No comma after a conjunction

Not Parents of adolescents notice increased conflict at puberty, <u>and,</u> they complain of bickering.

Key terms

compound construction Two or more words, phrases, or clauses connected by a coordinating conjunction, usually *and, but, or, nor*: *man and woman, old or young, leaking oil and spewing steam.*

conjunction A connecting word such as a **coordinating conjunction** (*and, but, or,* and so on) or a **subordinating conjunction** (*although, because, when,* and so on). (See 4 p. 171.)

But Parents of adolescents notice increased conflict at puberty, and they complain of bickering.

Not Although, other primates leave the family at adolescence, humans do not.

But Although other primates leave the family at adolescence, humans do not.

4 No commas around essential elements

Not Hawthorne's work, *The Scarlet Letter*, was the first major American novel. [The title is essential to distinguish the novel from the rest of Hawthorne's work.]

But Hawthorne's work *The Scarlet Letter* was the first major American novel.

Not The symbols, that Hawthorne uses, have influenced other novelists. [The clause identifies which symbols have been influential.]

But The symbols that Hawthorne uses have influenced other novelists.

5 No commas around a series

Commas separate the items *within* a series (p. 257) but do not separate the series from the rest of the sentence.

Not The skills of, hunting, herding, and agriculture, sustained the Native Americans.

But The skills of hunting herding, and agriculture sustained the Native Americans.

6 No comma before an indirect quotation

Not The report concluded, that dieting could be more dangerous than overeating.

But The report concluded that dieting could be more dangerous than overeating.

Key term

essential element Limits the word it refers to and thus can't be omitted without leaving the meaning too general. (See pp. 253–54.)

40 The Semicolon

The semicolon (;) separates equal and balanced sentence elements—usually main clauses (below) and occasionally items in series (p. 276).

Grammar checkers A grammar checker can spot a few errors in the use of semicolons. For example, a checker suggested using a semicolon after *perfect* in *The set was perfect, the director had planned every detail,* thus correcting a comma splice. But it missed the incorrect semicolon in *The set was perfect; deserted streets, dark houses, and gloomy mist* (a colon would be correct).

40a Use a semicolon between main clauses not joined by *and, but,* or another coordinating conjunction.

When no coordinating conjunction links two main clauses, the clauses should be separated by a semicolon.

> A new ulcer drug arrived on the market with a mixed reputation; doctors find that the drug works but worry about its side effects.

> The side effects are not minor; some leave the patient quite uncomfortable or even ill.

Note This rule prevents the errors known as comma splices and fused sentences. (See **4** pp. 241–42.)

40b Use a semicolon between main clauses related by *however, for example,* and so on.

When a conjunctive adverb or another transitional expression relates two main clauses in a single sentence, the clauses should be separated with a semicolon:

> An American immigrant, Levi Strauss, invented blue jeans in the 1860s; eventually, his product clothed working men throughout the West.

Key terms

main clause A word group that can stand alone as a sentence because it contains a subject and a predicate and does not begin with a subordinating word: *Parks help cities breathe.* (See **4** p. 179.)

coordinating conjunctions *And, but, or, nor,* and sometimes *for, so, yet.*

---

mycomplab

Visit *mycomplab.com* for more resources as well as exercises on the semicolon.

The position of the semicolon between main clauses never changes, but the conjunctive adverb or transitional expression may move around within the second clause. Wherever the adverb or expression falls, it is usually set off with a comma or commas. (See pp. 255–56.)

> Blue jeans have become fashionable all over the world; however, the American originators still wear more jeans than anyone else.

> Blue jeans have become fashionable all over the world; the American originators, however, still wear more jeans than anyone else.

> Blue jeans have become fashionable all over the world; the American originators still wear more jeans than anyone else, however.

Note This rule prevents the errors known as comma splices and fused sentences. (See **4** pp. 241–42.)

40c Use semicolons between main clauses or series items containing commas.

Normally, commas separate main clauses linked by coordinating conjunctions (*and, but, or, nor*) and separate items in a series. But when the clauses or series items contain commas, a semicolon between them makes the sentence easier to read.

> Lewis and Clark led the men of their party with consummate skill, inspiring and encouraging them, doctoring and caring for them; and they kept voluminous journals.   —Page Smith

> The custody case involved Amy Dalton, the child; Ellen and Mark Dalton, the parents; and Ruth and Hal Blum, the grandparents.

40d Delete or replace unneeded semicolons.

Too many semicolons can make writing choppy. And semicolons are often misused in certain constructions that call for other punctuation or no punctuation.

Key terms

conjunctive adverb A modifier that describes the relation of the ideas in two clauses, such as *consequently, hence, however, indeed, instead, nonetheless, otherwise, still, then, therefore, thus*. (See **4** p. 243.)

transitional expression A word or phrase that shows the relationship between ideas. Transitional expressions include conjunctive adverbs as well as *for example, in fact, of course*, and many other words and phrases. (See **1** pp. 36–37.)

1 No semicolon between a main clause and a subordinate clause or phrase

The semicolon does not separate unequal parts, such as main clauses and subordinate clauses or phrases.

> Not Pygmies are in danger of extinction; because of encroaching development.
>
> But Pygmies are in danger of extinction because of encroaching development.

> Not According to African authorities; only about 35,000 Pygmies exist today.
>
> But According to African authorities, only about 35,000 Pygmies exist today.

2 No semicolon before a series or explanation

Colons and dashes, not semicolons, introduce series, explanations, and so forth. (See the next page and p. 276.)

> Not Teachers have heard all sorts of reasons why students do poorly; psychological problems, family illness, too much work, too little time.
>
> But Teachers have heard all sorts of reasons why students do poorly: psychological problems, family illness, too much work, too little time.

41 The Colon

The colon (:) is mainly a mark of introduction: it signals that the words following will explain or amplify (next page). The colon also has several conventional uses, such as in expressions of time (p. 266).

Grammar checkers Many grammar checkers cannot recognize missing or misused colons and instead simply ignore them.

Visit *mycomplab.com* for more resources as well as exercises on the colon.

41a Use a colon to introduce a concluding explanation, a series, an appositive, and some quotations.

As an introducer, a colon is always preceded by a complete main clause. It may or may not be followed by a main clause. This is one way the colon differs from the semicolon, which generally separates main clauses only. (See pp. 262–63.)

Explanation
Soul food has a deceptively simple definition: the ethnic cooking of African Americans.

Sometimes a concluding explanation is preceded by *the following* or *as follows* and a colon:

A more precise definition might be the following: soul food draws on ingredients, cooking methods, and dishes that originated in Africa, were brought to the New World by slaves, and were modified or supplemented in the Caribbean and the American South.

Note A complete sentence *after* a colon may begin with a capital letter or a small letter (as in the preceding example). Just be consistent throughout an essay.

Series
At least three soul food dishes are familiar to most Americans: fried chicken, barbecued spareribs, and sweet potatoes.

Appositive
Soul food has only one disadvantage: fat.

Namely, that is, and other expressions that introduce appositives *follow* the colon: *Soul food has only one disadvantage: namely, fat.*

Quotation
One soul food chef has a solution: "Soul food doesn't have to be greasy to taste good. Instead of using ham hocks to flavor beans, I use smoked turkey wings. The soulful, smoky taste remains, but without all the fat of pork."

Use a colon before a quotation when the introduction is a complete sentence.

Key terms

main clause A word group that can stand alone as a sentence because it contains a subject and a predicate and does not begin with a subordinating word: *Soul food is a varied cuisine.* (See **4** p. 179.)

appositive A noun or noun substitute that renames another noun immediately before it: *my brother, Jack.* (See **4** p. 179.)

41b Use a colon after the salutation of a business letter, between a title and subtitle, and between divisions of time.

Salutation of business letter
Dear Ms. Burak:

Title and subtitle
Charles Dickens: An Introduction to His Novels

Time
12:26 AM   6:00 PM

41c Delete or replace unneeded colons.

Use the colon only at the end of a main clause, not in the following situations:

■ **Delete a colon after a verb.**

Not   The best-known soul food dish is: fried chicken.
But   The best-known soul food dish is fried chicken.

■ **Delete a colon after a preposition.**

Not   Soul food recipes can be found in: mainstream cookbooks as well as specialized references.
But   Soul food recipes can be found in mainstream cookbooks as well as specialized references.

■ **Delete a colon after *such as* or *including*.**

Not   Many Americans have not tasted delicacies such as: chitlins and black-eyed peas.
But   Many Americans have not tasted delicacies such as chitlins and black-eyed peas.

Key term

preposition *In, on, outside,* or another word that takes a noun or pronoun as its object: *in the house.* (See **4** p. 170.)

42 The Apostrophe

The apostrophe (') appears as part of a word to indicate possession (below), the omission of one or more letters (p. 270), or sometimes plural number (p. 270).

Grammar checkers A grammar checker usually has mixed results in recognizing apostrophe errors. For instance, it may flag missing apostrophes in contractions (as in *isnt*) but may not distinguish between *its* and *it's*, *their* and *they're*, *your* and *you're*, *whose* and *who's*. A checker may identify some apostrophe errors in possessives but overlook others, and it may flag correct plurals. Instead of relying on your checker, try using your computer's Search or Find function to hunt for all words you have ended in *-s*. Then check them to ensure that apostrophes are used correctly.

42a Use the apostrophe to show possession.

A noun or indefinite pronoun shows possession with an apostrophe and, usually, an *-s: the dog's hair, everyone's hope*. Only personal pronouns such as *hers* and *its* do not use apostrophes for possession.

Note Apostrophes are easy to misuse. Always check your drafts to be sure that all words ending in *-s* neither omit needed apostrophes nor add unneeded ones. Also, remember that the apostrophe or apostrophe-plus-*s* is an *addition*. Before this addition, always spell the name of the owner or owners without dropping or adding letters.

1 Singular words: Add -'s.

Bill Boughton's skillful card tricks amaze children.
Anyone's eyes would widen.
Most tricks will pique an adult's curiosity, too.

The *-'s* ending for singular words pertains also to singular words ending in *-s,* as the next examples show.

Henry James's novels reward the patient reader.
The business's customers filed suit.

> **Key term**
>
> **indefinite pronoun** A pronoun that does not refer to a specific person or thing, such as *anyone, each, everybody, no one,* or *something.* (See **4** p. 217.)

mycomplab

Visit *mycomplab.com* for more resources as well as exercises on the apostrophe.

Uses and misuses of the apostrophe

Uses of the apostrophe

■ **Use an apostrophe to form the possessives of nouns and indefinite pronouns** (previous page).

Singular	Plural
Ms. Park's	the Parks'
lawyer's	lawyers'
everyone's	two weeks'

■ **Use an apostrophe to form contractions** (p. 270).

it's a girl	shouldn't
you're	won't

■ **The apostrophe is optional for plurals of abbreviations, dates, and words or characters named as words** (p. 270).

MAs or MA's	Cs or C's
1960s or 1960's	ifs or if's

Misuses of the apostrophe

■ **Do not use an apostrophe plus -s to form the possessives of plural nouns ending in -s** (next page). Instead, use an apostrophe alone after the -s that forms the plural.

Not	But
the Kim's car	the Kims' car
boy's fathers	boys' fathers

■ **Do not use an apostrophe to form plurals of nouns** (p. 269).

Not	But
book's are	books are
the Freed's	the Freeds

■ **Do not use an apostrophe with verbs ending in -s** (p. 269).

Not	But
swim's	swims

■ **Do not use an apostrophe to form the possessives of personal pronouns** (p. 270).

Not	But
it's toes	its toes
your's	yours

Exception An apostrophe alone may be added to a singular word ending in -s when another s would make the word difficult to say: *Moses'* mother, *Joan Rivers'* jokes. But the added -s is never wrong (*Moses's*, *Rivers's*).

2 Plural words ending in *-s:* Add -' only.

<u>Workers</u>' incomes have fallen slightly over the past year.

Many students benefit from several <u>years</u>' work after high school.

The <u>Jameses</u>' talents are extraordinary.

Note the difference in the possessives of singular and plural words ending in *-s*. The singular form usually takes the apostrophe plus *-s: James's.* The plural takes only the apostrophe: *Jameses'.*

3 Plural words not ending in -s: Add -'s.

<u>Children</u>'s educations are at stake.

We need to attract the <u>media</u>'s attention.

4 Compound words: Add -'s only to the last word.

The <u>brother-in-law</u>'s business failed.

Taxes are always <u>somebody else</u>'s fault.

5 Two or more owners: Add -'s depending on possession.

Individual possession

<u>Zimbale</u>'s and <u>Mason</u>'s comedy techniques are similar. [Each comedian has his own technique.]

Joint possession

The child recovered despite her <u>mother and father</u>'s neglect. [The mother and father were jointly neglectful.]

42b Delete or replace any apostrophe in a plural noun, a singular verb, or a possessive personal pronoun.

1 Plural nouns

The plurals of nouns are generally formed by adding *-s* or *-es*, never with an apostrophe: *boys, families, Joneses, Murphys.*

Not   The <u>Jones</u>' controlled the <u>firm's</u> until 2001.
But   The <u>Joneses</u> controlled the <u>firms</u> until 2001.

2 Singular verbs

Verbs ending in *-s* never take an apostrophe:

Not   The subway <u>break's</u> down less often now.
But   The subway <u>breaks</u> down less often now.

3 | Possessives of personal pronouns

His, hers, its, ours, yours, theirs, and *whose* are possessive forms of *he, she, it, we, you, they,* and *who.* They do not take apostrophes:

Not The house is her's. It's roof leaks.
But The house is <u>hers</u>. <u>Its</u> roof leaks.

Don't confuse possessive pronouns with contractions. See below.

42c | Use the apostrophe to form contractions.

A **contraction** replaces one or more letters, numbers, or words with an apostrophe, as in the following examples:

it is, it has	it's	cannot	can't
they are	they're	does not	doesn't
you are	you're	were not	weren't
who is, who has	who's	class of 2012	class of '12

Note Don't confuse contractions with personal pronouns:

Contractions	Personal pronouns
It's a book.	Its cover is green.
They're coming.	Their car broke down.
You're right.	Your idea is good.
Who's coming?	Whose party is it?

42d | The apostrophe is optional to mark plural abbreviations, dates, and words or characters named as words.

You'll sometimes see apostrophes used to form the plurals of abbreviations (BA's), dates (1900's), and words or characters named as words (*but*'s). However, most current style guides recommend against the apostrophe in these cases.

BAs	PhDs
1990s	2000s

The sentence has too many *buts*.
Two *3s* end the zip code.

Note Italicize or underline a word or character named as a word (see **6** p. 293), but not the added -*s*.

43 Quotation Marks

Quotation marks—either double (" ") or single (' ')—mainly enclose direct quotations from speech or writing, enclose certain titles, and highlight words used in a special sense. These are the uses covered in this chapter, along with placing quotation marks outside or inside other punctuation marks. Additional information on using quotations appears elsewhere in this book:

- Using commas with signal phrases introducing quotations. See pp. 258–59.
- Using the ellipsis mark and brackets to indicate changes in quotations. See pp. 277–79.
- Quoting sources versus paraphrasing or summarizing them. See **7** pp. 323–26.
- Integrating quotations into your text. See **7** pp. 326–30.
- Acknowledging the sources of quotations to avoid plagiarism. See **7** pp. 333–35.
- Formatting long prose quotations and poetry quotations. See **MLA** p. 401.

Note Always use quotation marks in pairs, one at the beginning of a quotation and one at the end.

Grammar checkers A grammar checker will help you use quotation marks in pairs by flagging a lone mark. It may also look for punctuation inside or outside quotation marks, but it may not detect errors when punctuation should actually fall outside quotation marks.

43a Use double quotation marks to enclose direct quotations.

A **direct quotation** reports what someone said or wrote, in the exact words of the original:

> "Life," said the psychoanalyst Karen Horney, "remains a very efficient therapist."

Note Do not use quotation marks with a direct quotation that is set off from your text. See **MLA** p. 401. Also do not use quotation

Visit *mycomplab.com* for more resources as well as exercises on the quotation marks.

271

marks with an **indirect quotation,** which reports what someone said or wrote but not in the exact words.

> The psychoanalyst Karen Horney claimed that ~~"~~life is a good therapist.~~"~~

43b Use single quotation marks to enclose a quotation within a quotation.

> "In formulating any philosophy," Woody Allen writes, "the first consideration must always be: What can we know? Descartes hinted at the problem when he wrote, 'My mind can never know my body, although it has become quite friendly with my leg.' "

Notice that two different quotation marks appear at the end of the sentence—one single (to finish the interior quotation) and one double (to finish the main quotation).

43c Set off quotations of dialog according to standard practice.

When quoting conversations, begin a new paragraph for each speaker.

> "What shall I call you? Your name?" Andrews whispered rapidly, as with a high squeak the latch of the door rose.
> "Elizabeth," she said. "Elizabeth."
>
> —Graham Greene, *The Man Within*

When you quote a single speaker for more than one paragraph, put quotation marks at the beginning of each paragraph but at the end of only the last paragraph.

Note Quotation marks are optional for quoting unspoken thoughts or imagined dialog:

> I asked myself, "How can we solve this?"
> I asked myself, How can we solve this?

43d Put quotation marks around the titles of works that are parts of other works.

Use quotation marks to enclose the titles of works that are published or released within larger works. (See the following box.) Use single quotation marks for a quotation within a quoted title, as in the article title and essay title in the box. And enclose all punctuation in the title within the quotation marks, as in the article title.

Titles to be enclosed in quotation marks

Other titles should be italicized or underlined. (See **6** p. 292.)

Song "The Star-Spangled Banner"	Page or document on a Web site "Readers' Page" (on the site *Friends of Prufrock*)
Short poem "Mending Wall"	
Short story "The Gift of the Magi"	Episode of a television or radio program "The Mexican Connection" (on *60 Minutes*)
Article in periodical "Does 'Scaring' Work?"	
Essay "Joey: A 'Mechanical Boy'"	Subdivision of a book "The Mast Head" (Chapter 35 of *Moby-Dick*)

Note Some academic disciplines do not require quotation marks for titles within source citations.

43e Quotation marks may enclose words being used in a special sense.

On movie sets movable "wild walls" make a one-walled room seem four-walled on film.

Note Use italics or underlining for defined words. (See **6** p. 293.)

43f Delete quotation marks where they are not required.

Title of your paper

Not "The Death Wish in One Poem by Robert Frost"

But The Death Wish in One Poem by Robert Frost

Or The Death Wish in "Stopping by Woods on a Snowy Evening"

Common nickname

Not As President, "Jimmy" Carter preferred to use his nickname.

But As President, Jimmy Carter preferred to use his nickname.

Slang or trite expression

Quotation marks will not excuse slang or a trite expression that is inappropriate to your writing. If slang is appropriate, use it without quotation marks.

Not We should support the President in his "hour of need" rather than "wimp out on him."

But We should give the President the support he needs rather than turn away like cowards.

43g Place other punctuation marks inside or outside quotation marks according to standard practice.

1 Commas and periods: Inside quotation marks

Swift uses irony in his essay "A Modest Proposal."

Many first-time readers are shocked to see infants described as "delicious."

"'A Modest Proposal,'" writes one critic, "is so outrageous that it cannot be believed."

Exception When a parenthetical source citation immediately follows a quotation, place any period or comma *after* the citation:

One critic calls the essay "outrageous" (Olms 26).

Partly because of "the cool calculation of its delivery" (Olms 27), Swift's satire still chills a modern reader.

2 Colons and semicolons: Outside quotation marks

A few years ago the slogan in elementary education was "learning by playing"; now educators are concerned with basic skills.

We all know what is meant by "inflation": more money buys less.

3 Dashes, question marks, and exclamation points: Inside quotation marks only if part of the quotation

When a dash, question mark, or exclamation point is part of the quotation, place it *inside* quotation marks. Don't use any other punctuation, such as a period or comma:

"But must you—" Marcia hesitated, afraid of the answer.

"Go away!" I yelled.

Did you say, "Who is she?" [When both your sentence and the quotation would end in a question mark or exclamation point, use only the mark in the quotation.]

When a dash, question mark, or exclamation point applies only to the larger sentence, not to the quotation, place it *outside* quotation marks—again, with no other punctuation:

One evocative line in English poetry—"After many a summer dies the swan"—comes from Alfred, Lord Tennyson.

Who said, "Now cracks a noble heart"?

The woman called me "stupid"!

44 Other Marks

The other marks of punctuation are the dash (below), parentheses (p. 276), the ellipsis mark (p. 277), brackets (p. 279), and the slash (p. 279).

Grammar checkers A grammar checker may flag a lone parenthesis or bracket so that you can match it with another parenthesis or bracket. But most checkers cannot recognize other misuses of the marks covered here and instead simply ignore the marks.

44a Use the dash or dashes to indicate shifts and to set off some sentence elements.

The dash (—) is mainly a mark of interruption: it signals a shift, insertion, or break. In your papers, form a dash with two hyphens (--) or use the character called an em dash on your word processor. Do not add extra space around or between the hyphens or around the em dash.

Note When an interrupting element starting with a dash falls in the middle of a sentence, be sure to add the closing dash to signal the end of the interruption. See the first example below.

1 Shifts in tone or thought

The novel—if one can call it that—appeared in 2005.
If the book had a plot—but a plot would be conventional.

2 Nonessential elements

Dashes may be used instead of commas to set off and emphasize modifiers, parenthetical expressions, and other nonessential elements, especially when these elements are internally punctuated:

The qualities Monet painted—sunlight, rich shadows, deep colors—abounded near the rivers and gardens he used as subjects.

Though they are close together—separated by only a few blocks—the two neighborhoods could be in different countries.

Key term

nonessential element Gives added information but does not limit the word it refers to. (See pp. 253–54.)

---

mycomplab

Visit *mycomplab.com* for more resources as well as exercises on the dash, parentheses, the ellipsis mark, brackets, and the slash.

3 Introductory series and concluding series and explanations

Shortness of breath, skin discoloration or the sudden appearance of moles, persistent indigestion, the presence of small lumps—all these may signify cancer. [Introductory series.]

The patient undergoes a battery of tests—MRI, bronchoscopy, perhaps even biopsy. [Concluding series.]

Many patients are disturbed by the MRI—by the need to keep still for long periods in an exceedingly small space. [Concluding explanation.]

A colon could be used instead of a dash in the last two examples. The dash is more informal.

4 Overuse

Too many dashes can make writing jumpy or breathy.

Not   In all his life—eighty-seven years—my great-grandfather never allowed his picture to be taken—not even once. He claimed the "black box"—the camera—would steal his soul.

But   In all his eighty-seven years, my great-grandfather did not allow his picture to be taken even once. He claimed the "black box"—the camera—would steal his soul.

44b Use parentheses to enclose parenthetical expressions and labels for lists within sentences.

Note Parentheses *always* come in pairs, one before and one after the punctuated material.

1 Parenthetical expressions

Parenthetical expressions include explanations, facts, digressions, and examples that may be helpful or interesting but are not essential to meaning. Parentheses de-emphasize parenthetical expressions. (Commas emphasize them more than parentheses do, and dashes emphasize them still more.)

The population of Philadelphia (now about 1.5 million) has declined since 1950.

Note Don't put a comma before a parenthetical expression enclosed in parentheses. Punctuation after the parenthetical expres-sion should be placed outside the closing parenthesis.

Not   The population of Philadelphia compares with that of Phoenix, (just over 1.6 million.)

But   The population of Philadelphia compares with that of Phoenix (just over 1.6 million).

If you enclose a complete sentence in parentheses, capitalize the sentence and place the closing period *inside* the closing parenthesis:

In general, coaches will tell you that scouts are just guys who can't coach. (But then, so are brain surgeons.)
—Roy Blount

2 Labels for lists within sentences

Outside the Middle East, the countries with the largest oil reserves are (1) Venezuela (63 billion barrels), (2) Russia (57 billion barrels), and (3) Mexico (51 billion barrels).

When you set a list off from your text, do not enclose such labels in parentheses.

44c Use the ellipsis mark to indicate omissions from quotations.

The ellipsis mark, consisting of three periods separated by space (. . .), generally indicates an omission from a quotation. All the following examples quote from this passage about environmentalism:

Original quotation

"At the heart of the environmentalist world view is the conviction that human physical and spiritual health depends on sustaining the planet in a relatively unaltered state. Earth is our home in the full, genetic sense, where humanity and its ancestors existed for all the millions of years of their evolution. Natural ecosystems—forests, coral reefs, marine blue waters—maintain the world exactly as we would wish it to be maintained. When we debase the global environment and extinguish the variety of life, we are dismantling a support system that is too complex to understand, let alone replace, in the foreseeable future."

—Edward O. Wilson, "Is Humanity Suicidal?"

1. Omission of the middle of a sentence

"Natural ecosystems . . . maintain the world exactly as we would wish it to be maintained."

2. Omission of the end of a sentence, without source citation

"Earth is our home. . . ." [The sentence period, closed up to the last word, precedes the ellipsis mark.]

3. Omission of the end of a sentence, with source citation

"Earth is our home . . ." (Wilson 27). [The sentence period follows the source citation.]

4. Omission of parts of two or more sentences

Wilson writes, "At the heart of the environmentalist world view is the conviction that human physical and spiritual health depends on sustaining the planet . . . where humanity and its ancestors existed for all the millions of years of their evolution."

5. Omission of one or more sentences

As Wilson puts it, "At the heart of the environmentalist world view is the conviction that human physical and spiritual health depends on sustaining the planet in a relatively unaltered state. . . . When we debase the global environment and extinguish the variety of life, we are dismantling a support system that is too complex to understand, let alone replace, in the foreseeable future."

6. Omission from the middle of a sentence through the end of another sentence

"Earth is our home. . . . When we debase the global environment and extinguish the variety of life, we are dismantling a support system that is too complex to understand, let alone replace, in the foreseeable future."

7. Omission of the beginning of a sentence, leaving a complete sentence

a. Bracketed capital letter

"[H]uman physical and spiritual health," Wilson writes, "depends on sustaining the planet in a relatively unaltered state." [No ellipsis mark is needed because the brackets around the *H* indicate that the letter was not capitalized originally and thus that the beginning of the sentence has been omitted.]

b. Small letter

According to Wilson, "human physical and spiritual health depends on sustaining the planet in a relatively unaltered state." [No ellipsis mark is needed because the small *h* indicates that the beginning of the sentence has been omitted.]

c. Capital letter from the original

Hami comments, ". . . Wilson argues eloquently for the environmentalist world view." [An ellipsis mark *is* needed because the quoted part of the sentence begins with a capital letter and it is otherwise not clear that the beginning of the original sentence has been omitted.]

8. Use of a word or phrase

Wilson describes the earth as "our home." [No ellipsis mark needed.]

Note these features of the examples:

- **Use an ellipsis mark when it is not otherwise clear that you have left out material from the source,** as when you omit one or more sentences (examples 5 and 6) or when the words you quote form a complete sentence that is different in the original (examples 1–4 and 7c).
- **You don't need an ellipsis mark when it is obvious that you have omitted something,** such as when a bracketed letter or a

small letter indicates omission (examples 7a and 7b) or when a phrase clearly comes from a larger sentence (example 8).

■ **Place an ellipsis mark after a sentence period *except* when a parenthetical source citation follows the quotation,** as in example 3. Then the sentence period falls after the citation.

If you omit one or more lines of poetry or paragraphs of prose from a quotation, use a separate line of ellipsis marks across the full width of the quotation to show the omission.

In "Song: Love Armed" from 1676, Aphra Behn contrasts two lovers' experiences of a romance:

> Love in fantastic triumph sate,
>> Whilst bleeding hearts around him flowed,
>
> . . . .
>
> But my poor heart alone is harmed,
>> Whilst thine the victor is, and free. (lines 1-2, 15-16)

(See **MLA** p. 403 for the format of such displayed quotations.)

44d Use brackets to indicate changes in quotations.

Brackets have specialized uses in mathematical equations, but their main use for all kinds of writing is to indicate that you have altered a quotation to explain, clarify, or correct it.

"That Texaco station [just outside Chicago] is one of the busiest in the nation," said a company spokesperson.

The word *sic* (Latin for "in this manner") in brackets indicates that an error in the quotation appeared in the original and was not made by you. Do not use *sic* to make fun of a writer or to note errors in a passage that is clearly nonstandard.

According to the newspaper report, "The car slammed thru [sic] the railing and into oncoming traffic."

44e Use the slash between options and between lines of poetry run into the text.

Option
Some teachers oppose pass/fail courses.

Poetry

Many readers have sensed a reluctant turn away from death in Frost's lines "The woods are lovely, dark and deep, **/** But I have promises to keep" (13-14).

When separating lines of poetry in this way, leave a space before and after the slash. (See **MLA** p. 401 for more on quoting poetry.)

PART 6

Spelling and Mechanics

MICHIGAN STATE
UNIVERSITY

45 Spelling and the Hyphen

You can train yourself to spell better, and this chapter will tell you how. But you can improve instantly by acquiring three habits:

- Carefully proofread your writing.
- Cultivate a healthy suspicion of your spellings.
- Check a dictionary *every time* you doubt a spelling.

Spelling checkers A spelling checker can help you find and track spelling errors in your papers. But its usefulness is limited, mainly because it can't spot the confusion of words with similar spellings, such as *now/not, to/too,* and *their/they're/there.* See **1** pp. 27–29 for more on spelling checkers.

45a Anticipate typical spelling problems

Certain situations, such as misleading pronunciation, commonly lead to misspelling.

1 Pronunciation

In English, pronunciation of words is an unreliable guide to how they are spelled. Pronunciation is especially misleading with **homonyms,** words pronounced the same but spelled differently. Some homonyms and near-homonyms appear in the following box.

Words commonly confused

accept (to receive)
except (other than)

affect (to have an influence on)
effect (a result)

all ready (prepared)
already (by this time)

allusion (an indirect reference)
illusion (an erroneous belief or
perception)

ascent (a movement up)
assent (to agree, or an agreement)

bare (unclothed)
bear (to carry, or an animal)

board (a plane of wood)
bored (uninterested)

brake (to stop)
break (to smash)

---

mycomplab

Visit *mycomplab.com* for more resources as well as exercises on spelling and the hyphen.

buy (to purchase)
by (next to)

cite (to quote an authority)
sight (the ability to see)
site (a place)

desert (to abandon)
dessert (after-dinner course)

discreet (reserved, respectful)
discrete (individual, distinct)

fair (average, or lovely)
fare (a fee for transportation)

forth (forward)
fourth (after *third*)

hear (to perceive by ear)
here (in this place)

heard (past tense of *hear*)
herd (a group of animals)

hole (an opening)
whole (complete)

its (possessive of *it*)
it's (contraction of *it is* or *it has*)

know (to be certain)
no (the opposite of *yes*)

loose (not attached)
lose (to misplace)

meat (flesh)
meet (to encounter, or a competition)

passed (past tense of *pass*)
past (after, or a time gone by)

patience (forbearance)
patients (persons under medical care)

peace (the absence of war)
piece (a portion of something)

plain (clear)
plane (a carpenter's tool, or an airborne vehicle)

presence (the state of being at hand)
presents (gifts)

principal (most important, or the head of a school)
principle (a basic truth or law)

rain (precipitation)
reign (to rule)
rein (a strap for an animal)

right (correct)
rite (a religious ceremony)
write (to make letters)

road (a surface for driving)
rode (past tense of *ride*)

scene (where an action occurs)
seen (past participle of *see*)

stationary (unmoving)
stationery (writing paper)

their (possessive of *they*)
there (opposite of *here*)
they're (contraction of *they are*)

to (toward)
too (also)
two (following *one*)

waist (the middle of the body)
waste (discarded material)

weak (not strong)
week (Sunday through Saturday)

weather (climate)
whether (*if*, or introducing a choice)

which (one of a group)
witch (a sorcerer)

who's (contraction of *who is* or *who has*)
whose (possessive of *who*)

your (possessive of *you*)
you're (contraction of *you are*)

2 Different forms of the same word

Often, the noun form and the verb form of the same word are spelled differently: for example, *advice* (noun) and *advise* (verb). Sometimes the noun and the adjective forms of the same word differ: *height* and *high*. Similar changes occur in the parts of some irregular verbs (*know, knew, known*) and the plurals of irregular nouns (*man, men*).

3 American vs. British spellings

If you learned English outside the United States, you may be accustomed to British rather than American spellings. Here are the chief differences:

American	British
color, humor	colour, humour
theater, center	theatre, centre
canceled, traveled	cancelled, travelled
judgment	judgement
realize, civilize	realise, civilise
connection	connexion

Your dictionary may list both spellings, but it will specially mark the British one with *chiefly Brit* or a similar label.

45b Follow spelling rules

1 *ie* vs. *ei*

To distinguish between *ie* and *ei*, use the familiar jingle:

I before *e*, except after *c*, or when pronounced "ay" as in *neighbor* and *weigh*.

i before *e*	believe	thief	hygiene
ei after *c*	ceiling	conceive	perceive
ei sounded as "ay"	sleigh	eight	beige

Exceptions For some exceptions, remember this sentence:

The weird foreigner neither seizes leisure nor forfeits height.

2 Final *e*

When adding an ending to a word with a final *e*, drop the *e* if the ending begins with a vowel:

advise + able = advisable   surprise + ing = surprising

Keep the *e* if the ending begins with a consonant:

> care + ful = care*ful*   like + ly = like*ly*

Exceptions Retain the *e* after a soft *c* or *g*, to keep the sound of the consonant soft rather than hard: *courageous, changeable*. And drop the *e* before a consonant when the *e* is preceded by another vowel: *argue + ment = argument, true + ly = truly*.

3 | Final *y*

When adding an ending to a word with a final *y*, change the *y* to *i* if it follows a consonant:

> beauty, beaut*ies*   worry, worr*ied*   supply, suppl*ies*

But keep the *y* if it follows a vowel, if it ends a proper name, or if the ending is *-ing:*

> day, da*ys*   Minsky, Minsk*ys*   cry, cr*ying*

4 | Final consonants

When adding an ending to a one-syllable word ending in a consonant, double the final consonant when it follows a single vowel. Otherwise, don't double the consonant.

> slap, slap*ping*   park, par*king*   pair, pai*red*

In words of more than one syllable, double the final consonant when it follows a single vowel *and* when it ends a stressed syllable once the new ending is added. Otherwise, don't double the consonant.

> refer, refer*ring*   refer, refe*rence*   relent, relen*ted*

5 | Prefixes

When adding a prefix, do not drop a letter from or add a letter to the original word:

> *un*necessary   *dis*appoint   *mis*spell

6 | Plurals

Most nouns form plurals by adding *s* to the singular form. Add *es* for the plural of nouns ending in *s, sh, ch,* or *x*.

> boy, boy*s*   kiss, kiss*es*   church, church*es*

Nouns ending in *o* preceded by a vowel usually form the plural with *s*. Those ending in *o* preceded by a consonant usually form the plural with *es*.

> ratio, ratio*s*   hero, hero*es*

Some very common nouns form irregular plurals.

child, chil<u>dren</u>   woman, wom<u>en</u>   mouse, m<u>ice</u>

Some English nouns that were originally Italian, Greek, Latin, or French form the plural according to their original language:

analysis, analys<u>es</u>   criterion, criter<u>ia</u>   piano, piano<u>s</u>
basis, bas<u>es</u>   datum, dat<u>a</u>   thesis, thes<u>es</u>
crisis, cris<u>es</u>   medium, med<u>ia</u>

A few such nouns may form irregular *or* regular plurals: for instance, *index, ind<u>ices</u>, index<u>es</u>; curriculum, curricul<u>a</u>, curriculum<u>s</u>*. The regular plural is more contemporary.

   With compound nouns, add *s* to the main word of the compound. Sometimes this main word is not the last word.

city-state<u>s</u>   father<u>s</u>-in-law   passer<u>s</u>by

   CULTURE   Noncount nouns do not form plurals, either regu-
   LANGUAGE   larly (with an added *s*) or irregularly. Examples of
noncount nouns include *equipment, intelligence,* and *wealth.* See **4**
p. 227.

45c   Use the hyphen to form or divide words

   The hyphen is used either to form compound words or to divide words at the ends of lines.

1   Compound adjectives

   When two or more words serve together as a single modifier before a noun, a hyphen forms the modifying words clearly into a unit.

She is a <u>well-known</u> actor.
Some <u>Spanish-speaking</u> students work as translators.

When such a compound adjective follows the noun, the hyphen is unnecessary.

The actor is <u>well known</u>.
Many students are <u>Spanish speaking</u>.

The hyphen is also unnecessary in a compound modifier containing an *-ly* adverb, even before the noun: *clearly defined terms.*
   When part of a compound adjective appears only once in two or more parallel compound adjectives, hyphens indicate which words the reader should mentally join with the missing part.

School-age children should have <u>eight-</u> or <u>nine-o'clock</u> bedtimes.

2 Fractions and compound numbers

Hyphens join the numerator and denominator of fractions: *one-half, three-fourths.* Hyphens also join the parts of the whole numbers *twenty-one* to *ninety-nine.*

When a hyphenated number is part of a compound adjective before a noun, join all parts of the modifier with hyphens: *sixty-three-foot wall.*

3 Prefixes and suffixes

Do not use hyphens with prefixes except as follows:

- **With the prefixes *self-*, *all-*, and *ex-*:** *self-control, all-inclusive, ex-student.*
- **With a prefix before a capitalized word:** *un-American.*
- **With a capital letter before a word:** *T-shirt.*
- **To prevent misreading:** *de-emphasize, re-create a story.*

The only suffix that regularly requires a hyphen is *-elect*, as in *president-elect.*

4 Words at the ends of lines

You can avoid occasional short lines in your documents by setting your word processor to divide words automatically at appropriate breaks. (In the Tools menu, select Language and then Hyphenation.) To divide words manually, follow these guidelines:

- **Divide words only between syllables**—for instance, *win-dows,* not *wi-ndows.* Check a dictionary for correct syllable breaks.
- **Never divide a one-syllable word.**
- **Leave at least two letters on the first line and three on the second line.** If a word cannot be divided to follow this rule (for instance, *a-bus-er*), don't divide it.

If you must break an electronic address—for instance, in a source citation—do so only after a slash. Do not hyphenate, because readers may perceive any added hyphen as part of the address.

Not	http://www.library.miami.edu/staff/lmc/soc-race.html
But	http://www.library.miami.edu/staff/lmc/socrace.html

46 Capital Letters

Generally, capitalize a word only when a dictionary or conventional use says you must. Consult one of the style guides listed in **8** pp. 352 and 355 for special uses of capitals in the social, natural, and applied sciences.

Grammar checkers A grammar checker will flag overused capital letters and missing capitals at the beginnings of sentences. It will also spot missing capitals at the beginnings of proper nouns and adjectives—*if* the nouns and adjectives are in the checker's dictionary. For example, a checker caught *christianity* and *europe* but not *china* (for the country) or *Stephen king*.

CULTURE LANGUAGE Conventions of capitalization vary from language to language. English, for instance, is the only language to capitalize the first-person singular pronoun (*I*), and its practice of capitalizing proper nouns but not most common nouns also distinguishes it from some other languages.

46a Capitalize the first word of every sentence.

No one expected the outcome.

When quoting other writers, you should reproduce the capital letters beginning their sentences or indicate that you have altered the source's capitalization. Whenever possible, integrate the quotation into your own sentence so that its capitalization coincides with yours:

"Psychotherapists often overlook the benefits of self-deception," the author argues.

The author argues that "the benefits of self-deception" are not always recognized by psychotherapists.

If you need to alter the capitalization in the source, indicate the change with brackets:

"[T]he benefits of self-deception" are not always recognized by psychotherapists, the author argues.

The author argues that "[p]sychotherapists often overlook the benefits of self-deception."

mycomplab

Visit *mycomplab.com* for more resources as well as exercises on capital letters.

Note Capitalization of questions in a series is optional. Both of the following examples are correct:

Is the population a hundred? Two hundred? More?
Is the population a hundred? two hundred? more?

Also optional is capitalization of the first word in a complete sentence after a colon.

> **46b** Capitalize proper nouns, proper adjectives, and words used as essential parts of proper nouns

1 Proper nouns and proper adjectives

Proper nouns name specific persons, places, and things: *Shake-speare, California, World War I*. **Proper adjectives** are formed from some proper nouns: *Shakespearean, Californian*. Capitalize all proper nouns and proper adjectives but not the articles (*a, an, the*) that precede them:

Proper nouns and adjectives to be capitalized

Specific persons and things

Stephen King | Boulder Dam
Napoleon Bonaparte | the Empire State Building

Specific places and geographical regions

New York City | the Mediterranean Sea
China | the Northeast, the South

But: northeast of the city, going south

Days of the week, months, holidays

Monday | Yom Kippur
May | Christmas

Historical events, documents, periods, movements

the Vietnam War | the Renaissance
the Constitution | the Romantic Movement

Government offices or departments and institutions

House of Representatives | Polk Municipal Court
Department of Defense | Northeast High School

Political, social, athletic, and other organizations and associations and their members

Democratic Party, Democrats | League of Women Voters
Sierra Club | Boston Celtics
B'nai B'rith | Chicago Symphony Orchestra

(continued)

Proper nouns and adjectives to be capitalized

(continued)

Races, nationalities, and their languages

Native American	Germans
African American	Swahili
Caucasian	Italian

But: blacks, whites

Religions, their followers, and terms for the sacred

Christianity, Christians	God
Catholicism, Catholics	Allah
Judaism, Orthodox Jews	the Bible [**but** biblical]
Islam, Muslims	the Koran, the Qur'an

2 Common nouns used as essential parts of proper nouns

Capitalize the common nouns *street, avenue, park, river, ocean, lake, company, college, county,* and *memorial* when they are part of proper nouns naming specific places or institutions:

Main Street	Lake Superior
Central Park	Ford Motor Company
Mississippi River	Madison College
Pacific Ocean	George Washington Memorial

3 Compass directions

Capitalize compass directions only when they name a specific region instead of a general direction:

Students from the West often melt in eastern humidity.

4 Relationships

Capitalize the names of relationships only when they precede or replace proper names:

Our aunt scolded us for disrespecting Father and Uncle Jake.

5 Titles with persons' names

Before a person's name, capitalize his or her title. After or apart from the name, do not capitalize the title.

Professor Otto Osborne	Otto Osborne, a professor
Doctor Jane Covington	Jane Covington, a doctor
Governor Ella Moore	Ella Moore, the governor

Note Many writers capitalize a title denoting very high rank even when it follows a name or is used alone: *Ronald Reagan, past President of the United States.*

46c Capitalize most words in titles and subtitles of works

Within your text, capitalize all the words in a title *except* the following: articles (*a, an, the*); *to* in infinitives; and connecting words (prepositions and conjunctions) of fewer than five letters. Capitalize even these short words when they are the first or last word in a title or when they fall after a colon or semicolon.

"Courtship Through the Ages"	*Management: A New Theory*
A Diamond Is Forever	"Once More to the Lake"
"Knowing Whom to Ask"	*An End to Live For*
Learning from Las Vegas	*File Under Architecture*

Note The style guides of the academic disciplines have their own rules for capitals in titles. For instance, MLA style for English and some other humanities capitalizes all subordinating conjunctions but no prepositions. In addition, APA style for the social sciences and CSE style for the sciences capitalize only the first word and proper names in book and article titles within source citations.

46d Use capitals according to convention in online communication

Online messages written in all-capital letters or with no capital letters are difficult to read. Further, messages in all-capital letters may be taken as rude (see also **2** p. 104). Use capital letters according to rules 46a–46c in all your online communication.

47 Italics or Underlining

Italic type and <u>underlining</u> indicate the same thing: the word or words are being <u>distinguished</u> or emphasized. Italic type is now used almost universally in academic and business writing, and it has recently become the preferred style of the Modern Language Association (see **MLA** p. 360). Some instructors recommend underlining, so ask your instructor for his or her preference.

mycomplab

Visit *mycomplab.com* for more resources as well as exercises on italics or underlining.

Always use either italics or underlining consistently throughout a document in both text and source citations. If you are using italics, make sure that the italic characters are clearly distinct from the regular type. If you are using underlining and you underline two or more words in a row, underline the space between the words, too: Criminal Statistics: Misuses of Numbers.

Grammar checkers A grammar checker cannot recognize problems with italics or underlining. Check your work to ensure that you have used highlighting appropriately.

47a | Italicize or underline the titles of works that appear independently

Within your text, underline or italicize the titles of works that are published, released, or produced separately from other works. (See the box below.) Use quotation marks for all other titles. (See **5** p. 273.)

Titles to be italicized or underlined

Other titles should be placed in quotation marks. (See **5** p. 273.)

Books
War and Peace
And the Band Played On

Plays
Hamlet
The Phantom of the Opera

Computer software
Microsoft Internet Explorer
Acrobat Reader

Web sites
Google
Friends of Prufrock

Pamphlets
The Truth About Alcoholism

Long musical works
Tchaikovsky's *Swan Lake*
But: Symphony in C

Television and radio programs
The Shadow
NBC Sports Hour

Long poems
Beowulf
Paradise Lost

Periodicals
Time
Philadelphia Inquirer

Published speeches
Lincoln's *Gettysburg Address*

Movies, DVDs, and videos
Schindler's List
How to Relax

Works of visual art
Michelangelo's *David*
Picasso's *Guernica*

Exceptions Legal documents, the Bible, the Koran, and their parts are generally not italicized or underlined:

Not We studied the *Book of Revelation* in the *Bible*.

But We studied the Book of Revelation in the Bible.

47b Italicize or underline the names of ships, aircraft, spacecraft, and trains

Challenger	*Orient Express*	*Queen Mary 2*
Apollo XI	*Montrealer*	*Spirit of St. Louis*

47c Italicize or underline foreign words that are not part of the English language

Italicize or underline a foreign expression that has not been absorbed into English. A dictionary will say whether a word is still considered foreign to English.

The scientific name for the brown trout is *Salmo trutta*. [The Latin scientific names for plants and animals are always italicized or underlined.]

The Latin *De gustibus non est disputandum* translates roughly as "There's no accounting for taste."

47d Italicize or underline words or characters named as words

Use italics or underlining to indicate that you are citing a character or word as a word rather than using it for its meaning. Words you are defining fall under this convention.

The word *syzygy* refers to a straight line formed by three celestial bodies, as in the alignment of the earth, sun, and moon.

Some people say *th*, as in *thought*, with a faint *s* or *f* sound.

47e Occasionally, italics or underlining may be used for emphasis

Italics or underlining can stress an important word or phrase, especially in reporting how someone said something. But use such emphasis very rarely, or your writing may sound immature or hysterical.

47f In online communication, use alternatives for italics or underlining

Some forms of online communication do not allow conventional highlighting such as italics or underlining for the purposes described in this chapter. (On Web sites, for instance, underlining often indicates a link to another site.)

To distinguish book titles and other elements that usually require italics or underlining, type an underscore before and after the element: *Measurements coincide with those in _Joule's Handbook_.* You can also emphasize words with asterisks before and after: *I *will not* be able to attend.*

Don't use all-capital letters for emphasis; they yell too loudly. (See also p. 291.)

48 Abbreviations

The following guidelines on abbreviations pertain to the text of a nontechnical document. All academic disciplines use abbreviations in source citations, and much technical writing, such as in the sciences and engineering, uses many abbreviations in the document text. For the in-text requirements of the discipline you are writing in, consult one of the style guides listed in **8** pp. 349 (humanities), 352 (social sciences), and 355 (natural and applied sciences).

Usage varies, but writers increasingly omit periods from abbreviations that consist of or end in capital letters: *US, BA, USMC, PhD.* See **5** p. 248 on punctuating abbreviations.

Grammar and spelling checkers A grammar checker may flag some abbreviations, such as *ft.* (for *foot*) and *st.* (for *street*). A spelling checker will flag abbreviations it does not recognize. But neither checker can tell you whether an abbreviation is appropriate for your writing situation or will be clear to your readers.

Visit *mycomplab.com* for more resources as well as exercises on abbreviations.

48a Use standard abbreviations for titles immediately before and after proper names

Before the name	After the name
Dr. James Hsu	James Hsu, MD
Mr., Mrs., Ms., Hon.,	DDS, DVM, PhD,
St., Rev., Msgr., Gen.	EdD, OSB, SJ, Sr., Jr.

Do not use abbreviations such as *Rev., Hon., Prof., Rep., Sen., Dr.,* and *St.* (for *Saint*) unless they appear before a proper name.

48b Familiar abbreviations and acronyms are acceptable in most writing

An **acronym** is an abbreviation that spells a pronounceable word, such as WHO, NATO, and AIDS. These and other abbreviations using initials are acceptable in most writing as long as they are familiar to readers.

Institutions	LSU, UCLA, TCU
Organizations	CIA, FBI, YMCA, AFL-CIO
Corporations	IBM, CBS, ITT
People	JFK, LBJ, FDR
Countries	US, USA

Note If a name or term (such as *operating room*) appears often in a piece of writing, then its abbreviation (*OR*) can cut down on extra words. Spell out the full term at its first appearance, indicate its abbreviation in parentheses, and then use the abbreviation.

48c Use *BC, BCE, AD, CE, AM, PM, no.,* and *$* only with specific dates and numbers

44 BC	AD 1492	11:26 AM (*or* a.m.)	no. 36 (*or* No. 36)
44 BCE	1492 CE	8:05 PM (*or* p.m.)	$7.41

The abbreviations BC ("before Christ"), BCE ("before the common era"), and CE ("common era") always follow a date. In contrast, AD (*anno Domini,* Latin for "in the year of the Lord") precedes a date.

48d Generally reserve Latin abbreviations for source citations and comments in parentheses

Latin abbreviations are generally not italicized or underlined.

i.e.	*id est:* that is
cf.	*confer:* compare

e.g.	*exempli gratia:* for example
et al.	*et alii:* and others
etc.	*et cetera:* and so forth
NB	*nota bene:* note well

He said he would be gone a fortnight (i.e., two weeks).
Bloom et al., editors, *Anthology of Light Verse*
Trees, too, are susceptible to disease (e.g., Dutch elm disease).

Some writers avoid these abbreviations in formal writing, even within parentheses.

48e Use *Inc., Bros., Co.,* or & (for *and*) only in official names of business firms

Not The Santini bros. operate a large moving firm in New York City & environs.

But The Santini brothers operate a large moving firm in New York City and environs.

Or Santini Bros. is a large moving firm in New York City and environs.

48f Generally spell out units of measurement and names of places, calendar designations, people, and courses

In most academic, general, and business writing, the types of words listed below should always be spelled out. (In source citations and technical writing, however, these words are more often abbreviated.)

Units of measurement
The dog is thirty inches [not in.] high.

Geographical names
The publisher is in Massachusetts [not Mass. or MA].

Names of days, months, and holidays
The truce was signed on Tuesday [not Tues.], April [not Apr.] 16.

Names of people
Robert [not Robt.] Frost wrote accessible poems.

Courses of instruction
I'm majoring in political science [not poli. sci.].

49 Numbers

This chapter addresses the use of numbers (numerals versus words) in the text of a document. All disciplines use many more numerals in source citations.

Grammar checkers A grammar checker will flag numerals beginning sentences and can be customized to ignore or to look for numerals. But it can't tell you whether numerals or spelled-out numbers are appropriate for your writing situation.

49a Use numerals according to standard practice in the field you are writing in

Always use numerals for numbers that require more than two words to spell out:

> The leap year has 366 days.
> The population of Minot, North Dakota, is about 32,800.

In nontechnical academic writing, spell out numbers of one or two words:

> Twelve nations signed the treaty.
>
> The ball game drew forty-two thousand people. [A hyphenated number may be considered one word.]

In much business writing, use numerals for all numbers over ten: *five reasons, 11 participants*. In technical academic and business writing, such as in science and engineering, use numerals for all numbers over ten, and use numerals for zero through nine when they refer to exact measurements: *2 liters, 1 hour*. (Consult one of the style guides listed in **8** pp. 352 and 355 for more details.)

Note Use a combination of numerals and words for round numbers over a million: *26 million, 2.45 billion*. And use either all numerals or all words when several numbers appear together in a passage, even if convention would require a mixture.

CULTURE LANGUAGE In standard American English, a comma separates the numerals in long numbers (*26,000*), and a period functions as a decimal point (*2.06*).

mycomplab

Visit *mycomplab.com* for more resources as well as exercises on numbers.

49b Use numerals according to convention for dates, addresses, and other information

Days and years

June 18, 1985   AD 12
456 BCE   2010

The time of day

9:00 AM   3:45 PM

Addresses

355 Clinton Avenue
Washington, DC 20036

Exact amounts of money

$3.5 million $4.50

Decimals, percentages, and fractions

22.5   3½
48% (*or* 48 percent)

Scores and statistics

21 to 7   a ratio of 8 to 1
a mean of 26

Pages, chapters, volumes, acts, scenes, lines

Chapter 9, page 123
Hamlet, act 5, scene 3

Exceptions Round dollar or cent amounts of only a few words may be expressed in words: *seventeen dollars; sixty cents*. When the word *o'clock* is used for the time of day, also express the number in words: *two o'clock* (not *2 o'clock*).

49c Spell out numbers that begin sentences

For clarity, spell out any number that begins a sentence. If the number requires more than two words, reword the sentence so that the number falls later and can be expressed as a numeral.

Not   3.9 billion people live in Asia.

But   The population of Asia is 3.9 billion.

Research Writing

MICHIGAN STATE
UNIVERSITY

50 Research Strategy

Research writing gives you the chance to explore your questions through the wealth of information available to you. Sometimes the sheer amount of information, both on the open Web and through specialized sources like library books and databases, can seem overwhelming. Your best resource for help with your information search is an MSU librarian. Librarians are trained to help you tame the information flow from a gushing fire hydrant to a more manageable stream, as well as suggest new places for you to try. On the MSU Libraries' website, http://www.lib.msu.edu, you will find the "Ask a Librarian" link at the top of every page. Librarians are available 24-7 through chat, and can also be found at the Reference Desk on the first floor of the Main Library during the day and in the evenings. For more information, click on the Ask a Librarian Link.

50a Planning your work

Set deadlines for each step: finding a researchable subject and question, evaluating and synthesizing sources, drafting your paper, and revising and editing. In addition to planning your time for your research project from assignment to due date, look at when work in other classes will be coming due.

Research writing is a *writing* process:

- You work within a particular situation of subject, purpose, audience, and other factors (see **1** pp. 2–6).
- You gather ideas and information about your subject (**1** pp. 7–16).
- You focus and arrange your ideas (**1** pp. 17–20).
- You draft to explore your meaning (**1** pp. 21–22).
- You revise and edit to develop, shape, and polish (**1** pp. 22–29).

Although the process seems neatly sequential in this list, you know from experience that the stages overlap-that, for instance, you may begin drafting before you've gathered all the information you expect to find, and then while drafting you may discover a source that causes you to rethink your approach. Anticipating the process of research writing can free you to be flexible in your search and open to discoveries.

Visit *mycomplab.com* for more resources as well as exercises on research strategy.

You may want to begin with the MSU Libraries' Undergraduate Resources page, which you can find at http://www.lib.msu.edu/undergrad/index.jsp or by clicking on "Undergraduate Page" from the Libraries' website. Here you can find helpful tools for beginning your work, such as the MSU Libraries' Assignment Calculator. Input the date your assignment is due, and the Calculator will lay out a timeline for steps to take, as well as suggest sources for you to try along the way.

50b Keeping a research journal

While working on a research project, carry a notebook or a computer with you at all times to use as a **research journal,** a place to record your activities and ideas. (See **1** p. 7 on journal keeping.) In the journal's dated entries, you can write about the sources you consult, the leads you want to pursue, and any difficulties you encounter. Most important, you can record your thoughts about sources, leads, dead ends, new directions, relationships, and anything else that strikes you. The very act of writing in the journal can expand and clarify your thinking.

1 Using a journal to begin thinking about the assignment

As you analyze the assignment in front of you, use your research journal to list ideas on possible topics and questions. Have seen something on the Internet that left you with unanswered questions? Have you heard something in conversation that you would like to know more about? Was material introduced in class that you would like to explore in more depth? As you think of subjects or questions, keep notes to think about; leave space to add ideas as they occur to you. These journal entries will provide a starting point for your first searches for background information.

As you search for source material to answer your research question keep a log in your research journal that indicates which keywords give the best results, and which library databases provide the most information on your topic.

2 Keeping a working, annotated bibliography

To track where sources are, compile a **working bibliography** as you uncover possibilities. Recording the publication information in the style you have been assigned means that you will have already written entries for your paper's bibliography. Annotations will give you a "snapshot" of what each source is about.

a Source information

When you turn in your paper, you will be expected to attach a list of the sources you have used. So that readers can check or follow up on your sources, your list must include all the information needed to find the sources, in a format readers can understand. (See pp. 336–37.) The box on the next page shows the information you should record for each type of source so that you will not have to retrace your steps later.

Note Whenever possible, record source information in the correct format for the documentation style you will be using. Then you will be less likely to omit needed information or to confuse numbers, dates, and other data when it's time to write your citations. This book describes MLA (see **MLA** p. 358). For others, consult one of the guides listed in **8** pp. 352 and 355.

b Annotations

Creating annotations for a working bibliography converts it from a simple list into a tool for assessing sources. When you discover a possible source, record not only its publication information but also the following:

- **What you know about the content of the source.** Periodical databases and book catalogs generally include abstracts, or summaries, of sources that can help with this part of the annotation.
- **How you think the source may be helpful in your research.** Does it offer expert opinion, statistics, an important example, or a range of views? Does it place your subject in a historical, social, or economic context?

Taking the time with your annotations can help you discover gaps that may remain in your sources and will later help you decide which sources to pursue in depth. One student annotated a bibliography entry on his computer with a summary and a note on the source features he thought would be most helpful to him:

Entry for an annotated working bibliography

Publication information for source

> Gore, Al. *An Inconvenient Truth: The Planetary Emergency of Global Warming and What We Can Do about It.* Emmaus: Rodale, 2006. Print.

Summary of source

Ideas on use of source

> Book version of the documentary movie supporting Gore's argument that global warming is a serious threat to the planet. Includes summaries of scientific studies, short essays on various subjects, and dozens of images, tables, charts, and graphs. Last chapter offers several suggestions for ways to solve the problem, with an emphasis on changing individual buying habits.

As you become more familiar with your sources, you can use your initial annotated bibliography to record your evaluations of them as well as more detailed thoughts on how they fit into your research.

3 | Synthesizing sources

Using your research journal, you can begin to identify prevailing ideas you locate in your sources, and you can begin to note where ideas from one source to another connect or differ.

When you begin to locate the differences and similarities among sources, you move into the most significant part of research writing: forging relationships for your own purpose. This **synthesis** is an essential step in reading sources critically, and it continues through the drafting and revision of a research paper. As you infer connections—say, between one writer's opinions and another's or between two works by the same author—you create new knowledge.

Your synthesis of sources will grow more detailed and sophisticated as you proceed through the process of working with sources described in the balance of this chapter: gathering information from sources (pp. 304–05); deciding whether to summarize, paraphrase, or quote directly from sources (pp. 323–26); and integrating sources into your sentences (pp. 326–30). Unless you are analyzing primary sources such as the works of a poet, at first read your sources quickly and selectively to obtain an overview of your subject and a sense of how the sources approach it. Don't get bogged down in gathering detailed information, but *do* record your ideas about sources in your research journal (p. 301) or your annotated bibliography (p. 301).

Respond to sources

Write down what your sources make you think. Do you agree or disagree with the author? Do you find his or her views narrow, or do they open up new approaches for you? Is there anything in the source that you need to research further before you can understand it? Does the source prompt questions that you should keep in mind while reading other sources?

Connect sources

When you notice a link between sources, jot it down. Do two sources differ in their theories or their interpretations of facts? Does one source illuminate another—perhaps commenting or clarifying or supplying additional data? Do two or more sources report studies that support a theory you've read about or an idea of your own?

Heed your insights

Apart from ideas prompted by your sources, you are sure to come up with independent thoughts: a conviction, a point of confusion that suddenly becomes clear, a question you haven't seen anyone else ask. These insights may occur at unexpected times, so it's good practice to keep a notebook or computer handy to record them.

Draw your own conclusions

As your research proceeds, the responses, connections, and insights you form through synthesis will lead you to answer your starting research question with a statement of your thesis. They will also lead you to the main ideas supporting your thesis—conclusions you have drawn from your synthesis of sources, forming the main divisions of your paper.

Use sources to support your conclusions

Effective synthesis requires careful handling of evidence from sources so that it meshes smoothly into your sentences and yet is clearly distinct from your own ideas. When drafting your paper, make sure that each paragraph focuses on an idea of your own, with the support for the idea coming from your sources. Generally, open each paragraph with your idea, provide evidence from a source or sources with appropriate citations, and close with an interpretation of the evidence. (Avoid ending a paragraph with a source citation; instead, end with your own idea.) In this way, your paper will synthesize others' work into something wholly your own. For more on structuring paragraphs in academic writing, see **2** p. 82.

4 Gathering information from sources

You can accomplish a great deal of synthesis while gathering information from your sources. This information gathering is not a mechanical process. Rather, as you read you assess and organize the information in your sources.

As you are synthesizing ideas from your sources, you will also be gathering information as well. As you begin to see what is being written and how your topic is being approached, you will have a clearer idea of which information will help you shape your research paper.

Researchers vary in their methods for working with sources, but all methods share the same goals:

- **Keep accurate records of what sources say.** Accuracy helps prevent misrepresentation and plagiarism.
- **Keep accurate records of how to find sources.** These records are essential for retracing steps and for citing sources in the final paper. (See pp. 301–03 on keeping a working bibliography.)
- **Synthesize sources.** Information gathering is a critical process, leading to an understanding of sources, the relationships among them and your own ideas, and their support for your ideas.

To achieve these goals, you can take handwritten notes, type notes into your computer, annotate photocopies or printouts of sources, or annotate downloaded documents. On any given project, you may use all the methods. Each has advantages and disadvantages.

- **Handwritten notes:** Taking notes by hand is especially useful if you come across a source with no computer or photocopier handy. But handwritten notes can be risky. It's easy to introduce errors as you work from source to paper. And it's possible to copy source language and then later mistake and use it as your own, thus plagiarizing the source. Always take care to make accurate notes and to place big quotation marks around any passage you quote.

- **Notes on computer:** Taking notes on a computer can streamline the path of source to note to paper, because you can import the notes into your draft as you write. However, computer notes have the same disadvantages as handwritten notes: the risk of introducing errors and the risk of plagiarizing. As with handwritten notes, be a stickler for accuracy and use quotation marks for quotations.

- **Photocopies and printouts:** Photocopying from print sources or printing out online sources each has the distinct advantages of convenience and reduction in the risks of error and plagiarism during information gathering. But each method has disadvantages, too. The busywork of copying or printing can distract you from the crucial work of synthesizing sources. And you have to make a special effort to annotate copies and printouts with the publication information for sources. If you don't have this information for your final paper, you can't use the source.

- **Downloads:** Researching online, you can usually download full-text articles, Web pages, discussion-group messages, and other materials onto your computer. While drafting, you can import source information from one file into another. Like photocopies and printouts, though, downloads can distract you from interacting with sources and can easily become separated from the publication information you must have in order to use the sources. Even more important, directly importing source material creates a high risk of plagiarism. You must keep clear boundaries between your own ideas and words and those of others.

50c Finding a researchable subject and question

When thinking about a subject for research, you can seek inspiration in various places—from class readings to YouTube videos to articles posted on Facebook. When something has caught your attention or made you curious, write down a few notes on why it interests you as well as any questions it might bring up. Keep a list of ideas, terms, and questions that you can refer to as you search for information.

1 Appropriate subject

Seek a research subject that interests you and that you care about. (It may be a subject you've already written about without the benefit of research.) Starting with your own views will motivate you, and you will be a participant in a dialog when you begin examining sources.

2 Research question

Asking a question about your subject can give direction to your research by focusing your thinking on a particular approach. To discover your question, consider what about your subject intrigues or perplexes you, what you'd like to know more about. (See below for suggestions on using your own knowledge.)

Try to narrow your research question so that you can answer it in the time and space you have available. The question *How does human activity affect the environment?* is very broad, encompassing issues as diverse as pollution, distribution of resources, climate change, population growth, land use, biodiversity, and the ozone layer. In contrast, the question *How can buying environmentally friendly products help the environment?* or *How, if at all, should carbon emissions be taxed?* is much narrower. Each question also requires more than a simple *yes* or *no* answer, so that answering, even tentatively, demands thought about pros and cons, causes and effects.

As you read and write, your question will probably evolve to reflect your increasing knowledge of the subject, and eventually its answer will become your main idea, or focus.

50d Setting goals for sources

Before you start looking for sources, consider what you already know about your subject and where you are likely to find information on it.

1 Your own knowledge

Discovering what you already know about your topic will guide you in discovering what you don't know. Take some time to spell out facts you have learned, opinions you have heard or read elsewhere, and of course your own opinions. Use one of the discovery techniques discussed in **1** pp. 7–16 to explore and develop your ideas: keeping a journal, observing your surroundings, freewriting, brainstorming, clustering, and asking questions.

When you've explored your thoughts, make a list of questions for which you don't have answers, whether factual (*How much do Americans spend on green products?*) or more open-ended (*Are green products worth the higher prices?*). These questions will give you clues about the sources you need to look for first.

2 Kinds of sources

For many research projects, you'll want to consult a mix of sources, as described on the next two pages. You may start by seeking the outlines of your topic—the range and depth of opinions about it—in reference works and articles in popular periodicals or through a Web search. Then, as you refine your views and your research question, you'll move on to more specialized sources, such as scholarly books and periodicals and your own interviews or surveys. (See pp. 309–16 for more on each kind of source.)

The mix of sources you choose depends heavily on your subject. For example, a paper on green consumerism would require the use of very recent sources because environmentally friendly products are fairly new to the marketplace. Your mix of sources may also be specified by your instructor or limited by the requirements of your assignment.

Background information sources

Building a working knowledge of a subject can begin with consulting background sources, such as encyclopedias and other reference works. Often encyclopedias will contain histories, timelines, dates, names of people, outlines, keywords and terms, and links to other resources on particular subjects. The MSU Libraries have several online encyclopedias as well as a print collection on the first floor of the Main Library. If your research area is very new, such as a current event, trend, or technology, you may need to search the Web and news articles for background information. Wikipedia can be helpful for identifying keywords and finding links to other resources; you will need to be sure to critically evaluate the content of Wikipedia articles as you would other web sources (see evaluation section).

Primary and secondary sources

Use **primary sources** when they are available or are required by your assignment. These sources are firsthand accounts, such as works of literature, historical documents (letters, speeches, and so on), eyewitness reports (including articles by journalists who are on location), reports on experiments or surveys conducted by the writer, and your own interviews, experiments, observations, or correspondence.

Many assignments will allow you to use **secondary sources,** which report and analyze information drawn from other sources, often primary ones. Examples include a reporter's summary of a controversial issue, a historian's account of a battle, a critic's reading of a poem, and a psychologist's evaluation of several studies.

Secondary sources may contain helpful summaries and interpretations that direct, support, and extend your own thinking. However, most research-writing assignments expect your own ideas to go beyond those in such sources.

Scholarly and popular sources

The scholarship of acknowledged experts is essential for depth, authority, and specificity. Most instructors expect students to emphasize scholarly sources in their research. But the general-interest views and information of popular sources can help you apply more scholarly approaches to daily life.

- **Check the title.** Is it technical, or does it use a general vocabulary?
- **Check the publisher.** Is it a scholarly journal (such as *Cultural Geographies*) or a publisher of scholarly books (such as Harvard University Press), or is it a popular magazine (such as *Consumer Reports* or *Newsweek*) or a publisher of popular books (such as Little, Brown)?
- **Check the length of periodical articles.** Scholarly articles are generally much longer than magazine and newspaper articles.
- **Check the author.** Can you find any background information about the author, for example: are they affiliated with a university or professional organization?

Older and newer sources

Check the publication date. For most subjects a combination of older, established sources (such as books) and current sources (such as newspaper articles, interviews, or Web sites) will provide both background and up-to-date information. Only historical subjects or very current subjects require an emphasis on one extreme or another.

Viewpoint sources

Seek a range of viewpoints. Sources that attempt to be impartial can offer an overview of your subject and trustworthy facts. Sources with clear biases can offer a diversity of opinion. Of course, to discover bias, you may have to read the source carefully (see pp. 317–30); but you can infer quite a bit just from a bibliographical listing.

- **Check the language.** The word choices that an author uses often reveal a bias.
- **Check the publisher or affiliation.** Is the sources published by a group that has an obvious agenda or viewpoint that it promotes?

Note All material that you find will have some type of bias. If you are looking for hard facts, try to locate the most objective source that you can. Viewpoint sources are excellent for understanding different takes on a controversy or framing the debate on an issue.

51 Finding Sources

This chapter discusses conducting electronic searches (next page) and taking advantage of the range of sources, both print and electronic, that you have access to: reference works (p. 309); books (p. 309); periodicals (p. 310); the Web (p. 311); other online sources (p. 311); government publications (p. 313); images, audio, and video (p. 313); and your own interviews, surveys, and other primary sources (p. 314).

Note As you look for sources, avoid the temptation to seek a "silver bullet"—that is, to locate two or three perfect sources that already say everything you want to say about your subject. Instead of merely repeating others' ideas, read and synthesize many sources so that you develop your own ideas. For more on synthesis, see pp. 303–04.

Note You will probably have to use trial and error in developing your keywords, sometimes running dry (turning up few or no sources) and sometimes hitting uncontrollable gushers (turning up thousands or millions of mostly irrelevant sources). But the process is not busywork—far from it. Besides leading you eventually to worthwhile sources, it can also teach you a great deal about your subject: how you can or should narrow it, how it is and is not described by others, what others consider interesting or debatable about it, and what the major arguments are.

51a Finding background information

Reference works, often available online, include encyclopedias, dictionaries, digests, bibliographies, indexes, atlases, almanacs, and handbooks. Your research *must* go beyond these sources, but they can help you decide whether your topic really interests you and whether it meets the requirements for a research paper (p. 305). Preliminary research in reference works can also help you develop keywords for electronic searches and can direct you to more detailed sources on your topic.

51b Finding books

No matter what you find in a book, whether it's on the open Web or through the MSU Libraries' site, remember to check the library

mycomplab

Visit *mycomplab.com* for more resources as well as
exercises on finding sources.

catalog to see if the book is available. On the MSU Libraries' home page, http://www.lib.msu.edu, use the search box labeled "Library Catalog." When you find the book that you're looking for, click its title until you get to a screen which displays the book's location, call number, and status. Clicking on the book's location should give you a map or more information about where the book is stored. Before you go to the shelves to look for the book, make sure to write down the entire call number as this will guide you to a specific point on the shelf. If you have any questions at all about the book's location, please stop by the reference desk on the first floor of the Main Library and ask a librarian.

In searching the library shelves for a book, you will notice that the books are grouped by subject. Occasionally you will find other helpful books near the original one that you located. Browsing the shelves can be a source for generating new ideas about a subject.

Note If you can't find a specific book in the MSU Libraries' catalog, it is usually possible to borrow a copy from a different library for you at no charge. Click the "Ask A Librarian" link at the top of any library web page for directions on how to request a book from another library. This service can take from 5 days to 2 weeks, so if you're starting your project early you will have a lot more options for getting books.

51c Finding articles

You can find articles almost anywhere, from the open Web to library shelves. Articles are usually found within a larger publication — a periodical – which is published on an ongoing basis. Periodicals traditionally include newspapers, magazines, and scholarly journals.

To streamline your search, there are two places on the MSU Libraries' website (http://www.lib.msu.edu) where you can begin. The "Basic Search for Articles" search box will retrieve a broad range of articles, including selections from popular magazines, scholarly journals, newspapers, and trade publications. This is a good place to test the waters and see what types of information may be available related to your research interest.

If you need to dig deeper for more scholarly articles on a subject, try the "Browse Indexes by Subject" menu, also on the MSU Libraries' website (http://www.lib.msu.edu). Indexes are searchable databases, usually based on a specific area or subject, filled with articles and article citations. The "Browse Indexes by Subject" links will take you to pages which list all the MSU Libraries' article indexes related to the subject. At the top of these pages should be a link that says "Getting Started." Clicking "Getting Started" will list the most popular indexes in that subject, along with the name and contact information of a librarian who specializes in that area.

51d Finding sources on the Web

Internet or open Web searching is by far the most popular method of beginning a search for information, and can yield unique and plentiful results. There are a few things that you should keep in mind during your Web searching:

- **The Web is a wide-open network.** Anyone with the right hardware and software can place information on the Internet, and even a carefully conceived search can turn up sources with widely varying reliability: journal articles, government documents, scholarly data, term papers written by high school students, sales pitches masked as objective reports, wild theories. You must be especially diligent about evaluating Internet sources (see pp. 319–23).
- **The Web changes constantly.** No search engine can keep up with the Web's daily additions and deletions, and a source you find today may be different or gone tomorrow. You should not put off consulting an online source that you think you may want to use.
- **The Web provides limited information on the past.** Sources dating from before the 1980s or even more recently probably will not appear on the Web.
- **The Web is not all-inclusive.** Most books and many periodicals are available only via the library, not directly via the Web.

51e Finding other online sources

Several online sources can put you directly in touch with experts and others whose ideas and information may inform your research. Because these sources, like Web sites, are unfiltered, you must always evaluate them carefully. (See pp. 321–23.)

1 E-mail

As a research tool, e-mail allows you to communicate with others who are interested in your topic. You might, for instance, carry on an e-mail conversation with a teacher at your school or interview an expert in another state to follow up on a scholarly article he or she published. (See **2** pp. 103–05 for more on using e-mail.)

2 Blogs

Blogs (Web logs) are personal sites on which an author posts time-stamped comments, generally centering on a common theme, in a format that allows readers to respond to the author or to each other. You can find a directory of blogs at *blogcatalog.com*.

Like all other online media discussed in this section, blogs consulted as potential sources must be evaluated carefully. Some are reliable sources of opinion, news, or evolving scholarship, and many refer to worthy books, articles, Web sites, and other resources. But lots of blogs are little more than outlets for their authors' gripes and prejudices. See pp. 321–23 for tips on telling the good from the bad.

3 Discussion lists

A **discussion list** (sometimes called a **listserv** or just a **list**) uses e-mail to connect individuals who are interested in a common subject, often with a scholarly or technical focus. By sending a question to an appropriate list, you may be able to reach scores of people who know something about your topic. For an index of discussion lists, see *tile.net/lists*.

When conducting research on a discussion list, follow the guidelines for writing e-mail (**2** pp. 103–05) as well as these:

- *Lurk* for a while—read without posting messages. Make sure the discussion is relevant to your topic, and get a sense of how the group interacts.
- **Consult the list's archive.** Your question may already have been answered.
- **Don't ask for information you can find elsewhere.** Most list members are glad to help with legitimate questions but resent messages that rehash familiar debates or that ask them to do someone else's work.
- **Evaluate messages carefully.** Many list subscribers are passionate experts with fair-minded approaches to their topics, but almost anyone with an Internet connection can post a message to a list. See pp. 321–23 on evaluating online sources.

4 Web forums and newsgroups

Web forums and newsgroups are more open and less scholarly than discussion lists, so their messages require even more diligent evaluation. **Web forums** allow participants to join a conversation simply by selecting a link on a Web page. For a directory of forums, see *delphiforums.com*. **Newsgroups** are organized under subject headings such as *soc* for social issues and *biz* for business. For a directory of newsgroups, see *groups.google.com*.

5 Professional Organization Sites

When looking for information about a specific field, the websites of professional organizations can be valuable sources. Searching Google or another search engine for the name of your subject field/area (for example math, engineering, or marketing) with the word organizations (or professional societies, professional groups, and associations) should provide some initial results. Information on a professional organization's web site can include a history of the organization, what they do, what publications they sponsor, how to find a job in the field, and other relevant information.

51f Using government publications

Government publications can provide authoritative statistics and information from US government agencies and sponsored programs. A quick way to search for government documents, both in print at the MSU Libraries and line, is to use the "Advanced Catalog Search" online the Libraries' website, http://www.lib.msu.edu/. Enter your search terms and set the Location to "GOVERNMENT DOCUMENT."

51g Finding images, audio, and video

Images, audio, and video can be used as both primary and secondary sources in a research project. A painting, an advertisement, or a video of a speech might be the subject of a paper and thus a primary source. A podcast of a radio interview with an expert on your subject or a college lecture might serve as a secondary source. Because many of these sources are unfiltered—they can be posted by anyone—you must always evaluate them as carefully as you would any source you find on the open Web.

Note You must also cite every image, audio, and video source fully in your paper, just as you cite text sources, with author, title, and publication information. In addition, some sources will require that you seek permission from the copyright holder, either the source itself or a third party such as a photographer or the creator of video. Permission is especially likely to be required if you are submitting your paper on the public Web. See p. 336 for more about online publication.

1 Images

The use of images to support an argument is discussed in **2** pp. 96–102. To find images, you have a number of options.

- **Scout for images while reading sources.** Your sources may include charts, graphs, photographs, and other images that can support your ideas. When you find an image you may want to use, photocopy or download it so you'll have it available later.
- **Create your own images,** such as photographs or charts. See **1** pp. 52–56 for examples.
- **Use an image search engine.** *Google, Yahoo!, AlltheWeb,* and some other search engines conduct specialized image searches. They can find scores of images, but the results may be inaccurate

or incomplete because the sources surveyed often do not include descriptions of the images. (The engines will search file names and any text accompanying the images.)

■ Try the MSU Libraries' guide "Finding & Storing Images" at http://libguides.msu.edu/Images. This guide includes public image databases, directories, and links to subscription image resources from the MSU Libraries.

2 Audio and video

Audio and video, widely available on the Web and on CD-ROM, can provide your readers with the experience of "being there." For example, if you are researching the media response to Martin Luther King's famous "I Have a Dream" speech and you are publishing your paper electronically, you might insert links to the speech and to TV and radio coverage of it.

■ **Audio files** such as podcasts, Webcasts, and CDs record radio programs, interviews, speeches, lectures, and music. They are available on the Web and through your library. Online sources of audio include Congress's *American Memory* (see the previous page) and podcasts at *www.podcastdirectory.com*.

■ **Video files** capture performances, public presentations and speeches, news events, and other activities. They are available on the Web and through your library on DVD. Online sources of video include the Library of Congress's *American Memory* (see the previous page); *YouTube*, which includes commercials, historical footage, current events, and much more (*youtube.com*); and search engines such as *Google* (*video.google.com*).

51h Generating your own sources

Academic writing will often require you to conduct primary research for information of your own. For instance, you may need to analyze a poem, conduct an experiment, or interview an expert. Three common forms of primary research are observation, personal interviews, and surveys.

1 Observation

Observation can be an effective way to gather fresh information on your subject. You may observe in a controlled setting—for instance, watching the behavior of children playing in a child-development lab. Or you may observe in a more open setting—for instance, watching the interactions among students at a cafeteria on your campus. Be sure your observation has a well-defined purpose that relates to your research project. Throughout the observation, take careful notes, either on paper or on a handheld computer, and always record the date, time, and location for each session.

2 Personal interviews

An interview can be especially helpful for a research project because it allows you to ask questions precisely geared to your topic. You can conduct an interview in person, over the telephone, or online. A personal interview is preferable if you can arrange it, because you can see the person's expressions and gestures as well as hear his or her tone.

Here are a few guidelines for interviews:

- **Call or write for an appointment.** Tell the person exactly why you are calling, what you want to discuss, and how long you expect the interview to take. Be true to your word on all points.
- **Prepare a list of open-ended questions to ask**—perhaps ten or twelve for a one-hour interview. Plan on doing some research for these questions to discover background on the issues and your subject's published views on the issues.
- **Pay attention to your subject's answers** so that you can ask appropriate follow-up questions. Take care in interpreting answers, especially if you are online and thus can't depend on facial expressions, gestures, and tone of voice to convey the subject's attitudes.
- **Keep thorough notes.** Take notes during an in-person or telephone interview, or record the interview if you have the equipment and your subject agrees. For online interviews, save the discussion in a file of its own.
- **Verify quotations.** Before you quote your subject in your paper, check with him or her to ensure that the quotations are accurate.
- **Send a thank-you note immediately after the interview.** Promise your subject a copy of your finished paper, and send the paper promptly.

3 Surveys

Asking questions of a defined group of people can provide information about respondents' attitudes, behavior, backgrounds, and expectations. Use the following tips to plan and conduct a survey:

- **Decide what you want to find out.** The questions you ask should be dictated by your purpose. Formulating a **hypothesis** about your subject—a generalization that can be tested—will help you refine your purpose.
- **Define your population.** Think about the kinds of people your hypothesis is about—for instance, college men or preschool children. Plan to sample this population so that your findings will be representative.
- **Write your questions.** Surveys may contain closed questions that direct the respondent's answers (checklists and multiple-choice, true/false, or yes/no questions) or open-ended questions that allow

brief, descriptive answers. Avoid loaded questions that reveal your own biases or make assumptions about subjects' answers.

■ **Test your questions.** Use a few respondents with whom you can discuss the answers. Eliminate or recast questions that respondents find unclear, discomforting, or unanswerable.

■ **Tally the results.** Count the actual numbers of answers, including any nonanswers.

■ **Seek patterns in the raw data.** Such patterns may confirm or contradict your hypothesis. Revise the hypothesis or conduct additional research if necessary.

52 Working with Sources

Research writing is much more than finding sources and reporting their contents. The challenge and interest come from interacting with and synthesizing sources: reading them critically to discover their meanings, judge their relevance and reliability, and create relationships among them; and using them to extend and support your own ideas so that you make your subject your own.

‹CULTURE LANGUAGE› Making a subject your own requires thinking critically about sources and developing independent ideas. These goals may at first be uncomfortable if your native culture emphasizes understanding and respecting established authority more than questioning and enlarging it. The information here will help you work with sources so that you can become an expert in your own right and convincingly convey your expertise to others.

52a Evaluating sources

Before you gather information and ideas from sources, scan them to evaluate what they have to offer and how you might use them.

When evaluating any written information source, it's helpful to view the source as a piece of someone else's writing. Looking at the source through the lens of revision, arrangement, invention, delivery, and style—concepts you use in your own writing—will give you a foundation for understanding the purpose of the information and help you to decide whether and how to use the source for your project.

In addition to using the RAIDS concepts, the criteria in the following sections will help you to think critically about all types of

mycomplab

Visit *mycomplab.com* for more resources as well as exercises on working with sources.

information sources that you may encounter in your searching—from scholarly articles to Wikipedia entries.

Note If you have any questions about a source–where it comes from, whether it's appropriate to use in your project, or anything else—please ask your instructor and also talk to an MSU librarian. You can find librarian contact information by going to the MSU Libraries' website (http://www.lib.msu.edu) and clicking on the "Ask a Librarian" link at the top of the page.

1 Relevance and reliability

Not all the sources you find will prove worthwhile: some may be irrelevant to your subject, and others may be unreliable. Gauging the relevance and reliability of sources is the essential task of evaluating them. If you haven't already done so, read this book's chapter on critical thinking and reading (**2** pp. 68–80). It provides a foundation for answering the questions in the following box.

Questions for evaluating sources

For online sources, supplement these questions with those on pp. 319 and 322.

Relevance

- **Does the source devote some attention to your subject?** Does it focus on your subject or cover it marginally? How does it compare to other sources you've found?
- **Is the source appropriately specialized for your needs?** Check the source's treatment of a topic you know something about, to ensure that it is neither too superficial nor too technical.
- **Is the source up to date enough for your subject?** When was it published? If your subject is current, your sources should be, too.

Reliability

- **Where does the source come from?** Did you find it through your library or directly through the Internet? (If the latter, see pp. 319 and 319–323.) Is the source popular or scholarly?
- **Is the author an expert in the field?** Check the author's credentials in a biography (if the source includes one), in a biographical reference, or by a keyword search of the Web.
- **What is the author's bias?** How do the author's ideas relate to those in other sources? What areas does the author emphasize, ignore, or dismiss?
- **Is the source fair, reasonable, and well-written?** Does it provide sound reasoning and a fair picture of opposing views? Is the tone calm and objective? Is the source logically organized and error-free?
- **Are the author's claims well supported?** Does the author provide accurate, relevant, representative, and adequate evidence to back up his or her claims? Does the author cite sources, and if so are they reliable?

2 | Evaluating library sources

To evaluate sources you find through your library, either in print or on the library's Web site, look at dates, titles, summaries, introductions, headings, author biographies, and any source notes. The following criteria expand on the most important tips in the preceding box.

Identify the origin of the source

Check whether a library source is popular or scholarly. Scholarly sources, such as refereed journals and university press books, are generally deeper and more reliable, though some popular sources, such as first-hand newspaper accounts and books for a general audience, are often appropriate for research projects.

Check the author's expertise

The authors of scholarly publications tend to be experts whose authority can be verified. Check the source to see whether it contains a biographical note about the author, check a biographical reference, or check the author's name in a keyword search of the Web. Look for other publications by the author and for his or her job and any affiliation, such as teacher at a university, researcher with a nonprofit organization, author of general-interest books, or writer for popular magazines.

Identify the author's bias

Every author has a point of view that influences the selection and interpretation of evidence. You may be able to learn about an author's bias from biographies, citation indexes, and review indexes. But also look at the source itself. How do the author's ideas relate to those in other sources? What areas does the author emphasize, ignore, or dismiss? When you're aware of sources' biases, you can attempt to balance them.

Determine whether the source is fair, reasonable, and well written

Even a strongly biased work should present solid reasoning and give balanced coverage to opposing views—all in an objective tone. Any source should be organized logically and should be written in clear, error-free sentences. The absence of any of these qualities should raise a warning flag.

Analyze support for the author's claims

Evidence should be accurate, relevant to the argument, representative of its context, and adequate for the point being made (see **2** pp. 89–90). The author's sources should themselves be reliable.

3 Evaluating Web sites

> ## Questions for evaluating Web sites
> Supplement these questions with those on p. 317.
>
> - **What type of site are you viewing?** What does the type lead you to expect about the site's purpose and content?
> - **Who is the author or sponsor?** How credible is the person or group responsible for the site?
> - **What is the purpose of the site?** What does the site's author or sponsor intend to achieve?
> - **What does context tell you?** What do you already know about the site's subject that can inform your evaluation? What kinds of support or other information do the site's links provide?
> - **What does presentation tell you?** Is the site's design well thought out and effective? Is the writing clear and error-free?
> - **How worthwhile is the content?** Are the site's claims well supported by evidence? Is the evidence from reliable sources? When was the site last updated?

Determine the type of site

When you search the Web, you're likely to encounter various types of sites. Although they overlap—a primarily informational site may include scholarship as well—the types can usually be identified by their content and purposes. Here are the main types:

- **Scholarly sites:** These sites have a knowledge-building interest and include research reports with supporting data and extensive documentation of scholarly sources. The URLs of the sites generally end in *edu* (originating from an educational institution), *org* (a nonprofit organization), or *gov* (a government department or agency). Such sites are more likely to be reliable than the others described below.
- **Informational sites:** Individuals, nonprofit organizations, corporations, schools, and government bodies all produce sites intended to centralize information on particular subjects. The sites' URLs may end in *edu, org, gov,* or *com* (originating from a commercial organization). Such sites generally do not have the knowledge-building focus of scholarly sites and may omit supporting data and documentation, but they can provide useful information and often include links to scholarly sources.
- **Advocacy sites:** Many sites present the views of individuals or organizations that promote certain policies or actions. Their URLs usually end in *org,* but they may end in *edu* or *com.*

Some advocacy sites include serious, well-documented research to support their positions, but others select or distort evidence.

- **Commercial sites:** Corporations and other businesses maintain Web sites to explain or promote themselves or to sell goods and services. The URLs of commercial sites end in *com*. The information on such a site furthers the sponsor's profit-making purpose, but it can include reliable data.

- **Personal sites:** The sites maintained by individuals range from diaries of a family's travels to opinions on political issues to reports on evolving scholarship. The sites' URLs usually end in *com* or *edu*. Personal sites are only as reliable as their authors, but some do provide valuable eyewitness accounts, links to worthy sources, and other usable information. A particular kind of personal site, the blog, is discussed on pp. 311 and 322.

Identify the author and sponsor

A reputable site will list its authors, will name the group responsible for the site, and will provide information or a link for contacting the author and the sponsor. If none of this information is provided, you should not use the source. If you have only the author's or the sponsor's name, you may be able to discover more in a biographical dictionary, through a keyword search, or in your other sources. Make sure the author and the sponsor have expertise on the subject they're presenting: if an author is a doctor, for instance, what is he or she a doctor of?

Gauge purpose and bias

A Web site's purpose determines what ideas and information it offers. Inferring that purpose tells you how to interpret what you see on the site. If a site is intended to sell a product or an opinion, it will likely emphasize favorable ideas and information while ignoring or even distorting what is unfavorable. In contrast, if a site is intended to build knowledge—for instance, a scholarly project or journal—it will likely acknowledge diverse views and evidence.

Determining the purpose of a site often requires looking beyond the first page and beneath the surface of words and images. To start, read what the site says about itself, usually found on a page labeled "About." Be suspicious of any site that doesn't provide information about itself and its goals.

Consider context

Your evaluation of a Web site should be informed by considerations outside the site itself. Chief among these is your own knowledge. What do you already know about the site's subject and the prevailing views of it? Where does this site seem to fit into that picture? What can you learn from this site that you don't already know?

In addition, you can follow some of the site's links to see how they support, or don't support, the site's credibility. For instance, links to scholarly sources lend authority to a site—but *only* if the scholarly sources actually relate to and back up the site's claims.

Look at presentation

Considering both the look of a site and the way it's written can illuminate its intentions and reliability. Are the site's elements all functional and well integrated, or is the site cluttered with irrelevant material and graphics? Does the site seem carefully constructed and well maintained, or is it sloppy? Does the design reflect the apparent purpose of the site, or does it undercut or conceal that purpose in some way? Is the text clearly written, or is it difficult to understand? Is it error-free, or does it contain typos and grammatical errors?

Analyze content

With information about a site's author, purpose, and context, you're in a position to evaluate its content. Are the ideas and information current, or are they dated? (Check the publication date.) Are they slanted and, if so, in what direction? Are the views and data authoritative, or do you need to balance them—or even reject them? Are claims made on the site supported by evidence drawn from reliable sources? These questions require close reading of both the text and its sources.

4 Evaluating other online sources

Blogs, online discussions, and online images, video, and audio require the same critical scrutiny as Web sites do. Blogs and discussion groups can be sources of reliable data and opinions, but you will also encounter wrong or misleading data and skewed opinions. One podcast may provide an interview with a recognized expert while another claims authority that it doesn't deserve. A *YouTube* search using "I have a dream" brings up videos of Martin Luther King, Jr., delivering his famous speech as well as videos of people speaking hatefully about King and the speech.

Use the following strategy for evaluating blogs, discussion groups, and multimedia sources:

Questions for evaluating blogs, online discussions, images, video, and audio

Supplement these questions with those on pp. 316–18.

- ▪ **Who is the author or creator?** How credible is he or she?
- ▪ **What is the author's or creator's purpose?** What can you tell about why the author or creator is publishing the work?
- ▪ **What does the context reveal?** What do other responses to the work, including responses to a blog posting or the other messages in a discussion thread, indicate about the source's balance and reliability?
- ▪ **How worthwhile is the content?** Are the claims made by the author or creator supported by evidence? Is the evidence from reliable sources?
- ▪ **How does the source compare with other sources?** Do the claims made by the author or creator seem accurate and fair given what you've seen in sources you know to be reliable?

Identify the author or creator

Checking out the author or creator of a blog, online posting, video file, or podcast can help you judge its reliability. If the author or creator uses a screen name, write directly to him or her requesting full name and credentials. Do not use the source if you don't get a response. Once you know the person's name, you may be able to obtain background information from a keyword search of the Web or a biographical dictionary.

You can also get a sense of the interests and biases of an author or creator by tracking down his or her other publications. For a blog, check whether the author cites or links to other publications. For a discussion-group posting, look for an archive or other feature that allows you to find additional messages by the same author. For multimedia sources, try to gain an overview of the creator's work.

Analyze the author's or creator's purpose

What can you tell about *why* the author or creator is publishing the work? Look for claims, the use (or lack) of evidence, and the treatment of opposing views. All these convey the person's stand on the subject and general fairness, and they will help you position the source among your other sources.

Consider the context

Blogs, discussion-group postings, and multimedia sources are often difficult to evaluate in isolation. Looking beyond a particular contribution to the responses of others will give you a sense of how the author or creator is regarded. On a blog, look at the comments others have posted. Do the same with postings, going back to the initial posting in the discussion thread and reading forward.

Analyze content

A reliable source will offer evidence for claims and sources for evidence. If you don't see such supporting information, ask the author or creator for it. (If he or she fails to respond, don't use the source.) Then verify the sources with your own research: are they reputable?

The tone of writing can also be a clue to its purpose and reliability. Blogs, online discussions, and some podcasts tend to be more informal and often more heated than other kinds of dialog, but look askance at writing that's contemptuous, dismissive, or shrill.

Compare with other sources

Always consider blogs, postings, and multimedia sources in comparison to other sources so that you can distinguish singular, untested views from more mainstream views that have been subject to verification. Don't assume that a blog author's information and opinions are mainstream just because you see them on other blogs. The technology allows content to be picked up instantly by other blogs, so widespread distribution indicates only popularity, not reliability.

Be wary of blogs or postings that reproduce periodical articles, reports, or other publications. Try to locate the original version of the publication to be sure it has been reproduced fully and accurately, not quoted selectively or distorted. If you can't locate the original version, don't use the publication as a source.

52b Using summary, paraphrase, and quotation

Deciding whether to summarize, paraphrase, or quote directly from sources is an important step in synthesizing the sources' ideas and your own. You engage in synthesis when you use your own words to summarize an author's argument or paraphrase a significant example or when you select a significant passage to quote. Choosing summary, paraphrase, or quotation should depend on why you are using a source.

Note Summaries, paraphrases, and quotations all require source citations. A summary or paraphrase without a source citation or a quotation without quotation marks and a source citation is plagiarism. (See pp. 330–36 for more on plagiarism.)

1 Summary

When you **summarize,** you condense an extended idea or argument into a sentence or more in your own words. (See **2** pp. 69–70 for tips.) **Summary** is most useful when you want to record the gist of an author's idea without the background or supporting evidence.

Following is a passage from a scholarly essay about consumption and its impact on the environment. Then a sample computer note shows a summary of the passage.

Original quotation

Such intuition is even making its way, albeit slowly, into scholarly circles, where recognition is mounting that ever-increasing pressures on ecosystems, life-supporting environmental services, and critical natural cycles are driven not only by the sheer number of resource users and the inefficiencies of their resource use, but also by the patterns of resource use themselves. In global environmental policymaking arenas, it is becoming more and more difficult to ignore the fact that the overdeveloped North must restrain its consumption if it expects the underdeveloped South to embrace a more sustainable trajectory.

—Thomas Princen, Michael Maniates, and Ken Conca, "Confronting Consumption," p. 4

Summary of source

Environmental consequences of consumption

Princen, Maniates, and Conca 4

Overconsumption may be a more significant cause of environmental problems than increasing population is.

---

2 Paraphrase

When you **paraphrase,** you follow much more closely the author's original presentation, but you restate it using your own words and sentence structures. Paraphrase is most useful when you want to present or examine an author's line of reasoning but you don't feel the original words merit direct quotation. Here is a paraphrase of the quotation from the essay "Confronting Consumption."

Paraphrase of source

Environmental consequences of consumption

Princen, Maniates, and Conca 4

Scholars are coming to believe that consumption is partly to blame for changes in ecosystems, reduction of essential natural resources, and changes in natural cycles. Policy makers increasingly see that wealthy nations have to start consuming less if they want developing nations to adopt practices that reduce pollution and waste. Rising population around the world does cause significant stress on the environment, but consumption is increasing even more rapidly than population.

Notice that the paraphrase follows the original but uses different words and different sentence structures. In contrast, an unsuccessful paraphrase—one that plagiarizes—copies the author's words or sentence structures or both *without quotation marks*. (See pp. 334–35 for examples.)

Paraphrasing a source

■ **Read the relevant material several times to be sure you understand it.**

■ **Restate the source's ideas in your own words and sentence structures.** You need not put down in new words the whole passage or all the details. Select what is relevant to your topic, and restate only that. If complete sentences seem too detailed or cumbersome, use phrases.

■ **Be careful not to distort meaning.** Don't change the source's emphasis or omit connecting words, qualifiers, and other material whose absence will confuse you later or cause you to misrepresent the source.

(CULTURE LANGUAGE) If English is not your native language and you have difficulty paraphrasing the ideas in sources, try this. Before attempting a paraphrase, read the original passage several times. Then, instead of "translating" line by line, try to state the gist of the passage without looking at it. Check your effort against the original to be sure you have captured the source author's meaning and emphasis without using his or her words and sentence structures. If you need a synonym for a word, look it up in a dictionary.

3 Direct quotation

Your notes from sources may include many quotations, especially if you rely on photocopies, printouts, or downloads. Whether to use a quotation in your draft, instead of a summary or paraphrase, depends on how important the exact words are and on whether the source is primary or secondary (p. 307):

■ **Quote extensively when you are analyzing primary sources,** such as literary works and historical documents. The quotations will often be both the target of your analysis and the chief support for your ideas.

■ **Quote selectively when you are drawing on secondary sources.** Favor summaries and paraphrases over quotations, and put every quotation to both tests in the box on the next page. Most papers of ten or so pages should not need more than two or three quotations that are longer than a few lines each.

When you quote a source, either in your notes or in your draft, take precautions to avoid plagiarism or misrepresentation of the source:

- **Copy the material carefully.** Take down the author's exact wording, spelling, capitalization, and punctuation.
- **Proofread every direct quotation at least twice.**

Tests for direct quotations from secondary sources

The author's original satisfies one of these requirements:

- The language is unusually vivid, bold, or inventive.
- The quotation cannot be paraphrased without distortion or loss of meaning.
- The words themselves are at issue in your interpretation.
- The quotation represents and emphasizes a body of opinion or the view of an important expert.
- The quotation emphatically reinforces your own idea.
- The quotation is an illustration, such as a graph, diagram, or table.

The quotation is as short as possible:

- It includes only material relevant to your point.
- It is edited to eliminate examples and other unneeded material, using ellipsis marks and brackets (**5** pp. 277–79).

- **Use quotation marks around the quotation** so that later you won't confuse it with a paraphrase or summary. Be sure to transfer the quotation marks into your draft as well, unless the quotation is long and is set off from your text. For advice on handling long quotations, see **MLA** p. 401.
- **Use brackets** to add words for clarity or to change the capitalization of letters (see **5** p. 279 and **6** p. 288).
- **Use ellipsis marks** to omit irrelevant material (see **5** pp. 277–79).
- **Cite the source** of the quotation in your draft. See pp. 336–37 on documentation.

52c Integrating sources into your text

Integrating sources into your sentences is key to synthesizing others' ideas and information with your own. Evidence drawn from sources should *back up* your conclusions, not *be* your conclusions:

you don't want to let your evidence overwhelm your own point of view. The point of research is to investigate and go beyond sources, to interpret them and use them to support your own independent ideas.

Note The examples in this section use the MLA style of source documentation and also present-tense verbs (such as *disagrees* and *claims*). Several other conventions governing quotations are discussed elsewhere in this book:

- Using commas to punctuate signal phrases (**5** pp. 258–59).
- Placing other punctuation marks with quotation marks (**5** p. 274).
- Using brackets and the ellipsis mark to indicate changes in quotations (**5** pp. 277–79).
- Punctuating and placing parenthetical citations (**MLA** pp. 364–66).
- Formatting long prose quotations and poetry quotations (**MLA** p. 401).

---

1 Introduction of borrowed material

Readers will be distracted from your point if borrowed material does not fit into your sentence. In the passage below, the writer has not meshed the structures of her own and her source's sentences:

Awkward | One editor disagrees with this view and "a good reporter does not fail to separate opinions from facts" (Lyman 52).

In the following revision the writer adds words to integrate the quotation into her sentence:

Revised | One editor disagrees with this view, maintaining that "a good reporter does not fail to separate opinions from facts" (Lyman 52).

To mesh your own and your source's words, you may sometimes need to make a substitution or addition to the quotation, signaling your change with brackets:

Words added | "The tabloids [of England] are a journalistic case study in bad reporting," claims Lyman (52).

Verb form changed | A bad reporter, Lyman implies, is one who "[fails] to separate opinions from facts" (52). [The bracketed verb replaces *fail* in the original.]

Capitalization changed | "[T]o separate opinions from facts" is the work of a good reporter (Lyman 52). [In the original, *to* is not capitalized.]

| Noun supplied for pronoun | The reliability of a news organization "depends on [reporters'] trustworthiness," says Lyman (52). [The bracketed noun replaces *their* in the original.] |

2 Interpretation of borrowed material

You need to work borrowed material into your sentences so that readers see without effort how it contributes to the points you are making. If you merely dump source material into your paper without explaining how you intend it to be interpreted, readers will have to struggle to understand your sentences and the relationships you are trying to establish. For example, the following passage forces us to figure out for ourselves that the writer's sentence and the quotation state opposite points of view:

| Dumped | Many news editors and reporters maintain that it is impossible to keep personal opinions from influencing the selection and presentation of facts. "True, news reporters, like everyone else, form impressions of what they see and hear. However, a good reporter does not fail to separate opinions from facts" (Lyman 52). |

In the revision, the underlined additions tell us how to interpret the quotation:

| Revised | Many news editors and reporters maintain that it is impossible to keep personal opinions from influencing the selection and presentation of facts. Yet not all authorities agree with this view. One editor grants that "news reporters, like everyone else, form impressions of what they see and hear." But, he insists, "a good reporter does not fail to separate opinions from facts" (Lyman 52). |

Signal phrases

The words *One editor grants* and *he insists* in the revised passage above are **signal phrases:** they tell readers who the source is and what to expect in the quotations that follow. Signal phrases usually contain (1) the source author's name (or a substitute for it, such as *One editor* and *he*) and (2) a verb that indicates the source author's attitude or approach to what he or she says.

Some verbs for signal phrases appear in the following list. These verbs are in the present tense, which is typical of writing in the humanities. In the social and natural sciences, the past tense (*noted*) or present perfect tense (*has noted*) is more common.

Author is neutral	Author infers or suggests	Author argues	Author is uneasy or disparaging
comments	analyzes	claims	belittles
describes	asks	contends	bemoans
explains	assesses	defends	complains
illustrates	concludes	holds	condemns
notes	considers	insists	deplores
observes	finds	maintains	deprecates
points out	predicts		derides
records	proposes	Author agrees	disagrees
relates	reveals		laments
reports	shows	admits	warns
says	speculates	agrees	
sees	suggests	concedes	
thinks	supposes	concurs	
writes		grants	

Vary your signal phrases to suit your interpretation of borrowed material and also to keep readers' interest. A signal phrase may precede, interrupt, or follow the borrowed material:

Precedes	Lyman insists that "a good reporter does not fail to separate opinions from facts" (52).
Interrupts	"However," Lyman insists, "a good reporter does not fail to separate opinions from facts" (52).
Follows	"[A] good reporter does not fail to separate opinions from facts," Lyman insists (52).

Background information

You can add information to a quotation to integrate it into your text and to inform readers why you are using it. In most cases, provide the author's name in the text, especially if the author is an expert or if readers will recognize the name:

Author named	Harold Lyman grants that "news reporters, like everyone else, form impressions of what they see and hear." But, Lyman insists, "a good reporter does not fail to separate opinions from facts" (52).

If the source title contributes information about the author or the context of the quotation, you can provide it in the text:

Title given	Harold Lyman, in his book *The Conscience of the Journalist*, grants that "news reporters, like everyone else, form impressions of what they see and hear." But, Lyman insists, "a good reporter does not fail to separate opinions from facts" (52).

If the quoted author's background and experience reinforce or clarify the quotation, you can provide these credentials in the text:

> **Credentials given** Harold Lyman, <u>a newspaper editor for more than forty years</u>, grants that "news reporters, like everyone else, form impressions of what they see and hear." But, Lyman insists, "a good reporter does not fail to separate opinions from facts" (52).

You need not name the author, source, or credentials in your text when you are simply establishing facts or weaving together facts and opinions from varied sources. In the following passage, the information is more important than the source, so the name of the source is confined to a parenthetical acknowledgment:

> To end the abuses of the British, many colonists were urging three actions: forming a united front, seceding from Britain, and taking control of their own international relations (Wills 325–36).

53 Avoiding Plagiarism and Documenting Sources

The knowledge building that is the focus of academic writing rests on the integrity of everyone who participates in using and crediting sources, including students. The work of a writer or creator is his or her intellectual property. You and others may borrow the work's ideas and even its words or an image, but you *must* acknowledge that what you borrowed came from someone else.

When you acknowledge sources in your writing, you are doing more than giving credit to the writer or creator of the work you consulted. You are also showing what your own writing is based on, which in turn gives you credibility as a researcher and writer. Acknowledging sources creates the trust among scholars, students, writers, and readers that knowledge building requires.

Plagiarism (from a Latin word for "kidnapper") is the presentation of someone else's work as your own. Whether deliberate or accidental, plagiarism is a serious offense. It breaks trust, and it undermines or even destroys your credibility as a researcher and writer. In most colleges, a code of academic honesty calls for severe consequences for plagiarism: a reduced or failing grade, suspension from school, or expulsion.

mycomplab

Visit *mycomplab.com* for more resources as well as exercises on avoiding plagiarism and documenting sources.

■ *Deliberate* plagiarism:

Copying or downloading a phrase, a sentence, or a longer passage from a source and passing it off as your own by omitting quotation marks and a source citation.

Summarizing or paraphrasing someone else's ideas without acknowledging your debt in a source citation.

Handing in as your own work a paper you have bought, copied off the Web, had a friend write, or accepted from another student.

■ *Accidental* plagiarism:

Reading a wide variety of sources on a subject without taking notes on them, and then not remembering the difference between what you recently learned and what you already knew.

Forgetting to place quotation marks around another writer's words.

Carelessly omitting a source citation for a paraphrase.

Omitting a source citation for another's idea because you are unaware of the need to acknowledge the idea.

The way to avoid plagiarism is to acknowledge your sources by documenting them. This chapter discusses plagiarism and the Internet, shows how to distinguish what doesn't require acknowledgment from what does, and provides an overview of source documentation.

CULTURE LANGUAGE The concept of intellectual property and thus the rules governing plagiarism are not universal. In some other cultures, for instance, students may be encouraged to copy the words of scholars without acknowledgment in order to demonstrate their mastery of or respect for the scholars' work. In the United States, however, using an author's work without a source citation is considered theft. When in doubt about the guidelines in this chapter, ask your instructor for advice.

53a Committing and detecting plagiarism on the Internet

The Internet has made it easier to plagiarize than ever before, but it has also made plagiarism easier to catch.

Even honest students risk accidental plagiarism by downloading sources and importing portions into their drafts. Dishonest students may take advantage of downloading to steal others' work. They may also use the term-paper businesses on the Web, which offer both ready-made research and complete papers, usually for a fee. **Paying for research or a paper does not make it the buyer's work.** Anyone who submits someone else's work as his or her own is a plagiarist.

Checklist for avoiding plagiarism

Type of source

Are you using

- your own independent material,
- common knowledge, or
- someone else's independent material?

You must acknowledge someone else's material.

Quotations

- Do all quotations exactly match their sources? Check them.
- Have you inserted quotation marks around quotations that are run into your text?
- Have you shown omissions with ellipsis marks and additions with brackets?
- Does every quotation have a source citation?

Paraphrases and summaries

- Have you used your own words and sentence structures for every paraphrase and summary? If not, use quotation marks around the original author's words.
- Does every paraphrase and summary have a source citation?

The Web

- Have you obtained any necessary permission to use someone else's material on the Web?

Source citations

- Have you acknowledged every use of someone else's material in each place you used it?
- Does your list of works cited include entries for all the sources you have used?

Students who plagiarize from the Internet both deprive themselves of an education in honest research and expose themselves to detection. Teachers can use search engines to locate specific phrases or sentences anywhere on the Web, including among scholarly publications, all kinds of Web sites, and term-paper collections. They can search the term-paper sites as easily as students can, looking for similarities with papers they've received. They can also use detection programs such as *Turnitin* that compare students' work with other work anywhere on the Internet, seeking matches as short as a few words.

Some instructors suggest that their students use plagiarism-detection programs to verify that their own work does not include accidental plagiarism from the Internet.

53b Knowing what you need not acknowledge

1 Your independent material

Your own observations, thoughts, compilations of facts, or experimental results—expressed in your words and format—do not require acknowledgment. You should describe the basis for your conclusions so that readers can evaluate your thinking, but you need not cite sources for them.

2 Common knowledge

Common knowledge consists of the standard information on a subject as well as folk literature and commonsense observations.

- **Standard information** includes the major facts of history, such as the dates during which Charlemagne ruled as emperor of Rome (800–14). It does *not* include interpretations of facts, such as a historian's opinion that Charlemagne was sometimes needlessly cruel in extending his power.
- **Folk literature,** such as the fairy tale "Snow White," is popularly known and cannot be traced to a particular writer. Literature traceable to a writer is *not* folk literature, even if it is very familiar.
- **Commonsense observations** are things most people know, such as that inflation is most troublesome for people with low and fixed incomes. However, a particular economist's argument about the effects of inflation on Chinese immigrants is *not* a commonsense observation.

If you do not know a subject well enough to determine whether a piece of information is common knowledge, make a record of the source as you would for any other quotation, paraphrase, or summary. As you read more about the subject, the information may come up repeatedly without acknowledgment, in which case it is probably common knowledge. But if you are still in doubt when you finish your research, always acknowledge the source.

53c Knowing what you *must* acknowledge

You must always acknowledge other people's independent material—that is, any facts or ideas that are not common knowledge or your own. The source may be anything, including a book, an article, a movie, an interview, a microfilmed document, a Web page, a newsgroup posting, or an opinion expressed on the radio. You must acknowledge summaries or paraphrases of ideas or facts as well as quotations of the language and format in which ideas or facts appear: wording, sentence structures, arrangement, and special graphics (such as a diagram). You must acknowledge another's material no matter how you use it, how much of it you use, or how often you use it.

---

1 Copied language: Quotation marks and a source citation

The following example baldly plagiarizes the original quotation from Jessica Mitford's *Kind and Usual Punishment*, p. 7. Without quotation marks or a source citation, the example matches Mitford's wording (underlined) and closely parallels her sentence structure:

Original quotation	"The character and mentality of the keepers may be of more importance in understanding prisons than the character and mentality of the kept."
Plagiarism	But the character of prison officials (the keepers) is of more importance in understanding prisons than the character of prisoners (the kept).

To avoid plagiarism, the writer can paraphrase and cite the source (see the examples on the next page) or use Mitford's actual words *in quotation marks* and *with a source citation* (here, in MLA style):

Revision (quotation)	According to one critic of the penal system, "The character and mentality of the keepers may be of more importance in understanding prisons than the character and mentality of the kept" (Mitford 9).

Even with a source citation and with a different sentence structure, the next example is still plagiarism because it uses some of Mitford's words (underlined) without quotation marks:

Plagiarism	According to one critic of the penal system, the psychology of the kept may say less about prisons than the psychology of the keepers (Mitford 9).
Revision (quotation)	According to one critic of the penal system, the psychology of "the kept" may say less about prisons than the psychology of "the keepers" (Mitford 9).

2 Paraphrase or summary: Your own words and sentence structure and a source citation

The following example changes the sentence structure of the original Mitford quotation above, but it still uses Mitford's words (underlined) without quotation marks and without a source citation:

Plagiarism	In understanding prisons, we should know more about the character and mentality of the keepers than of the kept.

To avoid plagiarism, the writer can use quotation marks and cite the source (see the previous page) or *use his or her own words* and still *cite the source* (because the idea is Mitford's, not the writer's):

Revision (paraphrase)	Mitford holds that we may be able to learn more about prisons from the psychology of the prison officials than from that of the prisoners (9).
Revision (paraphrase)	We may understand prisons better if we focus on the personalities and attitudes of the prison workers rather than those of the inmates (Mitford 9).

In the next example, the writer cites Mitford and does not use her words but still plagiarizes her sentence structure:

Plagiarism	One critic of the penal system maintains that the psychology of prison officials may be more informative about prisons than the psychology of prisoners (Mitford 9).
Revision (paraphrase)	One critic of the penal system maintains that we may be able to learn less from the psychology of prisoners than from the psychology of prison officials (Mitford 9).

53d Using and acknowledging online sources

Online sources are so accessible and so easy to download into your own documents that it may seem they are freely available, exempting you from the obligation to acknowledge them. They are not. Acknowledging online sources is somewhat trickier than acknowledging print sources, but no less essential. Further, if you are publishing your work on the Web, you need to take account of sources' copyright restrictions as well.

1 Online sources in an unpublished project

When you use material from an online source in a print or online document to be distributed just to your class, your obligation to cite sources does not change: you must acknowledge someone else's independent material in whatever form you find it. With online sources, that obligation can present additional challenges:

- **Record complete publication information each time you consult an online source.** Online sources may change or even disappear entirely.

- **Acknowledge linked sites.** If you use a Web site and one or more of its linked sites, you must acknowledge the linked sites as well. One person's use of a second person's work does not release you from the responsibility to cite the second work.

■ **Seek the author's permission before using an e-mail message, discussion-group posting, or blog contribution.** Obtaining permission advises the author that his or her ideas are about to be distributed more widely and lets the author verify that you have not misrepresented the ideas.

2 Print and online sources in a Web composition

When you use material from print or online sources in a composition for the Web, you must not only acknowledge your sources but also take the additional precaution of observing copyright restrictions.

A Web site is a medium of publication just as a book or magazine is and so involves the same responsibility to obtain reprint permission from copyright holders. The exception is a password-protected site (such as a course site), which many copyright holders regard as private. You can find information about copyright holders and permissions on the copyright page of a print publication (following the title page) and on a page labeled something like "Terms of Use" on a Web site. If you don't see an explicit release for student use or publication on private Web sites, assume you must seek permission.

The legal convention of fair use allows an author to reprint a small portion of copyrighted material without obtaining the copyright holder's permission, as long as the author acknowledges the source. The online standards of fair use differ for print and online sources and are not fixed in either case. The guidelines below are conservative:

■ **Print sources:** Quote without permission fewer than fifty words from an article or fewer than three hundred words from a book. You'll need permission to use any longer quotation from an article or book; any quotation at all from a play, poem, or song; and any use of an entire work, such as a photograph, chart, or other illustration.

■ **Online sources:** Quote without permission text that represents just a small portion of the whole—say, up to forty words out of three hundred. Follow the print guidelines above for plays, poems, songs, and illustrations, adding multimedia elements (audio or video clips) to the list of works that require reprint permission for any use.

■ **Links:** You may need to seek permission to link your site to another one—for instance, if you rely on the linked site to substantiate your claims or to provide a multimedia element.

53e Documenting sources

Every time you borrow the words, facts, or ideas of others, you must **document** the source—that is, supply a reference (or document) telling readers that you borrowed the material and where you borrowed it from.

Editors and teachers in most academic disciplines require special documentation formats (or styles) in their scholarly journals and in students' papers. All the styles use a citation in the text that serves two purposes: it signals that material is borrowed, and it refers readers to detailed information about the source so that they can locate both the source and the place in the source where the borrowed material appears. The detailed source information appears either in footnotes or at the end of the paper.

Aside from these essential similarities, the disciplines' documentation styles differ markedly in citation form, arrangement of source information, and other particulars. Each discipline's style reflects the needs of its practitioners for certain kinds of information presented in certain ways.

Always ask your instructor which documentation style you should use. If your instructor does not require a particular style, use the one in this book that's most appropriate for the discipline in which you're writing. Do follow a single system for citing sources so that you provide all the necessary information in a consistent format.

Note Bibliography software—*Zotero, Refworks, Endnote,* and others—can help you format your source citations in the style of your choice. Always ask your instructors if you may use such software for your papers. The programs prompt you for needed information (author's name, book title, and so on) and then arrange, capitalize, underline, and punctuate the information as required by the style. But no program can anticipate all the varieties of source information, nor can it substitute for your own care and attention in giving your sources complete acknowledgment using the required form.

54 Writing the Paper

As you compose your research essay you will want to review Part One—The Writing Process. At this point, with information you have gathered and the answers you have formulated for your research question, you should be clear on Subject, Writer, Audience, and Purpose (SWAP) for your essay. However, writing and researching are both recursive processes. In other words, as you

Visit *mycomplab.com* for more resources as well as exercises on writing and revising a research paper.

write with your audience in mind, you may discover that there is additional information needed to communicate or support your position, requiring additional research. As you review what you have written, rethink questions suggested by using **RAIDS**.

Invention What have you invented? What changes have you made in attitudes, beliefs, etc. with your reader?

Arrangement What organizational plan have you used as you developed relationships between your sources and your analysis to help your reader easily understand your essay?

Revision What changes will facilitate your goals to communicate with your audience? What new strategies might better connect your work to your audience?

Style How does your style in this essay help you relate to your audience?

Delivery How does this mode of delivery affect your position in relationship to your reader?

MICHIGAN STATE
U N I V E R S I T Y

55 Working with the Goals and Requirements of the Disciplines

As you write your disciplinary literacy paper for your First-Year Writing class, and as you begin to explore the reading, writing, and researching that is done in your major—and later, as you begin to do more work in the major itself—you can apply both the RAIDS and SWAP strategies in effective and meaningful ways. When looking at and writing about the texts produced in your field, consider:

Revision (What is revision? What is being revised?) In most if not all disciplines, new knowledge rests on prior research and knowledge in the field. To what extent is the writer you are examining considering and revising that prior knowledge? How does this writer place him/herself in relationship to this past knowledge? How will you yourself, in writing about and in that discipline, place yourself in relationship to this past knowledge?

Invention (What is invention? What is being invented?) What cognitive, social and other activities did the writer/writers in your discipline have to engage in to create their texts? For example, what kinds of research did they do and make use of? How was this research conducted? Are they incorporating primary or secondary sources, and which will you use, in turn? What ideas will you invent about the nature of this prior research? How will you revise/add to this research?

Arrangement (What is arrangement? What is being arranged?) How have the writers and scholars in your field arranged the knowledge they present? Are they using inductive or deductive methods of reasoning? How is past knowledge in the field put into relationship with the knowledge-at-hand? How are their ideas developed?

Delivery (How is the text delivered to the readers, and what factors affect and are affected by the mode of delivery?) In what form is the knowledge in this field delivered? Are you looking at a textbook, or at a scholarly article from a journal, and how might the audience and purpose of each delivery mode affect the way the information is presented?)

Style (What is the style? How does the style contribute to the message?) Is the style formal or informal? To what extent do the

Visit *mycomplab.com* for more resources as well as exercises on the writing in the disciplines.

340

writers in this field use the personal voice ("I")? Is the tone objective or subjective, the verbs active or passive? Ultimately, how does the style then contribute to the message conveyed?

In conjunction with RAIDS, you can also use the SWAP strategies to strengthen your understanding of how writing, reading, and research are done in a particular discipline. For starters, consider the relationships among subject, writer, audience, and purpose. Even though the subject of any given assignment you compose in your major or even in your profession will be assigned, you will discover that you have much latitude in how you will approach and examine your topic. For example, while the subject of the disciplinary literacy paper—that is, an exploration of writing, reading, and research in a field of your choosing—is assigned, you have great freedom in how you approach and develop your ideas. Moreover, the approaches you choose and the writing decisions you make will be strongly tied both to the other aspects of SWAP (that is, writer, audience, and purpose), as well as to RAIDS. Your choice of subject will be tightly linked to the decisions you make about how best to create a meaningful relationship between your reader's assumptions and knowledge about your subject, and the new knowledge your paper will present.

For example, if you are writing to explain the field of engineering (how reading, writing, and research looks in this field) to an audience of fellow writer-readers in a first-year writing course, you will have to decide what kind of writing voice and what kinds of information will make this explanation most clear to your readers. However, if you are writing a case study that explains to other engineers the results of an engineering experiment that you and your fellow students in an upper-level engineering class have just completed, you will choose a very different writing voice as well as different kinds of information. The audience and purpose of each writing task will help determine the choices you make as a writer, in terms of your subject and the knowledge you invent, revise, and arrange in the process. Thinking of yourself as a writer who both expresses and communicates meaning in specific situations will deepen your success within specific disciplinary contexts.[1]

55a Using methods and evidence

The **methodology** of a discipline is the way its practitioners study their subjects—that is, how they proceed when investigating

---

[1] Introduction contributed by the MSU Custom Team.

Guidelines for academic writers

- Become familiar with the methodology and the kinds of evidence appropriate for the discipline in which you are writing.
- Analyze the special demands of each assignment. The questions you set out to answer, the assertions you wish to support, will govern how you choose your sources and evidence.
- Become familiar with the discipline's specialized tools and language.
- Use the discipline's style for source citations and document format.

the answers to questions. Methodology relates to the way practitioners analyze evidence and ideas. For instance, a literary critic and a social historian would probably approach Shakespeare's *Hamlet* quite differently: the literary critic might study the play for a theme among its poetic images; the historian might examine the play's relation to Shakespeare's context—England at the turn of the seventeenth century.

Whatever their approach, academic writers do not compose entirely out of their personal experience. Rather, they combine the evidence of their experience with that appropriate to the discipline, drawing well-supported conclusions about their subjects. The evidence of the discipline comes from research using primary or secondary sources.

- **Primary sources** are firsthand or original accounts, such as historical documents, works of art, and reports on experiments that the writer has conducted. When you use primary sources, you conduct original research and generate your own evidence. You might use your analysis of a painting as evidence for an interpretation of the painting. Or you might use data from your own survey of students to support your conclusions about students' attitudes.
- **Secondary sources** are books and articles written *about* primary sources. Much academic writing requires that you use such sources to spark, extend, or support your own ideas, as when you review the published opinions on your subject before contributing conclusions from your original research.

55b Understanding writing assignments

For most academic writing, your primary purpose will be either to explain something to your readers or to persuade them to accept your conclusions. To achieve your purpose, you will adapt your writing process to the writing situation, particularly to your reader's likely expectations for evidence and how you use it. Most assignments will contain keywords that imply some of these expectations—words such as *compare*, *define*, *analyze*, and *illustrate* that express customary ways of thinking about and organizing a vast range of subjects. (See **1** p. 11 for more on these so-called patterns of development.) You should be aware of such keywords and alert to them in the wording of assignments.

55c Using tools and language

When you write in an academic discipline, you use the scholarly tools of that discipline, particularly its periodical indexes. In addition, you may use the aids developed by practitioners of the discipline for efficiently and effectively approaching research, conducting it, and recording the findings. Many of these aids, such as a system for recording evidence from sources, are discussed in **7** pp. 300–37 and can be adapted to any discipline. Other aids are discussed in the next two chapters.

Pay close attention to the texts assigned in a course and any materials given out in class, for these items may introduce you to valuable references and other research aids, and they will use the specialized language of the discipline. This specialized language allows practitioners to write to each other both efficiently and precisely. It also furthers certain concerns of the discipline, such as accuracy and objectivity. Scientists, for example, try to interpret their data objectively, so they avoid *undoubtedly, obviously,* and other words that slant conclusions. Some of the language conventions like this one are discussed in the following chapters. As you gain experience in a particular discipline, keep alert for such conventions and train yourself to follow them.

55d Using vocabulary in the disciplines

Different disciplines use different vocabularies, and it is good for you, as a student in a specific major, to learn the vocabulary of the academic and professional community of which you are becoming a member. For example, people who do composition studies may use words such as *literacy, discourse, rhetorical situation,* and *multilingual.* People in psychology may speak of *behaviorism,* the *unconscious,* and *cognition.* Those in biology may talk of *nucleotides, autotrophs,* and *eukaryotes.* Engineering majors speak of *alkylation* and *moving-bed catalytic cracking,* while accounting majors may talk of *accrual basis, amoritzaion,* and *contingent liabilities.* Sometimes specific majors will use specific abbreviations and acronyms: *ROI* (*return on investment,* in accounting), *SCM* (*supply chain management*—in business and in the SCM field itself), and *ADP* (*adenosine diphosphate*—in biology), *RAIDS* and *SWAP* (first-year writing). Moreover, sometimes these letters may be intermixed with numeric symbols, as in the field of chemistry and chemical engineering. Within each of these fields, such "languages" operate as a kind of shorthand that enables the members to communicate efficiently and well with each other. Learning not just to recognize but to become conversant in the new "language" of your discipline will be key to your success.[2]

55e Disciplinary fields and chief characteristics[3]

As you look through the chart on the next page, be aware that there can be vast differences even within a specific discipline: that your economics professor, for example, may ask you to write a paper using the personal voice; that a film teacher may want a "history of film" paper that is more objective in tone. As you begin to make writing choices in response to specific assignments, always be sure to ask your professor about the precise audience and purpose. Will you be explaining a process or a series of concepts? Will you be arguing for a specific action? Will you be analyzing and interpreting an art work? Knowing your purpose and audience will help determine your writing choices, form, and language. (See Section 55b for more on this subject.)[4]

55f Following styles for source citations and document format

Most disciplines publish journals that require authors to use a certain style for source citations and a certain format for documents. In turn, most instructors in a discipline require the same of students writing papers for their courses.

When you cite your sources, you tell readers which ideas and information you borrowed and where they can find your sources. Thus source citations indicate how much knowledge you have and how broad and deep your research was. They also help you avoid **plagiarism**, the serious offense of presenting the words, ideas, and data of others as if they were your own. (See **7** pp. 330–36 on avoiding plagiarism.)

Document format specifies such features as margins and the placement of the title. But it also extends to special elements of the manuscript, such as tables or an abstract, that may be required by the discipline.

The style guides for various disciplines are listed on pp. 349 (humanities), 352 (social sciences), and 355 (natural and applied sciences). If your instructor does not require a particular style, use that of the Modern Language Association, which is described and illustrated at length in **MLA** pp. 358–411.

---

[2] Section 55e contributed by the MSU Custom Team.

[3] Because this list is more suggestive than comprehensive, there are many exceptions to the information presented. Also, not all of MSU's many majors are included here. For convenience, education and its many sub-disciplines have been folded into the humanities. Majors in MSU's College of Communication Arts and Sciences are closely allied to the fields of social sciences or business, while MSU pre-health majors, and majors in the College of Agriculture and Natural Studies, would most likely be connected with the natural sciences field.

[4] Contributed by the MSU Custom Team.

	Purpose	Majors	Forms	Language
Humanities	To create and analyze works of art, their modes of production and reception; to interpret and understand the human experience and its meaning	Composition studies, professional writing, the fine arts (i.e., art and art history, literature, creative writing, film, music, theater), history, the classics, foreign languages, philosophy, education	Poetry/fiction, personal essays, musical compositions, creative works in the plastic arts and/or in multimedia, interpretive analyses/critiques of these art forms, essays, research papers, abstracts, oral histories, process reflections, portfolios	Often creative, can sometimes use the "I," exploratory, critical, analytical
Social Sciences	To study human behavior, past and present, on both an individual and group/societal level	Anthropology, psychology, sociology, social work, child development, family studies, criminal justice, geography, political science, economics, women's and gender studies, African American and African studies, Chicano/Latino studies	Field notes and observations, case studies (including methodology), observations, discussion), abstracts, research papers	Abstract, often objective and formal, passive verbs

(continued)

(Continued)

	Purpose	Majors	Forms	Language
Natural Sciences	To systematically study living and non-living things, and processes	Astrophysics, astronomy, biochemistry, biology, microbiology, chemistry, earth science, physiology, human nutrition, genetics, geology, neuroscience, zoology, mathematics, applied statistics	Lab reports (focusing on methods, procedures, and results), abstracts, summaries, reports on experiments and case studies (including methodology, observations, and discussion)	Formal, objective, passive verbs, research-driven, hypothesis-oriented
Business	To educate and develop business leaders and successful businesses	Hospitality studies, human resource management, supply chain management, logistics, marketing, finance, business administration, accounting	Letters, e-mails, memos, case studies, annual reports	Ranges from the formal to the more informal, professional tone, active verbs, short crisp sentences
Engineering	To design and produce new technologies that are practical and useful to society	Chemical, biosystems, civil, industrial, aerospace, biomedical, mechanical, electrical	Case studies, design reports, project reports, lab reports, proposals; focus on methodology and design process	Formal and objective, with passive voice, though researcher/writers often work in teams

56 Writing in the Disciplines

56a Writing in the humanities

The humanities include literature, the visual arts, music, film, dance, history, philosophy, and religion. The preceding chapter discusses the particular requirements of reading and writing about literature. This section concentrates on history. Although the arts, religion, and other humanities have their own concerns, they share many important goals and methods with literature and history.

1 Methods and evidence in the humanities

Writers in the humanities record and speculate about the growth, ideas, and emotions of human beings. Based on the evidence of written words, artworks, and other human traces and creations, humanities writers explain, interpret, analyze, and reconstruct the human experience.

The discipline of history focuses on reconstructing the past. In Greek the word for history means "to inquire": historians inquire into the past to understand the events of the past. Then they report, explain, analyze, and evaluate those events in their context, asking such questions as what happened before or after the events or how the events were related to then existing political and social structures.

Historians' reconstructions of the past—their conclusions about what happened and why—are always supported with reference to the written record. The evidence of history is mainly primary sources, such as eyewitness accounts and contemporary documents, letters, commercial records, and the like. For history papers, you might also be asked to support your conclusions with those in secondary sources.

In reading historical sources, you need to weigh and evaluate their evidence. If, for example, you find conflicting accounts of the same event, you need to consider the possible biases of the authors. In general, the more a historian's conclusions are supported by public records such as deeds, marriage licenses, and newspaper accounts, the more reliable the conclusions are likely to be.

2 Writing assignments in the humanities

Papers in the humanities generally perform one or more of the following operations.

mycomplab

Visit *mycomplab.com* for more resources as well as exercises on writing in the disciplines.

- **Explanation:** for instance, showing how a painter developed a particular technique or clarifying a general's role in a historical battle.
- **Analysis:** examining the elements of a philosophical argument or breaking down the causes of a historical event.
- **Interpretation:** inferring the meaning of a film from its images or the significance of a historical event from contemporary accounts of it.
- **Synthesis:** finding a pattern in a historical period or in a composer's works.
- **Evaluation:** judging the quality of an architect's design or a historian's conclusions.

Most likely, you will use these operations in combination—say, interpreting and explaining the meaning of a painting and then evaluating it. (These operations are discussed in more detail in **2** pp. 70–73.)

3 | Tools and language in the humanities

The tools and language of the humanities vary according to the discipline. Major reference works in each field, such as those listed on the next page, can clarify specific tools you need and language you should use.

Writing tools

A useful tool for the arts is to ask a series of questions to analyze and evaluate a work. In any humanities discipline, a journal—a log of questions, reactions, and insights—can help you discover and record your thoughts.

In history the tools are those of any thorough and efficient researcher: a system for finding and tracking sources; a methodical examination of sources, including evaluating and synthesizing them; a system for gathering source information; and a separate system, such as a research journal, for tracking one's own evolving thoughts.

Language considerations

Historians strive for precision and logic. They do not guess about what happened or speculate about "what if." They avoid trying to influence readers' opinions with words having strongly negative or positive connotations, such as *stupid* or *brilliant*. Instead, historians show the evidence and draw conclusions from that. Generally, they avoid using *I* because it tends to draw attention away from the evidence and toward the writer.

Writing about history demands some attention to the tenses of verbs to maintain consistency. Generally, historians use the past tense to refer to events that occurred in the past. They reserve the present tense only for statements about the present or statements of general truths. For example:

> Franklin Delano Roosevelt <u>died</u> in 1945. Many of Roosevelt's economic reforms <u>persist</u> in programs such as Social Security, unemployment compensation, and farm subsidies.

4 Documentation and format in the humanities

Writers in the humanities generally rely on one of the following guides for source-citation style:

> *The Chicago Manual of Style*, 15th ed., 2003
> *A Manual for Writers of Research Papers, Theses, and Dissertations,* by Kate L. Turabian, 7th ed., rev. Wayne C. Booth, Gregory G. Colomb, and Joseph M. Williams, 2007
> *MLA Handbook for Writers of Research Papers,* 6th ed., by Joseph Gibaldi, 2003
> *MLA Style Manual and Guide to Scholarly Publishing,* 3rd ed., 2008

> See **MLA** pp. 358–411 for the recommendations of the *MLA Handbook.* Unless your instructor specifies otherwise, use these recommendations for papers in English and foreign languages. In history, art history, and many other disciplines, however, writers rely on *The Chicago Manual of Style* or the student reference adapted from it, *A Manual for Writers.* Both books detail two documentation styles. One, used mainly by scientists and social scientists, closely resembles the style of the American Psychological Association. The other style, used more in the humanities, calls for footnotes or endnotes and an optional bibliography.

56b Writing in the social sciences

The social sciences—including anthropology, economics, education, management, political science, psychology, and sociology—focus on the study of human behavior. As the name implies, the social sciences examine the way human beings relate to themselves, to their environment, and to one another.

1 Methods and evidence in the social sciences

Researchers in the social sciences systematically pose a question, formulate a **hypothesis** (a generalization that can be tested), collect data, analyze those data, and draw conclusions to support, refine, or disprove their hypothesis. This is the scientific method developed in the natural sciences (see p. 352).

Social scientists gather data in several ways:

- **They make firsthand observations of human behavior,** recording the observations in writing or electronically.
- **They interview subjects about their attitudes and behavior,** recording responses in writing or electronically. (See **7** p. 315 for guidelines on conducting an interview.)
- **They conduct broader surveys using questionnaires,** asking people about their attitudes and behavior. (See **7** pp. 315–16 for guidelines on conducting a survey.)
- **They conduct controlled experiments,** structuring an environment in which to encourage and measure a specific behavior.

In their writing, social scientists explain their own research or analyze and evaluate others' research.

The research methods of social science generate two kinds of data:

- *Quantitative data* **are numerical,** such as statistical evidence based on surveys, polls, tests, and experiments. When public-opinion pollsters announce that 47 percent of US citizens polled approve of the President's leadership, they are offering quantitative data gained from a survey. Social science writers present quantitative data in graphs, charts, and other illustrations that accompany their text.
- *Qualitative data* **are not numerical but more subjective:** they are based on interviews, firsthand observations, and inferences, taking into account the subjective nature of human experience. Examples of qualitative data include an anthropologist's description of the initiation ceremonies in a culture she is studying or a psychologist's interpretation of interviews he conducted with a group of adolescents.

2 Writing assignments in the social sciences

Depending on what social science courses you take, you may be asked to complete a variety of assignments:

- **A summary or review of research** reports on the available research literature on a subject, such as infants' perception of color.
- **A case analysis** explains the components of a phenomenon, such as a factory closing.
- **A problem-solving analysis** explains the elements of a problem, such as unreported child abuse, and suggests ways to solve it.
- **A research paper** interprets and sometimes analyzes and evaluates the writings of other social scientists about a subject, such as the effect of national appeals in advertising.

■ **A research report** explains the author's own original research or the author's attempt to replicate someone else's research.

Many social science disciplines have special requirements for the content and organization of each kind of paper. The requirements appear in the style guides of the disciplines, listed on p. 349. Because of the differences among disciplines and even among different kinds of papers in the same discipline, you should always ask your instructor what he or she requires for an assignment.

3 | Tools and language in the social sciences

The following guidelines for tools and language apply to most social sciences. However, the particular discipline you are writing in, or an instructor in a particular course, may have additional requirements.

Writing tools

Many social scientists rely on a **research journal** or **log,** in which they record their ideas throughout the research-writing process. Even if a research journal is not required in your courses, you may want to use one. As you begin formulating a hypothesis, you can record preliminary questions. Then when you are in the field conducting research, you can use the journal to react to the evidence you are collecting, to record changes in your perceptions and ideas, and to assess your progress.

To avoid confusing your reflections on the evidence with the evidence itself, keep records of actual data—notes from interviews, observations, surveys, and experiments—separately from the journal.

Language considerations

Each social science discipline has specialized terminology for concepts basic to the discipline. In sociology, for example, the words *mechanism, identity,* and *deviance* have specific meanings different from those of everyday usage. And *identity* means something different in sociology, where it applies to groups of people, than in psychology, where it applies to the individual. Social scientists also use precise terms to describe or interpret research. For instance, they say *The subject expressed a feeling of* rather than *The subject felt* because human feelings are not knowable for certain; or they say *These studies indicate* rather than *These studies prove* because conclusions are only tentative.

Just as social scientists strive for objectivity in their research, they also strive to demonstrate their objectivity through language in their writing. They avoid expressions such as *I think* in order to focus attention on what the evidence shows rather than on the researcher's opinions. (However, many social scientists prefer *I* to the artificial *the researcher* when they refer to their own actions, as in *I then interviewed the subjects.* Ask your instructor for his or her preferences.) Social scientists also avoid direct or indirect expression of their personal biases or emotions, either in discussions of other researchers' work or in descriptions of research subjects. Thus one social scientist does not call another's work *sloppy* or *immaculate* and does not refer to his or her own subjects as *drunks* or *innocent victims.* Instead, the writer uses neutral language and ties conclusions strictly to the data.

4 Documentation and format in the social sciences

Some of the social sciences publish style guides that advise practitioners how to organize, document, and type papers. The following is a partial list:

American Anthropological Association, *AAA Style Guide,* 2003 (*www.aaanet .org/publications/guidelines.cfm*)

American Political Science Association, *Style Manual for Political Science,* 2006

American Psychological Association, *Publication Manual of the American Psychological Association,* 5th ed., 2001, and *APA Style Guide to Electronic References,* 2007

American Sociological Association, *ASA Style Guide,* 3rd ed., 2007

Linguistic Society of America, "LSA Style Sheet," published every December in *LSA Bulletin*

A Uniform System of Citation (law), 18th ed., 2005

By far the most widely used style is that of the American Psychological Association. Always ask your instructor in any discipline what style you should use.

56c Writing in the natural and applied sciences

The natural and applied sciences include biology, chemistry, physics, mathematics, engineering, computer science, and their branches. Their purpose is to understand natural and technological phenomena. (A *phenomenon* is a fact or event that can be known by the senses.) Scientists conduct experiments and write to explain the step-by-step processes in their methods of inquiry and discovery.

1 Methods and evidence in the sciences

Scientists investigate phenomena by the **scientific method**, a process of continual testing and refinement:

Scientific evidence is almost always quantitative—that is, it consists of numerical data obtained from the measurement of

The scientific method

- **Observe carefully.** Accurately note all details of the phenomenon being researched.
- **Ask questions about the observations.**
- **Formulate a** *hypothesis,* or preliminary generalization, that explains the observed facts.
- **Test the hypothesis** with additional observations or controlled experiments.
- **If the hypothesis proves accurate,** formulate a *theory,* or unified model, that explains *why.*
- **If the hypothesis is disproved, revise it or start anew.**

phenomena. These data are called **empirical** (from a Greek word for "experience"): they result from observation and experience, generally in a controlled laboratory setting but also (as sometimes in astronomy or biology) in the natural world. Often the empirical evidence for scientific writing comes from library research into other people's reports of their investigations. Surveys of known data or existing literature are common in scientific writing.

2 Writing assignments in the sciences

No matter what your assignment, you will be expected to document and explain your evidence carefully so that anyone reading can check your sources and replicate your research. It is important for your reader to know the context of your research—both the previous experimentation and research on your particular subject (acknowledged in the survey of the literature) and the physical conditions and other variables surrounding your own work.

Assignments in the natural and applied sciences include the following:

- **A summary** distills a research article to its essence in brief, concise form. (Summary is discussed in detail in **2** pp. 63–65.)
- **A critique** summarizes and critically evaluates a scientific report.
- **A laboratory report** explains the procedure and results of an experiment conducted by the writer.
- **A research report** explains the experimental research of other scientists and the writer's own methods, findings, and conclusions.
- **A research proposal** reviews the relevant literature and explains a plan for further research.

A laboratory report has four or five major sections:

1. **"Abstract":** a summary of the report.
2. **"Introduction"** or **"Objective":** a review of why the study was undertaken, a summary of the background of the study, and a statement of the problem being studied.
3. **"Method"** or **"Procedure":** a detailed explanation of how the study was conducted, including any statistical analysis.
4. **"Results":** an explanation of the major findings (including unexpected results) and a summary of the data presented in graphs and tables.
5. **"Discussion":** an interpretation of the results and an explanation of how they relate to the goals of the experiment. This section also describes new hypotheses that might be tested as a result of the experiment. If the discussion is brief, it may be combined with the results in a single section labeled "Conclusions."

In addition, laboratory or research reports may include a list of references (if other sources were consulted). They almost always include tables and figures (graphs and charts) containing the data from the research.

3 Tools and language in the sciences

Tools and language concerns vary from discipline to discipline in the sciences. Consult your instructor for specifics about the field in which you are writing.

Writing tools

In the sciences a **lab notebook** or **scientific journal** is almost indispensable for accurately recording the empirical data from observations and experiments. Use such a notebook or journal for these purposes:

- **Record observations** from reading, from class, or from the lab.
- **Ask questions and refine hypotheses.**
- **Record procedures.**
- **Record results.**
- **Keep an ongoing record of ideas and findings** and how they change as data accumulate.
- **Sequence and organize your material** as you compile your findings and write your report.

Make sure that your records of data are clearly separate from your reflections on the data so that you don't mistakenly confuse the two in drawing your conclusions.

Language considerations

Science writers use objective language that removes the writer as a character in the situation and events being explained, except as the impersonal agent of change, the experimenter. Although usage is changing, scientists still rarely use *I* in their reports and evaluations, and they often resort to the passive voice of verbs, as in *The mixture was then subjected to centrifugal force.* This conscious objectivity focuses attention (including the writer's) on the empirical data and what they show. It discourages the writer from, say, ascribing motives and will to animals and plants. For instance, instead of asserting that the sea tortoise *evolved* its hard shell *to protect* its body, a scientist would write only what could be observed: that the hard shell *covers and thus protects* the tortoise's body.

Science writers typically change verb tenses to distinguish between established information and their own research. For established information, such as that found in journals and other reliable sources, use the present tense: *Baroreceptors monitor blood pressure.* For your own and others' research, use the past tense: *The bacteria died within three hours. Marti reported some success.*

Each discipline in the natural and applied sciences has a specialized vocabulary that permits precise, accurate, and efficient communication. Some of these terms, such as *pressure* in physics, have different meanings in the common language and must be handled carefully in science writing. Others, such as *enthalpy* in chemistry, have no meanings in the common language and must simply be learned and used correctly.

4 Documentation and format in the sciences

Within the natural and applied sciences, practitioners use one of two styles of documentation, varying slightly from discipline to discipline. Following are some of the style guides most often consulted:

American Chemical Society, *ACS Style Guide: A Manual for Authors and Editors,* 3rd ed., 2006

American Institute of Physics, *Style Manual for Guidance in the Preparation of Papers,* 4th ed., 1997

American Medical Association Manual of Style, 10th ed., 2007

Council of Science Editors, *Scientific Style and Format: The CSE Manual for Authors, Editors, and Publishers,* 7th ed., 2006

The most thorough and widely used of these guides is the last one, *Scientific Style and Format.*

MLA Documentation
and Format

MICHIGAN STATE
UNIVERSITY

MLA Documentation and Format

English, foreign languages, and some other humanities use the documentation style of the Modern Language Association, detailed in the *MLA Handbook for Writers of Research Papers* (6th ed., 2003) and substantially updated in the *MLA Style Manual and Guide to Scholarly Publishing* (3rd ed., 2008). This chapter presents the updated citation formats of the *MLA Style Manual*. In MLA documentation style, you twice acknowledge the sources of borrowed material:

- In your text, a brief parenthetical citation adjacent to the borrowed material directs readers to a complete list of all the works you cite.
- At the end of your paper, the list of works cited includes complete bibliographical information for every source.

Every entry in the list of works cited has at least one corresponding citation in the text, and every in-text citation has a corresponding entry in the list of works cited.

This chapter describes MLA documentation: writing text citations (below), placing citations (p. 364), using supplementary notes (p. 366), and preparing the list of works cited (p. 367). A detailed discussion of MLA document format (p. 399) and a sample MLA paper (p. 403) conclude the chapter.

Visit *mycomplab.com* for more resources as well as exercises on MLA documentation and format.

57a Writing parenthetical text citations

1 Citation formats

In-text citations of sources must include just enough information for the reader to locate the following:

- The *source* in your list of works cited.
- The *place* in the source where the borrowed material appears.

For any kind of source, you can usually meet both these requirements by providing the author's last name and (if the source uses them) the page numbers where the material appears. The reader can find the source in your list of works cited and find the borrowed material in the source itself.

The following models illustrate the basic text-citation forms and also forms for more unusual sources, such as those with no named author or no page numbers. See the **MLA** divider for an index to all the models.

Note Models 1 and 2 show the direct relationship between what you include in your text and what you include in a parenthetical citation. If you do *not* name the author in your text, you include the name in parentheses before the page reference (model 1). If you *do* name the author in your text, you do not include the name in parentheses (model 2).

1. Author not named in your text

When you have not already named the author in your sentence, provide the author's last name and the page number(s), with no punctuation between them, in parentheses.

> One researcher concludes that "women impose a distinctive construction on moral problems, seeing moral dilemmas in terms of conflicting responsibilities" (Gilligan 105-06).

See model 6 for the form to use when the source does not have an author. And see models 10 and 11 for the forms to use when the source does not provide page numbers.

2. Author named in your text

When you have already given the author's name with the material you're citing, do not repeat it in the parenthetical citation. Give just the page number(s).

> Carol Gilligan concludes that "women impose a distinctive construction on moral problems, seeing moral dilemmas in terms of conflicting responsibiiities" (105-06).

See model 6 for the form to use when the source does not list an author. And see models 10 and 11 for the forms to use when the source does not provide page numbers.

3. A work with two or three authors

If the source has two or three authors, give all their last names in the text or in the citation. Separate two authors' names with and.

> As Frieden and Sagalyn observe, "The poor and the minorities were the leading victims of highway and renewal programs" (29).

> According to one study, "The poor and the minorities were the leading victims of highway and renewal programs" (Frieden and Sagalyn 29).

With three authors, add commas and also and before the final name.

> The textbook by Wilcox, Ault, and Agee discusses the "ethical dilemmas in public relations practice" (125).

> One textbook discusses the "ethical dilemmas in public relations practice" (Wilcox, Ault, and Agee 125).

4. A work with more than three authors

If the source has more than three authors, you may list all their last names or use only the first author's name followed by et al. (the abbreviation for the Latin *et alii,* "and others"). The choice depends on what you do in your list of works cited (see pp. 367–68).

> Increased competition means that employees of public relations firms may find their loyalty stretched in more than one direction (Cameron et al. 417).

> Increased competition means that employees of public relations firms may find their loyalty stretched in more than one direction (Cameron, Wilcox, Reber, and Shin 417).

5. A work by an author of two or more cited works

If your list of works cited includes two or more works by the same author, then your citation must tell the reader which of the author's works you are referring to. Give the title either in the text or in a parenthetical citation. In a parenthetical citation, give the full title only if it is brief; otherwise, shorten the title to the first one, two, or three main words (excluding *A, An,* or *The*).

> At about age seven, children begin to use appropriate gestures with their stories (Gardner, *Arts* 144-45).

The full title of Gardner's book is *The Arts and Human Development* (see the works-cited entry on p. 369). This shortened title is italicized because the source is a book.

6. An anonymous work

For a work with no named author or editor (whether an individual or an organization), use a full or shortened version of the title, as explained above. In your list of works cited, you alphabetize an anonymous work by the first main word of the title (see p. 369), so the first word of a shortened title should be the same. The following citations refer to an unsigned source titled "The Right to Die." The title appears in quotation marks because the source is a periodical article.

> One article notes that a death-row inmate may demand his own execution to achieve a fleeting notoriety ("Right" 16).

> "The Right to Die" notes that a death-row inmate may demand execution to achieve a fleeting notoriety (16).

If two or more anonymous works have the same title, distinguish them with additional information in the text citation, such as the publication date.

7. A work with a corporate author

Some works list as author a government body, association, committee, company, or other group. Cite such a work by the organization's name. If the name is long, work it into the text to avoid an intrusive parenthetical citation.

> A 2008 report by the Hawaii Department of Education provides evidence of an increase in graduation rates (12).

8. A nonprint source

Cite a nonprint source such as a Web page or a DVD just as you would any other source. If your works-cited entry lists the source under the name of an author or other contributor, use that name in the text citation. The following example cites an authored source that has page numbers.

> Business forecasts for the fourth quarter tended to be optimistic (White 4).

If your works-cited entry lists the work under its title, cite the work by title in your text, as explained in model 6. The next example cites an entire work (a film on DVD) and gives the title in the text, so it omits a parenthetical citation (see model 10).

> Seven decades after its release, *Citizen Kane* is still remarkable for its rich black-and-white photography.

9. A multivolume work

If you consulted only one volume of a multivolume work, your list of works cited will say so (see model 30 on p. 379), and you can treat the volume as you would any book.

If you consulted more than one volume of a multivolume work, give the appropriate volume in your text citation.

> After issuing the Emancipation Proclamation, Lincoln said, "What I did, I did after very full deliberations, and under a very heavy and solemn sense of responsibility" (5: 438).

The number 5 indicates the volume from which the quotation was taken; the number 438 indicates the page number in that volume. When the author's name appears in such a citation, place it before the volume number with no punctuation: (Lincoln 5: 438).

If you are referring generally to an entire volume of a multivolume work and are not citing specific page numbers, add the abbreviation vol. before the volume number as in (vol. 5) or (Lincoln, vol. 5) (note the comma after the author's name). Then readers will not misinterpret the volume number as a page number.

10. An entire work or a work with no page or other reference numbers

When you cite an entire work rather than a part of it, you may omit any page or other reference number. If the work you cite has an author, try to work the author's name into your text. You will not need a parenthetical citation then, but the source still must appear in your list of works cited.

> Boyd deals with the need to acknowledge and come to terms with our fear of nuclear technology.

Use the same format when you cite a specific passage from a work with no page, paragraph, or other reference numbers, such as a Web source.

If the author's name does not appear in your text, put it in a parenthetical citation.

> Almost 20 percent of commercial banks have been audited for the practice (Friis).

11. A work with numbered paragraphs or sections instead of pages

Some electronic sources number each paragraph or section instead of each page. In citing passages in these sources, give the paragraph or section number(s) and distinguish them from page numbers: after the author's name, put a comma, a space, and par. (one paragraph), pars. (more than one paragraph), sec., or secs.

Twins reared apart report similar feelings (Palfrey, pars. 6-7).

12. An indirect source

When you want to use a quotation that is already in quotation marks—indicating that the author you are reading is quoting someone else—try to find the original source and quote directly from it. If you can't find the original source, then your citation must indicate that your quotation of it is indirect. In the following citation, qtd. in ("quoted in") says that Davino was quoted by Boyd.

George Davino maintains that "even small children have vivid ideas about nuclear energy" (qtd. in Boyd 22).

The list of works cited then includes only Boyd (the work consulted), not Davino.

13. A literary work

Novels, plays, and poems are often available in many editions, so your instructor may ask you to provide information that will help readers find the passage you cite no matter what edition they consult.

- **Novels:** The page number comes first, followed by a semicolon and then information on the appropriate part or chapter of the work.

  Toward the end of James's novel, Maggie suddenly feels "the thick breath of the definite—which was the intimate, the immediate, the familiar, as she hadn't had them for so long" (535; pt. 6, ch. 41).

- **Poems that are not divided into parts:** You may omit the page number and supply the line number(s) for the quotation. To prevent confusion with page numbers, precede the numbers with line or lines in the first citation; then use just the numbers.

  In Shakespeare's Sonnet 73 the speaker identifies with the trees of late autumn, "Bare ruined choirs, where late the sweet birds sang" (line 4). "In me," Shakespeare writes, "thou seest the glowing of such fire / That on the ashes of his youth doth lie . . ." (9-10).

- **Verse plays and poems that are divided into parts:** Omit a page number and cite the appropriate part—act (and scene, if any), canto, book, and so on—plus the line number(s). Use Arabic numerals for parts, including acts and scenes (3.4), unless your instructor specifies Roman numerals (III.iv).

> Later in Shakespeare's *King Lear* the disguised Edgar says, "The prince of darkness is a gentleman" (3.4.147).

- **Prose plays:** Provide the page number followed by the act and scene, if any. For an example, see the reference to *Death of a Salesman* on p. 366.

14. The Bible

When you cite passages of the Bible in parentheses, abbreviate the title of any book longer than four letters—for instance, Gen. (Genesis), 1 Sam. (1 Samuel), Ps. (Psalms), Prov. (Proverbs), Matt. (Matthew), Rom. (Romans). Then give the chapter and verse(s) in Arabic numerals.

> According to the Bible, at Babel God "did . . . confound the language of all the earth" (Gen. 11.9).

15. Two or more works in the same citation

When you refer to more than one work in a single parenthetical citation, separate the references with a semicolon.

> Two recent articles point out that a computer badly used can be less efficient than no computer at all (Gough and Hall 201; Richards 162).

Since long citations in the text can distract the reader, you may choose to cite several or more works in an endnote or footnote rather than in the text. See pp. 366–67.

2 Placement and punctuation of parenthetical citations

The following guidelines will help you place and punctuate text citations to distinguish between your own and your sources' ideas and to make your own text readable. See also **7** pp. 326–30 on editing quotations and using signal phrases to integrate source material into your sentences.

Where to place citations

Position text citations to accomplish two goals:

- Make it clear exactly where your borrowing begins and ends.
- Keep the citation as unobtrusive as possible.

You can accomplish both goals by placing the parenthetical citation at the end of the sentence element containing the borrowed material. This sentence element may be a phrase or a clause, and it may begin, interrupt, or conclude the sentence. Usually, as in the following examples, the element ends with a punctuation mark.

> The inflation rate might climb as high as 30 percent (Kim 164), an increase that could threaten the small nation's stability.
>
> The inflation rate, which might climb as high as 30 percent (Kim 164), could threaten the small nation's stability.
>
> The small nation's stability could be threatened by its inflation rate, which, one source predicts, might climb as high as 30 percent (Kim 164).

In the last example the addition of one source predicts clarifies that Kim is responsible only for the inflation-rate prediction, not for the statement about stability.

When your paraphrase or summary of a source runs longer than a sentence, clarify the boundaries by using the author's name in the first sentence and placing the parenthetical citation at the end of the last sentence.

> Juliette Kim studied the effects of acutely high inflation in several South American and African countries since World War II. She discovered that a major change in government accompanied or followed the inflationary period in 56 percent of cases (22-23).

When you cite two or more sources in the same paragraph, position authors' names and parenthetical citations so that readers can see who said what. In the following example, the beginnings and ends of sentences clearly mark the different sources.

> Schools use computers extensively for drill-and-practice exercises, in which students repeat specific skills such as spelling words, using the multiplication facts, or, at a higher level, doing chemistry problems. But many education experts criticize such exercises for boring students and failing to engage their critical thinking and creativity. Jane M. Healy, a noted educational psychologist and teacher, takes issue with "interactive" software for children as well as drill-and-practice software, arguing that "some of the most popular 'educational' software . . . may be damaging to independent thinking, attention, and motivation" (20). Another education expert, Harold Wenglinsky of the Educational Testing Service, found in a well-regarded 1998 study that fourth and eighth graders who used computers frequently, including for drill and practice, actually did worse on tests than their peers who used computers less often (*Does It Compute?* 21). In a later article, Wenglinsky concludes that "the quantity

of use matters far less than the quality of use." In schools, he says, high-quality computer work, involving critical thinking, is still rare ("In Search" 17).

How to punctuate citations

Generally place a parenthetical citation *before* any punctuation required by your sentence. If the borrowed material is a quotation, place the citation *between* the closing quotation mark and the punctuation:

Spelling argues that during the 1970s American automobile manufacturers met consumer needs "as well as could be expected" (26), but not everyone agrees with him.

The exception is a quotation ending in a question mark or exclamation point. Then use the appropriate punctuation inside the closing quotation mark, and follow the quotation with the text citation and a period.

"Of what use is genius," Emerson asks, "if the organ . . . cannot find a focal distance within the actual horizon of human life?" ("Experience" 60). Mad genius is no genius.

When a citation appears at the end of a quotation set off from the text, place it one space *after* the punctuation ending the quotation. Do not use additional punctuation with the citation or quotation marks around the quotation.

In Arthur Miller's *Death of a Salesman,* the most poignant defense of Willie Loman comes from his wife, Linda:

> He's not the finest character that ever lived. But he's a human being, and a terrible thing is happening to him. So attention must be paid. He's not to be allowed to fall into his grave like an old dog. Attention, attention must finally be paid to such a person. (56; act 1)

(This citation of a play includes the act number as well as the page number. See p. 364.)

3 | Footnotes or endnotes in special circumstances

Footnotes or endnotes may replace parenthetical citations when you cite several sources at once, when you comment on a source, or when you provide information that does not fit easily in the text. Signal a footnote or endnote in your text with a numeral raised above the appropriate line. Then write a note with the same numeral.

Text   At least five studies have confirmed these results.[1]

Note   1. Abbott and Winger 266-68; Casner 27; Hoyenga 78-79; Marino 36; Tripp, Tripp, and Walk 179-83.

In a note, the numeral is not raised, is indented one-half inch, and is followed by a period and a space. If the note appears as a footnote, place it at the bottom of the page on which the citation appears, set it off from the text with quadruple spacing, and single-space the note itself. If the note appears as an endnote, place it in numerical order with the other endnotes on a page between the text and the list of works cited. Double-space all the endnotes.

57b Preparing the MLA list of works cited

At the end of your paper, a list titled Works Cited includes all the sources you quoted, paraphrased, or summarized in your paper. (If your instructor asks you to include sources you examined but did not cite, title the list Works Consulted.)

Follow this format for the list of works cited:

- **Arrange your sources in alphabetical order** by the last name of the author. If an author is not given in the source, alphabetize the source by the first main word of the title (excluding *A*, *An*, or *The*).
- **Type the entire list double-spaced**, both within and between entries.
- **Indent the second and subsequent lines of each entry one-half inch from the left.** Your word processor can format this so-called hanging indent automatically.

For a complete list of works cited, see the paper by Justin Malik (p. 410).

MLA works-cited page

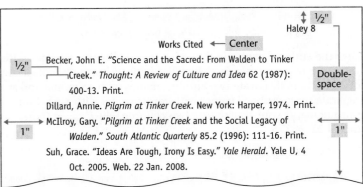

Haley 8

Works Cited ← Center

Becker, John E. "Science and the Sacred: From Walden to Tinker Creek." *Thought: A Review of Culture and Idea* 62 (1987): 400-13. Print.

Dillard, Annie. *Pilgrim at Tinker Creek*. New York: Harper, 1974. Print.

McIlroy, Gary. "*Pilgrim at Tinker Creek* and the Social Legacy of Walden." *South Atlantic Quarterly* 85.2 (1996): 111-16. Print.

Suh, Grace. "Ideas Are Tough, Irony Is Easy." *Yale Herald*. Yale U, 4 Oct. 2005. Web. 22 Jan. 2008.

An index to all the following models appears at the **MLA** divider. Use your best judgment in adapting the models to your particular sources. If you can't find a model that exactly matches a source you used, locate and follow the closest possible match. You will certainly need to combine formats—for instance, drawing on model 2 ("Two or three authors") and model 10 ("An article in a national newspaper") for a national newspaper article with two authors.

Note MLA style now requires that you give the medium for every source you cite, such as print, Web, DVD, or television. For example, if you consulted an article in a print magazine, your works-cited entry should list the medium as Print. If you consulted a book on the Web, your works-cited entry should list the medium as Web. The models here all conform to this standard.

1 Listing authors

The following models show how to handle authors' names in citing any kind of source.

1. One author

Ehrenreich, Barbara. *Dancing in the Streets: A History of Collective Joy*. New
York: Metropolitan-Holt, 2006. Print.

Give the author's full name—last name first, a comma, first name, and any middle name or initial. Omit any title, such as *Dr.* or *PhD*. End the name with a period. If your source lists an editor as author, see model 22, p. 375.

2. Two or three authors

Lifton, Robert Jay, and Greg Mitchell. *Who Owns Death: Capital Punishment,
the American Conscience, and the End of Executions*. New York: Morrow,
2000. Print.

Wilcox, Dennis L., Phillip H. Ault, and Warren K. Agee. *Public Relations: Strategies and Tactics*. 8th ed. New York: Irwin, 2006. Print.

Give the authors' names in the order provided on the title page. Reverse the first and last names of the first author *only*, not of any other authors. Separate two authors' names with a comma and and; separate three authors' names with commas and with and before the third name. If your source lists two or three editors as authors, see model 22, p. 375.

3. More than three authors

Cameron, Glen T., Dennis L. Wilcox, Bryan H. Reber, and Jae-Hwa Shin. *Public
Relations Today: Managing Competition and Conflict*. New York: Pearson,
2007. Print.

Cameron, Glen T., et al. *Public Relations Today: Managing Competition and Conflict.* New York: Pearson, 2007. Print.

You may, but need not, give all authors' names if the work has more than three authors. If you choose not to give all names, provide the name of the first author only, and follow the name with a comma and the abbreviation et al. (for the Latin *et alii,* meaning "and others"). If your source lists more than three editors as authors, see model 22, p. 375.

4. The same author(s) for two or more works

Gardner, Howard. *The Arts and Human Development.* New York: Wiley, 1973. Print.

---. *Five Minds for the Future.* Boston: Harvard Business School P, 2007. Print.

Give the author's name only in the first entry. For the second and any subsequent works by the same author, substitute three hyphens for the author's name, followed by a period. Note that the three hyphens stand for *exactly* the same name or names. If the second Gardner source were by Gardner and somebody else, both names would have to be given in full.

Place an entry or entries using three hyphens immediately after the entry that names the author. Within the set of entries by the same author, arrange the sources alphabetically by the first main word of the title, as in the Gardner examples (*Arts,* then *Five*).

If you cite two or more sources that list as author(s) exactly the same editor(s), follow the hyphens with a comma and ed. or eds. as appropriate. (See model 22, p. 375.)

5. A corporate author

Vault Technologies. *Turnkey Parking Solutions.* Salt Lake City: Mills, 2008. Print.

Corporate authors include associations, committees, institutions, government bodies, companies, and other groups. List the name of the group as author when a source gives only that name and not an individual's name.

6. Author not named (anonymous)

The Dorling Kindersley World Reference Atlas. London: Dorling, 2007. Print.

List a work that names no author—neither an individual nor a group—by its full title. If the work is a book, italicize the title. If the work is a periodical article or other short work, enclose the title in quotation marks:

"Let the Horse Race Begin." *Time* 31 Mar. 2008: 22. Print.

Alphabetize the work by the title's first main word, excluding *A, An,* or *The* (*Dorling* in the first example and Let in the second).

2 Listing periodical print sources

Print periodicals include scholarly journals, newspapers, and magazines that are published at regular intervals (quarterly, monthly, weekly, or daily). To cite more than one author, two or more articles by the same author, a corporate author, or an article with no named author, see models 1–6.

Note The treatment of volume and issue numbers and publication dates varies depending on the kind of periodical being cited, as the models indicate.

Articles in scholarly journals

7. An article in a journal with volume and issue numbers (print)

Bee, Robert. "The Importance of Preserving Paper-Based Artifacts in a Digital Age." *Library Quarterly* 78.2 (2008): 174-94. Print.

The facing page shows the basic format for an article in a print journal and the location of the required information in the journal. See p. 373 for parallel information on a newspaper article.

8. An article in a journal with only issue numbers (print)

Rymhs, Deena. "David Collier's *Surviving Saskatoon* and New Comics." *Canadian Literature* 194 (2007): 75-92. Print.

If a scholarly journal numbers only issues, not volumes, give the issue number alone after the journal title.

9. An abstract of a journal article or a dissertation (print)

Lever, Janet. "Sex Differences in the Games Children Play." *Social Problems* 23.2 (1996): 478-87. *Psychological Abstracts* 63.5 (1996): item 1431. Print.

For an abstract of an article, first provide the publication information for the article, following model 7. Then give the information for the abstract. If the abstract publisher lists abstracts by item rather than page number, add item before the number.

For an abstract appearing in *Dissertation Abstracts* (*DA*) or *Dissertation Abstracts International* (*DAI*), give the author's name and the title, Diss. (for "Dissertation"), the institution granting the author's degree, the date of the dissertation, and the publication information.

Steciw, Steven K. "Alterations to the Pessac Project of Le Corbusier." Diss. U of Cambridge, England, 1986. *DAI* 46.10 (1986): 565C. Print.

Format for a print journal article

① ②
Bee, Robert. "The Importance of Preserving Paper-Based Artifacts in a Digital Age."
③ ④ ⑤ ⑥ ⑦
Library Quarterly 78.2 (2008): 179-94. Print.

Journal cover

THE LIBRARY QVARTERLY

VOLUME 78 · APRIL 2008 · NUMBER 2

First page of article

THE IMPORTANCE OF PRESERVING PAPER-BASED ARTIFACTS IN A
DIGITAL AGE

Robert Bee[1]

The preservation of paper-based artifacts is an essential issue for col
agement in academic libraries. In recent years, the library science p

[*Library Quarterly*, vol. 78, no. 2, pp. 179–194]
© 2008 by The University of Chicago. All rights reserved.
0024-2519/2008/7802-0002$10.00

179

⑦ **Medium.** Give the medium of the article, Print, followed by a period.

③ **Title of periodical,** in italics. Omit any *A*, *An*, or *The* from the beginning of the title. Do not end with a period.

④ **Volume and issue numbers,** in Arabic numerals, separated by a period. Do not add a period after the issue number.

⑤ **Year of publication,** in parentheses and followed by a colon.

② **Title of article,** in quotation marks. Give the full title and any subtitle, separating them with a colon. End the title with a period inside the final quotation mark.

① **Author.** Give the full name—last name first, a comma, first name, and any middle name or initial. Omit *Dr., PhD,* or any other title. End the name with a period.

⑥ **Inclusive page numbers of article,** without "pp." Provide only as many digits in the last number as needed for clarity, usually two.

See also model 40 on p. 382 (entire dissertation), model 63 on p. 393 (abstract on the Web), and model 65 on p. 393 (abstract in an online database).

Note Most instructors expect you to consult and cite full articles, not abstracts.

Articles in newspapers

10. An article in a national newspaper (print)

Stout, David. "Blind Win Court Ruling on US Currency." *New York Times* 21 May
2008, natl. ed.: A23. Print.

See the facing page for an analysis of this entry and the location of the required information in the newspaper.

11. An article in a local newspaper (print)

Arntaenius, Linda. "Merwick Rezoning Pushes Senior Housing Debate." *Town
Topics* [Princeton] 21 May 2008: 1+. Print.

If the city of publication does not appear in the title of a local newspaper, follow the title with the city name, not italicized, in brackets.

Articles in magazines

12. An article in a weekly or biweekly magazine (print)

Fortini, Amanda. "Pomegranate Princess." *New Yorker* 31 Mar. 2008: 92-99. Print.

Give the author, title of the article, and title of the magazine. Follow the magazine title with the day, the month, and the year of publication. (Abbreviate all months except May, June, and July.) Don't place the date in parentheses, and don't provide a volume or issue number. Give the page numbers of the article and the medium, Print.

13. An article in a monthly or bimonthly magazine (print)

Douthat, Ross. "The Return of the Paranoid Style." *Atlantic Monthly* Apr. 2008:
52-59. Print.

Follow the magazine title with the month and the year of publication. (Abbreviate all months except May, June, and July.) Don't place the date in parentheses, and don't provide a volume or issue number. Give the page numbers of the article and the medium, Print.

Reviews, editorials, letters to the editor, interviews

14. A review (print)

Glasswell, Kathryn, and George Kamberelis. "Drawing and Redrawing the Map
of Writing Studies." Rev. of *Handbook of Writing Research*, by Charles A.

Format for a print newspaper article

①   ②   ③   ④

Stout, David. "Blind Win Court Ruling on US Currency." *New York Times* 21 May 2008,

    ⑤   ⑥   ⑦

    natl. ed.: A23. Print.

⑥ **Page number of article,** without "pp." Include a section designation before the number when the newspaper does the same, as here. Otherwise, give the section between the edition and the colon. Add a plus sign to the page number when the article continues on a later page.

① **Author.** Give the full name—last name first, a comma, first name, and any middle name or initial. Omit *Dr., PhD,* or any other title. End with a period.

First page of article

THE NEW YORK TIMES **NATIONAL** WEDNESDAY, MAY 21, 2008   A23

Blind Win Court Ruling on U.S. Currency

By DAVID STOUT

WASHINGTON — In a decision that could radically change the size, the color and even the feel of American money, a federal appeals court ruled on Tuesday that the United States discriminates against the blind and those with limited vision because its paper currency is all the same size regardless of a bill's value.

blind or visually impaired," said Brookly McLaughlin, deputy assistant secretary for public affairs.

Ms. McLaughlin said the Bureau of Engraving and Printing, the Treasury agency that makes paper money, had already contracted with a research firm to study ways to help those who are blind or have poor vision. The re-

in the country could cost $3.5 billion is bill

Other fected in money-di er machi makers Judge Randolph said.

The suit was brought under the Rehabilitation Act of 1973, which addresses discrimination in fed-

② **Title of article,** in quotation marks. Give the full title and any subtitle, separating them with a colon. End with a period inside the final quotation mark.

③ **Name of newspaper,** in italics. Give the title as it appears on the first page, omitting any *A, An,* or *The* from the beginning.

First page of newspaper

"All the News That's Fit to Print" **The New York Times**   National Edition

VOL. CLVII .... No. 54,317   © 2008 The New York Times   WEDNESDAY, MAY 21, 2008   Printed in California $1.25

⑦ **Medium.** Give the medium of the article, Print, followed by a period.

④ **Date of publication.** Give the day of the month first, then month, then year. Abbreviate all months except May, June, and July. End the date with a comma if listing the newspaper edition and/or the section designation. Otherwise, end with a colon.

⑤ **Edition.** If the newspaper lists an edition at the top of the first page, include it after the date. End with a comma if listing the section designation. Otherwise, end with a colon.

MacArthur, Steve Graham, and Jill Fitzgerald. *Reading Research Quarterly*

    42.2 (2007): 304-23. Print.

Rev. is an abbreviation for "Review." The names of the authors of the work being reviewed follow the title of the work, a comma, and by. If the review has no title of its own, then Rev. of and the title of the reviewed work immediately follow the name of the reviewer.

15. An editorial (print)

"A Global AIDS Campaign Stalled." Editorial. *New York Times* 21 June 2008,
natl. ed.: A18. Print.

For an editorial with no named author, begin with the title and add the word Editorial after the title, as in the example. For an editorial with a named author, start with his or her name and then proceed as in the example.

16. A letter to the editor (print)

McBride, Thad. "Swapping the Suit and Tie." Letter. *Economist* 29 Mar. 2008:
30. Print.

Add the word Letter after the title, if there is one, or after the author's name.

17. An interview (print)

Aloni, Shulamit. Interview. *Palestine-Israel Journal of Politics, Economics, and
Culture* 14.4 (2007): 63-68. Print.

Begin with the name of the person interviewed. If the interview does not have a title (as in the example), add Interview after the name. (Replace this description with the title if there is one.) You may also add the name of the interviewer if you know it—for example, Interview by Benson Wright. See model 75 (p. 397) to cite a broadcast interview or an interview you conduct yourself.

Articles in series or in special issues

18. An article in a series (print)

Kleinfeld, N. R. "Living at an Epicenter of Diabetes, Defiance, and Despair."
New York Times 10 Jan. 2006, natl. ed.: A1+. Print. Pt. 2 of a series,
Bad Blood, begun 9 Jan. 2006.

Cite an article in a series following a model on pp. 370–75 (scholarly journal, newspaper, or magazine). If you wish, end the entry with a description to indicate that the article is part of a series.

19. An article in a special issue (print)

Rubini, Monica, and Michela Menegatti. "Linguistic Bias in Personnel Selec-
tion." *Celebrating Two Decades of Linguistic Bias Research.* Ed. Robbie
M. Sutton and Karen M. Douglas. Spec. issue of *Journal of Language and
Social Psychology* 27.2 (2008): 168-81. Print.

Cite an article in a special issue of a periodical by starting with the author and title of the article. Follow with the title of the special issue, Ed., and the names of the issue's editor(s). Add Spec. issue of before the periodical title. Conclude with publication information, using the appropriate model on pp. 370–72 for a journal or magazine.

3 Listing nonperiodical print sources

Nonperiodical print sources are works that are not published at regular intervals, such as books, government publications, and pamphlets. To cite more than one author, two or more articles by the same author, a corporate author, or a source with no named author, see models 1–6.

Books

20. Basic format for a book (print)

Lahiri, Jhumpa. *Unaccustomed Earth*. New York: Knopf, 2008. Print.

The next page shows the basic format for a book and the location of the required information in the book. When other information is required, put it between the author's name and the title or between the title and the publication information, as in the following models.

21. A second or subsequent edition (print)

Bolinger, Dwight L. *Aspects of Language*. 3rd ed. New York: Harcourt, 1981.
    Print.

For any edition after the first, place the edition number after the title. (If an editor's name follows the title, place the edition number after the name. See model 26.) Use the appropriate designation for editions that are named or dated rather than numbered—for instance, Rev. ed. for "Revised edition."

22. A book with an editor (print)

Holland, Merlin, and Rupert Hart-Davis, eds. *The Complete Letters of Oscar
    Wilde*. New York: Holt, 2000. Print.

Handle editors' names like authors' names (models 1–4), but add a comma and the abbreviation ed. (one editor) or eds. (two or more editors) after the last editor's name.

23. A book with an author and an editor (print)

Mumford, Lewis. *The City in History*. Ed. Donald L. Miller. New York: Pantheon,
    1986. Print.

When citing the work of the author, give his or her name first, and give the editor's name after the title, preceded by Ed. (singular only, meaning "Edited by"). When citing the work of the editor, use

Format for a print book

① ② ③ ④ ⑤ ⑥
Lahiri, Jhumpa. *Unaccustomed Earth*. New York: Knopf, 2008. Print.

Title page

② **Title,** in italics. Give the full title and any sub-title, separating them with a colon. End the title with a period.

① **Author.** Give the full name—last name first, a comma, first name, and any middle name or initial. Omit *Dr., PhD,* or any other title. End the name with a period.

④ **Publisher's name.** Shorten most publishers' names ("UP" for University Press, "Little" for Little, Brown). Give both imprint and publisher's names when they appear on the title page: e.g., "Vintage-Random" for Vintage Books and Random House.

③ **City of publication.** Precede the publisher's name with its city, followed by a colon. Use only the first city if the title page lists more than one.

⑥ **Medium.** Give the medium of the book, Print, followed by a period.

⑤ **Date of publication.** If the date doesn't appear on the title page, look for it on the next page. End the date with a period.

Unaccustomed Earth

Jhumpa Lahiri

Alfred A. Knopf ▓ New York • Toronto 2008

model 22 for a book with an editor, adding By and the author's name after the title:

> Miller, Donald L., ed. *The City in History*. By Lewis Mumford. New York:
>
> Pantheon, 1986. Print.

24. A book with a translator (print)

Alighieri, Dante. *The Inferno.* Trans. John Ciardi. New York: NAL, 1971. Print.

When citing the work of the author, as in the preceding example, give his or her name first, and give the translator's name after the title, preceded by Trans. ("Translated by").

When citing the work of the translator, give his or her name first, followed by a comma and trans. Follow the title with By and the author's name:

Ciardi, John, trans. *The Inferno.* By Dante Alighieri. New York: NAL, 1971. Print.

When a book you cite by author has a translator *and* an editor, give their names in the order used on the book's title page.

25. An anthology (print)

Kennedy, X. J., and Dana Gioia, eds. *Literature: An Introduction to Fiction, Poetry, and Drama.* 10th ed. New York: Longman, 2007. Print.

Cite an entire anthology only when citing the work of the editor or editors or when your instructor permits cross-referencing like that shown in model 27. Give the name of the editor or editors (followed by ed. or eds.) and then the title of the anthology.

26. A selection from an anthology (print)

Mason, Bobbie Ann. "Shiloh." *Literature: An Introduction to Fiction, Poetry, and Drama.* Ed. X. J. Kennedy and Dana Gioia. 10th ed. New York: Longman, 2007. 604-13. Print.

This listing adds the following to the anthology entry in model 25: author of selection, title of selection (in quotation marks), and inclusive page numbers for the selection (without the abbreviation "pp."). If you wish, you may also supply the original date of publication for the work you are citing, after its title. See model 32 on p. 379.

If the work you cite comes from a collection of works by one author that has no editor, use the following form:

Auden, W. H. "Family Ghosts." *The Collected Poetry of W. H. Auden.* New York: Random, 1945. 132-33. Print.

If the work you cite is a scholarly article that was previously printed elsewhere, provide the complete information for the earlier publication of the piece, followed by Rpt. in ("Reprinted in") and the information for the source in which you found the piece:

Molloy, Francis C. "The Suburban Vision in John O'Hara's Short Stories." *Critique: Studies in Modern Fiction* 25.2 (1984): 101-13. Rpt. in *Short Story Criticism: Excerpts from Criticism of the Works of Short Fiction Writers.* Ed. David Segal. Vol. 15. Detroit: Gale, 1989. 287-92. Print.

27. Two or more selections from the same anthology (print)

Erdrich, Louise. "Indian Boarding School: The Runaways." Kennedy and Gioia
1106.

Kennedy, X. J., and Dana Gioia, eds. *Literature: An Introduction to Fiction,
Poetry, and Drama*. 10th ed. New York: Longman, 2007. Print.

Merwin, W. S. "For the Anniversary of My Death." Kennedy and Gioia 877-78.

Stevens, Wallace. "Thirteen Ways of Looking at a Blackbird." Kennedy and
Gioia 880-82.

When you are citing more than one selection from the same source,
your instructor may allow you to avoid repetition by giving the
source in full (the Kennedy and Gioia entry) and then simply cross-
referencing it in entries for the works you used. Thus the Erdrich,
Merwin, and Stevens examples replace full publication information
with Kennedy and Gioia and the appropriate pages in that book. Note
that each entry appears in its proper alphabetical place among
other works cited. Because each entry cross-references the Kennedy
anthology, the medium is not required.

28. An article in a reference work (print)

"Reckon." *Merriam-Webster's Collegiate Dictionary*. 11th ed. 2008. Print.

Wenner, Manfred W. "Arabia." *The New Encyclopaedia Britannica: Macropaedia*.
15th ed. 2007. Print.

List an article in a reference work by its title (first example) unless
the article is signed (second example). For works with entries arranged alphabetically, you need not include volume or page numbers. For well-known works like those above, you may also omit the
editors' names and all publication information except any edition
number and the year of publication. For works that are not well
known, give full publication information:

"Hungarians in America." *The Ethnic Almanac*. Ed. Stephanie Bernardo Johns.
6th ed. New York: Doubleday, 2002. 121-23. Print.

See also models 48 (p. 387) and 68 (p. 395), respectively, to cite reference works appearing on the Web or on a CD-ROM or DVD-ROM.

29. An illustrated book or graphic narrative (print)

Wilson, G. Willow. *Cairo*. Illus. M. K. Perker. New York: Vertigo-DC Comics,
2005. Print.

When citing the work of the writer of a graphic narrative or illustrated book, follow the example above: author's name, title, Illus.
("Illustrated by"), and the illustrator's name. When citing the

work of an illustrator, list his or her name first, followed by a comma and illus. ("illustrator"). After the title and By, list the author's name.

> Garth Williams, illus. *Charlotte's Web*. By E. B. White. 1952. New York: Harper,
> 1999. Print.

30. A multivolume work (print)

> Lincoln, Abraham. *The Collected Works of Abraham Lincoln*. Ed. Roy P. Basler.
> Vol. 5. New Brunswick: Rutgers UP, 1953. Print. 8 vols.

If you use only one volume of a multivolume work, give that volume number before the publication information (Vol. 5 in the preceding example). You may add the total number of volumes at the end of the entry (8 vols. in the example).

If you use two or more volumes of a multivolume work, give the work's total number of volumes before the publication information (8 vols. in the following example). Your text citation will indicate which volume you are citing (see p. 362).

> Lincoln, Abraham. *The Collected Works of Abraham Lincoln*. Ed. Roy P. Basler.
> 8 vols. New Brunswick: Rutgers UP, 1953. Print.

If you cite a multivolume work published over a period of years, give the inclusive years as the publication date: for instance, Cambridge: Harvard UP, 1978-90.

31. A series (print)

> Bergman, Ingmar. *The Seventh Seal*. New York: Simon, 1995. Print. Mod. Film
> Scripts Ser. 12.

Place the name of the series (not quoted or italicized) at the end of the entry, followed by a period, a series number (if any), and another period. Abbreviate common words such as *modern* and *series*.

32. A republished book (print)

> James, Henry. *The Bostonians*. 1886. New York: Penguin, 2001. Print.

Republished books include books reissued under new titles and paperbound editions of books originally released in hard covers. Place the original publication date (but not the place of publication or the publisher's name) after the title, and then provide the full publication information for the source you are using. If the book was originally published under a different title, add this title after Rpt. of ("Reprint of") at the end of the entry (after Print) and move the original publication date after the title—for example, Rpt. of *Thomas Hardy: A Life*. 1941.

33. The Bible (print)

The Bible. Print. King James Vers.

The Holy Bible. Trans. Ronald Youngblood et al. Grand Rapids: Zondervan, 1984. Print. New Intl. Vers.

When citing a standard version of the Bible (first example), do not italicize the title or the name of the version at the end. You need not provide publication information. For an edition of the Bible (second example), italicize the title, provide editors' and/or translators' names, give full publication information, and add the version name at the end.

34. A book with a title in its title (print)

Eco, Umberto. *Postscript to* The Name of the Rose. Trans. William Weaver. New York: Harcourt, 1983. Print.

When a book's title contains another book title (here *The Name of the Rose*), do not italicize the second title. When a book's title contains a quotation or the title of a work normally placed in quotation marks, keep the quotation marks and italicize both titles: *Critical Response to Henry James's "The Beast in the Jungle."*

35. Published proceedings of a conference (print)

Stimpson, Bill, ed. *2007 Annual Conference and Exhibition.* Proc. of Amer. Wind Energy Assn. Conf., 3-6 June 2007, New York. Red Hook: Curran, 2008. Print.

To cite the published proceedings of a conference, use a book model—here, an edited book (model 22). Between the title and the publication data, add information about the conference, such as its name, date, and location. You may omit any of this information that already appears in the source title. Treat a particular presentation at the conference like a selection from an anthology (model 26).

36. An introduction, preface, foreword, or afterword (print)

Donaldson, Norman. Introduction. *The Claverings.* By Anthony Trollope. New York: Dover, 1977. vii-xv. Print.

An introduction, foreword, or afterword is often written by someone other than the book's author. When citing such a piece, give its name without quotation marks or italics, as with Introduction above. (If the piece has a title of its own, provide it, in quotation marks, between the name of the author and the name of the book.) Follow the title of the book with By and the book author's name. Give the inclusive page numbers of the part you cite. (In the example above, the small Roman numerals refer to the front matter of the book, before page 1.)

When the author of a preface or introduction is the same as the author of the book, give only the last name after the title:

> Gould, Stephen Jay. Prologue. *The Flamingo's Smile: Reflections in Natural History.* By Gould. New York: Norton, 1985. 13-20. Print.

37. A book lacking publication information or pagination (print)

> Carle, Eric. *The Very Busy Spider.* New York: Philomel, 1984. N. pag. Print.

Some books are not paginated or do not list a publisher or a place of publication. To cite such a book, provide as much information as you can and indicate the missing information with an abbreviation: N.p. if no city of publication, n.p. if no publisher, n.d. if no publication date, and N. pag. if no page numbers.

Other nonperiodical print sources

38. A government publication (print)

> United Nations. Dept. of Economic and Social Affairs. *World Youth Report 2007: Young People's Transition to Adulthood—Progress and Challenges.* New York: United Nations, 2008. Print.

> United States. Cong. House. Committee on Agriculture, Nutrition, and Forestry. *Food and Energy Act of 2007.* 110th Cong., 1st sess. Washington: GPO, 2007. Print.

> Wisconsin. Dept. of Public Instruction. *Bullying Prevention Program: Grades 6-8.* Madison: Wisconsin Dept. of Public Instruction, 2007. Print.

If a government publication does not list a person as author or editor, give the appropriate agency as author, as in the above examples. Provide information in the order illustrated, separating elements with periods: the name of the government, the name of the agency (which may be abbreviated), and the title and publication information. For a congressional publication (second example), give the house and committee involved before the title, and give the number and session of Congress after the title. In this example, GPO stands for the US Government Printing Office.

If a government publication lists a person as author or editor, treat the source as an authored or edited book:

> Putko, Michelle. *Women in Combat Compendium.* Carlisle: US Army War Coll., Strategic Studies Inst., 2008. Print.

See model 47 (p. 387) to cite a government publication you find on the Web.

39. A pamphlet or brochure (print)

Understanding Childhood Obesity. Tampa: Obesity Action Coalition, 2008. Print.

Most pamphlets and brochures can be treated as books. In this example, the pamphlet has no listed author, so the title comes first. If your source has an author, give his or her name first, followed by the title and publication information.

40. A dissertation (print)

McFaddin, Marie Oliver. *Adaptive Reuse: An Architectural Solution for Poverty and Homelessness*. Diss. U of Maryland, 2007. Ann Arbor: UMI, 2007. Print.

Treat a published dissertation like a book, but after the title insert Diss. ("Dissertation"), the institution granting the degree, and the year.

For an unpublished dissertation, use quotation marks rather than italics for the title and omit publication information.

Wilson, Stuart M. "John Stuart Mill as a Literary Critic." Diss. U of Michigan, 1990. Print.

41. A letter (print)

Buttolph, Mrs. Laura E. Letter to Rev. and Mrs. C. C. Jones. 20 June 1857. *The Children of Pride: A True Story of Georgia and the Civil War*. Ed. Robert Manson Myers. New Haven: Yale UP, 1972. 334-35. Print.

List a published letter under the writer's name. Specify that the source is a letter and to whom it was addressed, and give the date on which it was written. Treat the remaining information like that for a selection from an anthology (model 26, p. 379). (See also model 16, p. 376, for the format of a letter to the editor of a periodical.)

For an unpublished letter in the collection of a library or archive, specify the writer, recipient, and date, as for a published letter. Then provide the medium, either MS ("manuscript") or TS ("typescript"). End with the name and location of the archive.

James, Jonathan E. Letter to his sister. 16 Apr. 1970. MS. Jonathan E. James Papers. South Dakota State Archive, Pierre.

For a letter you received, give the name of the writer, note the fact that the letter was sent to you, provide the date of the letter, and add the medium, MS or TS.

Wynne, Ava. Letter to the author. 6 Apr. 2008. MS.

To cite an e-mail message or a discussion-group posting, see models 70–71 (p. 395).

4 Listing nonperiodical Web sources

This section shows how to cite nonperiodical sources that you find on the Web. These sources may be published only once or occasionally, or they may be updated frequently but not regularly. (Most online magazines and newspapers fall into the latter category, even if they relate to printed periodicals, because their content changes often and unpredictably. See models 45 and 46.) Some nonperiodical Web sources are available only on the Web (below); others are available in other media as well, such as print or film (pp. 390–91). See models 62–67 (pp. 392–94) to cite a scholarly journal that you find on the Web and any periodical that you find in an online database.

The MLA no longer recommends providing a URL (electronic address) in Web source citations because URLs change frequently and because users can search for documents using search engines. However, do include a URL if your source is hard to find without it, if your source could be confused with another one, or if your instructor requires you to include URLs. See model 61 (p. 391) for the form to use when citing a URL.

Note The *MLA Style Manual* does not label its examples of nonperiodical Web sources as particular types. For ease of reference, the following models identify and illustrate the kinds of Web sources you are likely to encounter. If you don't see just what you need, consult the index of models on the **MLA** tabbed divider for a similar source type whose format you can adapt. If your source does not include all of the information needed for a complete citation, find and list what you can.

Nonperiodical sources available only on the Web

Many nonperiodical Web sources are available only online. The following list, adapted from the *MLA Style Manual*, itemizes the possible elements in a nonperiodical Web publication, in order of their appearance in a works-cited entry:

1. **Name of the author or other person responsible for the source,** such as an editor, translator, director, or performer. See models 1–6 (pp. 368–69) for the handling of authors' names. For other kinds of contributors, see models 22–24 (editors and translators) and models 74, 76–77, and 83 (directors, performers, and so on).

2. **Title of the cited work.** Use quotation marks for titles of articles, blog entries, and other sources that are parts of larger works. Use italics for books, plays, and other sources that are published independently.

3. **Title of the Web site,** in italics.

4. **Version or edition cited,** if any, following model 21 (p. 375)— for example, *Index of History Periodicals.* 2nd ed.

5. **Publisher or sponsor of the site,** followed by a comma. If you cannot find a publisher or sponsor, use N.p. ("No publisher") instead.

6. **Date of electronic publication, latest revision, or posting.** If no date is available, use n.d. ("no date") instead.

7. **Medium of publication:** Web.

8. **Date of your access:** day, month, year.

For some Web sources, you may want to include information that is not on this list, such as the names of both the writer and the performers on a television show.

42. A short work with a title (Web)

Molella, Arthur. "Cultures of Innovation." *The Lemelson Center for the Study of Invention and Innovation.* Smithsonian Inst., Natl. Museum of Amer. Hist., Spring 2005. Web. 3 Aug. 2008.

See the facing page for an analysis of this entry and the location of the required information on the Web site. If the short work you are citing lacks an author, follow model 6 (p. 369) for an anonymous source, starting the entry with the title of the work:

"Clean Energy." *Union of Concerned Scientists: Citizens and Scientists for Environmental Solutions.* Union of Concerned Scientists, 5 Feb. 2008. Web. 11 Mar. 2008.

To cite a short Web source that also appears in another medium (such as print), see models 56–60 (pp. 390–91). To cite an article from a Web journal or from an online database, see models 62–67 (pp. 392–94).

43. A short work without a title (Web)

Crane, Gregory, ed. Home page. *The Perseus Digital Library.* Dept. of Classics, Tufts U, n.d. Web. 21 July 2008.

If you are citing an untitled short work from a Web site, such as the home page of a site or a posting to a blog, insert Home page, Online posting, or another descriptive label in place of the title. Do not use quotation marks or italics for this label.

Note that this source lacks a publication date, indicated by n.d. after the sponsor's name.

Format for a short work on the Web

①   ②   ③

Molella, Arthur. "Cultures of Innovation." *The Lemelson Center for the Study of Inven-*

                ④   ⑤

tion and Innovation. Smithsonian Inst., Natl. Museum of Amer. Hist., Spring

    ⑥   ⑦

2005. Web. 3 Aug. 2008.

Top of page

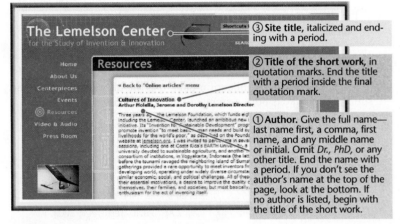

③ **Site title,** italicized and ending with a period.

② **Title of the short work,** in quotation marks. End the title with a period inside the final quotation mark.

① **Author.** Give the full name—last name first, a comma, first name, and any middle name or initial. Omit *Dr., PhD,* or any other title. End the name with a period. If you don't see the author's name at the top of the page, look at the bottom. If no author is listed, begin with the title of the short work.

Bottom of page

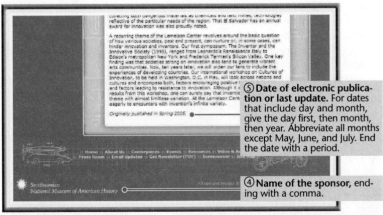

⑤ **Date of electronic publication or last update.** For dates that include day and month, give the day first, then month, then year. Abbreviate all months except May, June, and July. End the date with a period.

④ **Name of the sponsor,** ending with a comma.

⑥ **Medium.** Give the medium of the article, Web, followed by a period.

⑦ **Date of your access.** Give the day first, then month, then year. Abbreviate all months except May, June, and July. End the date with a period. (Since this date does not appear on the site, you'll need to record it separately.)

44. An entire site (Web)

Cheit, Ross E., ed. *The Recovered Memory Project.* Taubman Center for Public
and Amer. Insts., Brown U, July 2007. Web. 8 Oct. 2008.

When citing an entire Web site—for instance, a scholarly project or a foundation site—include the name of the editor, author, or compiler (if available); the title of the site; the sponsor; the date of publication or most recent update; the medium (Web); and your date of access.

If your source lacks a named author or editor, begin with the site title:

Union of Concerned Scientists: Citizens and Scientists for Environmental Solutions.
Union of Concerned Scientists, 5 Feb. 2008. Web. 11 Mar. 2008.

If your source lacks a sponsor, use the abbreviation N.p. ("No publisher"). If it lacks a publication date, use the abbreviation n.d. The source below lacks both a sponsor and a publication date:

Corbett, John. *STARN: Scots Teaching and Resource Network.* N.p., n.d. Web. 26
Nov. 2008.

45. An article in a newspaper (Web)

Carvajal, Doreen. "High-Tech Crime Is an Online Bubble That Hasn't Burst."
New York Times. New York Times, 7 Apr. 2008. Web. 8 Apr. 2008.

List the author, article title, and newspaper title as in model 10 or 11 (p. 372). Then give the publishers's name and the date. End with the medium of publication (Web) and the date of your access. (See model 66 to cite a newspaper article in an online database.)

Use the preceding format to adapt the models for print periodicals if you need to cite a Web newspaper review, editorial, letter to the editor, interview, or article in a series (models 14–18, pp. 372–74).

46. An article in a magazine (Web)

Yabroff, Jennie. "Art Aimed to Shock." *Newsweek.* Newsweek, 26 Apr. 2008.
Web. 15 May 2008.

List the author, article title, and magazine title as in model 12 or 13 (p. 372). Then give the publisher's name and the date. End with the medium (Web) and the date of your access. (See model 67 to cite a magazine article in an online database.)

Use the preceding format to adapt the models for print periodicals if you need to cite a Web magazine review, editorial, letter to the editor, interview, article in a series, or special issue (models 14–19, pp. 372–74).

47. A government publication (Web)

United States. Dept. of Agriculture. "Inside the Pyramid." *MyPyramid.gov.*
US Dept. of Agriculture, n.d. Web. 1 Mar. 2008.

See model 38 for examples of government publications in print. Provide the same information for online publications along with the facts of Web publication. The example above includes the names of the government and department; the title of the source, in quotation marks; the title of the Web site, in italics; the sponsor; n.d. (because there is no publication date); the medium (Web); and the date of access.

48. An article in a reference work (Web)

"Yi Dynasty." *Encyclopaedia Britannica Online.* Encyclopaedia Britannica, 2008.
Web. 7 Apr. 2008.

This source does not list an author, so the entry begins with the title of the article and then proceeds as for other Web sources. If a reference article has an author, place the name before the article title, as in model 42.

For reference works that you find in print or on CD-ROM or DVD-ROM, see models 28 (p. 378) and 68 (p. 395), respectively.

49. An image (Web)

To cite images that are available only on the Web, give the name of the artist or creator, the title of the work, the date of the work (if any), a word describing the type of image (if not otherwise clear from the image or site title), the title of the Web site, the sponsor, the date of the site, the medium (Web), and your date of access. The following examples show a range of possibilities.

A work of visual art:

Simpson, Rick. *Overload. Museum of Computer Art.* Museum of Computer Art,
2008. Web. 1 Apr. 2008.

A photograph:

Touboul, Jean. *Desert 1.* 2002. Photograph. *Artmuse.net.* Jean Touboul, 2007.
Web. 14 Nov. 2008.

An advertisement:

United States. Dept. of Educ. Federal Student Aid. Advertisement. *Facebook.*
Facebook, 2008. Web. 6 May 2008.

A map, chart, graph, or diagram:

"Greenhouse Effect." Diagram. *Earthguide.* Scripps Inst. of Oceanography,
2008. Web. 17 July 2008.

See also model 60 (p. 391) to cite an image that appears both on the Web and in another medium. And see models 78–82 (pp. 398–99) to cite images that aren't on the Web.

50. A television or radio program (Web)

Seabrook, Andrea, host. *All Things Considered*. Natl. Public Radio, 6 Apr. 2008.
    Web. 21 Apr. 2008.

The Web sites of television and radio networks and programs often include both content that was broadcast as part of a show and content that is unique to the site. Cite such material by its title or by the name of the person whose work you cite. Identify the role of anyone but an author (host in the example). Give the site title, the sponsor, the date, the medium (Web), and the date of your access. You may also cite other contributors (and their roles) after the title, as in model 52.

See also model 74 (p. 396) to cite a television or radio program that isn't on the Web.

51. A video recording (Web)

Green Children Foundation, prod. *The Green Children Visit China*. *YouTube*.
    YouTube, 7 Jan. 2008. Web. 28 June 2008.

Cite a video on the Web either by its title or by the name of the person whose work you are citing—in this example, the foundation that produced the video. Identify the role of anyone but an author (prod. in the example). Give the video title, the site title, the sponsor, the date, the medium (Web), and the date of your access. You may also cite other contributors (and their roles) after the title, as in model 52.

See also model 53 to cite a podcast of a video recording; model 59 (p. 390) to cite a video recording or film that appears both on the Web and in another medium (such as DVD); and model 77 (p. 397) to cite a film, DVD, or video recording that isn't on the Web.

52. A sound recording (Web)

Beglarian, Eve. *Five Things*. Perf. Beglarian et al. *Kalvos and Damian*. N.p., 23
    Oct. 2001. Web. 8 Mar. 2008.

Cite a musical sound recording by its title or by the name of the person whose work you are citing—in this example, the composer. (If the composer's name comes after the title, precede it with By. See the next example.) This example also gives the work title, the performers of the work, the site title, the sponsor (here unknown, so replaced with N.p.), the date, the medium (Web), and the date of access.

The same format may be used for a spoken-word recording that you find on the Web:

> Wasserstein, Wendy, narr. "Afternoon of a Faun." By Wasserstein. *The Borzoi Reader Online*. Knopf, 2001. Web. 14 Feb. 2008.

See also the next model to cite a sound podcast; model 58 to cite a sound recording that appears both on the Web and in another medium (such as CD); and model 76 (p. 397) to cite a sound recording that isn't on the Web.

53. A podcast (Web)

> Simon, Bob. "Exonerated." *60 Minutes*. *CBS News*. CBS News, 25 May 2008. Web. 6 June 2008.

This podcast from a news program lists the author of a story on the show, the title of the story (in quotation marks), and the program (italicized) as well as the site title, sponsor, date, medium (Web), and access date. If a podcast does not list an author or other creator, begin with the title.

54. A blog entry (Web)

> Marshall, Joshua Micah. "Asking the Tough Questions." *Talking Points Memo*. TPM Media, 15 May 2008. Web. 21 May 2008.

For a blog entry, give the author, the title of the entry, the title of the blog or site, the name of the sponsor (or N.p. if no sponsor is named), the publication date, the medium (Web), and the date of access. See model 43 (p. 384) to cite a blog entry without a title.

55. A wiki (Web)

> "Podcast." *Wikipedia*. Wikimedia, n.d. Web. 20 Nov. 2008.

To cite an entry from a wiki, follow the above example: entry title, site title, sponsor, publication date (here n.d. because the wiki entry is undated), medium (Web), and date of access. Begin with the site title if you are citing the entire wiki.

Nonperiodical Web sources also available in print

Some sources you find on the Web may be books, short stories, and other works that have been scanned from print versions. To cite such a source, generally provide the information for both original print publication and Web publication. Begin your entry as if you were citing the print work, consulting models 20–41 for an appropriate format. Then, instead of giving "Print" as the medium, provide the title of the Web site you used, any version or edition number, the medium you used (Web), and the date of your access.

56. A short work with print publication information (Web)

Wheatley, Phillis. "On Virtue." *Poems on Various Subjects, Religious and Moral.*
London, 1773. N. pag. *American Verse Project.* Web. 21 July 2008.

The print information for this poem follows model 26 (p. 377) for a selection from an anthology, but it omits the publisher's name because the anthology was published before 1900. The print information ends with N. pag. because the original source has no page numbers.

57. A book with print publication information (Web)

James, Henry. *The Ambassadors.* 1903. New York: Scribner's, 1909. *Oxford Text Archive.* Web. 5 May 2008.

The print information for this novel follows model 32 (p. 379) for a republished book, so it includes both the original date of publication (1903) and the publication information for the scanned book.

Nonperiodical Web sources also available in other media

Some images, films, and sound recordings that you find on the Web may have been published before in other media and then scanned or digitized for the Web. To cite such a source, generally provide the information for original publication as well as that for Web publication. Begin your entry as if you were citing the original, consulting models 74–84 (pp. 396–99) for an appropriate format. Then, instead of giving the original medium of publication, provide the title of the Web site you used, the medium you used (Web), and your date of access.

58. A sound recording with other publication information (Web)

"Rioting in Pittsburgh." CBS Radio, 1968. *Vincent Voice Library.* Web.
7 Dec. 2008.

For Web sound recordings with original publication information, base citations on model 76 (p. 397), adding the information for Web publication.

59. A film or video recording with other publication information (Web)

Coca Cola. Advertisement. Dir. Haskell Wexler. 1971. *American Memory.* Lib. of
Cong. Web. 8 Apr. 2008.

For Web films or videos with original publication information, base citations on model 77 (p. 397), adding the information for Web publication.

60. An image with other publication information (Web)

Pollock, Jackson. *Lavender Mist: Number 1*. 1950. Natl. Gallery of Art, Washington.
    WebMuseum. Web. 7 Apr. 2008.

Keefe, Mike. "FAA Inspector in a Quandary." Cartoon. *Denver Post* 5 Apr. 2008.
    PoliticalCartoons.com. Web. 7 Apr. 2008.

For Web images with original publication information, base citations on models 78–82 (pp. 398–99), adding the information for Web publication.

Citation of a URL

61. A source requiring citation of the URL

Joss, Rich. "Dispatches from the Ice: The Second Season Begins." *Antarctic*
    Expeditions. Smithsonian Natl. Zoo and Friends of the Natl. Zoo, 26 Oct.
    2007. Web. 26 Sept. 2008. <http://nationalzoo.si.edu/
    ConservationAndScience/AquaticEcosystems/Antarctica/Expedition/
    FieldNew/2-FieldNews.cfm>.

Because a URL does not always provide a convenient or usable route to a source, the MLA no longer recommends including URLs in works-cited entries. However, you should include URLs when your instructor requires them. You should also give a URL when readers may not be able to locate a source without one. For example, using a search engine to find "Dispatches from the Ice" (the title in the example) yields more than ten hits, one of which links to the correct site but the wrong document.

If you need to include a URL, ensure accuracy by using Copy and Paste to duplicate it in a file or an e-mail to yourself. In your list of works cited, give the URL after your date of access and a period. Put angle brackets on both ends of the URL, and end with a period. Break URLs *only* after slashes—do not hyphenate.

5 | Listing journals on the Web and periodicals in online databases

This section covers two kinds of periodicals: scholarly journals that you reach directly on the Web (next page) and journals, newspapers, and magazines that you reach in online databases (p. 393). Newspapers and magazines that you reach directly on the Web are typically not periodicals (because their content often changes), so they are covered in models 45 and 46 (p. 387).

Citations for Web journals and for periodicals in online databases resemble those for print periodicals, with some changes for the different medium.

Web journals consulted directly

The journals you find directly on the Web may be published only online or may be published in print versions as well. The citation format is the same in either case: begin with an appropriate print model (pp. 370–72), but replace "Print" with Web and add your access date. Because many Web journals are unpaged, you may have to substitute n. pag. for page numbers.

62. An article in a scholarly journal (Web)

Polletta, Francesca. "Just Talk: Public Deliberation after 9/11." *Journal of Public Deliberation* 4.1 (2008): n. pag. Web. 7 Apr. 2008.

Format for a journal article on the Web

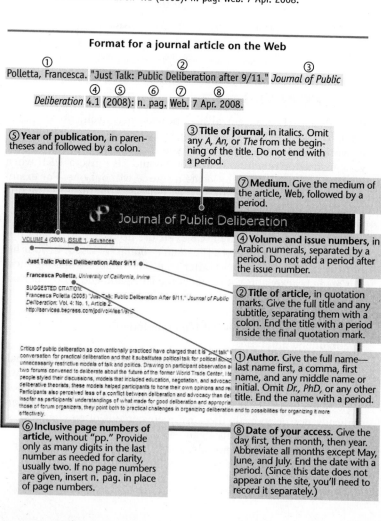

Polletta, Francesca. "Just Talk: Public Deliberation after 9/11." *Journal of Public Deliberation* 4.1 (2008): n. pag. Web. 7 Apr. 2008.

① ② ③ ④ ⑤ ⑥ ⑦ ⑧

⑤ **Year of publication,** in parentheses and followed by a colon.

③ **Title of journal,** in italics. Omit any *A, An,* or *The* from the beginning of the title. Do not end with a period.

⑦ **Medium.** Give the medium of the article, Web, followed by a period.

④ **Volume and issue numbers,** in Arabic numerals, separated by a period. Do not add a period after the issue number.

② **Title of article,** in quotation marks. Give the full title and any subtitle, separating them with a colon. End the title with a period inside the final quotation mark.

① **Author.** Give the full name—last name first, a comma, first name, and any middle name or initial. Omit *Dr., PhD,* or any other title. End the name with a period.

⑥ **Inclusive page numbers of article,** without "pp." Provide only as many digits in the last number as needed for clarity, usually two. If no page numbers are given, insert n. pag. in place of page numbers.

⑧ **Date of your access.** Give the day first, then month, then year. Abbreviate all months except May, June, and July. End the date with a period. (Since this date does not appear on the site, you'll need to record it separately.)

See the facing page for an analysis of the preceding example and the location of the required information in the Web journal. (For a journal article reached in an online database, see model 64.)

Use the same format to adapt the models for print periodicals if you need to cite a Web journal review, editorial, letter to the editor, interview, article in a series, or special issue (models 14–19, pp. 372–75).

63. An abstract of a journal article (Web)

Polletta, Francesca. "Just Talk: Public Deliberation after 9/11." *Journal of Public Deliberation* 4.1 (2008): n. pag. Abstract. Web. 7 Apr. 2008.

Treat a Web abstract like a Web journal article, but add Abstract between the publication information and the medium. (You may omit this label if the journal title clearly indicates that the cited work is an abstract.) See model 65 to cite an abstract in an online database.

Web periodicals consulted in online databases

Many articles in journals, newspapers, and magazines are available in online databases that you reach through your library's Web site, such as *Academic Search Premier, ProQuest,* and *Project Muse.* Follow models 7–19 (pp. 370–75) for print periodicals, but replace "Print" with the title of the database you consulted, the medium (Web), and the date of your access.

64. An article in a scholarly journal (online database)

Gorski, Paul C. "Privilege and Repression in the Digital Era: Rethinking the Sociopolitics of the Digital Divide." *Race, Gender and Class* 10.4 (2003): 145-76. *Ethnic NewsWatch.* Web. 23 Apr. 2008.

See the next page for an analysis of this entry and the location of the required information in the database.

65. An abstract of a journal article (online database)

Gorski, Paul C. "Privilege and Repression in the Digital Era: Rethinking the Sociopolitics of the Digital Divide." *Race, Gender and Class* 10.4 (2003): 145-76. Abstract. *Ethnic NewsWatch.* Web. 23 Apr. 2008.

Treat an abstract in an online database like a journal article in a database, but add Abstract between the publication information and the database title. (You may omit this label if the journal title clearly indicates that the cited work is an abstract.)

66. An article in a newspaper (online database)

Buckman, Rebecca. "Driver Cell Phone Bans Questioned." *Wall Street Journal* 13 May 2008, eastern ed.: D2+. *ProQuest.* Web. 12 Oct. 2008.

Format for a journal article in an online database

①   ②
Gorski, Paul C. "Privilege and Repression in the Digital Era: Rethinking the Socio-

                                  ③   ④   ⑤   ⑥
        politics of the Digital Divide." *Race, Gender and Class* 10.4 (2003): 145-76.

        ⑦   ⑧   ⑨
        Ethnic NewsWatch. Web. 23 Apr. 2008.

⑦ **Name of the database**, in italics, ending with a period.

② **Title of the article**, in quotation marks. End the title with a period inside the final quotation mark.

⑥ **Inclusive page numbers** of article, without "pp." Provide only as many digits in the last number as needed for clarity, usually two.

④ **Volume and issue numbers**, in Arabic numerals, separated by a period. Do not add a period after the issue number.

① **Author.** Give the full name—last name first, a comma, first name, and any middle name or initial. Omit *Dr.,* *PhD,* or any other title. End the name with a period.

⑤ **Year of publication**, in parentheses and followed by a colon.

③ **Title of journal**, in italics. Omit any *A, An,* or *The* from the beginning of the title. Do not end with a period.

⑧ **Medium.** Give the medium of the article, Web, followed by a period.

⑨ **Date of your access.** Give the day first, then month, then year. Abbreviate all months except May, June, and July. End the date with a period. (Since this date does not appear on the site, you'll need to record it separately.)

Follow model 10 or 11 (p. 372) for citing author, title of article, title of newspaper, publication date, edition (if any), and page numbers. Add the database title, the medium (Web), and your date of access.

67. An article in a magazine (online database)

> Brown, Kathryn. "The Skinny on the Environment." *Scientific American* Jan.
>
> 2008: 30-37. *Academic Search Premier.* Web. 3 Aug. 2008.

Follow model 12 or 13 (p. 372) for citing author, title of article, title of magazine, publication date, and page numbers. Add the title of the database, the medium (Web), and the date of your access.

6 Listing other electronic sources

Publications on CD-ROM or DVD-ROM

68. A nonperiodical CD-ROM or DVD-ROM

Nunberg, Geoffrey. "Usage in the Dictionary." *The American Heritage Dictionary of the English Language.* 4th ed. Boston: Houghton, 2000. CD-ROM.

Single-issue CD-ROMs may be encyclopedias, dictionaries, books, and other resources that are published just once, like print books. Follow models 20–37 for print books (pp. 375–381), but replace "Print" with CD-ROM or DVD-ROM. If the disc has a vendor that differs from the publisher of the work, add the vendor's place of publication, name, and publication date after the medium—for instance, Philadelphia: Soquest, 2006.

See also models 28 (p. 378) and 48 (p. 387) to cite reference works in print and on the Web.

69. A periodical CD-ROM or DVD-ROM

Kolata, Gina. "Gauging Body Mass Index in a Changing Body." *New York Times* 28 June 2005, natl. ed.: D1+. CD-ROM. *New York Times Ondisc.* UMI-ProQuest. Sept. 2005.

Databases on CD-ROM or DVD-ROM are issued periodically—for instance, every six months or every year. The journals, newspapers, and other publications included in such a database are generally available in print as well, so your works-cited entry should give the information for both formats. Start with information for the print version, following models 7–19 (pp. 370–74). Then replace "Print" with the medium (CD-ROM or DVD-ROM), the database title, the vendor's name (UMI-ProQuest in the example), and the database publication date.

E-mail and discussion-group postings

70. An e-mail message

Bailey, Elizabeth. "Re: London." Message to the author. 27 Mar. 2008. E-mail.

For e-mail, give the writer's name; the title, if any, from the e-mail's subject heading, in quotation marks; Message to the author (or the name of a recipient besides you); the date of the message; and the medium, E-mail. You do not need to include the date of your access.

71. A posting to a discussion group

Williams, Frederick. "Circles as Primitive." *The Math Forum @ Drexel.* Drexel U, 28 Feb. 2008. E-mail.

Cite a posting to a discussion group like a blog entry (model 54, p. 389). This example for a discussion-list posting includes author's name, title of the posting, title of the list, name of the sponsor, date of the posting, and medium (E-mail). If the posting is untitled, give Online posting instead. You need not add the date of your access.

Digital files

You may want to cite a digital file that is not on the Web or on a disc, such as a PDF document, a JPEG image, or an MP3 sound recording that you downloaded onto your computer. Use the appropriate model for your kind of source (for instance, model 79 for a personal photograph), but replace the medium with the file format you're using. If you don't know the file format, use Digital file.

72. A text file (digital)

Berg, John K. "Estimates of Persons Driving While Intoxicated." *Law Enforcement Today* 17 Apr. 2008. PDF file.

Fernandez, Carlos. "Summers in Spain." 2008. *Microsoft Word* file.

73. A media file (digital)

Springsteen, Bruce. "Empty Sky." *The Rising*. Columbia, 2002. MP3 file.

Boys playing basketball. Personal photograph by Granger Goetz. 2008. JPEG file.

7 Listing other sources

The source types covered in this section are not on a computer or, generally, in printed sources. Most of them have parallel citation formats elsewhere in this chapter when you reach them through electronic and print media. See model 17 (p. 374) to cite an interview in print. See models 49–52 (pp. 387–88) to cite images, television and radio programs, video recordings, and sound recordings that are available only on the Web. See models 58–60 (pp. 390–91) to cite such sources when they are available on the Web and in other media. And see model 73 to cite such sources in digital files.

74. A television or radio program

"Piece of My Heart." By Stacy McKee. Dir. Mark Tinker. *Grey's Anatomy*. ABC. KGO, San Francisco, 1 May 2008. Television.

Start with the title unless you are citing the work of a person or persons. The example here cites an episode title (in quotation marks) and the names of the episode's writer and director. By and Dir. identify their roles. Then the entry gives the program title (in italics), the name of the network, the call letters and city of the local station, the date, and the medium (Television). If you list individuals who worked on the entire program, put their names after the program title.

75. A personal or broadcast interview

Paul, William. Personal interview. 6 June 2008.

Diaz, Junot. Interview by Terry Gross. *Fresh Air*. Natl. Public Radio, WGBH, Boston, 18 Oct. 2007. Radio.

Begin with the name of the person interviewed. For an interview you conducted, specify Personal interview or the medium (such as Telephone interview or E-mail interview), and then give the date. For an interview you heard or saw, provide the title if any or Interview if there is no title. Add the name of the interviewer if he or she is identified. Then follow an appropriate model for the kind of source (here, a radio program), and end with the medium (here, Radio).

76. A sound recording

Rubenstein, Artur, perf. Piano Concerto no. 2 in B-flat. By Johannes Brahms. Cond. Eugene Ormandy. Philadelphia Orch. RCA, 1972. LP.

Springsteen, Bruce. "Empty Sky." *The Rising*. Columbia, 2002. CD.

Begin with the name of the individual whose work you are citing. Unless this person is the composer, identify his or her role, as with perf. ("performer") in the first example. If you're citing a work identified by form, number, and key (first example), do not use quotation marks or italics for the title. If you're citing a song or song lyrics (second example), give the title in quotation marks; then provide the title of the recording in italics. Following the title, identify the composer or author if you haven't already, after By, and name and identify other participants you want to mention. Then provide the manufacturer of the recording, the date of release, and the medium: LP in the first example, CD in the second.

77. A film, DVD, or video recording

A Beautiful Mind. Dir. Ron Howard. Universal, 2001. Film.

Start with the title of the work unless you are citing the work of a person (see the next example). Generally, identify and name the director. You may list other participants (writer, lead performers, and so on) as you judge appropriate. For a film, end with the distributor, date, and medium (Film).

For a DVD or videocassette, include the original release date (if any), the distributor's name, and the medium (DVD or Videocassette).

Balanchine, George, chor. *Serenade*. Perf. San Francisco Ballet. Dir. Hilary Bean. 1991. PBS Video, 2006. DVD.

78. A painting, photograph, or other work of visual art

Arnold, Leslie. *Seated Woman*. N.d. Oil on canvas. DeYoung Museum, San Francisco.

Sugimoto, Hiroshi. *Pacific Ocean, Mount Tamalpais*. 1994. Photograph.

Private collection.

To cite an actual work of art, name the artist and give the title (in italics) and the date of creation (or N.d. if the date is unknown). Then provide the medium of the work (such as Oil on canvas or Photograph) and the name and location of the owner, if known. (Use Private collection if not.)

For a work you see only in a reproduction, provide the complete publication information for the source you used. Omit the medium of the work itself, and replace it with the medium of the reproduction (Print in the following example). Omit such information only if you examined the actual work.

Hockney, David. *Place Furstenberg, Paris*. 1985. Coll. Art Gallery, New Paltz.

David Hockney: A Retrospective. Ed. Maurice Tuchman and Stephanie

Barron. Los Angeles: Los Angeles County Museum of Art, 1988. 247. Print.

79. A personal photograph

Common milkweed on Lake Michigan shoreline. Personal photograph by the

author. 22 Aug. 2008.

For a personal photograph by you or by someone else, describe the subject (without quotation marks or italics), say who took the photograph, and add the date.

80. A map, chart, graph, or diagram

"The Sonoran Desert." Map. *Sonoran Desert: An American Deserts Handbook*. By

Rose Houk. Tucson: Western Natl. Parks Assn., 2000. 12. Print.

Unless the creator of an illustration is given on the source, list the illustration by its title. Put the title in quotation marks if it comes from another publication or in italics if it is published independently. Then add a description (Map, Chart, and so on), the publication information, and the medium (here, Print).

81. A cartoon or comic strip

Trudeau, Garry. "Doonesbury." Comic strip. *San Francisco Chronicle* 28 Aug.

2008: E6. Print.

Cite a cartoon or comic strip with the artist's name, the title (in quotation marks), the description Cartoon or Comic strip, the publication information, and the medium (here, Print).

82. An advertisement

Escape Hybrid by Ford. Advertisement. *New Yorker* 10 Dec. 2007: 11. Print.

Cite an advertisement with the name of the product or company advertised, the description Advertisement, the publication information, and the medium (Print, Television, Radio, and so on).

83. A performance

Levine, James, cond. Boston Symphony Orch. Symphony Hall, Boston. 2 May 2008. Performance.

The New Century. By Paul Rudnick. Dir. Nicholas Martin. Mitzi E. Newhouse Theater, New York. 6 May 2008. Performance.

For a live performance, generally base your citation on film citations (model 77). Place the title first (second example) unless you are citing the work of an individual (first example). After the title, provide relevant information about participants as well as the theater, city, and performance date. Conclude with the medium (Performance).

84. A lecture, speech, address, or reading

Katrib, Ruba. "New Art: South Florida Exhibit." Museum of Contemporary Art. MOCA at Goldman Warehouse, Miami. 4 Sept. 2007. Address.

Give the speaker's name, the title if any (in quotation marks), the title of the meeting if any, the name of the sponsoring organization, the location of the presentation, and the date. End with a description of the type of presentation (Lecture, Speech, Address, Reading).

Although the MLA does not provide a specific style for citing classroom lectures in your courses, you can adapt the preceding format for this purpose.

Cavanaugh, Carol. Class lecture on teaching mentors. Lesley U. 4 Apr. 2008. Lecture.

57c Formatting a paper in MLA style

The MLA's manual for students, the *MLA Handbook*, provides guidelines for a fairly simple document format, with just a few elements. For guidelines on type fonts, headings, lists, illustrations, and other features that MLA style does not specify, see **1** pp. 45–51.

The samples on the next page show the formats for the first page and a later page of a paper. For the format of the list of works cited, see p. 367.

First page of MLA paper

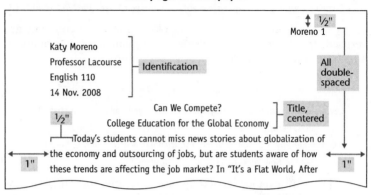

Later page of MLA paper

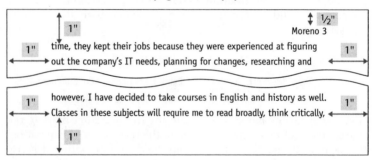

Margins Use minimum one-inch margins on all sides of every page.

Spacing and indentions Double-space throughout. Indent paragraphs one-half inch. (See opposite for indention of poetry and long prose quotations.)

Paging Begin numbering on the first page, and number consecutively through the end (including the list of works cited). Use Arabic numerals (1, 2, 3) positioned in the upper right, about one-half inch from the top. Place your last name before the page number in case the pages later become separated.

Identification and title MLA style does not require a title page for a paper. Instead, give your name, your instructor's name, the course title, and the date on separate lines in the upper left of the first page—one inch from the top of the paper. (See the sample above.) Double-space between all lines of this identification.

Double-space again, and center the title. Do not highlight the title with italics, underlining, boldface, larger type, or quotation marks. Capitalize the words in the title according to the guidelines in **6** p. 291. Double-space the lines of the title and between the title and the text.

Poetry and long prose quotations Treat a single line of poetry like any other quotation, running it into your text and enclosing it in quotation marks. You may run in two or three lines of poetry as well, separating the lines with a slash surrounded by space.

> An example of Robert Frost's incisiveness is in two lines from "Death of the Hired Man": "Home is the place where, when you have to go there **/** They have to take you in" (119-20).

Always set off from your text a poetry quotation of more than three lines. Use double spacing above and below the quotation and for the quotation itself. Indent the quotation one inch from the left margin. *Do not add quotation marks.*

> Emily Dickinson stripped ideas to their essence, as in this description of "A narrow Fellow in the Grass," a snake:
>
>> I more than once at Noon
>>
>> Have passed, I thought, a Whip lash
>>
>> Unbraiding in the Sun
>>
>> When stopping to secure it
>>
>> It wrinkled, and was gone – (12-16)

Also set off a prose quotation of more than four typed lines. (See **7** pp. 325–26 on when to use such long quotations.) Double-space and indent as with the preceding poetry example. *Do not add quotation marks.*

> In the influential *Talley's Corner* from 1967, Elliot Liebow observes that "unskilled" construction work requires more skill than is generally assumed:
>
>> A healthy, sturdy, active man of good intelligence requires from two to four weeks to break in on a construction job. . . . It frequently happens that his foreman or the craftsman he services is not willing to wait that long for him to get into condition or to learn at a glance the difference in size between a rough 2 x 8 and a finished 2 x 10. (62)

Do not use a paragraph indention for a quotation of a single complete paragraph or a part of a paragraph. Use paragraph indentions of one-quarter inch only for a quotation of two or more complete paragraphs.

57d Examining a sample paper in MLA style

The sample paper beginning on p. 403 follows MLA guidelines for overall format, parenthetical citations, and the list of works cited. Marginal annotations highlight features of the paper.

Note Because the sample paper addresses a current topic, many of its sources come from the Internet and do not use page or other reference numbers. Thus the in-text citations of these sources do not give reference numbers. In a paper relying solely on printed journals, books, and other traditional sources, most if not all in-text citations would include page numbers.

A note on outlines

This paper illustrates proper use of the MLA documentation style. It is not a model for our program's expectations for source-based written products.

Justin Malik

Ms. Rossi

English 112-02

18 Mar. 2008

The False Promise of Green Consumerism

They line the aisles of just about any store. They seem to dominate television and print advertising. Chances are that at least a few of them belong to you. From organic jeans to household cleaners to hybrid cars, products advertised as environmentally friendly are readily available and are so popular they're trendy. It's easy to see why Americans are buying these things in record numbers. The new wave of "green" consumer goods makes an almost irresistible promise: we can save the planet by shopping.

Saving the planet does seem to be urgent. Thanks partly to former Vice President Al Gore, who sounded the alarm in 1992 with *Earth in the Balance* and again in 2006 with *An Inconvenient Truth,* the threat of global warming has become a regular feature in the news media and a recurring theme in popular culture. Unfortunately, as Gore himself points out, climate change is just one of many environmental problems competing for our attention: the rainforests are vanishing, our air and our water are dangerously polluted, alarming numbers of species are facing extinction, and landfills are overflowing (*Earth* 23-28). All the bad news can be overwhelming, and most people feel powerless to halt the damage. Thus it is reassuring that we may be able to help by making small changes in what we buy—but it is not entirely true. Although green consumerism can help the environment, consumerism itself is the root of some of the most pressing ecological problems we face. To make a real difference, we must consume less.

The market for items perceived as ecologically sound is enormous. Experts estimate that spending on green products already approaches $200 billion a year (Adler et al.). Shoppers respond well to new options, whether the purchase is as minor as a bottle of chemical-free dish soap or as major as a front-loading washing machine. Not surprisingly, businesses are

---

Annotations (right margin):

Identification: writer's name, instructor's name, course title, date.

Title centered.

Double-space throughout.

Introduction: establishes the issue with examples (first paragraph) and background (second paragraph).

Citation form: no parenthetical citation because author and titles are named in the text and discussion cites entire works.

Citation form: shortened title for one of two works by the same author.

Thesis statement.

Background on green products (next two paragraphs).

Citation form: source with more than three authors; no page number because source from an online database is unnumbered.

Malik 2

responding by offering as many new eco-products as they can. Sandra Jones of the *Chicago Tribune* reports that "green product introductions [have] skyrocketed" lately. She cites a market research report by the Mintel International Group: in the first five years of this century, new household products labeled as green rose from zero to 153, eco-conscious health and beauty aids increased by more than a thousand percent, and organic food and beverage options nearly tripled (B1). These new products are offered for sale at stores like Wal-Mart, Target, Home Depot, Starbucks, and Pottery Barn. It seems clear that green consumerism has grown into a mainstream interest.

Determining whether or not a product is as green as advertised can be a challenge. Claims vary: a product might be labeled as organic, biodegradable, energy efficient, recycled, carbon neutral, renewable, or just about anything that sounds environmentally positive. However, none of these terms carries a universally accepted meaning, and no enforceable labeling regulations exist ("It's Not Easy"). Some of the new product options offer clear environmental benefits: for instance, compact fluorescent light bulbs last ten times as long as regular bulbs and draw about a third of the electricity (Gore, *Inconvenient* 306), and paper made from recycled fibers saves many trees. But other "green" products just as clearly do little or nothing to help the environment: a disposable razor made with less plastic is still a disposable razor, destined for a landfill after only a few uses.

Distinguishing truly green products from those that are not so green merely scratches the surface of a much larger issue. The products aren't the problem; it's our high rate of consumption that poses the real threat to the environment. We seek what's newer and better—whether cars, clothes, phones, computers, televisions, shoes, or gadgets—and they all require resources to make, ship, and use them. Political scientists Thomas Princen, Michael Maniates, and Ken Conca maintain that overconsumption is a leading force behind several ecological crises, warning that

> ever-increasing pressures on ecosystems, life-
> supporting environmental services, and critical

Brackets signal word added to clarify the quotation.

Source author named in text, so not named in parenthetical citation.

Common-knowledge examples of stores and products do not require source citations.

Citation form: shortened title for anonymous source; page number for a one-page source not required.

Citation form: author not named in the text; shortened title for one of two works by the same author. Position of citation clarifies which example comes from the source.

Environmental effects of consumption (next four paragraphs). Writer synthesizes information from half a dozen sources to develop his own ideas.

Quotation over four lines set off without quotation marks. See p. 401.

Malik 3

> natural cycles are driven not only by the sheer
> number of resource users . . . but also by the pat-
> terns of resource use themselves. (4)

Those patterns of resource use are disturbing. In just the second half of the twentieth century, gross world product (the global output of consumer goods) grew at five times the rate of population growth—a difference explained by a huge rise in consumption per person. (See fig. 1.) Such growth might be good for the economy, but it is bad for the environment. As fig. 1 shows, it is accompanied by the depletion of natural resources, increases in the carbon emissions that cause global warming, and increases in the amount of solid waste disposal.

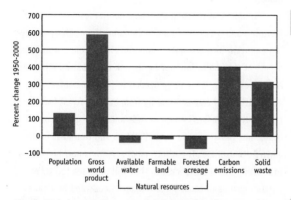

Fig. 1. Global population, consumption, and environmental impacts, 1950-2000. Data from United Nations Development Programme; *Human Development Report: Changing Today's Consumption Patterns—For Tomorrow's Human Development*; New York: Oxford UP; 1998, 4; print; and from Earth Policy Inst.; "Eco-Economy Indicators"; *Earth Policy Institute*; EPI, Feb. 2008; Web; 6 Mar. 2008.

The first negative effect of overconsumption, the depletion of resources, occurs because the manufacture and distribution of any consumer product depends on the use of water, land, and raw materials such as wood, metal, and oil. Paul Hawken, a respected environmentalist, explains that just in the United States "[i]ndustry moves, mines, extracts, shovels, burns, wastes, pumps, and disposes of *4 million pounds of*

Malik 4

Citation form: source with three authors; "qtd. in" indicates indirect source (Hawken quoted by DeGraaf, Wann, and Naylor); "emphasis added" indicates italics was not in original quotation.

Citation form: corporate author is named in the text, so page number only.

Citation form: no parenthetical citation because author is named in the text and online source has no page or other reference numbers.

Summary reduces six pages in the source to three sentences. Signal phrase and parenthetical citation mark boundaries of the summary.

Citation form: shortened title for one of two works by the same author; page numbers indicate exact locations of information in source.

Writer's own conclusion from preceding data.

Citation form: author (a US government body) named in text.

material in order to provide one average . . . family's needs for a year" (qtd. in DeGraaf, Wann, and Naylor 85; emphasis added). The United Nations Development Programme's 1998 *Human Development Report* (still the most comprehensive study of the environmental impacts of consumerism) warns that many regions in the world don't have enough water, productive soil, or forests to meet the basic needs of their populations (4). More recent data from the Earth Policy Institute show that as manufacturing and per-person consumption continue to rise, the supply of resources needed for survival continues to decline. Thus heavy consumption poses a threat not only to the environment but also to the well-being of the human race.

In addition to using up scarce natural resources, manufacturing and distributing products harms the earth by spewing pollution into the water, soil, and air. The most worrisome aspect of that pollution may be its link to global warming. As Al Gore explains, the energy needed to power manufacturing and distribution comes primarily from burning fossil fuels, a process that releases carbon dioxide and other greenhouse gases into the air. Those gases build up and trap heat in the earth's atmosphere. The result, most scientists now believe, is increasing global temperatures that will raise sea levels, expand deserts, and cause more frequent floods and hurricanes (*Inconvenient* 26-27, 81, 118-19, 184). As the preceding bar chart shows, carbon emissions, like production of consumer goods in general, are rising at rates out of proportion with population growth. The more we consume, the more we contribute to global warming.

As harmful as they are, gradual global warming and the depletion of resources half a world away can be difficult to comprehend or appreciate. A more immediate environmental effect of our buying habits can be seen in the volumes of trash those habits create. The US Environmental Protection Agency found that in a single year (2006), US residents, corporations, and institutions produced 251 million tons of municipal solid waste, amounting to "4.6 pounds per person per day" (1-2). Nearly a third of that trash came just from the

Malik 5

wrappers, cans, bottles, and boxes used for shipping consumer goods. Yet the mountains of trash left over from consumption are only a part of the problem. In industrial countries overall, 90 percent of waste comes not from what gets thrown out, but from the manufacturing processes of converting natural resources into consumer products (DeGraaf, Wann, and Naylor 192). Nearly everything we buy creates waste in production, comes in packaging that gets discarded immediately, and ultimately ends up in landfills that are already overflowing.

> Citation form: source with three authors; authors not named in text.

Unfortunately, the growing popularity of green products has not reduced the environmental effects of consumption. A study conducted by economists Jeff Rubin and Benjamin Tal for the research firm CIBC World Markets found that while eco-friendly and energy-efficient products have become more available, "consumption is growing by ever-increasing amounts." The authors give the example of automobiles: in the last generation, cars have become much more energy efficient, but the average American now drives 2500 more miles a year, for a net gain in energy use (4-5). At the same time, per-person waste production in the United States has risen by more than 20 percent (United States 1). Greener products may reduce our cost of consumption and even reduce our guilt about consumption, but they do not reduce consumption and its effects.

> Environmental effects of green consumption.

> Citation form: authors are named in the text, so page numbers only.

> Citation form: US government source not named in text.

> Writer's own conclusion from preceding data.

If buying green won't solve the problems caused by overconsumption, what will? Politicians, environmentalists, and economists have proposed an array of far-reaching ideas, including creating a financial market for carbon credits and offsets, aggressively taxing consumption and pollution, offering financial incentives for environmentally positive behaviors, and even abandoning market capitalism altogether (Muldoon). However, all of these are "top-down" solutions that require concerted government action. Gaining support for any one of them, putting it into practice, and getting results could take decades. In the meantime, the environment would continue to deteriorate. Clearly, short-term solutions are also essential.

> Solutions to problem of consumption (next three paragraphs).

> Citation form: author's name only, because scholarly article on the Web has no page or other reference numbers.

The most promising short-term solution is for individuals to change their own behavior as consumers. The greenest behavior that individuals can adopt may be precycling, the term widely used for avoiding purchases of products that involve the use of raw materials. Precycling includes choosing eco-friendly products made of recycled or nontoxic materials (such as aluminum-free deodorants and fleece made from soda bottles) and avoiding items wrapped in excessive packaging (such as kitchen tools strapped to cardboard and printer cartridges sealed in plastic clamshells). More important, though, precycling means not buying new things in the first place. Renting and borrowing, when possible, save money and resources; so do keeping possessions in good repair and not replacing them until absolutely necessary. Good-quality used items, from clothing to furniture to electronics, can be obtained for free, or very cheaply, through online communities like *Craigslist* and *Freecycle,* from thrift stores and yard sales, or by trading with friends and relatives. When consumers choose used goods over new, they can help to reduce demand for manufactured products that waste energy and resources, and they can help to keep unwanted items out of the waste stream.

Avoiding unnecessary purchases brings personal benefits as well. Brenda Lin, an environmental activist, explained in an e-mail interview that frugal living not only saves money but also provides pleasure:

> You'd be amazed at what people throw out or give away: perfectly good computers, oriental rugs, barely used sports equipment, designer clothes, you name it. . . . It's a game for me to find what I need in other people's trash or at Goodwill. You should see the shock on people's faces when I tell them where I got my stuff. I get almost as much enjoyment from that as from saving money and helping the environment at the same time.

Lin's experience relates to a study of the personal and social consequences of consumerism by the sociologist Juliet B. Schor. Schor found that the more people buy, the less happy they tend to feel because of the stress of working longer

---

Common-knowledge definition and writer's own examples do not require source citations.

Primary source: personal interview by e-mail.

Quotation of over four lines set off without quotation marks. See p. 401.

Ellipsis mark signals omission from quotation.

Citation form: no parenthetical citation because author is named in the text and interview has no page or other reference numbers.

hours to afford their purchases (11-12). Researching the opposite effect, Schor conducted interviews with hundreds of Americans who had drastically reduced their spending so that they would be less dependent on paid work. For these people, she discovered, a deliberately lower standard of living improved quality of life by leaving more time to spend with family and pursue personal interests (125-28). Reducing consumption, it turns out, does not have to translate into sacrifice.

> Writer's own conclusion from two sources.

For unavoidable purchases like food and light bulbs, buying green can make a difference by influencing corporate decisions. Some ecologists and economists believe that as more shoppers choose earth-friendly products over their traditional counterparts—or boycott products that are clearly harmful to the environment—more manufacturers and retailers will look for ways to limit the environmental effects of their industrial practices and the goods they sell (Gore, *Earth* 193; Muldoon). Indeed, as environmental business consultant Gregory C. Unruh points out in an article for *Harvard Business Review*, several major companies, among them Wal-Mart, Coca-Cola, General Electric, and Nike, have already taken up sustainability initiatives in response to market pressure. In the process, the companies have discovered that environmentally minded practices tend to raise profits and strengthen customer loyalty (102). By giving industry solid, bottom-line reasons to embrace ecological goals, consumer demand for earth-friendly products can magnify the effects of individual action.

> Benefits of green consumerism.

> Citation form: two works in the same citation.

> Citation form: author is named in the text, so page numbers only.

Careful shopping can help the environment, but green doesn't necessarily mean "Go." All consumption depletes resources, increases the likelihood of global warming, and creates waste, so even eco-friendly products must be used in moderation. As individuals, we can each play a small role in helping the environment—and help ourselves at the same time—by not buying anything we don't really need, even if it seems environmentally sound. Reducing our personal impact on the earth is a small price to pay for preserving a livable planet for future generations.

> Conclusion: summary and a call for action.

Works Cited

New page, double-spaced. Sources alphabetized by authors' last names.	
An article with more than three authors, from a weekly magazine in an online database.	Adler, Jerry, et al. "The Greening of America." *Newsweek* 14 Aug. 2006: 46-50. *Master File Premier*. Web. 20 Feb. 2008.
A print book with three authors.	DeGraaf, John, David Wann, and Thomas H. Naylor. *Affluenza: The All-Consuming Epidemic*. San Francisco: Berrett-Koehler, 2001. Print.
A short, titled work on a Web site, with a corporate author.	Earth Policy Inst. "Eco-Economy Indicators." *Earth Policy Institute*. EPI, Feb. 2008. Web. 6 Mar. 2008.
A print book with one author.	Gore, Al. *Earth in the Balance: Ecology and the Human Spirit*. Boston: Houghton, 1992. Print.
Second source by author of two or more cited works: three hyphens replace author's name.	---. *An Inconvenient Truth: The Planetary Emergency of Global Warming and What We Can Do about It*. Emmaus: Rodale, 2006. Print.
An anonymous article in a print monthly magazine, listed and alphabetized by title.	"It's Not Easy Buying Green." *Consumer Reports* Sept. 2007: 9. Print.
A print newspaper article.	Jones, Sandra. "Green! It's Easy Being Green When It's in Vogue." *Chicago Tribune* 27 May 2007, final ed.: B1+. Print.
A personal interview by e-mail.	Lin, Brenda. Message to the author. 7 Mar. 2008. E-mail.
An article in a Web scholarly journal that numbers only issues and does not use page numbers.	Muldoon, Annie. "Where the Green Is: Examining the Paradox of Environmentally Conscious Consumption." *Electronic Green Journal* 23 (2006): n. pag. Web. 28 Feb. 2008.
An introduction to a print anthology.	Princen, Thomas, Michael Maniates, and Ken Conca. Introduction. *Confronting Consumption*. Ed. Princen, Maniates, and Conca. Cambridge: MIT P, 2002. 1-20. Print.
A short, titled work on a Web site, by two authors.	Rubin, Jeff, and Benjamin Tal. "Does Energy Efficiency Save Energy?" *StrategEcon*. CIBC World Markets, 27 Nov. 2007. Web. 13 Mar. 2008.
A print book with one author.	Schor, Juliet B. *The Overspent American: Upscaling, Downshifting, and the New Consumer*. New York: Basic, 1998. Print.
A print book with a corporate author.	United Nations Development Programme. *Human Development Report 1998: Changing Today's Consumption Patterns— For Tomorrow's Human Development*. New York: Oxford UP, 1998. Print.
A US government source with no named author, so government body given as author.	United States. Environmental Protection Agency. Solid Waste and Emergency Response. *Municipal Solid Waste*

Malik 9

Generation, Recycling, and Disposal in the United States:
Facts and Figures for 2006. US Environmental Protection
Agency, Nov. 2007. Web. 4 Feb. 2008.

Unruh, Gregory C. "The Biosphere Rules." *Harvard Business Re-*
view 86.2 (2008): 111-17. *Business Source Premier*. Web.
14 Mar. 2008.

An article in a scholarly journal that numbers volumes and issues, consulted in an online database.

The First-Year Writing curriculum at Michigan State University invites students to explore multiple literacies to raise awareness of their current strengths and weaknesses and to invite them to begin a life-long process of developing creative, effective, ethical literacy practices. Our stretch program provides a year-long sequence (Preparation for College Writing and Tier I Writing) for students who need two semesters to meet our shared learning outcomes (see "Preface for Students") and a one-semester course for students who can meet those goals more quickly (Tier I Writing). The stretch program approach allows us to respond effectively to a diverse student population, opening access to a successful MSU education to as many students as possible. The base assignments that appear in this section can be adapted to accommodate any of our Program themes. Preparation for College Writing classes generally drop the disciplinary literacy assignment (usually the source-based research paper in Tier I classes) and adapt other assignments as needed to prepare students for Tier I Writing.

Rationale for the base assignment sequence

The base assignment sequence moves students and teachers through the study of the following types of literacy in relation to a major course theme:

- Personal Literacies
- Cultural Literacies
- Disciplinary Literacies (in Tier I Writing classes)
- Remix Literacies
- Revisionary Literacies

Our curriculum emphasizes the situated nature of literacy, encouraging the use of two sets of major concepts: RAIDS and SWAP. These concepts are explained at length in the "Writing Process" section of this book. SWAP, or Subject, Writer, Audience and Purpose, also creates a frame for the pedagogical motivations for these base assignments.

The five base assignments for Tier I Writing create composing situations that encourage teachers and students to successfully engage the Program learning outcomes as students transition to understanding and meeting the expectations for writing, reading and

Visit *mycomplab.com* for more resources as well as exercises on the spelling and the hyphen.

researching in the larger contexts that define higher education. Generally, the Disciplinary Literacy assignment is not used in Preparation for College Writing courses; these courses focus more on writing, reading and related inquiry practices and less on the production of more advanced academic research. In both threads of the First-Year Writing curriculum Subject, Writer, Audience and Purpose (SWAP) are not only parts of the writing situation for student-generated texts; they are also pedagogical elements of the assignments. Here we give examples of how SWAP can be used to understand the pedagogical frame for each base assignment.

58a Pedagogical SWAPS for base assignments

1 Pedagogical SWAP for the lived literacy assignment

Subject: varies by section but should create opportunities for students to explore the ways that a previously learned type of literacy (used inside or outside of school) can help enhance the transition to meeting some set of literacy expectations in higher education in the U.S.

Writer: varies, but should give students the opportunity to make new connections between and among at least one type of literacy they are familiar with and some aspects of academic writing that are less familiar. That is, the writer should have the chance to practice moving from known to new knowledge in an overt way.

Audience: in general, peers are the audience, although some subset of that group may be chosen (e.g., women, international students). The pedagogical goal is to start the process of thinking about audience in ways that move students away from decontextualized models for writing (e.g. the five-paragraph theme) and toward more situated notions of revision, arrangement invention, delivery, and style (RAIDS).

Purpose: the expectations for writing in higher education in America can be very different from the expectations for writing that students have experienced in previous educational settings. The purpose of this paper is to help students see that some of the literacy skills they bring with them can help them understand and meet new expectations in varied writing situations, especially those related to the learning outcomes associated with this assignment (below to see "Lived Literacy Assignment").

2 Pedagogical SWAP for the cultural literacies assignment

Subject: some form of cultural artifact(s) that can help faculty, staff, and administrators of higher education in America understand the lives of their students as learners.

Writer: a person who can help those in a different place on a hierarchy understand the lives of people at another place on that hierarchy by selecting materials well, developing a clear, specific purpose, and meeting the expectations of an academic audience.

Audience: faculty, staff, administrators of higher education in America or some sub-set of that group (e.g., professors who teach large classes, advisors).

Purpose: people often have to write, read, discuss, etc. with members of a community who have different positions in a structure or hierarchy than they themselves have. The pedagogical purpose of this assignment is to help students develop RAIDS strategies for participating in and contributing to conversations that include people from different structural positions in effective ways in contexts that call for academic writing. For the specific Program learning outcomes associated with this assignment (below to see "Cultural Literacies Assignment").

3 Pedagogical SWAP for the disciplinary literacies assignment

Subject: the writing, reading and researching practices of a discipline of interest to each individual student. Discussion and peer-response sessions should create opportunities for using student work to examine similarities and differences across disciplines and majors.

Writer: a person who needs to develop an understanding of the writing, reading, and researching practices that inform a discipline/major area of interest.

Audience: varies, but should encourage writers to move beyond researching merely to gather information and toward inquiry as vital to making good decisions and helping others to do the same.

Purpose: to build on the understanding about academic structure developed in the cultural literacies assignment in relation to disciplinary structures, especially those disciplinary structures of interest to individual students. This assignment give students the opportunity to develop deeper understandings of the types of literacy work associated with different disciplines so they can make informed decisions about pursuing particular areas of study and work and help others do the same.

4 Pedagogical SWAP for the remix/technological literacies assignment (often small or large group projects)

Subject: varies, but focuses on terms for effective transitions from written assignments to alternative media, applying RAIDS to this process to analyze effective means of communication other than those that require traditional alphabetic formats; for group projects: how to use RAIDS strategies in collaborative composing situations.

Writer: people who use communication forms other than traditional alphabetic literacies and who will benefit from developing more critical skills regarding their use, especially in relation to RAIDS.

Audience: varies, but the audience should be positioned as benefiting from the alternative delivery form in ways they would not benefit from the traditional forms of alphabetic textual delivery.

Purpose: to develop further understanding of SWAP and RAIDS by studying and practicing them outside of the frame of alphabetic literacies; practice meeting increasingly common expectations for delivering messages in varied forms, including graphic, video, audio and other media. This assignment helps students begin to understand the reasons for those expectations and to respond effectively. For group projects: working in groups to meet literacy expectations.

5 Pedagogical SWAP for the revising literacies assignment

Subject: varies, but focuses on how literacy skills, knowledge about literacies, and attitudes toward literate activities (e.g., writing, reading, researching) have changed over the course of study and the implications of those changes.

Writer: writers, readers and researchers who have developed knowledge and awareness of themselves, one another, and others as literate human beings in ways that make it possible for them to generate and disseminate new knowledge.

Audience: varies, but should be a person or people interested in expanding knowledge about the ways literacy resonates as a scholarly conversation (e.g. how forms of literacy from outside schools affect teaching and learning; how student literacy changes across writing situations; how building knowledge about diverse forms of literacy affects decisions, etc.).

Purpose: to create a writing situation that allows students to see, experience, and practice the ways that teaching and learning in higher education position them to participate in and contribute to generative, knowledge-building activities (rather than merely consuming and adapting to known and/or accepted practices, assumptions, etc.).

Note: Pedagogical SWAPS can be used as guides as teachers adapt the base assignments to individual course sections.

58b Base assignments

1 First-Year Writing

Michigan State University

Lived Literacies Base Assignment

Background: We began this semester exploring the literacy histories of ourselves, one another and others. In paper #1, each of you will have the opportunity to create a more formal version of your own literacy history. As our readings have illustrated, there are a number of ways to focus your literacy autobiography: working from a significant event or events, following a chronological pattern, discussing significant people involved in that history, etc. You can choose any one or any combination of these focusing methods or use one that you have seen at work in a literacy autobiography that we have not read together as a class. As you make these decisions, remember that your literacy history should do more than tell a story or strive for self-expression; it must also reflect on the significance of the literacy issues implied by the narrative. This means that you must explore your literacy history to identify and analyze the larger themes and issues raised by that history. Reviewing and analyzing information to identify its significance in some larger frame is a common expectation for students in higher education; this assignment will help you meet these expectations in effective ways.

Context: This assignment supports the following shared First-Year Writing learning outcomes and the following learning outcomes for undergraduate education (LOU) at MSU (LOU outcomes appear in parentheses)

Writing:

- Use writing for purposes of reflection, action, and participation in academic inquiry (analytical thinking; communication)
- Exercise a flexible repertoire of invention, arrangement, and revision strategies (integrated reasoning; communication)

Reading: .

- Engage in reading for purposes of reflection, critical analysis, decision-making, and inquiry (analytical thinking; integrated reasoning)

- Read in ways that improve writing, especially by demonstrating an ability to analyze invention, arrangement, and revision strategies at work in a variety of texts (analytical thinking; integrated reasoning;)

Inquiry/Researching

- Apply methods of inquiry and conventions to generate new understanding (analytical thinking; integrated reasoning)
- Demonstrate an understanding of research as epistemic and recursive processes that arise from and respond back to various communities (integrated reasoning; cultural understanding)

Rhetorical Situation: In Paper #1, then, you will reflect upon the different facets of your literacy history and upon your ideas of literacy more generally. Your purpose here is to discover how the reading we have done to date sheds new light on your own literacy history, and to communicate that discovery to others. It is important to remember that you are not only telling a story; you are also reflecting on the significance of your story in relation to the literacy themes we have studied to date. Like each assignment this semester, your paper must include a visual; for this paper your visual will be a cover page that prepares the audience to enter into your text as an engaged reader.

We will spend a significant amount of time discussing invention, arrangement, and revision activities for this assignment. Due dates appear on your syllabus.

Requirements: 3–5 pages in 12 point font; one-inch margins; a cover page with a visual that helps readers enter your paper in the right frame of mind; a short cover letter in which you explain your invention, arrangement, and revision choices for this assignment.

2 First-Year Writing

Michigan State University

Cultural Literacies Base Assignment

Background: Our study of critical discourse reveals to us that considering familiar things in new ways enhances our understandings of the artifacts that inform our everyday lives. In this paper you will have the opportunity to analyze an artifact or artifacts to shed new light on their cultural significance. Remember as you select your artifact(s) that your goal is to practice using critical analysis and writing to generate new insights from exploring familiar elements of our cultures.

Context: In a democracy people are confronted with various images, discourses, points of view, etc. Clearly, democratic consciousness requires us to do more than merely identify with these things. To make decisions about where we stand on political, ethical, commercial, etc. interests, we must use our critical abilities to analyze the artifacts that create and inform our realities. In this paper, your job is to select one or more cultural artifacts that share a common theme and use the critical concepts we have studied to discern what those artifacts mean and how they mean what they mean.

This assignment invites you to continue practicing the shared learning outcomes from Paper 1. It also asks you to practice effectively the additional outcomes listed below. As in the previous assignment, the learning outcomes for undergraduate education at MSU appear in parentheses after the First-Year Writing Program learning outcomes to which they are related.

Writing

- Work within a repertoire of genres and modes to meet appropriate rhetorical purposes (communication; analytical thinking; integrated reasoning) In the previous paper you wrote an exploratory essay; for this assignment your essay will be more formal and academic.

- Understand diction, usage, voice, and style, including standard edited English, as conventional and rhetorical features of writing (analytical thinking; cultural understanding; communication)

Reading

- Understand that academic fields and disciplines employ varied genre, styles, syntactical patterns, uses of evidence, and citation styles (analytical thinking; integrated reasoning; communication)

Inquiry/Research

- Demonstrate an ability to generate and apply research strategies that are purposeful, ethical, and balanced (integrated reasoning)
- Understand the logics and uses of citation systems and documentation styles and display competence with one citation system/documentation style (analytical thinking; cultural understanding)

Rhetorical Situation: To help the faculty, staff, and administrators of institutions of higher learning understand the cultures that inform the lives of their students, you have been asked to analyze some cultural artifacts commonly used by students in higher education in the United States for a column in the *Chronicle of Higher Education*. You have approximately 1500 words to get the job done. MSU students have been selected to submit columns because of their reputation as writers whose prose is engaging and in need of little editing; please remember this when you submit your piece for consideration. As with paper #1, you may choose to use invention, arrangement, and revision strategies we have seen at work in our readings and/or some you have created yourself or seen at work in other texts. Style and Delivery choices should be driven by the expectations of the publication you are writing for and its audience. Some visual representation of your artifacts is required by this assignment; in most cases, those visuals will appear within the text itself.

SWAP Analysis: In writing situations that define your audience in specific ways, it is often efficient and effective to get a clear idea of the components of the writing situation early in your process. You will discuss these concepts in class.

Subject

Writer

Audience

Purpose

3 First-Year Writing

Michigan State University

Disciplinary Literacy Base Assignment

Background: Earlier assignments for this course gave you opportunities to identify themes and terms for analysis so that you could begin to understand and practice meeting the expectations for writing in higher education. Paper three allows you to continue engaging effective invention, arrangement, revision, style, and delivery practices. It also introduces you to the ways that research and participating in important academic discussions prepare you to use literacy in successful ways across the kinds of writing situations you will find yourself in in higher education and, perhaps, beyond.

Requirements: Different academic disciplines have different ways of presenting and analyzing information, different ways of building knowledge, and different ways of presenting knowledge in written forms. This paper gives you the opportunity to begin building your own understanding of how writing, reading, and researching operate within a discipline of interest to you. You may choose any discipline you wish to examine for this project. Whichever you choose, you must engage in the following activities:

- Analysis of at least one scholarly article from that discipline
- Analysis of at least one article from a trade publication related to that discipline
- Conduct an interview with a person who teaches major courses and/or does research in that discipline
- Conduct an interview with a person who practices in a field related to that discipline

You may also want to analyze an introductory piece about economic and quality of life issues related to the literacy work done in that discipline or career field.

Your paper must be at least 7–9 pages long, in 12-point font, with one-inch margins. Your visual should communicate a specific, important piece of information; graphs and charts are commonly used for this purpose.

Writing Context: Many students come to higher education with only a vague idea of what it means to become a participating member of an academic discipline. Your purpose in this essay is to give students who are new to the academic discipline/field you have chosen an introduction to the expectations for writing, reading, and researching in that discipline. Ultimately, your paper should help your audience understand the ways that literacies are used to create and communicate knowledge in the discipline/field you choose to explore.

This assignment gives you the opportunity to continue practicing successfully meeting the learning goals connected with previous assignments. It also helps you begin to integrate the skills related to the following learning outcomes. As always, the learning outcomes that relate to our Undergraduate Learning Goals appear in parentheses.

Writing

- Demonstrate an understanding of writing as an epistemic and recursive process; effectively apply a variety of knowledge-making strategies in writing (integrated reasoning)

Reading

- Demonstrate an understanding of reading as an epistemic and recursive meaning making process (integrated reasoning; cultural understandng)

- Understand that various academic disciplines and fields employ varied genre, voice, syntactical choices, uses of evidence, and citation styles that call for a variety of reading strategies (analytical thinking; integrated reasoning; communication)

Inquiry/Researching

- Demonstrate the ability to locate, critically evaluate, and employ a variety of sources for a range of purposes (analytical thinking; integrated reasoning)

4 First-Year Writing

Michigan State University

Base Remix Assignment

For this project you will transform one of your essays into an alternative form. Keeping the same focus and purpose, you will transform the message in ways that effectively respond to a new writing situation. You might choose to create a video, a photo essay, a PowerPoint presentation, a web page, a painting, a brochure, a poster, a basket, jewelry, etc. Please bring all of your essays to class on ____ so that we can start discussing how we might select essays and alternative forms of presentation.

The remix assignment asks you to practice effectively the following learning outcomes (as always the goals for undergraduate learning related to these outcomes appear in parentheses):

Writing:

- Work within a repertoire of genres and modes to meet appropriate rhetorical purposes (analytical thinking; integrated reasoning; communication)
- Exercise a flexible repertoire of invention, arrangement, style, and delivery strategies (integrated reasoning; communication)
- Demonstrate an understanding of writing as an epistemic and recursive process and effectively apply a variety of knowledge-making strategies (integrated reasoning)
- Understand diction, usage, voice, and style, including standard edited English, as conventional and rhetorical features of writing (analytical thinking; cultural understanding; communication)

Reading

- Engage in reading for the purposes of reflection, critical analysis, decision-making and inquiry (analytical thinking; integrated reasoning)

■ Demonstrate an understanding of reading as an epistemic and recursive meaning-making process (integrated reasoning)

Inquiry/Researching

■ Apply methods of inquiry and conventions to generate new understanding (analytical thinking; integrated reasoning)
■ Demonstrate the ability to generate and apply research strategies that are purposeful, ethical, and balanced (integrated reasoning)

Remixing a text can give lots of texture to conversations about these learning goals because a remix forces us to revise in dramatic ways as we shift audience, purpose, and self to give the same message in a new context. Therefore, this assignment also prepares you to deal with course concepts in deep ways as you prepare for the final course assignment.

Your final project should be accompanied by a memo that explains:

■ the SWAP elements of your project
■ why you selected the essay and alternative presentational form(s) that you chose for this project
■ Your process (RAIDS) for creating the project
■ How your process helped you improve in learning outcomes areas listed above (and others if you choose to discuss those)

We will create an assessment guide for this project together in class.

> Note: SWAP refers to Subject, Writer, Audience, Purpose
> RAIDS refers to Revision, Arrangement, Invention, Delivery, Style

5 First-Year Writing

Michigan State University
Revising Literacies
Base Assignment for Final Papers

Learning Outcomes for Final Papers: This assignment asks you to reread the papers and projects that you (and, perhaps, your peers) have created this semester to meet the following major goals:

■ Use writing for purposes of reflection, action, and participation in academic inquiry
■ Engage in reading for the purposes of reflection, critical analysis, decision-making, and inquiry

- Read in ways that improve writing, especially by demonstrating an ability to analyze invention, arrangement and revision strategies at work in a variety of texts
- Exercise a flexible repertoire of invention, arrangement, and revision strategies
- Demonstrate an understanding of research as epistemic and recursive processes that arise from and respond back to various communities

This does not mean that other issues, such as style and delivery, are not important. But they should be made in relation to the elements of SWAP that you define for your paper; they will be evaluated in the larger frame of the project.

Requirements for this Assignment: Your final paper for this course gives you the opportunity to revisit and revise your literacy history for a specific purpose of your choosing. For example, you might choose to revisit and revise your literacy history to clarify how your writing, reading, and researching practices have changed this semester and how you will apply them and/or continue to develop them in the future. Or, you might decide to revisit and revise for the purpose of helping in-coming students understand the big picture of First-Year Writing to enhance their chances of success in the Program. Alternatively, you might decide to use this paper opportunity to explore and explain how what you have learned this semester will be applied to some form of non-academic writing that you have become interested in (e.g., songwriting). You may decide to explore the ways that our learning goals relate to the undergraduate learning goals at MSU.

The important thing to remember as you use Purpose, Audience, Subject, and Writer to define your final project is that the final product should help you both 1) revise your individual literacy autobiography in a significant way by drawing on course materials and activities and 2) create strong points of significance (i.e. strong purpose/audience/subject relationships).

Your visual(s) can be placed anywhere; visuals will be evaluated for effectiveness in relation to your purpose.

This paper should be 5–7 pages long; it counts for 25% of your final course grade and it is due at the scheduled final time for our course section.

During our final exam time, you will write a cover letter explaining:

1. which invention, arrangement, and revision strategies you used and why
2. which purpose, audience, subject, and writer you defined for the assignment and why
3. the ways in which exploring various kinds of literacy has enhanced your ability to compose this final academic essay.

GLOSSARY/
INDEX
CULTURE
LANGUAGE GUIDE

The Little, Brown
compact handbook

MICHIGAN STATE
UNIVERSITY

Glossary of Usage

This glossary provides notes on words or phrases that often cause problems for writers. The recommendations for standard American English are based on current dictionaries and usage guides. Items labeled **nonstandard** should be avoided in academic and business settings. Those labeled **colloquial** and **slang** occur in speech and in some informal writing but are best avoided in formal college and business writing. (Words and phrases labeled *colloquial* include those labeled by many dictionaries with the equivalent term *informal.*)

a, an Use *a* before words beginning with consonant sounds, including those spelled with an initial pronounced *h* and those spelled with vowels that are sounded as consonants: *a historian, a one-o'clock class, a university.* Use *an* before words that begin with vowel sounds, including those spelled with an initial silent *h: an organism, an L, an honor.*

The article before an abbreviation depends on how the abbreviation is to be read: *She was once an AEC undersecretary* (*AEC* is to be read as three separate letters). *Many Americans opposed a SALT treaty* (*SALT* is to be read as one word, *salt*).

See also **4** pp. 228–29 on the uses of *a/an* versus *the.*

accept, except *Accept* is a verb meaning "receive." *Except* is usually a preposition or conjunction meaning "but for" or "other than"; when it is used as a verb, it means "leave out." *I can accept all your suggestions except the last one. I'm sorry you excepted my last suggestion from your list.*

advice, advise *Advice* is a noun, and *advise* is a verb: *Take my advice; do as I advise you.*

affect, effect Usually *affect* is a verb, meaning "to influence," and *effect* is a noun, meaning "result": *The drug did not affect his driving; in fact, it seemed to have no effect at all.* But *effect* occasionally is used as a verb meaning "to bring about": *Her efforts effected a change.* And *affect* is used in psychology as a noun meaning "feeling or emotion": *One can infer much about affect from behavior.*

agree to, agree with *Agree to* means "consent to," and *agree with* means "be in accord with": *How can they agree to a treaty when they don't agree with each other about the terms?*

all ready, already *All ready* means "completely prepared," and *already* means "by now" or "before now": *We were all ready to go to the movie, but it had already started.*

all right *All right* is always two words. *Alright* is a common error.

all together, altogether *All together* means "in unison" or "gathered in one place." *Altogether* means "entirely." *It's not altogether true that our family never spends vacations all together.*

allusion, illusion An *allusion* is an indirect reference, and an *illusion* is a deceptive appearance: *Paul's constant allusions to Shakespeare created the illusion that he was an intellectual.*

almost, most *Almost* means "nearly"; *most* means "the greater number (or part) of." In formal writing, *most* should not be used as a substitute for *almost*: *We see each other almost* [not *most*] *every day.*

a lot *A lot* is always two words, used informally to mean "many." *Alot* is a common misspelling.

among, between In general, use *among* for relationships involving more than two people or for comparing one thing to a group to which it belongs. *The four of them agreed among themselves that the choice was between New York and Los Angeles.*

amount, number Use *amount* with a singular noun that names something not countable (a noncount noun): *The amount of food varies.* Use *number* with a plural noun that names more than one of something countable (a plural count noun): *The number of calories must stay the same.*

and/or *And/or* indicates three options: one or the other or both (*The decision is made by the mayor and/or the council*). If you mean all three options, *and/or* is appropriate. Otherwise, use *and* if you mean both, *or* if you mean either.

ante-, anti- The prefix *ante-* means "before" (*antedate, antebellum*); *anti-* means "against" (*antiwar, antinuclear*). Before a capital letter or *i*, *anti-* takes a hyphen: *anti-Freudian, anti-isolationist.*

anxious, eager *Anxious* means "nervous" or "worried" and is usually followed by *about*. *Eager* means "looking forward" and is usually followed by *to*. *I've been anxious about getting blisters. I'm eager* [not *anxious*] *to get new running shoes.*

anybody, any body; anyone, any one *Anybody* and *anyone* are indefinite pronouns; *any body* is a noun modified by *any*; *any one* is a pronoun or adjective modified by *any*. *How can anybody communicate with any body of government? Can anyone help Amy? She has more work than any one person can handle.*

any more, anymore *Any more* means "no more"; *anymore* means "now." Both are used in negative constructions. *He doesn't want any more. She doesn't live here anymore.*

apt, liable, likely *Apt* and *likely* are interchangeable. Strictly speaking, though, *apt* means "having a tendency to": *Horace is apt to forget his lunch in the morning. Likely means "probably going to": Horace is leaving so early today that he's likely to catch the first bus.*

Liable normally means "in danger of" and should be confined to situations with undesirable consequences: *Horace is liable to trip over that hose.* Strictly, *liable* means "responsible" or "exposed to": *The owner will be liable for Horace's injuries.*

are, is Use *are* with a plural subject (*books are*), *is* with a singular subject (*a book is*).

as *As* may be vague or ambiguous when it substitutes for *because, since,* or *while*: *As the researchers asked more questions, their money ran* *out.* (Does *as* mean "while" or "because"?) *As* should never be used as a substitute for *whether* or *who*. *I'm not sure whether* [not *as*] *we can make it. That's the man who* [not *as*] *gave me directions.*

as, like   In formal speech and writing, *like* should not introduce a full clause (with a subject and a verb) because it is a preposition. The preferred choice is *as* or *as if: The plan succeeded as* [not *like*] *we hoped. It seemed as if* [not *like*] *it might fail. Other plans like it have failed.*

as, than   In comparisons, *as* and *than* precede a subjective-case pronoun when the pronoun is a subject: *I love you more than he* [*loves you*]. *As* and *than* precede an objective-case pronoun when the pronoun is an object: *I love you as much as* [*I love*] *him.* (See also **4** p. 225.)

assure, ensure, insure   *Assure* means "to promise": *He assured us that we would miss the traffic. Ensure* and *insure* often are used interchangeably to mean "make certain," but some reserve *insure* for matters of legal and financial protection and use *ensure* for more general meanings: *We left early to ensure that we would miss the traffic. It's expensive to insure yourself against floods.*

at   The use of *at* after *where* is wordy and should be avoided: *Where are you meeting him?* is preferable to *Where are you meeting him at?*

awful, awfully   Strictly speaking, *awful* means "awe-inspiring." As intensifiers meaning "very" or "extremely" (*He tried awfully hard*), *awful* and *awfully* should be avoided in formal speech or writing.

a while, awhile   *Awhile* is an adverb; *a while* is an article and a noun. *I will be gone awhile* [not *a while*]. *I will be gone for a while* [not *awhile*].

bad, badly   In formal speech and writing, *bad* should be used only as an adjective; the adverb is *badly*. *He felt bad because his tooth ached badly.* In *He felt bad,* the verb *felt* is a linking verb and the adjective *bad* describes the subject. See also **4** p. 223.

being as, being that   Colloquial for *because*, the preferable word in formal speech or writing: *Because* [not *Being as*] *the world is round, Columbus never did fall off the edge.*

beside, besides   *Beside* is a preposition meaning "next to." *Besides* is a preposition meaning "except" or "in addition to" as well as an adverb meaning "in addition." *Besides, several other people besides you want to sit beside Dr. Christensen.*

better, had better   *Had better* (meaning "ought to") is a verb modified by an adverb. The verb is necessary and should not be omitted: *You had better* [not just *better*] *go.*

between, among   See *among, between.*

bring, take   Use *bring* only for movement from a farther place to a nearer one and *take* for any other movement. *First take these books to the library for renewal; then take them to Mr. Daniels. Bring them back to me when he's finished.*

but, hardly, scarcely   These words are negative in their own right; using *not* with any of them produces a double negative (see **4** pp. 225–26). *We have but* [not *haven't got but*] *an hour before our plane leaves. I could hardly* [not *couldn't hardly*] *make out her face.*

but, however, yet   Each of these words is adequate to express contrast. Don't combine them. *He had finished, yet* [not *but yet*] *he continued.*

can, may   Strictly, *can* indicates capacity or ability, and *may* indicates permission or possibility: *If I may talk with you a moment, I believe I can solve your problem.*

censor, censure   To *censor* is to edit or remove from public view on moral or some other grounds; to *censure* is to give a formal scolding. *The lieutenant was censured by Major Taylor for censoring the letters her soldiers wrote home from boot camp.*

center around   *Center on* is more logical than, and preferable to, *center around.*

cite, sight, site   *Cite* is a verb usually meaning "quote," "commend," or "acknowledge": *You must cite your sources. Sight* is both a noun meaning "the ability to see" or "a view" and a verb meaning "perceive" or "observe": *What a sight you see when you sight Venus through a strong telescope. Site* is a noun meaning "place" or "location" or a verb meaning "situate": *The builder sited the house on an unlikely site.*

climatic, climactic   *Climatic* comes from *climate* and refers to the weather: *Recent droughts may indicate a climatic change. Climactic* comes from *climax* and refers to a dramatic high point: *During the climactic duel between Hamlet and Laertes, Gertrude drinks poisoned wine.*

complement, compliment   To *complement* something is to add to, complete, or reinforce it: *Her yellow blouse complemented her black hair.* To *compliment* something is to make a flattering remark about it: *He complimented her on her hair. Complimentary* can also mean "free": *complimentary tickets.*

conscience, conscious   *Conscience* is a noun meaning "a sense of right and wrong"; *conscious* is an adjective meaning "aware" or "awake." *Though I was barely conscious, my conscience nagged me.*

contact   Often used imprecisely as a verb instead of a more exact word such as *consult, talk with, telephone,* or *write to.*

continual, continuous   *Continual* means "constantly recurring": *Most movies on television are continually interrupted by commercials. Continuous* means "unceasing": *Some cable channels present movies continuously without commercials.*

could of   See *have, of.*

credible, creditable, credulous   *Credible* means "believable": *It's a strange story, but it seems credible to me. Creditable* means "deserving of credit" or "worthy": *Steve gave a creditable performance. Credulous* means "gullible": *The credulous Claire believed Tim's lies.* See also *incredible, incredulous.*

criteria   The plural of *criterion* (meaning "standard for judgment"): *Our criteria are strict. The most important criterion is a sense of humor.*

data   The plural of *datum* (meaning "fact"). Though *data* is often used as a singular noun, most careful writers still treat it as plural: *The data fail* [not *fails*] *to support the hypothesis.*

device, devise *Device* is the noun, and *devise* is the verb: *Can you devise some device for getting his attention?*

different from, different than *Different from* is preferred: *His purpose is different from mine.* But *different than* is widely accepted when a construction using *from* would be wordy: *I'm a different person now than I used to be* is preferable to *I'm a different person now from the person I used to be.*

differ from, differ with To *differ from* is to be unlike: *The twins differ from each other only in their hairstyles.* To *differ with* is to disagree with: *I have to differ with you on that point.*

discreet, discrete *Discreet* (noun form *discretion*) means "tactful": *What's a discreet way of telling Maud to be quiet? Discrete* (noun form *discreteness*) means "separate and distinct": *Within a computer's memory are millions of discrete bits of information.*

disinterested, uninterested *Disinterested* means "impartial": *We chose Pete, as a disinterested third party, to decide who was right. Uninterested* means "bored" or "lacking interest": *Unfortunately, Pete was completely uninterested in the question.*

don't *Don't* is the contraction for *do not,* not for *does not: I don't care, you don't care,* and *he doesn't* [not *don't*] *care.*

due to the fact that Wordy for *because.*

eager, anxious See *anxious, eager.*

effect See *affect, effect.*

elicit, illicit *Elicit* is a verb meaning "bring out" or "call forth." *Illicit* is an adjective meaning "unlawful." *The crime elicited an outcry against illicit drugs.*

emigrate, immigrate *Emigrate* means "to leave one place and move to another": *The Chus emigrated from Korea. Immigrate* means "to move into a place where one was not born": *They immigrated to the United States.*

ensure See *assure, ensure, insure.*

enthused Used colloquially as an adjective meaning "showing enthusiasm." The preferred adjective is *enthusiastic: The coach was enthusiastic* [not *enthused*] *about the team's victory.*

et al., etc. Use *et al.,* the Latin abbreviation for "and other people," only in source citations: *Jones et al.* Avoid *etc.,* the Latin abbreviation for "and other things," in formal writing, and do not use it to refer to people or to substitute for precision, as in *The government provides health care, etc.*

everybody, every body; everyone, every one *Everybody* and *everyone* are indefinite pronouns: *Everybody* [*everyone*] *knows Tom steals. Every one* is a pronoun modified by *every,* and *every body* a noun modified by *every.* Both refer to each thing or person of a specific group and are typically followed by *of: The game commissioner has stocked every body of fresh water in the state with fish, and now every one of our rivers is a potential trout stream.*

everyday, every day *Everyday* is an adjective meaning "used daily" or "common"; *every day* is a noun modified by *every*: *Everyday problems tend to arise every day.*

everywheres Nonstandard for *everywhere*.

except See *accept, except*.

except for the fact that Wordy for *except that*.

explicit, implicit *Explicit* means "stated outright": *I left explicit instructions. Implicit* means "implied, unstated": *We had an implicit understanding.*

farther, further *Farther* refers to additional distance (*How much farther is it to the beach?*), and *further* refers to additional time, amount, or other abstract matters (*I don't want to discuss this any further*).

fewer, less *Fewer* refers to individual countable items (a plural count noun), *less* to general amounts (a noncount noun, always singular). *Skim milk has fewer calories than whole milk. We have less milk left than I thought.*

flaunt, flout *Flaunt* means "show off": *If you have style, flaunt it. Flout* means "scorn" or "defy": *Hester Prynne flouted convention and paid the price.*

flunk A colloquial substitute for *fail*.

fun As an adjective, *fun* is colloquial and should be avoided in most writing: *It was a pleasurable* [not *fun*] *evening.*

further See *farther, further*.

get This common verb is used in many slang and colloquial expressions: *get lost, that really gets me, getting on. Get* is easy to overuse: watch out for it in expressions such as *it's getting better* (substitute *improving*) and *we got done* (substitute *finished*).

good, well *Good* is an adjective, and *well* is nearly always an adverb: *Larry's a good dancer. He and Linda dance well together. Well* is properly used as an adjective only to refer to health: *You look well.* (*You look good*, in contrast, means "Your appearance is pleasing.")

good and Colloquial for "very": *I was very* [not *good and*] *tired.*

had better See *better, had better*.

had ought The *had* is unnecessary and should be omitted: *He ought* [not *had ought*] *to listen to his mother.*

hanged, hung Though both are past-tense forms of *hang*, *hanged* is used to refer to executions and *hung* is used for all other meanings: *Tom Dooley was hanged* [not *hung*] *from a white oak tree. I hung* [not *hanged*] *the picture you gave me.*

hardly See *but, hardly, scarcely*.

have, of Use *have*, not *of*, after helping verbs such as *could, should, would, may*, and *might*: *You should have* [not *should of*] *told me.*

he, she; he/she Convention has allowed the use of *he* to mean "he or she": *After the infant learns to creep, he progresses to crawling.* However, many writers today consider this usage inaccurate and unfair because it seems to exclude females. The construction *he/she*, one substitute for *he*, is awkward and objectionable to most readers. The better choice is to make the pronoun plural, to rephrase, or, sparingly, to use *he or she*. For instance: *After infants learn to creep, they progress to crawling. After learning to creep, the infant progresses to crawling. After the infant learns to creep, he or she progresses to crawling.* See also **3** p. 151 and **4** pp. 217–18.

herself, himself See *myself, herself, himself, yourself.*

hisself Nonstandard for *himself.*

hopefully *Hopefully* means "with hope": *Freddy waited hopefully for a glimpse of Eliza.* The use of *hopefully* to mean "it is to be hoped," "I hope," or "let's hope" is now very common; but since many readers continue to object strongly to the usage, try to avoid it. *I hope* [not *Hopefully*] *the law will pass.*

idea, ideal An *idea* is a thought or conception. An *ideal* (noun) is a model of perfection or a goal. *Ideal* should not be used in place of *idea*: *The idea* [not *ideal*] *of the play is that our ideals often sustain us.*

if, whether For clarity, use *whether* rather than *if* when you are expressing an alternative: *If I laugh hard, people can't tell whether I'm crying.*

illicit See *elicit, illicit.*

illusion See *allusion, illusion.*

immigrate, emigrate See *emigrate, immigrate.*

implicit See *explicit, implicit.*

imply, infer Writers or speakers *imply*, meaning "suggest": *Jim's letter implies he's having a good time.* Readers or listeners *infer*, meaning "conclude": *From Jim's letter I infer he's having a good time.*

incredible, incredulous *Incredible* means "unbelievable"; *incredulous* means "unbelieving": *When Nancy heard Dennis's incredible story, she was frankly incredulous.* See also *credible, creditable, credulous.*

individual, person, party *Individual* should refer to a single human being in contrast to a group or should stress uniqueness: *The US Constitution places strong emphasis on the rights of the individual.* For other meanings *person* is preferable: *What person* [not *individual*] *wouldn't want the security promised in that advertisement? Party* means "group" (*Can you seat a party of four for dinner?*) and should not be used to refer to an individual except in legal documents. See also *people, persons.*

infer See *imply, infer.*

in regards to Nonstandard for *in regard to, as regards,* or *regarding.*

inside of, outside of The *of* is unnecessary when *inside* and *outside* are used as prepositions: *Stay inside* [not *inside of*] *the house. The decision is outside* [not *outside of*] *my authority. Inside of* may refer colloquially to time, though in formal English *within* is preferred: *The law was passed within* [not *inside of*] *a year.*

insure See *assure, ensure, insure.*

irregardless Nonstandard for *regardless.*

is, are See *are, is.*

is because See *reason is because.*

is when, is where These are faulty constructions in sentences that define: *Adolescence is a stage* [not *is when a person is*] *between childhood and adulthood. Socialism is a system in which* [not *is where*] *government owns the means of production.* See also **4** p. 244.

its, it's *Its* is the pronoun *it* in the possessive case: *That plant is losing its leaves. It's* is a contraction for *it is* or *it has: It's* [*It is*] *likely to die. It's* [*It has*] *got a fungus.* Many people confuse *it's* and *its* because possessives are most often formed with *-'s*; but the possessive *its*, like *his* and *hers*, never takes an apostrophe.

-ize, -wise The suffix *-ize* changes a noun or adjective into a verb: *revolutionize, immunize.* The suffix *-wise* changes a noun or adjective into an adverb: *clockwise, otherwise, likewise.* Avoid the two suffixes except in established words: *I'm highly sensitive* [not *sensitized*] *to that kind of criticism. Financially* [not *Moneywise*], *it's a good time to buy real estate.*

kind of, sort of, type of In formal speech and writing, avoid using *kind of* or *sort of* to mean "somewhat": *He was rather* [not *kind of*] *tall.*

Kind, sort, and *type* are singular and take singular modifiers and verbs: *This kind of dog is easily trained.* Agreement errors often occur when these singular nouns are combined with the plural adjectives *these* and *those: These kinds* [not *kind*] *of dogs are easily trained. Kind, sort,* and *type* should be followed by *of* but not by *a: I don't know what type of* [not *type* or *type of a*] *dog that is.*

Use *kind of, sort of,* or *type of* only when the word *kind, sort,* or *type* is important: *That was a strange* [not *strange sort of*] *statement.*

lay, lie *Lay* means "put" or "place" and takes a direct object: *We could lay the tablecloth in the sun.* Its main forms are *lay, laid, laid. Lie* means "recline" or "be situated" and does not take an object: *I lie awake at night. The town lies east of the river.* Its main forms are *lie, lay, lain.* (See also **4** p. 184.)

leave, let *Leave* and *let* are interchangeable only when followed by *alone; leave me alone* is the same as *let me alone.* Otherwise, *leave* means "depart" and *let* means "allow": *Jill would not let Sue leave.*

less See *fewer, less.*

liable See *apt, liable, likely.*

lie, lay See *lay, lie.*

like, as See *as, like.*

like, such as Strictly, *such as* precedes an example that represents a larger subject, whereas *like* indicates that two subjects are comparable. *Steve has recordings of many great saxophonists such as Ben Webster and Lee Konitz. Steve wants to be a great jazz saxophonist like Ben Webster and Lee Konitz.*

likely See *apt, liable, likely.*

literally This word means "actually" or "just as the words say," and it should not be used to qualify or intensify expressions whose words are not to be taken at face value. The sentence *He was literally climbing the walls* describes a person behaving like an insect, not a person who is restless or anxious. For the latter meaning, *literally* should be omitted.

lose, loose *Lose* means "mislay": *Did you* lose *a brown glove? Loose* means "unrestrained" or "not tight": *Ann's canary got* loose. *Loose* also can function as a verb meaning "let loose": *They* loose *the dogs as soon as they spot the bear.*

lots, lots of Colloquial substitutes for *very many, a great many,* or *much*. Avoid *lots* and *lots of* in college or business writing.

may, can See *can, may.*

may be, maybe *May be* is a verb, and *maybe* is an adverb meaning "perhaps": *Tuesday* may be *a legal holiday.* Maybe *we won't have classes.*

may of See *have, of.*

media *Media* is the plural of *medium* and takes a plural verb: *All the news* media are *increasingly visual.* The singular verb is common, even in the media, but many readers prefer the plural verb and it is always correct.

might of See *have, of.*

moral, morale As a noun, *moral* means "ethical conclusion" or "lesson": *The* moral *of the story escapes me.* Morale *means "spirit" or "state of mind": *Victory improved the team's* morale.

most, almost See *almost, most.*

must of See *have, of.*

myself, herself, himself, yourself The *-self* pronouns refer to or intensify another word or words: *Paul helped* himself*; Jill* herself *said so.* The *-self* pronouns are often used colloquially in place of personal pronouns, but that use should be avoided in formal speech and writing: *No one except* me [not myself] *saw the accident. Our delegates will be Susan and* you [not yourself]. See also **4** p. 211 on the unchanging forms of the *-self* pronouns in standard American English.

nowheres Nonstandard for *nowhere.*

number See *amount, number.*

of, have See *have, of.*

off of *Of* is unnecessary. Use *off* or *from* rather than *off of: He jumped* off [or from*, not* off of] *the roof.*

OK, O.K., okay All three spellings are acceptable, but avoid this colloquial term in formal speech and writing.

on account of Wordy for *because of.*

on the other hand This transitional expression of contrast should be preceded by its mate, *on the one hand: On the one hand, we hoped for snow. On the other hand, we feared that it would harm the animals.* However, the two combined can be unwieldy, and a simple *but, however, yet,* or *in contrast* often suffices: *We hoped for snow.* Yet *we feared that it would harm the animals.*

outside of See *inside of, outside of.*

owing to the fact that Wordy for *because.*

party See *individual, person, party.*

people, persons In formal usage, *people* refers to a general group: *We the* people *of the United States.* . . . *Persons* refers to a collection of individuals: *Will the person or persons who saw the accident please notify.* . . . Except when emphasizing individuals, prefer *people* to *persons.* See also *individual, person, party.*

per   Except in technical writing, an English equivalent is usually preferable to the Latin *per: $10 an* [not *per*] *hour; sent by* [not *per*] *parcel post; requested in* [not *per* or *as per*] *your letter.*

percent (per cent), percentage   Both these terms refer to fractions of one hundred. *Percent* always follows a number (*40 percent of the voters*), and the word should be used instead of the symbol (%) in general writing. *Percentage* stands alone (*the percentage of voters*) or follows an adjective (*a high percentage*).

person   See *individual, person, party.*

persons   See *people, persons.*

phenomena   The plural of *phenomenon* (meaning "perceivable fact" or "unusual occurrence"): *Many phenomena are not recorded. One phenomenon is attracting attention.*

plenty   A colloquial substitute for *very: The reaction occurred very* [not *plenty*] *fast.*

plus   *Plus* is standard as a preposition meaning "in addition to": *His income plus mine is sufficient.* But *plus* is colloquial as a conjunctive adverb: *Our organization is larger than theirs; moreover* [not *plus*], *we have more money.*

precede, proceed   The verb *precede* means "come before": *My name precedes yours in the alphabet.* The verb *proceed* means "move on": *We were told to proceed to the waiting room.*

prejudice, prejudiced   *Prejudice* is a noun; *prejudiced* is an adjective. Do not drop the *-d* from *prejudiced: I was fortunate that my parents were not prejudiced* [not *prejudice*].

pretty   Overworked as an adverb meaning "rather" or "somewhat": *He was somewhat* [not *pretty*] *irked at the suggestion.*

previous to, prior to   Wordy for *before.*

principal, principle   *Principal* is an adjective meaning "foremost" or "major," a noun meaning "chief official," or, in finance, a noun meaning "capital sum." *Principle* is a noun only, meaning "rule" or "axiom." *Her principal reasons for confessing were her principles of right and wrong.*

proceed, precede   See *precede, proceed.*

question of whether, question as to whether   Wordy substitutes for *whether.*

raise, rise   *Raise* means "lift" or "bring up" and takes a direct object: *The Kirks raise cattle.* Its main forms are *raise, raised, raised. Rise* means "get up" and does not take an object: *They must rise at dawn.* Its main forms are *rise, rose, risen.* (See also **4** p. 184.)

real, really   In formal speech and writing, *real* should not be used as an adverb; *really* is the adverb and *real* an adjective. *Popular reaction to the announcement was really* [not *real*] *enthusiastic.*

reason is because   Although colloquially common, this expression should be avoided in formal speech and writing. Use a *that* clause after *reason is: The reason he is absent is that* [not *is because*] *he is sick.* Or: *He is absent because he is sick.* (See also **4** p. 245.)

respectful, respective *Respectful* means "full of (or showing) respect": *Be respectful of other people. Respective* means "separate": *The French and the Germans occupied their respective trenches.*

rise, raise See *raise, rise.*

scarcely See *but, hardly, scarcely.*

sensual, sensuous *Sensual* suggests sexuality; *sensuous* means "pleasing to the senses." *Stirred by the sensuous scent of meadow grass and flowers, Cheryl and Paul found their thoughts growing increasingly sensual.*

set, sit *Set* means "put" or "place" and takes a direct object: *He sets the pitcher down.* Its main forms are *set, set, set. Sit* means "be seated" and does not take an object: *She sits on the sofa.* Its main forms are *sit, sat, sat.* (See also **4** p. 184.)

shall, will *Will* is the future-tense helping verb for all persons: *I will go, you will go, they will go.* The main use of *shall* is for first-person questions requesting an opinion or consent: *Shall I order a pizza? Shall we dance? Shall* can also be used for the first person when a formal effect is desired (*I shall expect you around three*), and it is occasionally used with the second or third person to express the speaker's determination (*You shall do as I say*).

should of See *have, of.*

sight, site, cite See *cite, sight, site.*

since *Since* mainly relates to time: *I've been waiting since noon.* But *since* is also often used to mean "because": *Since you ask, I'll tell you.* Revise sentences in which the word could have either meaning, such as *Since I studied physics, I have been planning to major in engineering.*

sit, set See *set, sit.*

site, cite, sight See *cite, sight, site.*

so Avoid using *so* alone or as a vague intensifier: *He was so late. So* needs to be followed by *that* and a clause that states a result: *He was so late that I left without him.*

somebody, some body; someone, some one *Somebody* and *someone* are indefinite pronouns; *some body* is a noun modified by *some;* and *some one* is a pronoun or an adjective modified by *some. Somebody ought to invent a shampoo that will give hair some body. Someone told Janine she should choose some one plan and stick with it.*

sometime, sometimes, some time *Sometime* means "at an indefinite time in the future": *Why don't you come up and see me sometime? Sometimes* means "now and then": *I still see my old friend Joe sometimes. Some time* means "a span of time": *I need some time to make the payments.*

somewheres Nonstandard for *somewhere.*

sort of, sort of a See *kind of, sort of, type of.*

such Avoid using *such* as a vague intensifier: *It was such a cold winter. Such* should be followed by *that* and a clause that states a result: *It was such a cold winter that Napoleon's troops had to turn back.*

such as See *like, such as.*

supposed to, used to In both these expressions, the *-d* is essential: *I used to* [not *use to*] *think so. He's supposed to* [not *suppose to*] *meet us.*

sure Colloquial when used as an adverb meaning *surely: James Madison sure was right about the need for the Bill of Rights.* If you merely want to be emphatic, use *certainly: Madison certainly was right.* If your goal is to convince a possibly reluctant reader, use *surely: Madison surely was right.*

sure and, sure to; try and, try to *Sure to* and *try to* are the correct forms: *Be sure to* [not *sure and*] *buy milk. Try to* [not *Try and*] *find some decent tomatoes.*

take, bring See *bring, take.*

than, as See *as, than.*

than, then *Than* is a conjunction used in comparisons, *then* an adverb indicating time: *Holmes knew then that Moriarty was wilier than he had thought.*

that, which *That* introduces an essential clause: *We should use the lettuce that Susan bought* (*that Susan bought* limits the lettuce to a particular lettuce). *Which* can introduce both essential and nonessential clauses, but many writers reserve *which* only for nonessential clauses: *The leftover lettuce, which is in the refrigerator, would make a good salad* (*which is in the refrigerator* simply provides more information about the lettuce we already know of). Essential clauses (with *that* or *which*) are not set off by commas; nonessential clauses (with *which*) are. See also **5** p. 254.

that, which, who Use *that* for animals, things, and sometimes collective or anonymous people: *The rocket that failed cost millions. Infants that walk need constant tending.* Use *which* only for animals and things: *The river, which flows south, divides two countries.* Use *who* only for people and for animals with names: *Dorothy is the girl who visits Oz. Her dog, Toto, who accompanies her, gives her courage.*

their, there, they're *Their* is the possessive form of *they: Give them their money. There* indicates place (*I saw her standing there*) or functions as an expletive (*There is a hole behind you*). *They're* is a contraction for *they are: They're going fast.*

theirselves Nonstandard for *themselves.*

them In standard American English, *them* does not serve as an adjective: *Those* [not *them*] *people want to know.*

then, than See *than, then.*

these kind, these sort, these type, those kind See *kind of, sort of, type of.*

this, these *This* is singular: *this car* or *This is the reason I left. These* is plural: *these cars* or *These are not valid reasons.*

thru A colloquial spelling of *through* that should be avoided in all academic and business writing.

to, too, two *To* is a preposition; *too* is an adverb meaning "also" or "excessively"; and *two* is a number. *I too have been to Europe two times.*

too Avoid using *too* as a vague intensifier: *Monkeys are too mean.* If you do use *too*, explain the consequences of the excessive quality: *Monkeys are too mean to make good pets.*

toward, towards Both are acceptable, though *toward* is preferred. Use one or the other consistently.

try and, try to See *sure and, sure to; try and, try to.*

type of See *kind of, sort of, type of.* Don't use *type* without *of: It was a family type of* [not *type*] *restaurant.* Or better: *It was a family restaurant.*

uninterested See *disinterested, uninterested.*

unique *Unique* means "the only one of its kind" and so cannot sensibly be modified with words such as *very* or *most: That was a unique* [not *a very unique* or *the most unique*] *movie.*

usage, use *Usage* refers to conventions, most often those of a language: *Is "hadn't ought" proper usage? Usage* is often misused in place of the noun *use: Wise use* [not *usage*] *of insulation can save fuel.*

use, utilize *Utilize* can be used to mean "make good use of": *Many teachers utilize computers for instruction.* But for all other senses of "place in service" or "employ," prefer *use.*

used to See *supposed to, used to.*

wait for, wait on In formal speech and writing, *wait for* means "await" (*I'm waiting for Paul*) and *wait on* means "serve" (*The owner of the store herself waited on us*).

ways Colloquial as a substitute for *way: We have only a little way* [not *ways*] *to go.*

well See *good, well.*

whether, if See *if, whether.*

which, that See *that, which.*

which, who, that See *that, which, who.*

who's, whose *Who's* is the contraction of *who is* or *who has: Who's* [*Who is*] *at the door? Jim is the only one who's* [*who has*] *passed. Whose* is the possessive form of *who: Whose book is that?*

will, shall See *shall, will.*

-wise See *-ize, -wise.*

would be Often used instead of *is* or *are* to soften statements needlessly: *One example is* [not *would be*] *gun-control laws. Would* can combine with other verbs for the same unassertive effect: *would ask, would seem, would suggest,* and so on.

would have Avoid this construction in place of *had* in clauses that begin *if* and state a condition contrary to fact: *If the tree had* [not *would have*] *withstood the fire, it would have been the oldest in town.* See also **4** p. 201.

would of See *have, of.*

you In all but very formal writing, *you* is generally appropriate as long as it means "you, the reader." In all writing, avoid indefinite uses of *you,* such as *In one ancient tribe your first loyalty was to your parents.* See also **4** p. 221.

your, you're *Your* is the possessive form of *you: Your dinner is ready. You're* is the contraction of *you are: You're bound to be late.*

yourself See *myself, herself, himself, yourself.*

Credits

Text and Illustrations

Brooks, Gwendolyn. "The Bean Eaters" by Gwendolyn Brooks, 1991. Reprinted by consent of Brooks Permissions.

Cunningham, John A., and Peter Selby. "Relighting Cigarettes: How Common Is It?" by John A. Cunningham and Peter Selby, *Nicotine and Tobacco Research*, 9.5, 621–23. Copyright © 2007 by Informa Healthcare—Journals. Reproduced with permission of Informa Healthcare—Journals in the format Textbook via Copyright Clearance Center.

Davies, Antony. "Unemployment Rates of High School Graduates and College Graduates, 1984–2004," from *The Economics of College Tuition* by Antony Davies. Copyright © 2005. Reprinted by permission.

Dyson, Freeman J. From *Disturbing the Universe* by Freeman J. Dyson. Copyright © 1979 by Freeman J. Dyson. Reprinted by permission of Basic Books, a member of Perseus Books Group.

EBSCO. From *www.web.ebscohost.com*. Reprinted by permission.

Friedman, Thomas L. "It's a Flat World, After All" *New York Times*, April 3, 2005.

Google. *www.google.com*.

Goreau, Angeline. "Hers: Worthy Women Revisited" by Angeline Goreau. Copyright © 1986 by Angeline Goreau. Originally appeared in *New York Times*, December 11, 1986. Reprinted by permission of Georges Borchardt, Inc., for the author.

Ik, Kim Yong. Excerpt from "A Book-Writing Venture" by Kim Yong Ik. Originally published in *The Writer*, October 1965. Copyright © Kim Yong Ik. Reprinted by permission of Faith M. Leigh, literary heir to the estate of Kim Yong Ik.

Jackson, Tim. "Live Better by Consuming Less?" by Tim Jackson, *Journal of Industrial Ecology*, 9.1–2. Reprinted by permission of Blackwell Publishing Ltd.

Kuralt, Charles. *Dateline America*. Orlando: Harcourt, 1979.

Lahiri, Jhumpa. From *Unaccustomed Earth* by Jhumpa Lahiri, copyright © 2008 by Jhumpa Lahiri. Used by permission of Alfred A. Knopf, a division of Random House, Inc.

Mayer, Lawrence. "The Confounding Enemy of Sleep." *Fortune*, June, 1974.

Molella, Arthur. From "Cultures of Innovation" by Arthur Molella, Lemelson Center, National Museum of American History, Smithsonian Institution, *www.invention.smithsonian.org*. Used by permission.

Muldoon, Annie. Abstract of "Where the Green Is: Examining the Paradox of Environmentally Conscious Consumption" by Annie Muldoon, *Electronic Green Journal*, 23, April 2006, on the EBSCOhost database Web site, *www.web.ebscohost.com*. Reprinted by permission of EBSCO and UCLA Library.

Ouchi, William G. *Theory Z*. Reading: Addison-Wesley, 1981.

Polletta, Francesca. "Just Talk: Public Deliberation after 9/11" by Francesca Polletta, *Journal of Public Deliberation*, 4.1, Article 2, *www.services.bepress.com*. Used by permission.

ProQuest. From "Privilege and Repression in the Digital Era: Rethinking the Sociopolitics of the Digital Divide," *www.proquest.com*. Used by permission.

Rosen, Ruth. "Search for Yesterday" by Ruth Rosen from *Watching Television* edited by Todd Gitlin. New York: Pantheon Books, 1986.

Selwyn, Neil. "The Social Processes of Learning to Use Computers" by Neil Selwyn, *Social Science Computer Review*, 23.1, 122. Copyright © 2005 by Sage Publications Inc. Journals. Reproduced with permission of Sage Publications Inc. Journals in the format Textbook via Copyright Clearance Center.

Sowell, Thomas. "Student Loans" from *Is Reality Optional? and Other Essays* by Thomas Sowell, 1993. Reprinted by permission of Thomas Sowell and Creators Syndicate, Inc.

Stout, David. From "Blind Win Court Ruling on U.S. Currency" by David Stout, *New York Times*, May 21, 2008. All rights reserved. Used by permission and protected by the Copyright Laws of the United States. The printing, copying, redistribution, or retransmission of the Material without express written permission is prohibited.

Tuchman, Barbara. "The Decline of Quality" by Barbara Tuchman, *New York Times*, November 2, 1980. Reprinted by the permission of Russell & Volkening as agents for the author. Copyright © 1980 by Barbara Tuchman.

UNFPA. "AIDS Clock" from the UNFPA.org Web site, *www.unfpa.org*, 2008. Reprinted with permission.

Woolf, Virginia. *The Waves*. New York: Harcourt, 1931.

Photos

Title page, clockwise from top left: Jamie Grill/Iconica/Getty; The Image Bank/Getty; Stone/Getty; Andersen Ross/Blend Images/Getty; David Fischer/Digital Vision/Getty; **56:** NASA; **75:** *Boostup.org;* **98:** Getty; **100:** Michael Foujols/Corbis.

Index

441

essential vs. nonessential,
5 253, 254
as modifiers, **4** 177–79
prepositional. *See* Prepositional
phrases
subordination with, **3** 141–42
types of, **4** 177–79
verb, **4** 177, 186
verbal. *See* Verbals and verbal
phrases
Physics, research sources on, **8** 355
piece, peace, **6** 283
Place names
abbreviation of, **6** 296
capitalization of, **6** 289
commas in, **5** 258
Plagiarism
vs. academic integrity, **7** 330
accidental, **7** 331
avoiding, **7** 330–37
with computer notes, **7** 305
defined, **7** 330
deliberate, **7** 331
detecting, on the Internet, **7** 331
with downloaded sources, **7** 305
with handwritten notes, **7** 305
during information gathering,
7 305
and intellectual property, **7** 330
with Internet sources, **7** 331–32
with paraphrases, **7** 334–35
with photocopied or printed-out
sources, **7** 305
with quotations, **7** 334
with summaries, **2** 67, **7** 334–35
Turnitin to detect, **7** 332
vs. using common knowledge,
7 333
vs. using your own independent
material, **7** 333
plain, plane, **6** 283
Plain form, of verbs
defined, **4** 168
in forming past tense and past
participles, **4** 182
in forming simple present tense,
4 168
forms of *do* with, **4** 185
plane, plain, **6** 283
Plays
acts and scenes of, **MLA** 364
titles of, italics or underlining for,
6 292
plenty, **Gl** 435
Plurals. *See also* Agreement of
pronouns and antecedents;
Agreement of subjects and verbs
of abbreviations, dates, and
characters or words named as
words, **5** 268, 270

apostrophes misused to form,
5 268
apostrophes with possessives of,
5 269
defined, **4** 167
determiners with, **4** 227
formation of, **6** 286
grammar checkers for, **5** 271
of nouns, **4** 167, **5** 269
in pronoun-antecedent
agreement, **4** 221
in subject-verb agreement,
4 204–09
plus, **Gl** 435
PM, AM, **6** 295
Podcasts
documenting, **MLA** 389
Poetry
analyzing, **8** 345
omission of lines of, **5** 279
slashes between lines of, **5** 279,
MLA 401
titles of: italics or underlining for
long, **6** 292; quotation marks
for short, **5** 273
Point-by-point comparison and
contrast, **1** 40
Point of view
in illustrations, **2** 76
in literary works, **8** 327
Point size (type fonts), **1** 49
Political science, research sources
on, **8** 349
Portfolios, writing, **1** 31
Positive form, of adjectives and
adverbs, **4** 170, 224
Possessive case
apostrophes to indicate, **4** , **5**
267–69
defined, **4** 210
before gerunds, **4** 215
grammar checkers for, **5** 267
of nouns and indefinite pronouns,
4 167, **5** 267–69
of personal pronouns, **4** 269, **5** 270
Post hoc fallacy, **2** 95
PowerPoint, **2** 115–16
precede, proceed, **Gl** 435
Predicate adjectives. *See* Subject
complements
Predicate nouns. *See* Subject
complements
Predicates. *See also* Objects; Subject
complements; Verbs
agreement of subjects with, **4**
204–210
complete, **4** 173–74
compound, **4** 173, **5** 260
defined, **4** 172–73
patterns, **4** 174–76

U

Throughout this handbook, the symbol (CULTURE LANGUAGE) signals topics for students whose first language or dialect is not standard American English. These topics can be tricky because they arise from rules in standard English that are quite different in other languages and dialects. Many of the topics involve significant cultural assumptions as well.

No matter what your language background, as a college student you are learning the culture of US higher education and the language that is used and shaped by that culture. The process is challenging, even for native speakers of standard American English. It requires not just writing clearly and correctly but also mastering conventions of developing, presenting, and supporting ideas. The challenge is greater if, in addition, you are trying to learn standard American English and are accustomed to other conventions. Several habits can help you succeed:

- **Read.** Besides course assignments, read newspapers, magazines, and books in English. The more you read, the more fluently and accurately you'll write.
- **Write.** Keep a journal in which you practice writing in English every day.
- **Talk and listen.** Take advantage of opportunities to hear and use English.
- **Ask questions.** Your instructors, tutors in the writing lab, and fellow students can clarify assignments and help you identify and solve writing problems.
- **Don't try for perfection.** No one writes perfectly, and the effort to do so can prevent you from expressing yourself fluently. View mistakes not as failures but as opportunities to learn.
- **Revise first; then edit.** Focus on each essay's ideas, support, and organization before attending to grammar and vocabulary. See the revision and editing checklists in **1** pp. 24 and 26.
- **Set editing priorities.** Concentrate first on any errors that interfere with clarity, such as problems with word order or subject-verb agreement.

The following index leads you to text discussions of writing topics that you may need help with.

Contents

CULTURE LANGUAGE ◀ Guide on reverse

Editing Symbols

ab	Faulty abbreviation, **6** 294
ad	Misused adjective or adverb, **4** 222
agr	Error in agreement, **4** 204, 215
ap	Apostrophe needed or misused, **5** 267
appr	Inappropriate language, **3** 145
arg	Faulty argument, **2** 88
awk	Awkward construction
cap	Use capital letter, **6** 288
case	Error in case form, **4** 210
cit	Missing source citation or error in form of citation, **7** 330, 336–37
coh	Coherence lacking, **1** 33
con	Be more concise, **3** 159
coord	Coordination needed, **3** 233
crit	Think or read more critically, **2** 68
cs	Comma splice, **4** 240
d	Ineffective diction (word choice), **3** 145, 146
des	Ineffective or incorrect document design, **1** 45
det	Error in use of determiner, **4** 226
dm	Dangling modifier, **4** 234
emph	Emphasis lacking or faulty, **3** 130
exact	Inexact language, **3** 152
frag	Sentence fragment, **4** 236
fs	Fused sentence, **4** 240
gram	Error in grammar, **4** 166–181
hyph	Error in use of hyphen, **6** 286
inc	Incomplete construction, **3** 158
ital	Italicize or underline, **6** 291
k	Awkward construction
lc	Use lowercase (small) letter, **6** 288
mixed	Mixed construction, **4** 244
mm	Misplaced modifier, **4** 231
mng	Meaning unclear
no cap	Unnecessary capital letter, **6** 288
no ,	Comma not needed, **5** 259
no ¶	No new paragraph needed, **1** 32
num	Error in use of numbers, **6** 297
p	Error in punctuation, **5** 248–280
. ? !	Period, question mark, exclamation point, **5** 248
,	Comma, **5** 250
;	Semicolon, **5** 262
:	Colon, **5** 264
'	Apostrophe, **5** 267
" "	Quotation marks, **5** 271
— ( ) [ ] … /	Dash, parentheses, brackets, ellipsis mark, slash, **5** 275
par, ¶	Start new paragraph, **1** 32
¶ coh	Paragraph not coherent, **1** 33
¶ dev	Paragraph not developed, **1** 38
¶ un	Paragraph not unified, **1** 32
pass	Ineffective passive voice, **4** 202
pn agr	Error in pronoun-antecedent agreement, **4** 215
ref	Error in pronoun reference, **4** 219
rep	Unnecessary repetition, **3** 156
rev	Revise or proofread, **1** 22
run-on	Run-on (fused) sentence, **4** 231
shift	Inconsistency, **4** 198, 201, 203, 221
sp	Misspelled word, **6** 283
spec	Be more specific, **1** 38, **3** 243
sub	Subordination needed or faulty, **3** 136
t	Error in verb tense, **4** 194
t seq	Error in tense sequence, **4** 198
trans	Transition needed, **1** 36
und	Underline or italicize, **6** 291
usage	See Glossary of Usage, **Gl** 428
var	Vary sentence structure, **3** 141
vb	Error in verb form, **4** 182
vb agr	Error in subject-verb agreement, **4** 204
w	Wordy, **3** 159
ww	Wrong word, **3** 152
//	Faulty parallelism, **3** 139
◯	Close up the space
ℛ	Delete
t͡eh	Transpose letters or words
the	Capitalize, **6** 288
The	Use a small letter, **6** 288
X	Obvious error
^	Something missing, **3** 158
??	Document illegible or meaning unclear